Steinbeis-Edition

**Peter Dohm** ist Professor für Betriebswirtschaftslehre an der Hochschule für Polizei Villingen-Schwenningen sowie Direktor der Steinbeis Business Academy, ein Verbund von Steinbeis-Transfer-Instituten der Steinbeis-Hochschule Berlin (SHB). Seit 1988 lehrt Prof. Dr. Dohm BWL, VWL, Kosten- sowie Leistungsrechnung und Unternehmensführung in der Erwachsenenfortbildung. Prof. Dr. Dohm hat verschiedene Publikationen zur Allgemeinen Betriebs- und Volkswirtschaftslehre, zur Kosten- und Leistungsrechnung sowie zum betrieblichen Finanz- und Rechnungswesen verfasst.

**Peter Dohm** is Professor of Business Administration at the Police University Villingen-Schwenningen, as well as Director of the Steinbeis Business Academy. Since 1988, Prof. Dr. Dohm teaches business administration, economics, cost and performance accounting and management in the adult education setting. Prof. Dr. Dohm is the author of several publications on general business management and economics, costs and performance as well as operational finance and accounting.

**Rainer Esterer**, Dipl.-Kfm., ist Dozent für Volks- und Betriebswirtschaftslehre am Fortbildungsinstitut der Bayerischen Polizei in Ainring. Seit 2002 leitet Rainer Esterer Projektmanagementseminare im Rahmen der Erwachsenenfortbildung unter anderen an der SHB. Ein weiterer Schwerpunkt seiner Tätigkeit bildet die praktische Beratung von Projektverantwortlichen und deren Teams in der Anwendung von Techniken und Instrumenten des Projekt- und Qualitätsmanagements.

**Rainer Esterer**, Dipl.-Kfm., is a lecturer in Economics and Business Administration at the educational institute of the Bavarian police in Ainring. Since 2002, Rainer Esterer leads project management seminars in an adult education setting. A further focus of his activities is the practical advice to project managers and their teams in the application of techniques and instruments of project and quality management.

**Maximilian May**, MBA, ist als zertifizierter Senior Projektmanager (IPMA Level B, PRINCE2®-Practitioner) in der Beratung von Organisationen hinsichtlich Projekt- und Qualitätsmanagement sowie Organisationsentwicklung tätig. Des Weiteren ist er als Trainer, Coach und Moderator in verschiedenen Kontexten der Führungskräfteentwicklung tätig.

**Maximilian May**, MBA, is a certified Senior Project Manager (IPMA Level B, Prince2® practitioner) providing advice to organizations with regard to project and quality management as well as organizational development. Furthermore Mr. May acts as a trainer, coach and moderator in the various contexts of management development.

**Edda Schönberger**, Dipl.-Wirt.-Rom., ist im wissenschaftlichen Projektbetrieb eingebunden und konnte Erfahrungen in der internationalen Projektzusammenarbeit sammeln. Darüber hinaus war sie bereits bei der Young Crew der GPM e.V. (Deutsche Gesellschaft für Projektmanagement) aktiv, der Schwerpunkt lag hierbei auf agilen Projektmanagementmethode und der Kommunikation im Projekt.

**Edda Schönberger**, Dipl.-Wirt.-Rom., is involved in the scientific project operation and has gathered experience in international collaborations. In addition, Ms. Schönberger was early on active in the Young Crew of the GPM e.V. (German Association for Project Management), focusing on agile project management and communications in projects.

Steinbeis Business Acadmey (Hrsg./Publ.)
Peter Dohm, Rainer Esterer, Maximilian May, Edda Schönberger

# Projektmanagement
# Project Management

Deutsch | English

Seminarbegleitende Unterlagen zum Studienfach
Accompanying Documents for the Subject of Study

**Transfer-Dokumentation-Report**
Steinbeis Business Administration Basics

**Steinbeis Business Academy**
SBA ■ ■ ■ ☐ ☐ ☐
Steinbeis-Hochschule Berlin SHB

**Impressum | Imprint**

© 2014 Steinbeis-Edition

Alle Rechte der Verbreitung, auch durch Film, Funk und Fernsehen, fotomechanische Wiedergabe, Tonträger jeder Art, auszugsweisen Nachdruck oder Einspeicherung und Rückgewinnung in Datenverarbeitungsanlagen aller Art, sind vorbehalten.

All rights of the dissemination, including through film, radio and television, reprography, music playback of any kind, partial reproduction or storage and recovery in data processing equipment of all kinds, are reserved.

Steinbeis Business Academy (Hrsg. / Publ.)
Peter Dohm | Rainer Esterer | Maximilian May | Edda Schönberger
Projektmanagement | Project Management
Seminarbegleitende Unterlagen zum Studienfach | Accompanying documents for the subject of study

1. Auflage | Steinbeis-Edition, Stuttgart 2014 | 1. Edition | Steinbeis-Edition, Stuttgart 2014
ISBN: 978-3-943356-63-2
Übersetzer | Translator: Astrid Hall
Satz | Layout: Steinbeis-Edition
Titelbild | Cover picture: © Alexander Putyata, © George Paul – iStockphoto.com
Gedruckt in Deutschland | Printed in Germany

Steinbeis ist weltweit im unternehmerischen Wissens- und Technologietransfer aktiv. Zum Steinbeis-Verbund gehören derzeit rund 1.000 Steinbeis-Unternehmen sowie Kooperations- und Projektpartner in über 60 Ländern. Das Dienstleistungsportfolio der fachlich spezialisierten Steinbeis-Unternehmen im Verbund umfasst Beratung, Forschung & Entwicklung, Aus- und Weiterbildung sowie Analysen & Expertisen für alle Management- und Technologiefelder. Ihren Sitz haben die Steinbeis-Unternehmen überwiegend an Forschungseinrichtungen, insbesondere Hochschulen, die originäre Wissensquellen für Steinbeis darstellen. Rund 6.000 Experten tragen zum praxisnahen Transfer zwischen Wissenschaft und Wirtschaft bei. Dach des Steinbeis-Verbundes ist die 1971 ins Leben gerufene Steinbeis-Stiftung, die ihren Sitz in Stuttgart hat.

Steinbeis is an international service provider in entrepreneurial knowledge and technology transfer. The Steinbeis Transfer Network is made up of about 1,000 Steinbeis Enterprises and project partners in more than 60 countries. Specialized in chosen areas, Steinbeis Enterprises' portfolio of services covers consulting; research and development; training and employee development as well as evaluation and expert reports for every sector of technology and management. Steinbeis Enterprises are frequently based at research institutions, especially universities, which are constituting the Network's primary sources of expertise. The Steinbeis Network comprises around 6,000 experts committed to practical transfer between academia and industry. Founded in 1971, the Steinbeis-Stiftung is the umbrella organization of the Steinbeis Transfer Network. It is headquartered in Stuttgart, Germany.

164843-2014-07 | www.steinbeis-edition.de

## Wissen (vermitteln) alleine genügt nicht

Steinbeis ist und war von je her dem konkreten Transfer von Technologien und Wissen verpflichtet. Konkret bedeutet das v. a. auch die nutzenorientierte Anwendung von geschaffenem Wissen. Die Wissensvermittlung und das Wissen selbst sind notwendige, lange aber noch nicht hinreichende Bedingung für einen erfolgreichen Transfer.

Bei der Entwicklung des Konzepts des Projekt-Kompetenz-Studiums (PKS) haben wir darauf geachtet, dass nicht nur die Aneignung, sondern insbesondere auch die Anwendung von vermitteltem Wissen systembedingt gegeben ist. Daher steht das von uns transferorientiert betreute und in einem Unternehmen (bzw. einer Organisation) durchgeführte Projekt im Mittelpunkt jedes SHB-Studiums.

Erste Erfahrungen im Bachelor-Studiengang haben gezeigt, dass reine stoffanbietende Lehrbriefe im PKS weniger geeignet sind. Wir entwickelten daher das Konzept der Transfer-Dokumentation-Reports (TDR). Im Mittelpunkt der TDR steht konsequenterweise der praktische Transfer von bereits dokumentiertem (theoretischem) Wissen in die Praxis, d. h. in das Projekt und somit das Unternehmen. Die eigene Reflexion über sowie die Relevanz theoretischer Fundierung für das Projekt bzw. das Unternehmen wird im Report dokumentiert. Wird die gesamte Theorie notwendigerweise und klassisch in den Prüfungen abgefragt, stellt der Report für den Studenten und dessen Betreuer eine praxisorientierte Prüfung des Transfers dar.

Ich wünsche Ihnen (und auch uns), dass Sie durch die TDR relevantes Wissen für Ihren persönlichen Erfolg und den Ihres Unternehmens, noch besser, nutzenorientiert anwenden können.

*Prof. Dr. Dr. h. c. mult. Johann Löhn*
Präsident Steinbeis-Hochschule Berlin

## Knowledge (transfer) on its own is not enough

Steinbeis is and always has been committed to the specific transfer of technologies and knowledge. In more specific terms, this means, first and foremost, the benefit-oriented application of the generated knowledge. Knowledge transfer and knowledge itself are an essential, yet not sufficient condition for a successful transfer.

Developing the Project-Competence-Study (PCS) concept we have paid attention to the fact that not only the acquisition but particularly the use of transferred knowledge must be inherent to the system. Therefore, the focus of the SHB courses is centered on the particular transfer-oriented project which is supervised by us and realized in a company (or an organization).

First experiences with the Bachelor course have shown, merely learning-oriented preparatory papers are less suitable for the PCS. This is why we developed the concept of the Transfer-Documentation-Reports (TDRs). Consistently, the focus of the TDR is on the transfer of the already documented (theoretical) knowledge into practical use, that is, into the project and hence into the company. The own reflection on as well as the relevance of the theoretical framework for the project or the company are documented in the report. Necessarily, the whole theoretical knowledge is tested in classic exams. The report represents a practice-oriented examination of the transfer for the student and the tutor.

I wish you (and us) that you are enabled by the TDRs to apply relevant knowledge even better in a benefit-oriented way, for your personal success and your company's success.

*Prof. Dr. Dr. h. c. mult. Johann Löhn*
President Steinbeis University Berlin

## Aufbau TDR

**Titel:** Projektmanagement
TDR (Transfer-Dokumentation-Report)

**Lernziele:** Der Student sollte nach Bearbeitung des TDR in der Lage sein:
- einen Transfer zum Projekt leisten zu können,
- die Thematik im Unternehmen erkennen,
- ein wissenschaftliches Thema auf die Unternehmenspraxis anzuwenden,
- einen Zusammenhang zwischen dem Themengebiet und dem Unternehmen herzustellen,
- wiederzugeben, welche Instrumente im Unternehmen angewendet werden und welche für das Projekt relevant sind,
- zu erkennen, welche Aktivitäten das Unternehmen verfolgt,
- das Themengebiet ergebnisorientiert aufarbeiten zu können,
- das gesamte Themengebiet gedanklich zu durchdringen und anzuwenden,
- sowie die Reflexion des Themengebietes sowohl auf das Unternehmen als auch auf das Projekt zu leisten.

### Transferreport I (unternehmensbezogen):
Transfer des TDR-Themas auf das Unternehmen

### Transferreport II (projektbezogen):
Transfer des TDR-Themas auf das Projekt bzw. die Abteilung und Erstellung einer Präsentation

### Dokumentation:
Dokumentation der Literatur im Anhang

# Structure TDR

**Titel:** Project Management
TDR (Transfer Documentation Report)

**Learning objectives:** The student should, after the processing of the TDRs be able to:

- Perform a transfer to the project.
- Recognize the subject area in the company,
- Apply a scientific subject to the business practice,
- Connect the subject matter with a company environment,
- Express what instruments are applied in the company and which are relevant for the project,
- See what activities the company is pursuing,
- Process the subject area results oriented,
- Comprehend and apply the entire topic,
- Reflect the subject both in the company as well as in the project.

**Transfer report I (company related):**
Transfer of the TDR topics to the company

**Transfer report II (project related):**
Transfer of the TDR topic to the project or division, and drafting of a presentation

**Documentation:**
Documentation of the literature in the Appendix

## Transferreport I (unternehmensbezogen)

- Wie ist das Thema bzw. das Themengebiet Projektmanagement in Ihrem Unternehmen umgesetzt?
- Welche Bedeutung wird dem Projektmanagement in Ihrem Unternehmen beigemessen?
- Welchen konkreten unternehmerischen Nutzen hat das Themengebiet in Ihrem Unternehmen?

Beschreiben und erläutern Sie dies bitte auf mindestens einer, höchstens drei Seiten.

Fall es Ihnen nicht möglich ist die oben genannten Fragen auf Ihr Unternehmen zu übertragen, da in Ihrem Unternehmen keinerlei Projekte anfallen, setzen Sie sich beispielsweise mit folgenden Fragestellungen auseinander:

- In welcher Art wären Projekte in Ihrem Unternehmen denkbar?
- Welche Methode des Projektmanagements wäre für Ihr Unternehmen am geeignetsten?
- Stellen Sie einen Vergleich auf, warum genau diese Methode am besten geeignet ist und andere weniger.
- Welche Organisationsform wäre am sinnvollsten und warum?

## Transfer Report I (Company Related)

- How is the topic or the subject matter project management implemented in your company?
- Which importance is provided to the project management system in your company?
- What are the specific business benefits of the subject in your company?

Describe and explain this please on at least one, however no more than three pages.

If you are not able to apply the above-mentioned questions to your business, because your organization does not generate any projects, please discuss for example the following questions:

- In what would form would projects in your company be plausible?
- Which method of project management would be most suitable for your company?
- Compare why exactly this method is the most suitable and others are less suitable.
- What organizational form would be best and why?

## Transferreport II (projektbezogen)

Bitte beschreiben Sie die Relevanz und Transfermöglichkeit des Themengebiets bezogen auf Ihr Projekt. Betrachten Sie bitte auch das unternehmensinterne Projektmanagement für Ihr Projekt.

Bitte arbeiten Sie mindestens sieben, höchstens zehn Seiten Report zu diesen Fragestellungen aus. Bei der Bearbeitung können Sie bei Bedarf folgende Checkliste zur Hilfe bzw. als Anhaltspunkt nehmen:

- Wie sieht das aktuelle (unternehmensinterne) Projektmanagement aus?
- Wie ist Ihr Projekt strukturiert? Wie ist es in das Unternehmensumfeld einzuordnen?
- Stellen Sie die verschiedenen Phasen des Projektmanagements übertragen auf Ihr Projekt dar.
- Welchen Nutzen hat Ihr Projekt für das Unternehmen?
- Stellen Sie die Methode dar, mit der Sie Ihr Projekt managen.

# Transfer Report II (Project Related)

Please describe the relevance and applicability of the topic with respect to your project. Please also discuss the corporate project management for your project.

Please generate a report of at least seven, a maximum of 10 pages with respect to these questions. If necessary, you can use the following checklist for help or reference:

- What is the current (internal) project management?
- How is your project structured? How is it integrated in the business environment?
- Please discuss the various phases of project management as they apply to your project.
- What benefits has your project for the company?
- Discuss the method, which you use to manage your project.

# Inhaltsverzeichnis

Wissen (vermitteln) alleine genügt nicht .................................................................. VI
Aufbau TDR ................................................................................................................ VIII
Transferreport I (unternehmensbezogen) ................................................................ X
Transferreport II (projektbezogen) ........................................................................... XII
Abbildungsverzeichnis ............................................................................................... XVIII
Tabellenverzeichnis .................................................................................................... XXII
Vorwort ......................................................................................................................... XXIV

**1 Grundlagen des Projektmanagements** .............................................................. 2
   1.1 Definition „Projekt" ............................................................................................ 2
   1.2 Abgrenzung zwischen Projekt und Tagesgeschäft ....................................... 4
   1.3 Das magische Dreieck des Projektmanagements ......................................... 4
   1.4 Voraussetzungen zur Projektarbeit .................................................................. 8
   1.5 Projektmanagement ........................................................................................... 10
   1.6 Projektphasen ...................................................................................................... 10
   1.7 Phasenmodell ...................................................................................................... 14

**2 Vorphase (Projektinitialisierung)** ........................................................................ 18
   2.1 Vorstudie / Aufgabenanalyse im Rahmen eines Workshops ....................... 18
   2.2 Entscheidungshilfen und Priorisierungsmethoden ...................................... 38
   2.3 Vorhabensantrag (Projektantrag) ..................................................................... 40
   2.4 Projektorganisation ............................................................................................. 44
         2.4.1 Linien-Projektorganisation .................................................................... 44
         2.4.2 Stabs- oder Einfluss-Projektorganisation .......................................... 46
         2.4.3 Reine Projektorganisation .................................................................... 48
         2.4.4 Matrix-Projektorganisation .................................................................. 50
         2.4.5 Wechsel der Organisationsform ........................................................... 52
   2.5 Übersicht Organisationsformen ....................................................................... 52

**3 Definitionsphase** ..................................................................................................... 56
   3.1 Projekt-Start-up oder Kick-off ........................................................................... 56
         3.1.1 Aufgaben des Auftraggebers / Entscheiders ..................................... 56
         3.1.2 Anforderungen an den Projektleiter ................................................... 58
         3.1.3 Die Aufgaben des Projektleiters sind .................................................. 58
         3.1.4 Befugnisse des Projektleiters ................................................................ 58
         3.1.5 Anforderungen an das Projektteam .................................................... 60
         3.1.6 Festlegung der Aufbau- und Ablauforganisation ............................ 60
         3.1.7 Erstellung ................................................................................................ 62
   3.2 Werkzeuge in der Definitionsphase ................................................................. 62
         3.2.1 Planungsplan .......................................................................................... 62
         3.2.2 Zieldefinition – Projektziele und Zielstrukturplan ........................... 62

**4 Planungsphase** ......................................................................................................... 74
   4.1 Grobplanung ....................................................................................................... 74
   4.2 Fein- oder Detailplanung .................................................................................. 76
   4.3 Erforderliche Projektpläne in der Übersicht ................................................. 76
   4.4 Projektpläne als Beispiel ................................................................................... 78
         4.4.1 Projektstrukturplan ............................................................................... 78
         4.4.2 Projektablaufplan .................................................................................. 90
         4.4.3 Personal- / Ressourcenplanung ........................................................... 102

# Table of Contents

**Knowledge (transfer) on its own is not enough** ................................................. VII
**Structure TDR** ................................................................................................ IX
**Transfer Report I (Company Related)** ............................................................. XI
**Transfer Report II (Project Related)** ............................................................. XIII
**Figures** ........................................................................................................ XIX
**Tables** ........................................................................................................ XXIII
**Introduction** ................................................................................................ XXV

**1 Basics of Project Management** ................................................................. 3
   1.1 Definition of "Project" ............................................................................ 3
   1.2 Differentiation Between Project and Day-to-Day Business ........................ 5
   1.3 The Magic Triangle of Project Management ............................................ 5
   1.4 Prerequisites for Project Work ................................................................ 9
   1.5 Project Management ............................................................................ 11
   1.6 Project Phases .................................................................................... 11
   1.7 Phase Model ....................................................................................... 15

**2 Initial Phase (Project Initiation)** ............................................................. 19
   2.1 Initial Study / Analysis in the Context of a Workshop .............................. 19
   2.2 Decision Making Tools and Methods of Prioritization ............................. 39
   2.3 Project Application (Project Proposal) .................................................. 41
   2.4 Project Organization ........................................................................... 45
      2.4.1 Linear Project Organization ........................................................ 45
      2.4.2 Staff or Influence Project Organization ....................................... 47
      2.4.3 Pure Project Organization .......................................................... 49
      2.4.4 Matrix Project Organization ....................................................... 51
      2.4.5 Change of the Type of Organization ........................................... 53
   2.5 Overview Organizational Forms ........................................................... 53

**3 Definition Phase** ..................................................................................... 57
   3.1 Project Start-Up or Kick Off ................................................................. 57
      3.1.1 Tasks of the Client / Decision Maker .......................................... 57
      3.1.2 Requirements for the Project Manager ....................................... 59
      3.1.3 The Tasks of the Project Manager Are: ....................................... 59
      3.1.4 Competencies of the Project Leader ........................................... 59
      3.1.5 Requirements of the Project Team .............................................. 61
      3.1.6 Definition of the Organizational and Operational Structure ......... 61
      3.1.7 Creation ................................................................................... 63
   3.2 Tools in the Definition Phase ............................................................... 63
      3.2.1 Design Plan .............................................................................. 63
      3.2.2 Objective Definition – Project Objectives and Target Structure Plan ... 63

**4 Planning Phase** ....................................................................................... 75
   4.1 Rough Planning ................................................................................... 75
   4.2 Fine or Detailed Planning .................................................................... 77
   4.3 Necessary Project Plans in the Overview .............................................. 77
   4.4 Project Plans as an Example ................................................................ 79
      4.4.1 Work Breakdown Structure ....................................................... 79
      4.4.2 Project Schedule ....................................................................... 91
      4.4.3 Staff / Resource Planning .......................................................... 103

|  |  |  |
|---|---|---|
| | 4.4.4 Kostenplanung | 104 |
| | 4.4.5 EVA – Earned-Value-Analyse | 108 |
| **5** | **Realisierungsphase** | **120** |
| | 5.1 Projektsteuerung / Controlling | 120 |
| |     5.1.1 Controlling – Begriff | 120 |
| |     5.1.2 Grundregeln | 122 |
| |     5.1.3 Systematik des Projektcontrollings | 122 |
| |     5.1.4 Qualitätssicherung | 124 |
| |     5.1.5 Meilenstein-Trendanalyse | 126 |
| | 5.2 Projektstatussitzung | 128 |
| |     5.2.1 Arten von Sitzungen | 128 |
| |     5.2.2 Was soll bei Projektsitzungen beachtet werden? | 130 |
| **6** | **Abschlussphase** | **134** |
| **7** | **Teamentwicklung** | **140** |
| **8** | **Projektmanagementmethoden** | **144** |
| | 8.1 Klassisches Projektmanagement | 144 |
| | 8.2 Agiles Projektmanagement | 144 |
| | 8.3 Prince2 | 146 |
| | 8.4 Scrum | 164 |
| **9** | **Fallstudie** | **186** |
| | 9.1 Ausgangssituation | 186 |
| |     9.1.1 Projekt und Abgrenzung zum Tagesgeschäft | 186 |
| |     9.1.2 Das magische Dreieck des Projektmanagements | 186 |
| |     9.1.3 Phasenmodell | 188 |
| | 9.2 Vorphase | 188 |
| |     9.2.1 Vorstudie | 188 |
| |     9.2.2 Entscheidung | 198 |
| |     9.2.3 Projektorganisation | 198 |
| | 9.3 Definitionsphase | 198 |
| |     9.3.1 Projekt-Start-up | 198 |
| |     9.3.2 Anforderungen an den Projektleiter und das Projektteam | 200 |
| |     9.3.3 Verwendete Werkzeuge | 200 |
| | 9.4 Planungsphase | 202 |
| |     9.4.1 Grob- und Feinplanung | 202 |
| |     9.4.2 Projektpläne | 204 |
| | 9.5 Realisierungsphase | 210 |
| |     9.5.1 Projektcontrolling | 210 |
| |     9.5.2 Meilenstein-Trendanalyse | 212 |
| |     9.5.3 Qualitätssicherung | 212 |
| |     9.5.4 Projektstatussitzungen | 214 |
| | 9.6 Abschlussphase | 214 |
| | 9.7 Teamentwicklung | 214 |
| **10** | **Lösungshinweise der Aufgaben zur Selbstkontrolle** | **216** |
| **Literaturverzeichnis** | | **266** |
| **Quellen aus dem Internet** | | **267** |
| **Weiterführende Links zur ersten Orientierung** | | **268** |

|   |   |   |
|---|---|---|
| | 4.4.4 Cost Planning | 105 |
| | 4.4.5 EVA – Earned Value Analysis | 109 |

## 5 Implementation Phase ... 121
### 5.1 Project Management / Cost Control ... 121
    5.1.1 Cost Control – Concept ... 121
    5.1.2 General Rules ... 123
    5.1.3 Classification of Project Controlling ... 123
    5.1.4 Quality Assurance ... 125
    5.1.5 Milestone Trend Analysis ... 127
### 5.2 Project Progress Review ... 129
    5.2.1 Type of Reviews ... 129
    5.2.2 What Is Important to Note in Project Meetings? ... 131

## 6 Final Phase ... 135

## 7 Team Development ... 141

## 8 Project Management Methodologies ... 145
### 8.1 Classic Project Management ... 145
### 8.2 Agile Project Management ... 145
### 8.3 Prince2 ... 147
### 8.4 Scrum ... 165

## 9 Case Study ... 187
### 9.1 Initial Situation ... 187
    9.1.1 Project and the Boundaries to the Day-to-Day Business ... 187
    9.1.2 The Magic Triangle of Project Management ... 187
    9.1.3 Phase Model ... 189
### 9.2 Initial phase ... 189
    9.2.1 Preliminary Study ... 189
    9.2.2 Decision ... 199
    9.2.3 Project Organization ... 199
### 9.3 Definition Phase ... 199
    9.3.1 Project-Start-Up ... 199
    9.3.2 Requirements for the Project Manager and the Project Team ... 201
    9.3.3 Tools Used ... 201
### 9.4 Planning phase ... 203
    9.4.1 Outline and Detail Planning ... 203
    9.4.2 Project Plans ... 205
### 9.5 Implementation Phase ... 211
    9.5.1 Project Controlling ... 211
    9.5.2 Milestone Trend Analysis ... 213
    9.5.3 Quality Assurance ... 213
    9.5.4 Project Progress Meetings ... 215
### 9.6 Final Phase ... 215
### 9.7 Team Development ... 215

## 10 Solutions for the Tasks for Progress Review ... 217

**Bibliography** ... 266
**Sources from the Internet** ... 267
**Further Links for Basic Information** ... 268

## Abbildungsverzeichnis

Abb. 1: Das magisches Dreieck des Projektmanagements ................... 6
Abb. 2: Phasenmodell ................... 14
Abb. 3: Zielhierarchie ................... 24
Abb. 4: Projektumfeldanalyse ................... 28
Abb. 5: Projektbeteiligte ................... 30
Abb. 6: Projektrisikoanalyse ................... 32
Abb. 7: Projektstrukturplanung ................... 34
Abb. 8: Balkenplan (Screenshot MS-Project) ................... 38
Abb. 9: Eisenhower-Matrix ................... 38
Abb. 10: Portfolio-Analyse ................... 40
Abb. 11: Projektantrag 1 ................... 40
Abb. 12: Projektantrag 2 ................... 42
Abb. 13: Linien-Projektorganisation ................... 44
Abb. 14: Stabs- / Einfluss-Projektorganisation ................... 46
Abb. 15: Reine Projektorganisation ................... 48
Abb. 16: Matrix-Projektorganisation ................... 50
Abb. 17: Projektorganisationsformen ................... 52
Abb. 18: Planungsplan ................... 62
Abb. 19: Ziele ................... 66
Abb. 20: Zielarten ................... 66
Abb. 21: Zielstrukturplan ................... 68
Abb. 22: Pflichtenheft ................... 70
Abb. 23: Planungsphasen ................... 74
Abb. 24: Projektstrukturplan ................... 78
Abb. 25: Arbeitspaketbeschreibung ................... 84
Abb. 26: Projektstruktur EDV-Projektbibliothek
(Screenshot Ordnerstruktur Windows) ................... 88
Abb. 27: Projektablaufplan ................... 90
Abb. 28: Vorgangs- / Aktivitätenliste ................... 92
Abb. 29: Balkendiagramm ................... 92
Abb. 30: Netzplanknoten ................... 96
Abb. 31: Anordnungsbeziehungen im Netzplan ................... 100
Abb. 32: Personalplanung Listentechnik ................... 102
Abb. 33: Kapazitätsauslastungsdiagramm ................... 102
Abb. 34: Kostenstellen ................... 106
Abb. 35: Kostentableau ................... 106
Abb. 36: Basiswerte ................... 110
Abb. 37: Variances und Indices ................... 112
Abb. 38: Controlling ................... 120
Abb. 39: Systematik des Projektcontrollings ................... 122
Abb. 40: Meilenstein-Trendanalyse ................... 128
Abb. 41: Projektabschlussphase ................... 134
Abb. 42: Auswirkungsbeziehungen im Projekt ................... 140
Abb. 43: Teamentwicklung ................... 142
Abb. 44: Klassisches Projektmanagement ................... 144
Abb. 45: Agiles Projektmanagement ................... 146

# Figures

| | | |
|---|---|---|
| Fig. 1: | Magic Triangle of Project Management | 7 |
| Fig. 2: | Phase Model | 15 |
| Fig. 3: | Target Hierarchy | 25 |
| Fig. 4: | Project Environment Analysis | 29 |
| Fig. 5: | Project Participants | 31 |
| Fig. 6: | Project Risk Analysis | 33 |
| Fig. 7: | Project Structure Analysis | 35 |
| Fig. 8: | Gantt Chart (for Example MS-Project) | 39 |
| Fig. 9: | Eisenhower Matrix | 39 |
| Fig. 10: | Portfolio Analysis | 41 |
| Fig. 11: | Project Application 1 | 41 |
| Fig. 12: | Project Application 2 | 43 |
| Fig. 13: | Linear Project Organization | 45 |
| Fig. 14: | Staff / Influence-Project Organization | 47 |
| Fig. 15: | Pure Project Organization | 49 |
| Fig. 16: | Matrix Project Organization | 51 |
| Fig. 17: | Project Organization Forms | 53 |
| Fig. 18: | Design Plan | 63 |
| Fig. 19: | Objectives | 67 |
| Fig. 20: | Objective Types | 67 |
| Fig. 21: | Target Structure Plan | 69 |
| Fig. 22: | Performance Specifications | 71 |
| Fig. 23: | Graphic Planning Stages | 75 |
| Fig. 24: | Work Breakdown Structure | 79 |
| Fig. 25: | Work Package Description | 85 |
| Fig. 26: | Project Structure IT-Project Library (Screenshot Windows File Structure) | 89 |
| Fig. 27: | Project Schedule | 91 |
| Fig. 28: | Process / Activity list | 93 |
| Fig. 29: | Gantt chart | 93 |
| Fig. 30: | Activity Plan Node | 97 |
| Fig. 31: | Ordered Relationships Activity Network | 101 |
| Fig. 32: | Personnel Planning List Technique | 103 |
| Fig. 33: | Capacity Utilization Diagram | 103 |
| Fig. 34: | Cost Centers | 107 |
| Fig. 35: | Cost Tables | 107 |
| Fig. 36: | Base Values | 111 |
| Fig. 37: | Variances and Indices | 113 |
| Fig. 38: | Controlling | 121 |
| Fig. 39: | Classification of Project Controlling | 123 |
| Fig. 40: | Milestone Trend Analysis | 129 |
| Fig. 41: | Final Project Phase | 135 |
| Fig. 42: | Impact of Relationships in the Project | 141 |
| Fig. 43: | Team Development | 143 |
| Fig. 44: | Classic Project Management | 145 |
| Fig. 45: | Agile Project Management | 147 |

| | |
|---|---|
| Abb. 46: Modell Prince2 | 148 |
| Abb. 47: Managementaufbau Prince2 | 152 |
| Abb. 48: Prozesse Prince2 | 154 |
| Abb. 49: Überblick Prince2 | 158 |
| Abb. 50: Scrum-Prozess | 164 |
| Abb. 51: Scrum-Rollen | 166 |
| Abb. 52: Sprint Planning Meeting 1 & 2 | 172 |
| Abb. 53: Sprint & Daily Scrum | 174 |
| Abb. 54: Sprint Review & Retrospektive | 176 |
| Abb. 55: Sprint Burndown Chart | 178 |
| Abb. 56: Scrum-Beispiel-Projekt „Hausbau" | 182 |
| Abb. 57: Projekt-Workshop | 188 |
| Abb. 58: Ressourcenplan | 194 |
| Abb. 59: Balkenplan (Screenshot MS-Project) | 196 |
| Abb. 60: Projektorganisation | 198 |
| Abb. 61: Projektstrukturplan | 204 |
| Abb. 62: Arbeitspaketbeschreibung | 206 |
| Abb. 63: Projektablaufplan (Screenshot MS-Project) | 208 |
| Abb. 64: Ressourcenplan | 210 |
| Abb. 65: Projektantrag | 232 |
| Abb. 66: Projektorganisationsformen | 240 |
| Abb. 67: Klassisches Projektmanagement | 254 |
| Abb. 68: Agiles Projektmanagement | 256 |
| Abb. 69: Modell Prince2 | 256 |

Alle Abbildungen sind, sofern nicht anders angegeben, eigene Darstellung.

| | | |
|---|---|---|
| Fig. 46: | Modell Prince2 | 149 |
| Fig. 47: | Management structure Prince2 | 153 |
| Fig. 48: | Prince2 Processes | 155 |
| Fig. 49: | Overview Prince2 | 159 |
| Fig. 50: | Scrum-Process | 165 |
| Fig. 51: | Scrum-Roles | 167 |
| Fig. 52: | Sprint Planning Meeting 1 & 2 | 173 |
| Fig. 53: | Sprint & Daily Scrum | 175 |
| Fig. 54: | Sprint Review & Retrospektive | 177 |
| Fig. 55: | Sprint Burndown Chart | 179 |
| Fig. 56: | Scrum Example Project "House Construction" | 183 |
| Fig. 57: | Project Workshop | 189 |
| Fig. 58: | Resource Plan | 195 |
| Fig. 59: | Gantt Chart (Screenshot MS-Project) | 197 |
| Fig. 60: | Project Organization | 199 |
| Fig. 61: | Work Breakdown Structure | 205 |
| Fig. 62: | Work Package Description | 207 |
| Fig. 63: | Project Schedule (Screenshot MS-Project) | 209 |
| Fig. 64: | Resource Plan | 211 |
| Fig. 65: | Project Application | 233 |
| Fig. 66: | Project Organization Forms | 241 |
| Fig. 67: | Classic Project Management | 255 |
| Fig. 68: | Agile Project Management | 257 |
| Fig. 69: | Prince2 Model | 257 |

Unless otherwise stated or indicated, all figures are compiled by the authors.

# Tabellenverzeichnis

| | | |
|---|---|---|
| Tab. 1: | Abgrenzung Projekt und Tagesgeschäft | 4 |
| Tab. 2: | Vor- und Nachteile der Linien-Projektorganisation | 44 |
| Tab. 3: | Vor- und Nachteile der Stabs-/Einfluss-Projektorganisation | 46 |
| Tab. 4: | Vor- und Nachteile der reinen Projektorganisation | 48 |
| Tab. 5: | Vor- und Nachteile der Matrix-Projektorganisation | 50 |
| Tab. 6: | Vor- und Nachteile Balkendiagramm | 92 |
| Tab. 7: | Vor- und Nachteile Netzplan | 94 |
| Tab. 8: | Elemente des Netzplanes | 94 |
| Tab. 9: | Pufferberechnung | 98 |
| Tab. 10: | Übersicht Basiswerte | 112 |
| Tab. 11: | Übersicht Basiswerte | 114 |
| Tab. 12: | Übersicht Indices | 114 |
| Tab. 13: | Übersicht Kostenprognose | 116 |
| Tab. 14: | Übersicht Laufzeitprognose | 118 |
| Tab. 15: | Projektsitzung | 130 |
| Tab. 16: | Inhalte eines Abschlussberichts | 136 |
| Tab. 17: | Rolle und Verantwortlichkeiten Prince2 | 150 |
| Tab. 18: | Aufgaben Projektmanager Prince2 | 154 |
| Tab. 19: | Vor- und Nachteile Prince2 | 160 |
| Tab. 20: | Beispiel Prince2 – Grundprinzipien | 160 |
| Tab. 21: | Beispiel Prince2 – Themen | 162 |
| Tab. 22: | Beispiel Prince2 – Prozesse | 162 |
| Tab. 23: | Scrum-Komponenten | 164 |
| Tab. 24: | Übersicht Product Owner, Scrum Master und Entwicklerteam | 168 |
| Tab. 25: | Übersicht Zeremonien Scrum | 176 |
| Tab. 26: | Taskboard | 178 |
| Tab. 27: | Übersicht Artefakte Scrum | 180 |
| Tab. 28: | Vor- und Nachteile Scrum | 182 |
| Tab. 29: | Fallbeispiel Meilensteine und Zeitplan | 190 |
| Tab. 30: | Fallbeispiel Projektumfeldanalyse | 192 |
| Tab. 31: | Fallbeispiel Ressourcenplanung | 194 |
| Tab. 32: | Fallbeispiel Planungsplan | 200 |
| Tab. 33: | Fallbeispiel Zielstrukturplan | 202 |
| Tab. 34: | Fallbeispiel Meilenstein-Trendanalyse | 212 |
| Tab. 35: | Vor- und Nachteile der Linien-Projektorganisation | 234 |
| Tab. 36: | Vor- und Nachteile der Stabs-/Einfluss-Projektorganisation | 234 |
| Tab. 37: | Vor- und Nachteile der reinen Projektorganisation | 236 |
| Tab. 38: | Vor- und Nachteile der Matrix-Projektorganisation | 238 |
| Tab. 39: | Rolle und Verantwortlichkeiten Prince2 | 258 |
| Tab. 40: | Scrum-Komponenten | 260 |
| Tab. 41: | Übersicht Zeremonien Scrum | 262 |
| Tab. 42: | Übersicht Artefakte Scrum | 264 |

Alle Tabellen sind, sofern nicht anders angegeben, eigene Darstellung.

# Tables

| | | |
|---|---|---|
| Tab. 1: | Differentiation Day-to-Day Business and Project Work | 5 |
| Tab. 2: | Benefits and Disadvantages Linear Project Organization | 45 |
| Tab. 3: | Benefits and Disadvantages Staff / Influence Project Organization | 47 |
| Tab. 4: | Benefits and Disadvantages Pure Project Organization | 49 |
| Tab. 5: | Benefits and Disadvantages Matrix Project Organization | 51 |
| Tab. 6: | Benefits and Disadvantages Gantt-Chart | 93 |
| Tab. 7: | Benefits and Disadvantages Activity Network | 95 |
| Tab. 8: | Elements Activity Network | 95 |
| Tab. 9: | Float Time Calculation | 99 |
| Tab. 10: | Overview Base Values | 113 |
| Tab. 11: | Overview Base Values | 115 |
| Tab. 12: | Overview Indices | 115 |
| Tab. 13: | Overview Cost Forecast | 117 |
| Tab. 14: | Overview Forecast Schedule | 119 |
| Tab. 15: | Project Meeting | 131 |
| Tab. 16: | Contents of the Final Report | 137 |
| Tab. 17: | Roles and Responsibilities Prince2 | 151 |
| Tab. 18: | Tasks Project Manager Prince2 | 155 |
| Tab. 19: | Benefits and Disadvantages Prince2 | 161 |
| Tab. 20: | Example Prince2 – basic principles | 161 |
| Tab. 21: | Example Prince2 – Subjects | 163 |
| Tab. 22: | Example Prince2 – Processes | 163 |
| Tab. 23: | Scrum-Components | 165 |
| Tab. 24: | Overview Product Owner, Scrum Master and Development Team | 169 |
| Tab. 25: | Overview Scrum Ceremonies | 177 |
| Tab. 26: | Taskboard | 179 |
| Tab. 27: | Overview Scrum Artifacts | 181 |
| Tab. 28: | Benefits and Disadvantages Scrum | 183 |
| Tab. 29: | Case Study Milestones and Outline Schedule | 191 |
| Tab. 30: | Case Study Project Environment Analysis | 193 |
| Tab. 31: | Case Study Ressource Plan | 195 |
| Tab. 32: | Case Study Design Plan | 201 |
| Tab. 33: | Case Study Target Structure Plan | 203 |
| Tab. 34: | Case Study Milestone Trend Analysis | 213 |
| Tab. 35: | Benefits and Disadvantages Linear Project Organization | 235 |
| Tab. 36: | Benefits and Disadvantages Staff or Influence Project Organization | 235 |
| Tab. 37: | Benefits and Disadvantages Pure Project Organization | 237 |
| Tab. 38: | Benefits and Disadvantages Matrix Project Organization | 239 |
| Tab. 39: | Roles and Responsibilites Prince2 | 259 |
| Tab. 40: | Scrum Components | 261 |
| Tab. 41: | Overview Scrum Ceremonies | 263 |
| Tab. 42: | Overview Scrum Artifacts | 265 |

Unless otherwise stated or indicated, all tables are compiled by the authors.

## Vorwort

Der Ihnen vorliegende TDR Projektmanagement soll einen Einblick ins das Projektmanagement ermöglichen und ein Basiswissen aus diesem Bereich vermitteln.

Kapitel 1 befasst sich daher mit den Grundlagen des Projektmanagements. Die darauf folgenden Kapitel 2 bis 6 beschreiben die verschiedenen Phasen (Vorphase, Definition, Planung, Realisierung und Abschluss), die im Projektmanagement durchlaufen werden und entwickeln somit die klassische Vorgehensweise beim Managen und Durchführen von Projekten.

In Kapitel 7 wird auf die Entwicklung des Projektteams eingegangen. Das abschließende Kapitel 8 beleuchtet verschiedene Projektmanagementmethoden. Im letzten Abschnitt, Kapitel 9, wird das bisher gelernte noch einmal an einer Fallstudie verdeutlicht.

Im Anschluss an jedes Kapitel finden Sie Aufgaben zur Selbstkontrolle des Lern- und Verständnisprozesses. Die Lösungshinweise zu diesen Fragen sind in Kapitel 10 zusammengetragen.

*Die Autoren im Februar 2014*

# Introduction

The TDR project management being discussed should provide you with an insight into project management and basic knowledge of the subject matter.

For those reasons chapter 1 focuses on the basics of project management. The following chapters 2 to 6 describe the various phases (preparatory phase, definition, planning, implementation and completion), of project management and develop with it the classic approach to manage and execute projects.

chapter 7 will discuss the development of the project team. The final chapter 8 examines various project management methodologies. In the last section, chapter 9 will illustrate everything you have learned so far once again in a case study.

Following each chapter you will find tasks for checking your learning and comprehension progress. The suggestions for solutions to these questions are consolidated in chapter 10.

*The authors, February 2014*

**Notizen**

### Symbolik des TDR Books

 **Definitionen und Hinweise**

 **Orientierungshilfe**

Notes

### The Symbols of the TDR

| | |
|---|---|
|  | **Definition and General Information** |
|  | **Guide** |

# 1 Grundlagen des Projektmanagements

## Allgemeines

Unternehmen beschäftigen sich überwiegend mit wiederkehrenden Prozessen, die teilweise standardisiert sind und als Routine behandelt werden können. Neben solchen alltäglichen Arbeitsbereichen sind aber auch immer wieder Innovationen und Umstrukturierungen in Projektform notwendig. Im Folgenden soll, nach einer Begriffsdefinition und der Abgrenzung zwischen Tagesgeschäft und Projektarbeit, eine Einführung in den Bereich des Projektmanagements gegeben werden.

## 1.1 Definition „Projekt"

**Ein Projekt ist nach der DIN 69901[1]:**

„ein Vorhaben, das im Wesentlichen durch die Einmaligkeit der Bedingungen in ihrer Gesamtheit gekennzeichnet ist." – Projekte sind Aufgaben mit besonderen Merkmalen. Sie sind durch folgende Merkmale gekennzeichnet:

- Einmaligkeit
- klare Zielsetzung
- definierter(s) Anfang/Ende
- begrenzter Aufgabenumfang
- Neuartigkeit
- Risiko
- Komplexität
- spezielle Organisation
- begrenzte Mittel (zeitlich, finanziell, personell)
- besondere Größe und Bedeutung
- messbarer Erfolg
- mit außergewöhnlichen Kosten verbunden

---

[1] Vgl. Deutsches Institut für Normung (2009), DIN 69901.

# 1 Basics of Project Management

## General Information

Companies mainly deal with recurring processes, some of which are standardized and can be treated as routine. In addition to such everyday work processes innovation and restructuring in a project form are necessary on a recurring bases. The following is intended to provide a definition of terms and the boundaries between day-to-day business and project work, after an introduction to the area of project management is provided.

## 1.1 Definition of "Project"

A project is, according to the DIN 69901[1]:

"An undertaking, which is primarily defined through the uniqueness of the conditions in their entirety." Projects are tasks with special characteristics. They are characterized by:

- Uniqueness
- Clear objectives
- Defined start/end
- Limited scope
- Novelty
- Risk
- Complexity
- Special organization
- Limited resources (time, financial, manpower)
- Special magnitude and importance
- Measurable success
- Associated with extraordinary costs

---

[1] Cf. Deutsches Institut für Normung (2009), DIN 69901.

## 1.2 Abgrenzung zwischen Projekt und Tagesgeschäft

Wie bereits oben angeführt grenzen sich das Tagesgeschäft und die Projektarbeit gegenseitig ab, diese Unterschiede werden in der folgenden Tabelle dargestellt:

| Tagesgeschäft | Projekt |
| --- | --- |
| wiederholte Prozesse und Leistungen (Routinetätigkeit) | neuer Prozess und/oder neues Ergebnis (Einmaligkeit) |
| verschiedene Ziele werden verfolgt | ein konkretes und klar umrissenes Ziel (mit Detailzielen) wird angestrebt |
| andauernde Tätigkeit | einmalige, zeitlich begrenzte Aktivität |
| in der Regel homogene Mitarbeiterzusammensetzung | möglichst heterogene Mitarbeiterzusammensetzung |
| bestehendes System für gemeinsame Anstrengungen | neu aufzubauendes System |
| Arbeiten innerhalb der Linie | Arbeiten außerhalb der Linie |
| Bestimmtheit des Ablaufs bezüglich Ergebnis, Kosten und Zeitbedarf | hohe Unsicherheit bezüglich Ergebnis, Kosten und Zeitbedarf |
| Anwendung von etablierten Verfahren und Methoden | Bruch mit etablierten Verfahren und Methoden |
| Unterstützung des Status Quo | Veränderung des Status Quo |

Tab. 1: Abgrenzung Projekt und Tagesgeschäft.

## 1.3 Das magische Dreieck des Projektmanagements

In Projekten lassen sich drei wesentliche Größen identifizieren, welche die Ecken eines „magischen" Dreiecks darstellen und voneinander abhängen. Diese werden als Haupteinflussfaktoren bezeichnet, weil in ihnen der gesamte Einsatz an Arbeitsstunden, die Sach- und Finanzausstattung und alle „Projekt-Leistungserstellungsprozesse" sowie das Projektergebnis enthalten sind. Die Veränderung einer dieser voneinander abhängigen Größen bedingt eine Veränderung auch (von mindestens einer) der beiden anderen Größen!

**Haupteinflussfaktor „Leistung/Qualität":**
Je höher die Ansprüche an den Umfang und/oder die Qualität der Projektergebnisse gestellt werden, umso größer wird wahrscheinlich der aufzuwendende Einsatz (Input) an Personalstunden und Ressourcen (Sachmittel, Geld etc.) sein. Wird nachträglich eine höhere Qualität des Projektergebnisses oder zusätzliche Funktionalitäten gefordert, dann wird sich auch höchstwahrscheinlich der Endtermin des Projekts zeitlich nach hinten verzögern.

## 1.2 Differentiation Between Project and Day-to-Day Business

As previously mentioned the day-to-day business and project work are differentiated from each other, these differences are shown in the following table:

| Day-to-Day Business | Project |
| --- | --- |
| Repeated processes and services (routine activity) | New process and / or new result (uniqueness) |
| Different goals are pursued | A concrete and clearly defined objective (with sub objectives) is being sought |
| Enduring activities | One-off, time-limited activity |
| Generally homogeneous organizational participation | Where possible a heterogeneous organizational participation |
| Existing system for joint efforts | Newly-to-be-established system |
| Work within the line | Work outside the line |
| Certainty of the process on results, costs and time required | High uncertainty of the process on results, costs and time required |
| Application of established procedures and methodology | Departure from established procedures and methodology |
| Support of the status quo | Departure from the status quo |

Tab. 1: Differentiation Day-to-Day Business and Project Work.

## 1.3 The Magic Triangle of Project Management

There are three essential elements in projects, which identify the corners of a "magic triangle" and which depend on each other. These are known as major influence factors, because they contain the entire effort of working hours, the property and financial envelope and all "project performance processes" as well as the result of the project. The change one of these interdependent variables necessitates also a change of (at least one) of the other two variables!

**Primary Variable "Performance / Quality":**
The higher the demands on the extent and / or the quality of the project results, the greater will be probably the expended use (input) of HR Hours and resources (material, money, etc.). If a higher quality or additional functionalities of the project result are subsequently required, most likely the completion date of the project will be delayed.

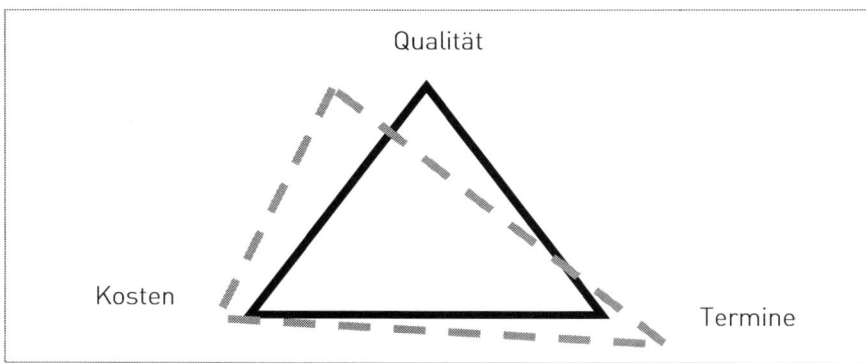

Abb. 1: Das magisches Dreieck des Projektmanagements.

Mehr Personal einzusetzen wäre eine denkbare Lösung, welche aber nicht unbedingt Erfolg bringen wird, weil dieses zusätzliche Personal eventuell zunächst eingearbeitet werden muss (Kosten- und Zeitfaktor). Schwierigkeiten könnten hier ebenfalls nicht ausreichend vorhandene Ressourcen verursachen, wenn zum Beispiel für 20 Mitarbeiter nur fünf PCs zur Verfügung stehen.

**Haupteinflussfaktor Termine:**
Zu starres Einhalten der in der Planungsphase festgelegten Termine schränkt die Flexibilität der Projektgruppe zu stark ein. Es besteht die Gefahr der Reduktion von (Teil-)Ergebnissen, wenn unter Zeitdruck, quasi über Nacht, eine Leistung erstellt werden muss.

Werden Termine verändert, dann werden sicherlich im Falle einer Terminvorverlegung Auswirkungen auf die Faktoren Kosten (+) und Leistung / Qualität (-) entstehen. Werden Termine nach hinten verschoben, besteht zumindest das Risiko, dass Freiräume nicht effizient (= wirtschaftlich) ausgenutzt werden.

**Haupteinflussfaktor Kosten:**
Kosten in einem Projekt entstehen durch den Einsatz von Personal und den Verbrauch von Ressourcen zur Erbringung des Projektergebnisses. Wenn Kosten gesenkt werden, beziehungsweise das dem Projekt zur Verfügung stehende Budget geschmälert wird, liegt es auf der Hand, dass das angestrebte Projektziel nicht in vollem Umfang und / oder nicht zum ursprünglich avisierten Zeitpunkt erfüllt werden kann.

Eine wesentliche und wichtige Aufgabe aller Projektverantwortlichen liegt darin, diese Abhängigkeiten zunächst zu erkennen und zu verstehen.

Im Zusammenhang mit dem „magischen Dreieck" kann in der Projektarbeit ein Spannungsfeld darin bestehen, dass Projekte zwar einerseits über eine entsprechende Aufbau- und Ablauforganisation mit Budget-, Termin- und Ablaufplänen usw. abgebildet werden müssen, aber dass andererseits zu viele und vor allem zu starre Regelungen die Flexibilität und Kreativität des Teams sowie die Innovationsfreude (als wesentliche Forderung an Projektergebnisse) erheblich dämpfen können.

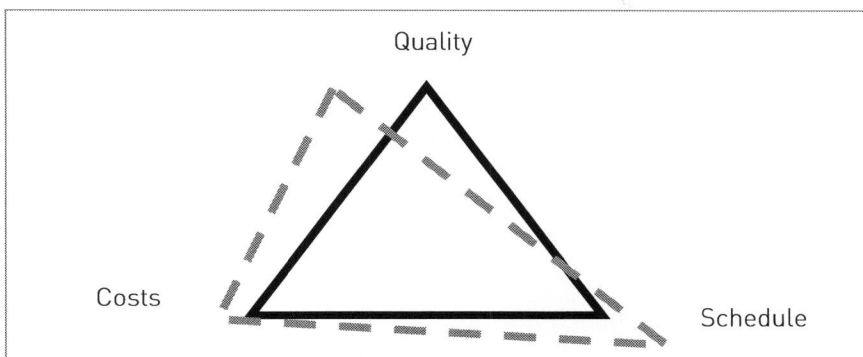

Fig. 1: Magic Triangle of Project Management.

A possible solution would be to use more staff, which may however not necessarily achieve the expected results, as the additional staff may need to first be "incorporated" (cost and time factor). Insufficient resources could cause further complications. For example, if only 5 PCs are available for 20 employees.

**Primary Variable "Schedule":**
Excessively rigid adherence to the milestones defined in the planning phase limits the "flexibility" of the project group too much. There is a danger of the reduction of (part-) results, when quasi "over night" results need to be achieved under time pressure.

If milestones are changed, in the case of a compression of the time line a certain impact on the variables of costs ( + ) and performance / quality ( – ) is created. If the time line is relaxed, there is at least the risk that the additional time is not efficiently (= economically) used.

**Primary Variable "Costs":**
Costs in a project are incurred by the use of personnel and the "consumption" of resources to achieve the project result. If costs are reduced, and / or the budget available for the project is shrunk, it is obvious that the project can neither meet the target fully nor the originally planned completion date.

An essential and important task of all responsible for the project lies first in the identification and then the understanding of these dependencies.

In the context of the "magic triangle" the project work can create tensions between the dependencies of the organizational structure and process organization on the one hand with budget, time and flow charts, etc., on the other, which have to be mapped, however too many rigid rules can significantly dampen in particular the flexibility and creativity of the team as well as the innovation (as a key requirement of project results).

Ein weiterer Konfliktbereich bei der Bearbeitung eines Projekts kann entstehen, wenn bei der Zielformulierung widersprüchliche, sich gegenseitig ausschließende oder entgegenstehende Ziele formuliert werden.

## 1.4 Voraussetzungen zur Projektarbeit

Bevor das Projektmanagement näher erläutert wird, sollen erst die zur Projektarbeit benötigten Voraussetzungen aufgezeigt werden:

- Erteilung des Projektauftrages
- Fähigkeit und Verpflichtung zu ganzheitlichem Denken
- Einteilung der Projektlaufzeit in Projektphasen
- Einhaltung der definierten Projektphasen
- projektspezifische Organisation der Aufbauorganisation
- technisch und wirtschaftlich sinnvolle Ablaufgestaltung
- formalisierte Abläufe und Verfahren, methodisches Vorgehen
- Definition von klaren Zielen und Vorgaben, die allen bekannt sind und von allen gleich verstanden werden
- Vorhandensein einer Aufgabenanalyse oder Vorstudie
- detaillierte Planungsunterlagen
- Gestaltung der konkreten Projektarbeit (Definition, Zielsetzung, Vernetzung der Arbeitspakete)
- Transparenz über den jeweiligen Projektstand
- frühzeitiges Erkennen von Projektrisiken
- sorgfältige Auswahl der Projektgruppenmitglieder
- Integrationsfähigkeit der Beteiligten
- Gestaltung von Teamarbeit und Kommunikation
- Berücksichtigung psycho-sozialer Faktoren
- Selbstdisziplin und Selbstkritik der Beteiligten
- ständiger Informationsfluss im Projekt
- ständiges Controlling
- verbindlicher Abschlusstermin
- konkrete Umsetzungsempfehlungen

A further conflict area in the processing of a project can be created when during the objective formulation conflicting, mutually exclusive or conflicting objectives are stated.

## 1.4　Prerequisites for Project Work

Before project management is explained in greater detail, the necessary conditions for the project work will be discussed:

- Issuing of the project mandate
- Ability and commitment to holistic thinking
- Classification of the project schedule in project phases
- Compliance with the defined project phases
- Project-specific organization of the organizational structure
- Technically and economically feasible process planning
- Formalized processes and procedures, a methodical approach
- Definition of clear objectives and targets, which are well known to and understood by all the same.
- Presence of a job task analysis or a preliminary study
- Detailed planning documents
- Draft of the project work details (definition, goal setting, networking of the work packages)
- Transparency about the respective project status
- Early identification of project risks
- Careful selection of project group members
- Integration capacity of the parties
- Plan for teamwork and communication
- Considering psycho-social factors
- Self-discipline, and self-criticism on the part of the parties
- Constant flow of information on the project
- Constant controlling
- Mandatory completion date
- Specific recommendations

## 1.5 Projektmanagement

**Projektmanagement bedeutet:** Gesamtheit aller Führungsaufgaben, Führungsorganisationen, Führungstechniken und Führungsmittel für die Abwicklung eines Projekts.

Als essenzielle Aufgaben des Projektmanagements lassen sich folgende Punkte festhalten:

- Strukturierung von Projekten
- starke Betonung der Definitions- und Zielfindungsphase
- starke Betonung der Planungsphase
- klare Ziele und Vorgaben für alle Beteiligten
- Transparenz über den jeweiligen Projektstand
- frühes Erkennen von Risiken
- konsequente Planung, Steuerung und Kontrolle (Projektcontrolling)
- schnelle Reaktion auf Störungen
- Qualitätssicherung
- klare Regelung der Verantwortlichkeiten
- Prinzip der Schriftlichkeit

## 1.6 Projektphasen

Das zu managende Projekt lässt sich in fünf Phasen unterteilen. Diese Projektphasen umfassen die Vor-, Definitions-, Planungs-, Realisierungs- und Abschlussphase.

**Vorphase**
Die Vorphase dient der Problembeschreibung, der Aufgabenanalyse sowie der Erarbeitung des Projektauftrages und der Erteilung des Projektantrages. Nach Abschluss der Vorphase ist das Projekt gegründet.

**Definitionsphase**
In der Definitionsphase werden grundlegende Bestimmungen für das erteilte Projekt erarbeitet. Darunter befinden sich beispielsweise die Projektziele, die Organisation des Ablaufes, die Erstellung eines Pflichtenheftes. Auch der Punkt, an dem das Projekt als beendet gilt, wird hier vereinbart.

Wurde das Projekt direkt von einem Auftraggeber erteilt und nicht innerhalb einer Vorphase entwickelt, findet in der Definitionsphase eine Problem- und Aufgabenanalyse statt.

## 1.5 Project Management

> **Project management means:** All management tasks, management organization, techniques and resources for the conduct of a project.

The following points can be documented as essential tasks of project management:

- Structuring of projects
- Strong emphasis on the definition, objectives and goals in the initial phase of the project
- Strong emphasis on the planning phase
- Clear objectives and targets for all those involved
- Transparency about the respective project status
- Early identification of risks
- Consistent planning, management and control (project reporting)
- Fast response to problems
- Quality assurance
- Clear delineation of responsibilities
- Principle of the written form

## 1.6 Project Phases

The project to be managed can be divided into five phases. These phases include the initial, definitions, planning, realization and final phase. The five typical phases of a project will be discussed in more detail in the following chapters.

**Initial Phase**
The initial phase serves the problem description, the task analysis and the elaboration of the project mandate and the issue of the project application. After the completion of the initial phase the project is launched.

**Definition Phase**
During the definition phase the basic provisions for the project will be developed. Included are the project objectives, the organization of the processes, and the preparation of specifications. Equally the completion phase will be agreed to at this time.

If a customer tasked the project rather than the project developed from an initial phase the definition phase will include a problem and task analysis.

**Planungsphase**

In der nun folgenden Planungsphase wird das weitere Vorgehen zur Umsetzung des Projektes geplant. Es wird unter anderem auf Basis der zu erledigenden Arbeitspakete ein zeitlicher Rahmen gesetzt und Ressourcen, Kosten und Abläufe geplant.

**Realisierungsphase**

Nach der Planung folgt in der Realisierungsphase die Umsetzung der Pläne. Weiter findet auch eine Kontrolle und Steuerung des Ablaufes statt (Projektcontrolling). Das Projektcontrolling dient zur Qualitätssicherung und zur Möglichkeit, gegebenenfalls Anpassungen und Ergänzungen durchführen zu können.

**Abschlussphase**

Ist der vorher definierte Endpunkt des Projektes erreicht, tritt die Abschlussphase ein. Das Projektergebnis wird präsentiert und durch den Auftraggeber formell abgenommen. Anschließend wird das Projektergebnis gesichert, ein Abschlussbericht erstellt und gewonnene Erfahrungen dokumentiert. Zuletzt wird das Projekt aufgelöst.

Die fünf typischen Phasen eines Projektes werden in den folgenden Kapiteln näher betrachtet.

**Planning Phase**
In the following planning phase the procedures for the implementation of the project are planned. Among other things, work packages will be prepared on which basis a schedule is drafted and resources, costs, and operations are planned.

**Implementation Phase**
After the planning phase follows the implementation phase. Control and management of the process takes place (project controlling). Project reporting is used for quality assurance and the ability to perform adjustments and additions as necessary.

**Final Phase**
The pre-determined end point is reached, the final phase of the project. The result of the project will be presented and formally accepted by the customer. The result of the project is then backed up, a final report written and lessons learned documented. At last the project will be stood down

The five typical stages of a project will be explained in the following chapters.

## 1.7 Phasenmodell

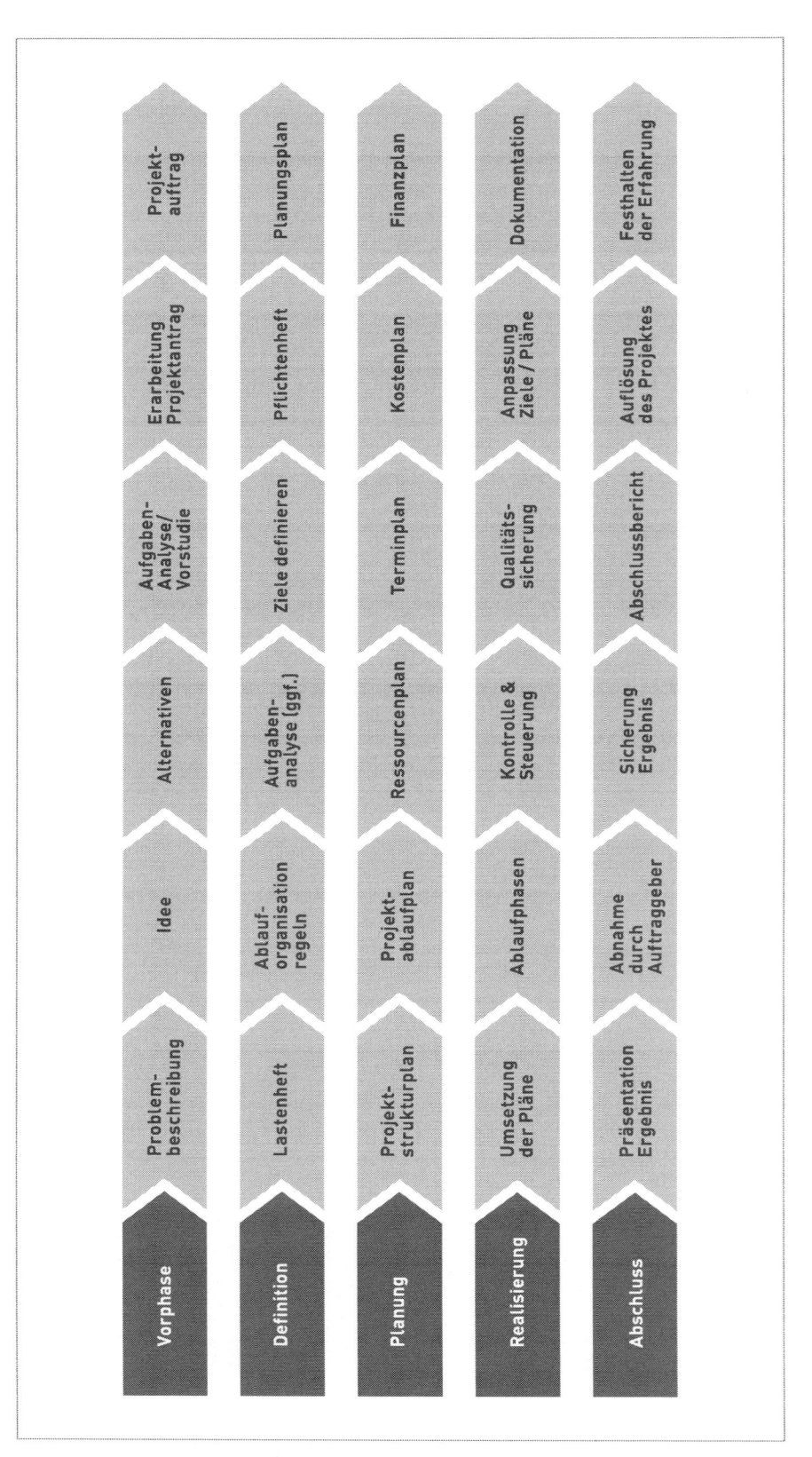

| Vorphase | Definition | Planung | Realisierung | Abschluss |
|---|---|---|---|---|
| Problembeschreibung | Lastenheft | Projektstrukturplan | Umsetzung der Pläne | Präsentation Ergebnis |
| Idee | Ablauforganisation regeln | Projektablaufplan | Ablaufphasen | Abnahme durch Auftraggeber |
| Alternativen | Aufgabenanalyse (ggf.) | Ressourcenplan | Kontrolle & Steuerung | Sicherung Ergebnis |
| Aufgaben-Analyse/Vorstudie | Ziele definieren | Terminplan | Qualitätssicherung | Abschlussbericht |
| Erarbeitung Projektantrag | Pflichtenheft | Kostenplan | Anpassung Ziele / Pläne | Auflösung des Projektes |
| Projektauftrag | Planungsplan | Finanzplan | Dokumentation | Festhalten der Erfahrung |

Abb. 2: Phasenmodell.

## 1.7 Phase Model

| Initial phase | Definition | Planning | Implementation | Conclusion |
|---|---|---|---|---|
| Problem description | Specifications | Project work breakdown | Implementation of the plans | Presentation of the result |
| Idea | Process organization rules | Project schedule | Process phases | Acceptance by the client |
| Alternatives | Tasks analysis (if applicable) | Resources plan | Monitoring & control | Backup copy of the result |
| Tasks analysis / Initial study | Define objectives | Schedule | Quality assurance | Final report |
| Develop project request | Specifications | Budget | Adaptation of objectives / plans | Stand down of the project |
| Project mandate | Design plan | Financial plan | Documentation | After action report |

Fig. 2: Phase Model.

**Notizen**

**Aufgaben zur Selbstkontrolle**

*1.1   Definieren Sie, wodurch ein Projekt gekennzeichnet ist.*

*1.2   Beschreiben Sie, in welche Phasen ein Projekt eingeteilt werden kann.*

**Tasks for Progress Review**

*1.1  Define the salient characteristics of a project.*

*1.2  Describe the individual phases of the project.*

**Notes**

## 2 Vorphase (Projektinitialisierung)

Am Anfang eines Projekts steht grundsätzlich eine Idee zur Lösung eines Problems. Soll zu dieser Idee ein Vorhabensantrag formuliert werden, so hilft das Instrument der Vorstudie / Aufgabenanalyse diesen Antrag zu konkretisieren. Die Aufgabenanalyse hilft ebenso bei der Entscheidungsfindung, ob und wie diese Idee verwirklicht wird. Bei der Entscheidung, die Idee weiter zu verfolgen und außerhalb der allgemeinen Aufbauorganisation zu bearbeiten, gibt es zwei grundsätzliche Möglichkeiten, dies zu tun: entweder im Rahmen einer Arbeitsgruppe unter Anlehnung an die Richtlinien zum Projektmanagement (nur ein Teil der Formalien ist zu erfüllen), oder aber als Projekt nach den Richtlinien zum Projektmanagement. Hier sind grundsätzlich alle Regelungen zu beachten und zu erfüllen. Eine Anpassung an die tatsächlichen Erfordernisse ist mit Zustimmung des Auftraggebers möglich.

Wurde allerdings ein Projektauftrag / Lastenheft direkt durch den Auftraggeber erteilt, so dient die Aufgabenanalyse zur Konkretisierung dieses Auftrages und zur Klärung von noch offenen Fragen mit dem Auftraggeber.

Bei einem Arbeitsgruppenauftrag gilt das gleiche wie im vorhergehenden Absatz angeführt.

### 2.1 Vorstudie / Aufgabenanalyse im Rahmen eines Workshops

Die Vorstudie oder Aufgabenanalyse dient dazu, die Aufgabe, die sich durch ein (mögliches) Projekt ergibt, in ihrer Gesamtheit wahrzunehmen und zu beschreiben. Anstatt sich zu Anfang schon in Details zu verlieren, soll die Aufgabe aus allen denkbaren Blickwinkeln dargestellt und verstanden werden. Sie soll dem Bearbeiter ein Bild über die erforderlichen Tätigkeiten und Teilaufgaben liefern und ihm einen schnellen Einstieg in die Projektproblematik ermöglichen.

> Die Fragen der Analyse nach dem WAS, WER, WO, WANN, WIE und WAS NICHT bilden einen „roten Faden", um den Projektrahmen festzulegen, und ermöglichen dem Bearbeiter und dem Auftraggeber den Umfang des Vorhabens / Projektes zu erkennen.

## 2  Initial Phase (Project Initiation)

At the beginning of a project is principally an idea to solve a "problem". If this idea is the basis of a project an initial study or task analysis is used as a tool to definitize the mandate. This task analysis helps in the decision-making, if and how this idea is put into practice. In the decision to pursue the idea and to work it outside of the general organizational structure, are two basic possibilities: either in the context of a working group, based on the guidelines for project management (only a part of the formal framework is met), or as a project, according to the guidelines for project management. In this case principally all rules have to be observed and met. A customization to the actual requirements is possible with the consent of the client.

However, if a project mandate / specification is issued directly by the client, the task analysis is used for the definition of this mandate and to clarify remaining questions with the client.

In case of a working group mandate the same as discussed in the preceding paragraph applies.

### 2.1  Initial Study / Analysis in the Context of a Workshop

The initial study, or task analysis, serves to get and describe a holistic view of the task, which results in a (potential) project. Instead of getting lost in the details at the beginning, the task should be viewed and understood from all possible angles. The aim is to provide the individual a picture of the required activities and subtasks and enables the project operator to get a quick start into the project objectives.

> The questions of the analysis for the WHAT, WHO, WHERE, WHEN, HOW, and WHAT NOT constitute a common theme in order to determine the scope of the project and allow the project operator and the client to recognize the scale of the undertaking / project.

**Vorgehensweise bei der Aufgabenanalyse bzw. Vorstudie:**
Die nachfolgende Vorlage gibt einen Anhaltspunkt zur Erfüllung dieser Aufgabe.

## Vorstudie / Aufgabenanalyse

*A) Problembeschreibung und anzustrebende Situation*

### a) Hintergrundinformation
Dieser Abschnitt beschreibt den dienstlichen Aufgabenbereich des Auftraggebers und gibt an, warum das Projekt/Vorhaben für erforderlich gehalten wird. Hintergrund für ein Projekt/Vorhaben können zum Beispiel neue Tätigkeitsfelder, die Reaktion auf gesellschaftliche Veränderungen oder auch der Bedarf an Rationalisierungsmaßnahmen sein.

### b) Problembeschreibung (Ist-Stand)
Hier wird in einer informativen und knappen Weise die Problematik dargestellt, die durch die Umsetzung der Idee in Form eines Projektes oder sonstigen Vorhabens einer Lösung zugeführt werden soll.

Gefordert ist eine Untermauerung des Änderungsbedarfs durch die Nennung von Kenngrößen, wie zum Beispiel Ist-Aufwand, Informationsaufkommen, Kosten, Anzahl der beteiligten Mitarbeiter, Anzahl der Medienbrüche, unnötige Redundanzen usw.

Sofern es ähnliche Projekte oder Vorhaben gibt, die beabsichtigt, bereits begonnen oder abgeschlossen sind, sind diese hier zu nennen.

### c) Anzustrebende Situation
In diesem Punkt fasst der Antragsteller alle Aspekte zusammen, welche die mit dem Vorhaben angestrebte künftige Situation beschreiben. Beschrieben werden auch die Aufbau- und Ablauforganisation sowie die bisherigen Arbeitsergebnisse, an denen Änderungen vorgenommen werden müssen. Auch die Form der Änderungen ist hier deutlich zu machen.

### d) Wesentliche Teilaufgaben
In welche Aufgabenblöcke als Teilaufgaben oder gar Teilprojekte ist die Aufgabe unterteilt? Werden Teilprojekte gebildet, so sind für diese unter einer Gesamtprojektleitung Teilprojektleiter zu bestimmen.

### e) Orte und Termine
Wo wird die Aufgabe gelöst? Seit wann besteht die Aufgabe? Ab wann wird das Vorhaben in Angriff genommen? Bis wann soll das Vorhaben beendet sein?

**Procedure for the Task Analysis or Initial Study:**
The following template provides tips for the accomplishment of this task.

## Initial Study / Task Analysis

*A) Problem Description and Desired Results*

**a) Background Information**
This section describes the official mandate from the client and specifies why the project / undertaking is considered necessary. Background for a project / undertaking may for example be a new field of activity, the response to social changes, or the need for rationalization measures.

**b) Problem Description (Status Quo)**
Here the objectives are described in an informative and concise way, which should contribute to a solution of the implementation of the idea in the form of a project or another undertaking.

Required is a confirmation of the changes necessary by the definition of parameters, such as current expenditures, required information, cost, number of the employees involved, the changes of media format, avoiding unnecessary redundancy, etc.

If there are similar projects or undertakings, which are intended, have already begun, or are completed, these should be listed here.

**c) Desired Objectives**
At this point in time, the applicant summarizes all aspects, which describe the objectives of the project. Equally described are the structure and processes, as well as the previous results, where changes need to be made. Also the type of the changes is to be specified clearly.

**d) Essential Subtasks**
In what task units as subtasks or even subprojects is the project divided? If subprojects will be created subproject managers below the main project management need to be named.

**e) Locations and Schedule**
Where will the problem be solved? Since when exists the task? When will the project be started? By when will the project be completed?

*Notes*

### f) Projektabschlusskriterien

Dieser Abschnitt identifiziert die wichtigsten Arbeitsergebnisse, damit das Projekt als erfolgreich abgeschlossen betrachtet werden kann. Sie sind vom Auftraggeber am Ende des Projektes abzunehmen. Es ist festzustellen, was das Projekt unbedingt erbringen muss und was als zusätzlich zwar wünschenswert, aber nicht zwingend erforderlich zu betrachten ist.

### g) Alternativen

Gibt es Alternativen? Warum hat man sich für die gewählte Alternative entschieden?

### h) Rahmenbedingungen

Gibt es Einschränkungen oder Vorgaben, die auf die Arbeit an dem Vorhaben Einfluss haben? Hierzu zählen beispielsweise die anzuwendende Projektmethode, Prioritäten, Personal, Zeit, Technologie, Umgebung, Entscheidungszyklen, Werkzeuge und Techniken.

Eine wesentliche Rahmenbedingung bei Beschaffungsvorhaben stellt das Haushalts- und Vergaberecht dar. Die Durchführung eines Vergabeverfahrens hat stets Auswirkungen auf das Gesamtprojekt bezüglich Projektlaufzeit, formalen Zuständigkeiten und Vorgehensweisen, Projektrisiken und ggf. auf die Zusammensetzung der Projektgruppe. Deshalb wird dringend empfohlen, bereits im Vorfeld bzw. in der Definitionsphase die zuständigen Spezialdienststellen zu kontaktieren.

Rahmenbedingungen können sich auch durch die Rechtsordnung, wie beispielsweise durch das Datenschutzrecht, ergeben.

Die Identifizierung von Rahmenbedingungen bestärkt das Management, diese zu kontrollieren, um den Erfolg sicherzustellen.

### i) Annahmen

Annahmen beziehen sich beispielsweise auf vorgesehene Ergebnisse anderer Vorhaben, die ihrerseits aber Einfluss auf das Ergebnis des eigenen Projektes ausüben. Sie können sich auch auf die Erfüllung der oben genannten Regulierungsaufgaben beziehen. Eine derartige Annahme wäre beispielsweise, dass bis zum Abschluss des Projektes die dann erforderlichen technischen Voraussetzungen, die derzeit noch von einem anderen Projekt zu schaffen sind, auch tatsächlich erfüllt sind.

### j) Verantwortung des Auftraggebers

Dieser Abschnitt identifiziert die Verantwortung des Auftraggebers. Ihm muss nicht nur seine Verantwortung klar sein, sondern auch die Rückwirkung auf den Projektverlauf und das Projektergebnis, wenn er dieser Verantwortung nicht gerecht wird. Dies bedeutet, dass der Auftraggeber das Projekt in jeder Hinsicht unterstützen und für das erforderliche Budget sorgen muss.

#### f) Project Conclusion Criteria
This section identifies the most important results, so that the project can be considered as successfully completed when these are achieved. The client accepts these at the end of the project. It is to be noted which results are absolutely necessary and which are desirable, however not mandatory.

#### g) Alternatives
Are there alternatives? Why was the selected alternative chosen?

#### h) General Conditions
Are there any restrictions or requirements, which impact on the work of the project? For example, this includes the applicable project method, priorities, staff, time, technology, environment, decision cycles, tools, and techniques.

An essential precondition for procurement is the budget and procurement law. The execution of a contract award procedure has always an impact on the overall project regarding project duration, formal responsibilities and procedures, project risks and, potentially, on the composition of the project group. It is strongly recommended to contact the competent special agencies early in the initial or definition phase.

Basic conditions can result from the legal system, such as for example the Data Protection Law.

The identification of the condition encourages the management to control these, in order to ensure success.

#### i) Assumptions
Assumptions can, for example, refer to the intended results of other projects, which in turn influence the outcome of the current project. They can also refer to the compliance with the above-mentioned regulatory tasks. Such an assumption would be that, for example, that by the end of the project the then necessary technical conditions, which are still to be created by another project, will actually be in place.

#### j) Responsibility of the Client
This section identifies the responsibility of the client. He must not only be clear about his responsibility, but also the impact on the development of the project and the result of the project, if he does not meet this obligation. This means that the client supports the project in every respect and ensures the required budget is available.

*B) Vorplanung und Analysen*

> Ein **Ziel** ist ein gedanklich vorweggenommener Soll-Zustand,
> - der in der **Zukunft** liegt,
> - der **real** sein soll,
> - dessen Erreichen **wünschenswert** und **motivierend** ist und
> - der nur durch **Handlung** erreicht werden kann.

**a) Zielklärung – Zielhierarchie**

Hier sind die sich aus den vorhergehenden Punkten im Teil A ergebenden wesentlichen Ziele („Was soll durch das Projekt erreicht werden?") zu nennen. Das Detaillieren der Projektziele wird in der Regel über mehrere Ebenen in Form einer Hierarchie durchgeführt. Das Oberziel wird dabei in mehrere sinnvolle Unterziele aufgespalten. Jedes Unterziel (Subziel) steht dabei zum Oberziel in einer Ziel-Mittel-Relation, d. h. das Unterziel ist das Mittel, das zur Erreichung des Oberziels beiträgt. Durch schrittweises Vorgehen werden immer weitere Ebenen gebildet.

Durch die Aufführung der einzelnen Projektziele soll eine umfassende Projektbetrachtung ermöglicht werden. Ein Projekt als Ganzes besteht aus kleineren, eng zusammenhängenden Zielen.

Diese Projektziele müssen in Bezug auf Qualität und Quantität messbar und durchführbar sein. Darüber hinaus können inhaltliche Zusatzziele auftreten, wie zum Beispiel Organisationsentwicklungsziele, Personalentwicklungsziele und Marketingziele. Innerhalb des Projektprozesses sind Punkte wie Kosten, Nutzen, Zeit, Umsatz u. a. als zu erreichende Ziele definierbar.

Eine weitergehende detaillierte Definition und Operationalisierung der Projektziele erfolgt nach Abschluss der Vorstudie/Aufgabenanalyse in einem weiteren Arbeitsschritt in der Definitionsphase.

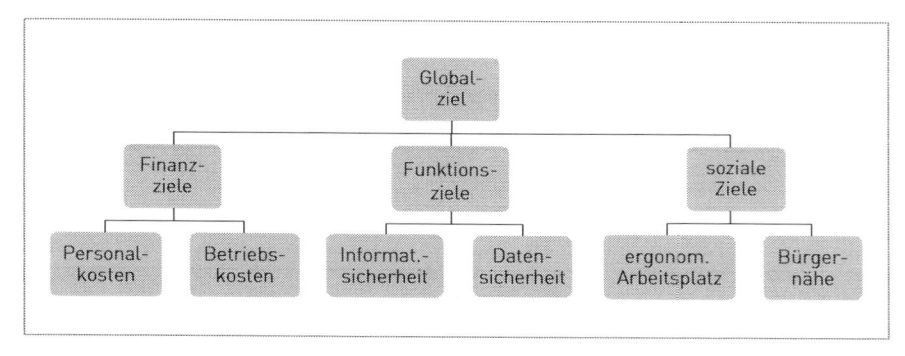

Abb. 3: Zielhierarchie.

*B) Pre-Planning and Analysis*

> An **objective** is a theoretically implemented target situation,
> - which lies in the **future**,
> - which should be **real**,
> - the achievement of which is **desirable** and **motivating**
> - which can only be achieved by **action**.

**a) Objectives Statement – Objectives Hierarchy**

Here the results of the essential objectives from the before mentioned points from Part A ("what should be achieved by the project?") are to be listed. The detailing of the project objectives is usually performed in the form of a hierarchy with several levels. The overall objective is split into several meaningful sub-objectives. Each sub-objective fits in the overall objective in a goal-means relationship, i. e., the sub-objective is the means, which contributes to achieve the main goal. Through an incremental approach more and more levels will be created.

The listing of individual project objectives facilitates a comprehensive project overview. A project as a whole consists of smaller, closely related objectives.

These project objectives must be measurable and feasible in terms of quality and quantity. Additionally, content objectives may develop, such as organizational, personnel, and marketing objectives. Within the project processes are issues, such as cost, benefit, time, sales, etc., which can be defined as objectives to be achieved.

A more detailed definition and operationalization of the project objectives are performed after completion of the initial study / analysis in a further step during the definition phase.

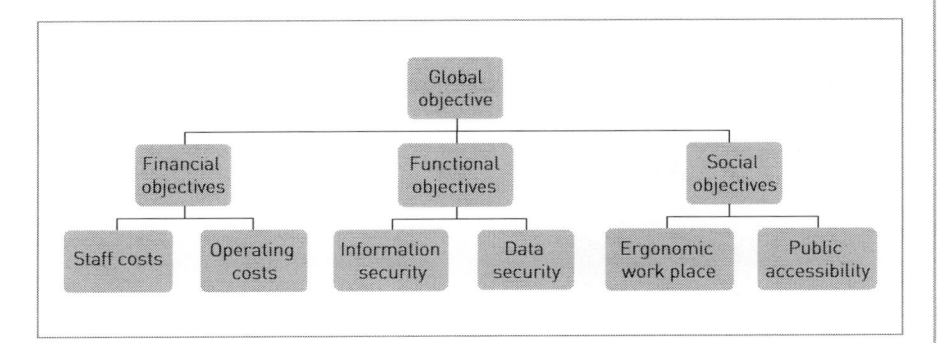

Fig. 3: Target Hierarchy.

### b) Projektumfeldanalyse (PUA)

Projekte sind immer in ein Umfeld eingebettet (siehe Abb. 4), das aus verschiedenen Institutionen und Personen besteht. Positive und negative Projektinteressenten sind frühzeitig zu ermitteln, um bei eventuell später auftretenden Schwierigkeiten sofort reagieren zu können oder bereits zu Beginn des Projekts Förderer zu gewinnen und Hinderern den Wind aus den Segeln zu nehmen.

Einflüsse aus dem Projektumfeld berühren die Ziele und Erfolgsaussichten des Projektes und sind somit kritische Erfolgsfaktoren.

Um innerhalb eines Projektes alle betroffenen Stakeholder zu identifizieren, wird die Projektumfeldanalyse (PUA) durchgeführt. Hierbei wird ein Projekt als ein System mit sozialen Strukturen betrachtet, wodurch eine Abgrenzung der Beteiligten im Projektumfeld möglich ist. Sie wird durchgeführt, um einerseits Betroffene zu Beteiligten zu machen, indem man sie in die Projektorganisation einbindet, und um andererseits Maßnahmen für kritische Beteiligte setzen zu können.

Ziele der Projektumfeldanalyse sind:

- Erkennung und Erfassung aller Randbedingungen und Einflussfaktoren für das Projekt
- Erfassung aller Interessengruppen am Projekt (Stakeholder) und der Art ihrer Interessen
- Früherkennung von Projektrisiken
- Erkennung der Anknüpfungspunkte für die Einbettung des Projektes in das Unternehmen
- Erkennung von Chancen und Potenzialen
- Aufzeigen von Handlungsmöglichkeiten zur Beeinflussung des Projektumfeldes
- Dokumentation dieser Erkenntnisse für die Projektplanung

Im Wesentlichen besteht die Projektumfeldanalyse aus den Phasen:

- Identifikation / Erfassung
- Strukturierung
- Analyse / Bewertung / Priorisierung
- Entwicklung von Empfehlungen für das Projekt
- laufende Beobachtung der veränderlichen Randbedingungen

## b) Project Environment Analysis (PEA)

Projects are always rooted in an environment (cf. Fig. 4), which is formed by different institutions and persons. Positive and negative project leads need to be identified at an early stage, to be able to react immediately if later on difficulties arise or to obtain sponsors early in the project and to eliminate the objections of obstructionists.

Influences from the project environment touch on the objectives and prospects of success of the project and are therefore critical success factors.

To identify all affected stakeholders within a project a project environment analysis (PEA) is performed. This is where a project is viewed as a system with social structures, which makes a distinction between the parties involved in the project context possible. The objective is to engage those affected to become involved in the project organization and initiate measures for critical stakeholders.

Objectives of the analysis of the project environment are:

- Recognition and documentation of all constraints and factors affecting the project
- Capturing of all stakeholders on the project and the nature of their interests
- Early detection of project risks
- Detection of the points of departure for the integration of the project in the company
- Detection of opportunities and potential
- Identification of suitable courses of action to influence the project environment
- Recording of these findings for the project planning

Essentially, the project environment analysis consists of these phases:

- Identification / recording
- Structuring
- Analysis / evaluation / prioritization
- Development of recommendations for the project
- Ongoing monitoring of the constraining variables

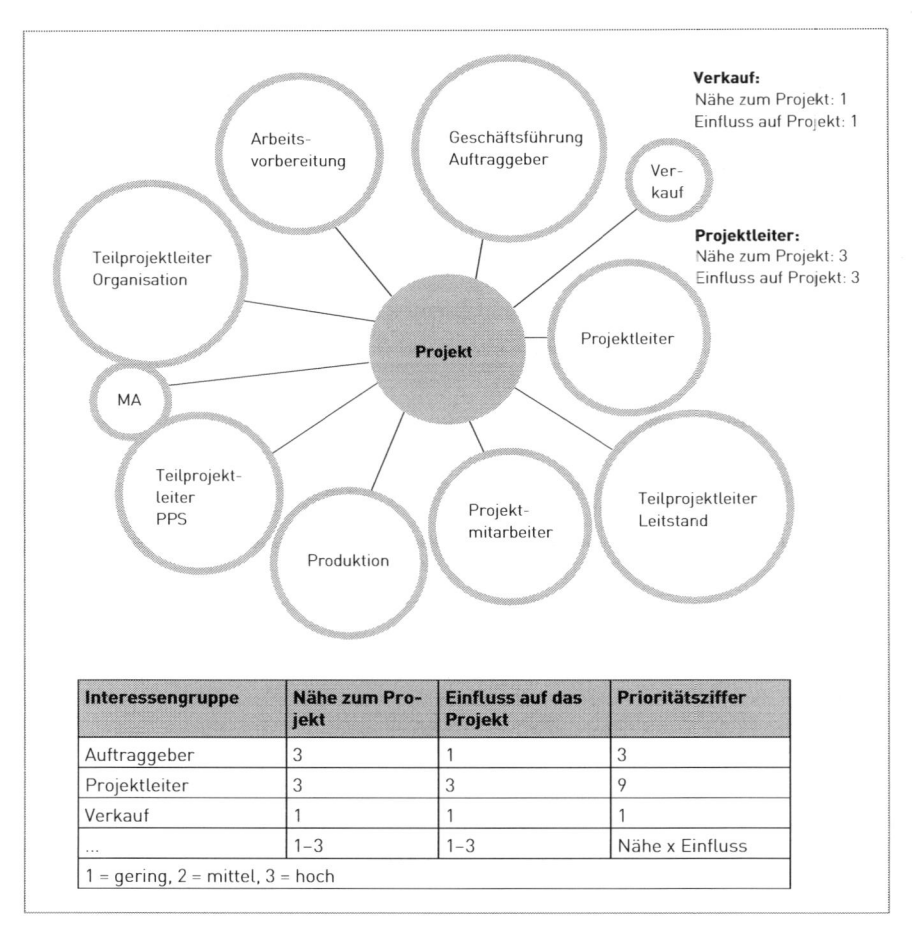

| Interessengruppe | Nähe zum Projekt | Einfluss auf das Projekt | Prioritätsziffer |
|---|---|---|---|
| Auftraggeber | 3 | 1 | 3 |
| Projektleiter | 3 | 3 | 9 |
| Verkauf | 1 | 1 | 1 |
| ... | 1–3 | 1–3 | Nähe x Einfluss |
| 1 = gering, 2 = mittel, 3 = hoch | | | |

Abb. 4: Projektumfeldanalyse.

**c) Projektumfeldanalyse: Betroffene und Beteiligte der Projektorganisation**
Wer stellt die Instanzen des Projekts dar (welche Institutionen – Auftraggeber, Projektausschuss, der den Projektleiter stellende Verband, Mitglieder des Projektteams, Projekt-Geschäftsstelle)? Wer ist Projektbetroffener beziehungsweise Kunde (späterer Anwender des Projektergebnisses)?

**Sales Department:**
Proximity to the project: 1
Influence on project: 1

**Project Manager:**
Proximity to the project: 3
Influence on project: 3

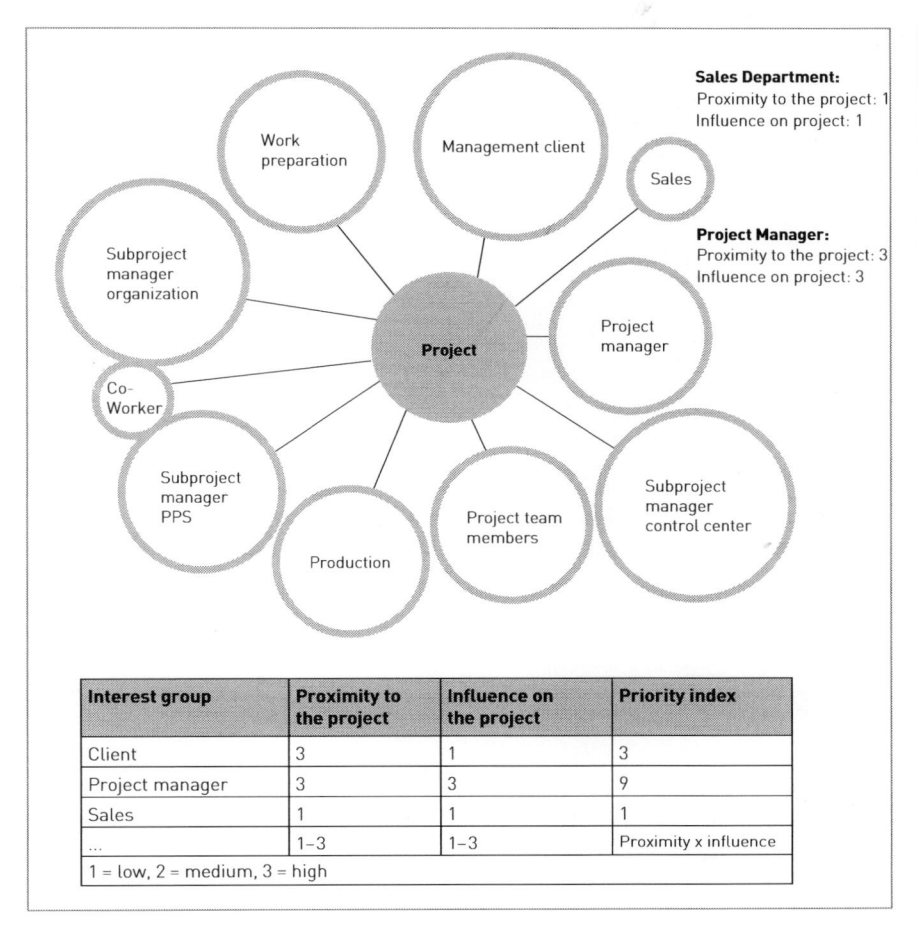

| Interest group | Proximity to the project | Influence on the project | Priority index |
|---|---|---|---|
| Client | 3 | 1 | 3 |
| Project manager | 3 | 3 | 9 |
| Sales | 1 | 1 | 1 |
| ... | 1–3 | 1–3 | Proximity x influence |
| 1 = low, 2 = medium, 3 = high | | | |

Fig. 4: Project Environment Analysis.

### c) Project Environment Analysis: Affected and Involved in the Project Organization

Who represents the authorities of the project (which institutions – client, project steering committee, the association providing the project manager, members of the project team, project administration office)? Who is affected by the project or customer (later on the user of the project result)?

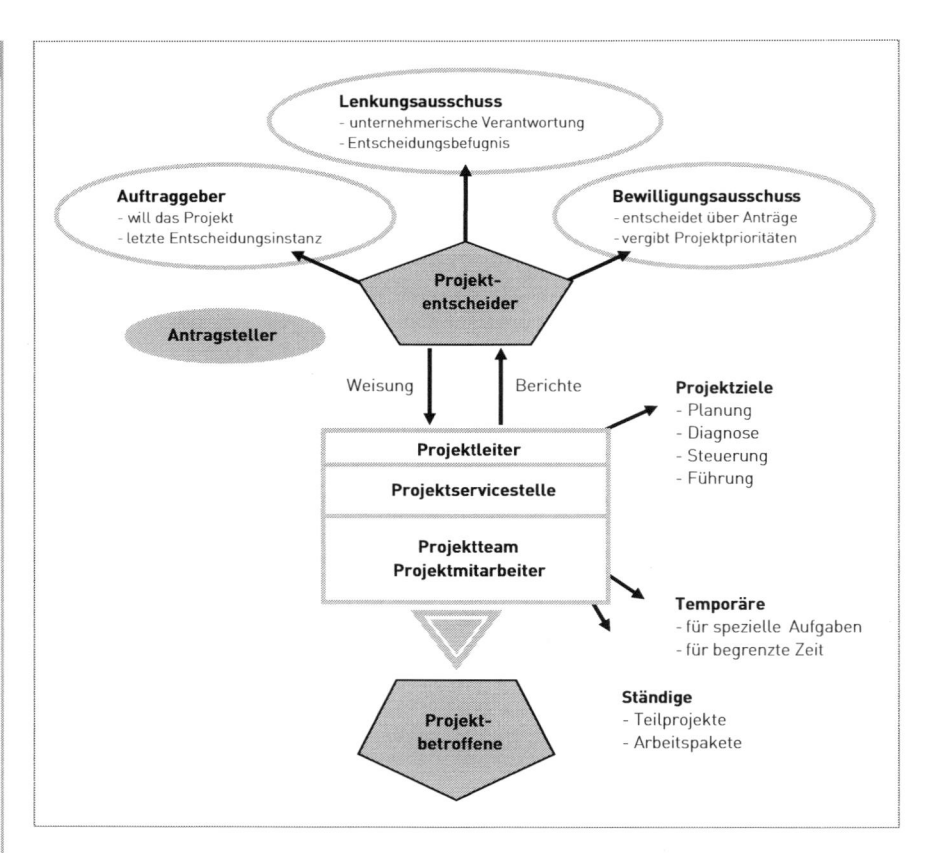

```
                    Lenkungsausschuss
                    - unternehmerische Verantwortung
                    - Entscheidungsbefugnis

    Auftraggeber                          Bewilligungsausschuss
    - will das Projekt                    - entscheidet über Anträge
    - letzte Entscheidungsinstanz         - vergibt Projektprioritäten
                    Projekt-
                    entscheider
    Antragsteller

              Weisung      Berichte      Projektziele
                                         - Planung
              Projektleiter              - Diagnose
                                         - Steuerung
              Projektservicestelle       - Führung

              Projektteam
              Projektmitarbeiter
                                         Temporäre
                                         - für spezielle Aufgaben
                                         - für begrenzte Zeit

                                         Ständige
              Projekt-                   - Teilprojekte
              betroffene                 - Arbeitspakete
```

Abb. 5: Projektbeteiligte.

**d) Projektrisikoanalyse**

Da komplexe Projekte eine Vielzahl unbekannter Faktoren aufweisen, besteht eine wichtige Aufgabe der Projektleitung darin, in der Zukunft liegende Risiken vorauszusehen.

Das Risiko definiert sich durch die Eintrittswahrscheinlichkeit und die zu erwartende Schadenshöhe.

Die genaue Vorgehensweise dabei ist wie folgt gegliedert:

- Identifikation der Risiken
- Abschätzen der Eintrittswahrscheinlichkeit
- Abschätzen der Tragweite / Auswirkung
- Planung der Gegenmaßnahmen

In der Projektrisikoanalyse sollen die Projektrisiken möglichst vollständig erfasst werden. Eine Orientierung am Projektstrukturplan und an der Projektumfeldanalyse fördert einerseits die Realisierung des Ziels der Vollständigkeit und sichert andererseits Konsistenz in der Projektdokumentation. Durch die Bestimmung von Projektrisiken werden gleichzeitig auch Maßnahmen zur Risikovermeidung und -vorsorge getroffen (siehe Abb. 6).

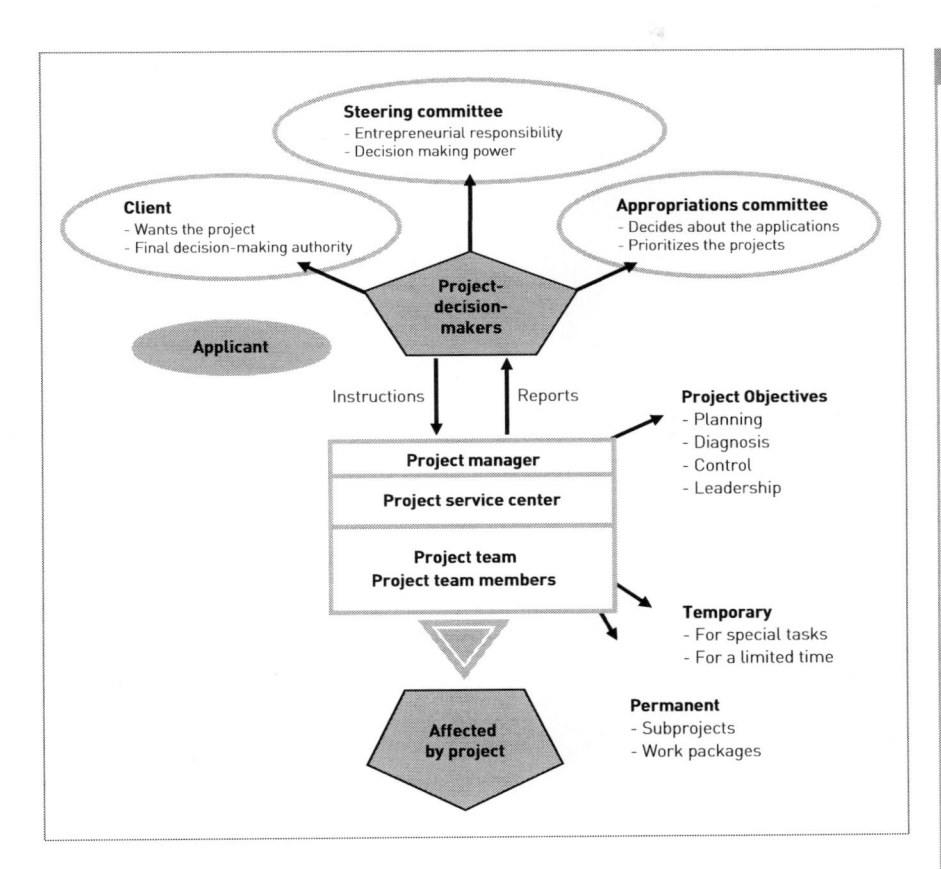

Fig. 5: Project Participants.

**d) Project Risk Assessment**

Because complex projects have a number of unidentified factors, an important task of the project management is to predict future risks.

The "risk" is defined by the probability of their occurrence and the expected financial loss.

The exact procedure is structured as follows:

- Identification of the risks
- Evaluation of the probability of occurrence
- Evaluation of the scope/impact
- Planning of countermeasures

The project risks as far as possible are to be fully documented in the project risk assessment. An orientation on the work breakdown structure, and on the project environment analysis enhances the realization of the objective completeness and increases the consistency in the project documentation. By identifying the project risks at the same time risk prevention measures and precautions are being put in place (cf. Fig. 6).

| Projekt | Teilprojekt | ☐ Projektplanung ☐ Projektstart | ☐ Zwischenbericht/Meilenstein ☐ Projektabschluss | Erstellt durch (Name/Abteilung) Datum: | Überarbeitet/Datum: |
|---|---|---|---|---|---|

| Risikoidentifizierung – derzeitiger Zustand | | | | | | | | Maßnahmen – verbesserter Zustand | | | | | |
|---|---|---|---|---|---|---|---|---|---|---|---|---|---|
| Arbeitsschritt | Risiko | Risikofolge | Risikoursache | Auftreten | Bedeutung | Entdeckbarkeit | Risiko Prioritätszahl (RPZ) | Maßnahme(n) | Verantwortlichkeit Termin | Auftreten | Bedeutung | Entdeckbarkeit | Risiko Prioritätszahl (RPZ) |
|  | Verzögerung im Projekt | Auftraggeber unzufrieden | Projektleiter erkrankt | 3 | 8 | 1 | 24 | Ernennung eines stellv. Projektleiters | TS | 1 | 8 | 1 | 8 |
|  | Mitarbeiter nehmen Aufgaben nicht richtig wahr | zu geringe Steuerung | Arbeitspakete werden nicht richtig erledigt | 5 | 5 | 5 | 125 | Nachhalten von Aufgaben durch den Projektleiter | RK | 5 | 5 | 1 | 25 |
|  | Budgetüberschreitung | Projekt kann nicht beendet werden | schlechtes Controlling | 5 | 10 | 8 | 400 | strategisches Controlling einrichten | TS | 5 | 10 | 2 | 100 |
|  | keine Akzeptanz der Lösungen | Mitarbeiter setzen Ergebnisse nicht um | zu geringe Schulungen | 7 | 8 | 7 | 392 | Feedback im Projekt einholen | RK | 7 | 4 | 7 | 196 |

Auftreten: kein 1, sehr gering 2–3, gering 4–6, mäßig 7–8, hoch 9–10

Bedeutung (Auswirkung aus Auftraggebersicht): nicht wahrnehmbar 1, geringe Auswirkung 2–3, mäßig schwere Auswirkung 4–6, schwere Auswirkung 7–8, äußerst schwerwiegende Auswirkung 9–10

Entdeckbarkeit (vor Projektabschluss): hoch 1, mäßig 2–5, gering 6–8, sehr gering 9, keine 10

Abb. 6: Projektrisikoanalyse.

### e) Grobplanung der Projektstruktur (Projektstrukturplanung)

Hier sind zunächst die wesentlichen Maßnahmenbündel (= Arbeitspakete) zur Zielerreichung zu benennen, welche Produkte, Prozesse und Anwendungen enthalten. Eine weitergehende Feinplanung der Projektstruktur ist erst nach Vorliegen einer mit dem Projektauftraggeber abgestimmten Zielhierarchie, nach Abschluss der Definitionsphase, möglich.

| Project | Subproject | | ☐ Project planning<br>☐ Project start | ☐ Interim report/milestones<br>☐ Project close-up | | | | | | Created by (name/division)<br>Date: | | Revision/Date: | |
|---|---|---|---|---|---|---|---|---|---|---|---|---|---|

| Risk identification – current conditions | | | | | | | | Actions – improved conditions | | | | | |
|---|---|---|---|---|---|---|---|---|---|---|---|---|---|
| Subtask | Risk | Outcome | Cause | Incidence | Meaning | Discoverability | Risk Priority Number (RPN) | Actions | Responsibility | Incidence | Meaning | Discoverability | Risk Priority Number (RPN) |
| Delay | Client dis-satisfied | Project manager got ill | | 3 | 8 | 1 | 24 | nominate an acting Project manager | TS | 1 | 8 | 1 | 8 |
| | Co-workers don't work | Working packages not done | Controlling too less | 5 | 5 | 5 | 125 | monitoring tasks by Project manager | RK | 5 | 5 | 1 | 25 |
| | Exceeding budget | Project can't be closed | Bad controlling | 5 | 10 | 8 | 400 | establish strategic controlling | TS | 5 | 10 | 2 | 100 |
| | Solutions not accepted | Co-workers don't realize solutions | Not enough training | 7 | 8 | 7 | 392 | solicit feedback from team | RK | 7 | 4 | 7 | 196 |

Incidence: none 1, very low 2–3, low 4–6, medium 7–8, high 9–10
Meaning (effect – clients view): unobservable 1, low impact 2–3, medium effect 4–6, serious effect 7–8, extremly serious effect 9–10
Discoverability (before project close-up): high 1, medium 2–5, low 6–8, very low 9, none 10

Fig. 6: Project Risk Analysis.

### e) Outline of the Project Structure (Project Structure Planning)

Here are the essential packages of measures (=work packages) for the achievements are being identified, which contain products, processes, and applications. Only after the submission of the target hierarchy as agreed to with project sponsor and after the completion of the definition phase is a more detailed planning of the project structure possible.

Die Darstellung der Maßnahmenbündel beinhaltet auch, welche externen Einflüsse und Entwicklungen zu berücksichtigen sind. Hierzu zählen zum Beispiel die Herstellung und Bedienung von Schnittstellen bestehender oder geplanter Systeme oder die Zusammenarbeit mit anderen Behörden und Organisationen.

Erforderliche Regulierungsaufgaben, wie beispielsweise die Einholung von Genehmigungen oder die Beschaffung bestimmter Hard- oder Software, bestimmen die Maßnahmenbündel ebenso wie die Initialisierung von erforderlichen Vorschriften- und / oder Rechtsänderungen.

Baut das Projekt auf andere Vorhaben auf, so sind die Arbeitsergebnisse, die von dort zu liefern sind, hier zu beschreiben.

Der Projektstrukturplan (PSP) wird auf der Grundlage der Zielhierarchie erstellt. Dazu werden Arbeitspakete (AP) als kleinste Einheit im Strukturplan definiert, mit denen das jeweilige Ziel erreicht wird. Die Arbeitspakete wiederum können in einzelne Vorgänge untergliedert werden. Die Aufschlüsselung Projektziel – Teilprojekt – Teilaufgabe – Arbeitspaket erfolgt durch das Projektteam. Die Aufschlüsselung der Arbeitspakete in Vorgänge erfolgt durch den für die Erledigung des Arbeitspaketes zuständigen Auftragnehmer. Ein Arbeitspaket gilt dann als „geschnürt", wenn das Projektteam eine weitere Untergliederung für nicht mehr sinnvoll hält.

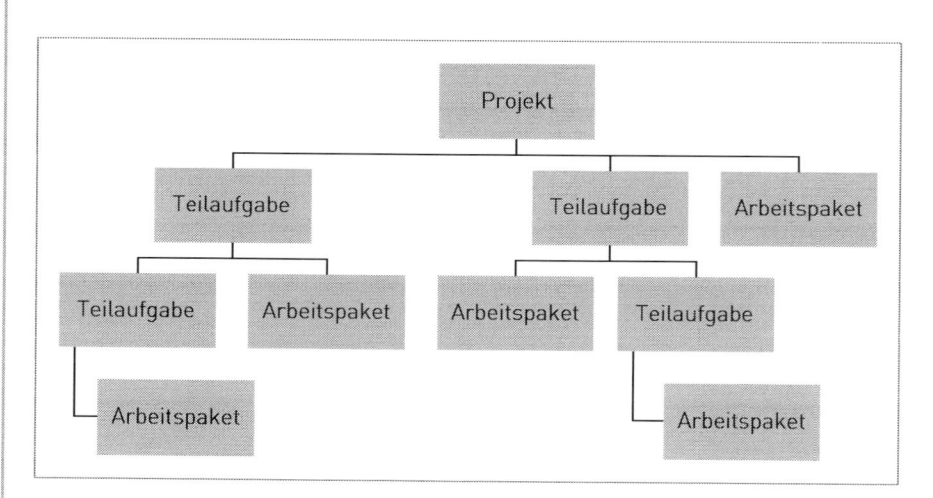

Abb. 7: Projektstrukturplanung.

**Ziele der Strukturierung:**

- Schaffung von Transparenz
- Bildung von Teilprojekten und Arbeitspaketen

**Zwei Vorgehensarten:**

- Induktives Vorgehen (Bottom up): Mittels Brainstorming werden alle Aufgaben gesammelt und anschließend mit Oberbegriffen versehen. So entsteht die Struktur nach und nach. Die Methode erleichtert den Einstieg in neuartige Projekte.

A presentation of the package of measures includes the type of external influences and developments, which are to be considered. These include, for example, the manufacture and operation interfaces of existing or planned systems or the co-operation with other authorities and organizations.

Required regulatory tasks, such as the collection of licenses or the procurement of hard- or software determine the packages of measures as well as the initialization of the required regulations and / or legislative changes.

If the project is based on other projects, the results, which are to be provided by that project are to be described here.

The work breakdown structure (WBS) will be created on the basis of the target hierarchy. To do this work packages (WP) are defined as the smallest unit in the work breakdown, with which each objective is achieved. The work packages, in turn, can be broken down into individual activities. The breakdown of the project – subproject – subtask – work package is performed by the project team. The contractor responsible for the execution of the work package carries out the breakdown of the work packages in operations. A work package will be considered a "package", when the project team does no longer consider a further breakdown useful.

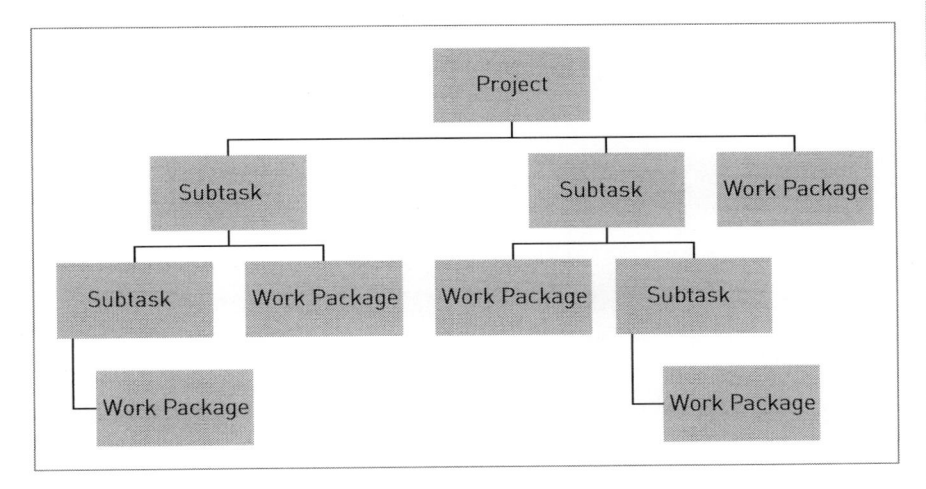

Fig. 7: Project Structure Analysis.

**Objectives of the Structure:**

- Creating transparency
- Formation of subprojects and work packages

**Two Approaches:**

- Inductive approach (bottom-up): using brainstorming all tasks are collected and then labeled with generic terms. This way, the structure is gradually formed. This method makes it easy to get started with new projects.

- Deduktives Vorgehen (Top down): Die einzelnen Elemente werden schrittweise zerlegt, wobei jede Ebene immer vollständig zu zergliedern ist. Bei dieser Vorgehensweise sollte Projekterfahrung vorhanden sein, weiterhin empfiehlt sich diese Vorgehensweise bei Standardprojekten.

**f) Ressourcenplan**

Ausgehend vom Projektstrukturplan und den dort definierten Arbeitspaketen als kleinste Einheit wird die Personal-, Sachmittel- und Einsatzmittelplanung vorgenommen. Die zentralen Fragen sind hier wer, wann, wie viel und wie lange. Aus dieser Planung lassen sich auch die Gesamtkosten eines Projektes relativ leicht ableiten, da man nur mit überschaubaren, d. h. gut schätzbaren, Größen rechnen muss.

Die Planung der verfügbaren Ressourcen muss aus verschiedenen Gründen erfolgen. Erstens ist das Projektergebnis maßgeblich von den zur Verfügung stehenden Ressourcen abhängig und zweitens ist die wirtschaftliche Betrachtung für alle projektspezifischen Tätigkeiten relevant.

Ebenso wie bei der Erarbeitung eines Projektstrukturplans unterscheidet man hier zwischen induktivem und deduktivem Vorgehen:

- Induktives Vorgehen eignet sich insbesondere bei komplexen, schwer überschaubaren Projekten. Dieses Vorgehen eignet sich in erster Linie zur Beseitigung punktueller Schwachstellen des Ist-Zustandes.
- Deduktives Vorgehen empfiehlt sich bei Projekten, die einen guten Überblick zulassen. Es eignet sich zur Erstellung idealtypischer, optimierender Lösungsmodelle.

In der Regel lösen sich beide Vorgehensweisen ab. Nach einer grundlegenden deduktiven (konzeptionellen) Bearbeitung folgt eine Phase der Pflege und punktuellen Verbesserung, bis auf diesem Weg keine nennenswerten Verbesserungen mehr möglich sind. Dann folgt wieder ein deduktiver Ansatz.

**g) Balkenplan**

Der Balkenplan dient dazu, eine übersichtliche Darstellung der Terminplanung und der zeitlichen Lage der Arbeitspakete zu erhalten und ist in folgende Teilaufgaben untergliedert:

- Ermittlung der Zeiten für die einzelnen Aktivitäten
- Ermittlung der Gesamtzeit für das Projekt
- Ermittlung von Anfangs- und Endterminen
- dadurch Ermittlung der kritischen Pfade

- Deductive approach (top-down): the individual elements are disassembled step-by-step and each level is disintegrated fully every time. Project experience is required to apply this approach and it is only recommended for "standard projects".

**f) Resource Plan**

The planning of staff, material resources and supply is performed based on the work breakdown structure and the work packages defined as the smallest unit. The central issues here are who, when, how much and for how long. From this planning the total cost of a project can be easily derived because only manageable, i. e. easily estimated variables are being considered.

The planning of the available resources must be performed for various reasons. First the result of the project largely depends on the resources available and, second, the economic view for all relevant project-specific activities is being considered.

A differentiation between inductive and deductive approach is made just as in the development of a work breakdown structure:

- Inductive approach is particularly suitable for complex, difficult manageable projects. This approach is used first and foremost to eliminate specific weaknesses of the status quo.
- A deductive approach is recommended for projects that allow a good overview. It is suitable for creating ideal, optimized solutions.

As a rule both practices alternate. After the basic deductive (conceptual) processing follows a phase of care and specific improvement, until significant improvements are no longer possible by this approach. Then follows the deductive approach.

**g) Gantt Chart**

A Gantt chart is used to show a clear representation of the scheduling and the temporal location of the work packages and is divided into the following subtasks:

- Determination of the schedule for the various activities
- Determination of the total time for the project
- Determination of start and end dates
- Determination of the critical paths through the above

**Festlegen markanter Zeitpunkte (Meilensteine) im Projekt**

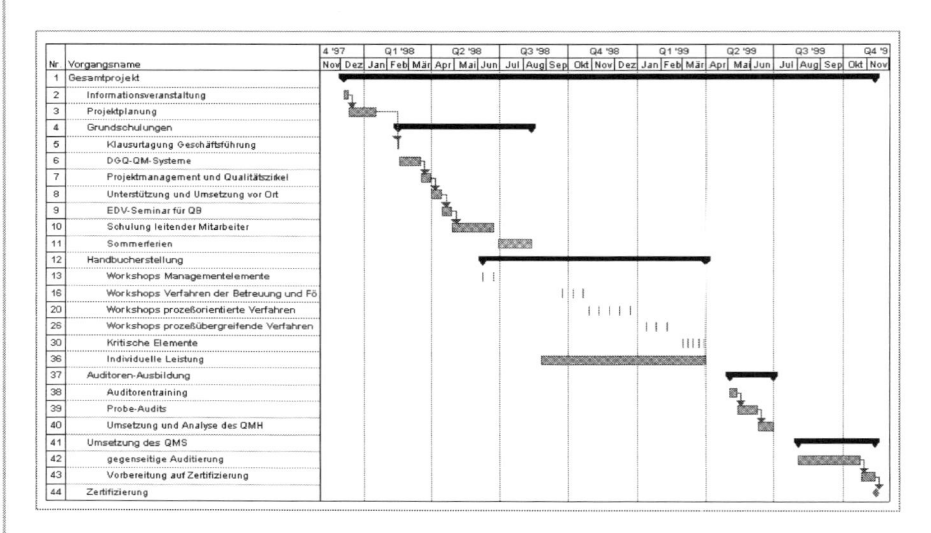

Abb. 8: Balkenplan (Screenshot MS-Project).

**h) Stellungnahme des Strategischen Controllings (optional)**

- Aussagen zur Strategieverträglichkeit
- Aussagen zur Portfolioverträglichkeit: Gibt es bereits gleiche oder ähnliche Vorhaben / Projekte oder sind diese bereits beantragt?

**Entscheidung „Go" oder „No-Go"**

Die Ergebnisse der durchgeführten Aufgabenanalyse bilden die Entscheidungsgrundlage zur Beantwortung der Fragen, ob das Projekt durchgeführt wird beziehungsweise ob es unter den erörterten Gesichtspunkten überhaupt durchgeführt werden kann.

## 2.2 Entscheidungshilfen und Priorisierungsmethoden

Um Aufgaben nach Wichtigkeit beziehungsweise Dringlichkeit zu selektieren und einzuordnen, bietet sich die Anwendung einer Eisenhower-Matrix oder einer Portfolio-Analyse an. Beide Analysearten werden unten dargestellt und erklärt (Abb. 9 und Abb. 10). Ein mögliches Anwendungsbeispiel ist die Priorisierung einer To-Do-Liste, was bis zur Genehmigung des Projektes noch geklärt werden muss.

**a) Eisenhower-Matrix**

A = 1. Priorität (wichtig und dringend; muss sofort erledigt werden)

B = 2. Priorität (wichtig, aber nicht dringend; Aufgabe terminieren)

C = 3. Priorität (dringend, aber nicht wichtig; gleich erledigen oder übergehen)

D = 4. Priorität (weder wichtig noch dringend; übergehen)

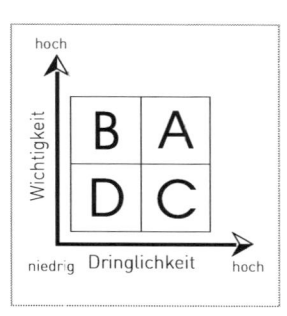

Abb. 9: Eisenhower-Matrix.

**Set Striking Dates (Milestones) in the Project**

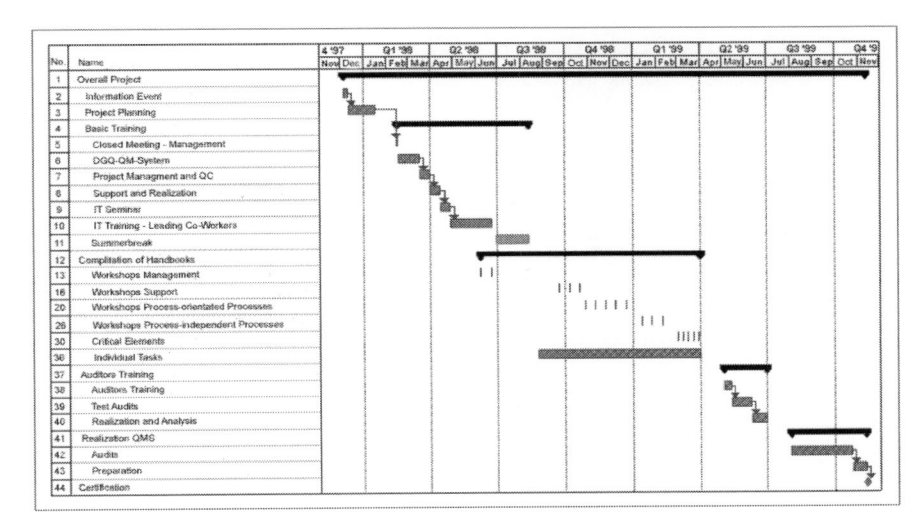

Fig. 8: Gantt Chart (for Example MS-Project).

**h) Position Statement of the Strategic Controlling Panel (Optional)**

- Statements on strategy compatibility
- Statements on portfolio compatibility – are there identical or similar plans / projects or are these applied for?

**Decision "Go" or "No Go"**

The results of the executed analysis form the basis for decision-making, whether the project will be carried out or if, in light of the addressed objectives it can be carried out at al.

## 2.2 Decision Making Tools and Methods of Prioritization

The application of an Eisenhower matrix or a portfolio analysis is used to select tasks based on the importance or urgency and to categorize it. Both types are shown and explained below (Fig. 9 and Fig. 10). A possible application is the prioritization of a to-do list of tasks, which have to be clarified prior the approval of the project.

**a) Eisenhower Matrix**

A = 1. Priority (important and urgent; must be done immediately)

B = 2. Priority (important, but not urgent; schedule task)

C = 3. Priority (important, but not urgent; schedule task)

D = 4. Priority (neither important nor urgent; skip)

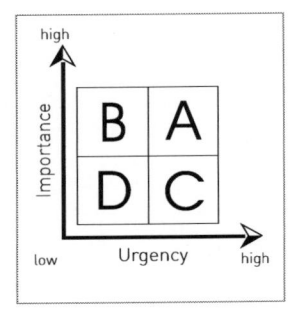

Fig. 9: Eisenhower Matrix.

**b) Portfolio-Analyse**

A = wichtig und dringend, sofort behandeln

B = terminieren oder / und überarbeiten

C = vernachlässigen, verwerfen

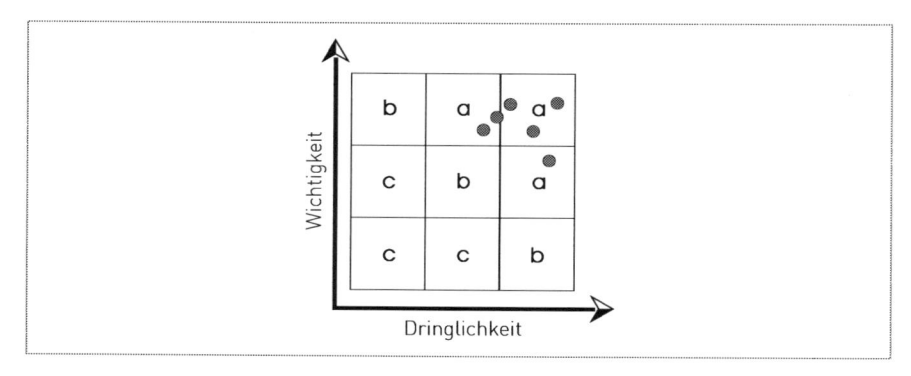

Abb. 10: Portfolio-Analyse.

## 2.3 Vorhabensantrag (Projektantrag)

Im Anschluss an die Aufgabenanalyse wird der Vorhabensantrag (Projektantrag) gestellt. Dieser sollte nachfolgende Punkte enthalten:

*1 Kurzbeschreibung (Hintergrund)*

*2 Problemdarstellung / Ist-Stand*

*3 Lösungsvorschlag*

*4 Nutzen*
  *4.1 Vorhabensziele*
  *4.2 Chancen und Risiken*

*5 Aufwandsschätzungen*
  *5.1 Umfang des Vorhabens*
  *5.2 Aufwand und Kosten*

*6 Weitere Informationen für den Entscheider (optional!)*
  *6.1 Projektumfeldanalyse; Betroffene und Beteiligte*
  *6.2 Rahmenbedingungen*
  *6.3 Annahmen*

*7 Anlagen*
  *7.1 Stellungnahme des Strategischen Controllings*
  *7.2 Sonstiges*

Abb. 11: Projektantrag 1.

Wie zu erkennen ist, können die entsprechenden Punkte der Aufgabenanalyse größtenteils unverändert oder leicht angepasst in den Projektantrag übernommen werden.

**b) Portfolio Analysis**

A = important and urgent, perform immediately

B = schedule and / or revise

C = neglect, discard

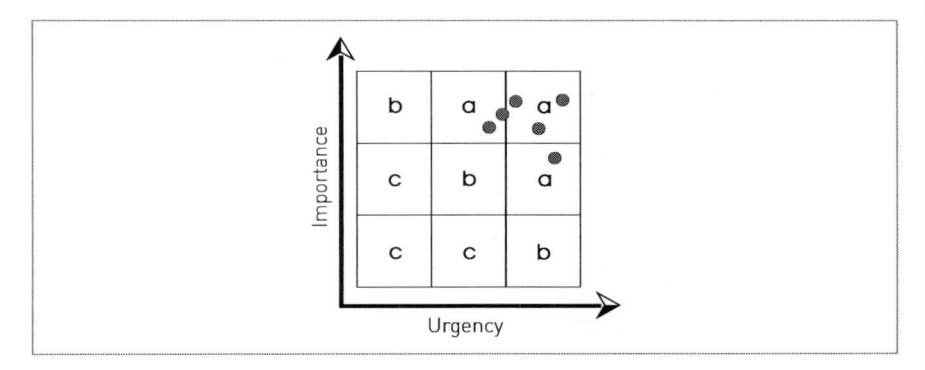

Fig. 10: Portfolio Analysis.

## 2.3 Project Application (Project Proposal)

Subsequent to the task analysis the project application (project proposal) is submitted. This should contain the following items:

1. Brief description (background)
2. Problem statement / status quo
3. Proposed solution
4. Benefit
   4.1 Objectives
   4.2 Opportunities and risks
5. Cost estimates
   5.1 Scope of the project
   5.2 Efforts and costs
6. For more information for the decision-makers (optional!)
   6.1 Project environment analysis, affected and interested parties
   6.2 General conditions
   6.3 Assumptions
7. Equipment
   7.1 Position statement of the Strategic Controlling Panel
   7.2 Other

Fig. 11: Project Application 1.

As you can see, the corresponding items of the task analysis can be inserted largely unchanged or slightly adapted into the project application.

Fortgeführt wird dies im Projektauftrag / Lastenheft, der / das wie folgt gegliedert ist:

> 1 *Projekt (Arbeitsgruppe)*
>   1.1 *Projektname (Arbeitsgruppenname)*
>   1.2 *Hintergrund*
>   1.3 *Auftragnehmer*
>       1.3.1 *Projektleiter (Arbeitsgruppenleiter)*
>       1.3.2 *Projektteam (Arbeitsgruppenmitglieder)*
>       1.3.3 *Organisationsform (Aufbauorganisation)*
>   1.4 *Projekt-Controlling-Stelle (entfällt bei Arbeitsgruppe)*
>   1.5 *Projektausschuss (entfällt bei Arbeitsgruppe)*
>
> 2 *Problembeschreibung / Ist-Stand*
>
> 3 *Lösungsvorschlag / Alternativenauswahl*
>
> 4 *Nutzen*
>   4.1 *Projektziele (Arbeitsgruppenziele)*
>   4.2 *Projektumfeldanalyse*
>   4.3 *Chancen und Risiken (Risikoanalyse)*
>   4.4 *Projektstruktur*
>
> 5 *Aufwandsschätzung*
>   5.1 *Umfang des Projektes*
>   5.2 *ausgeschlossene Leistungen*
>   5.3 *Aufwand und Kosten, Personal und Budget*
>   5.4 *Projektdauer, Termine (Balkenplan)*
>
> 6 *Weitere Informationen*
>   6.1 *Betroffene und Beteiligte*
>   6.2 *Rahmenbedingungen*
>       6.2.1 *Schnittstellen*
>       6.2.2 *Einordnung in die IT-Strategie, Priorisierung*
>
> 7 *Anlagen*

Abb. 12: Projektantrag 2.

Auch hier kann ein Großteil des Inhaltes aus dem Vorhabensantrag übernommen werden, wobei allerdings die Ergänzung dessen mit den Anforderungen des Auftraggebers erforderlich ist.

Aus der Praxis heraus bleibt aber zu sagen, dass sich der Projektleiter in aller Regel seinen Auftrag selbst erstellt und dieser nur vom Auftraggeber unterzeichnet wird.

This will be continued in the project order / specification structured as follows:

1 Project (working group)
   1.1 Project name (workgroup name)
   1.2 Background
   1.3 Contractor
      1.3.1 Project manager (work group leader)
      1.3.2 Project team (work group member)
      1.3.3 Organizational structure (company organization)
   1.4 Project controlling body (not applicable for working group)
   1.5 Project steering committee (not applicable for working group)

2 Problem description (status quo)

3 Suggested solution / alternative selection

4 Benefit
   4.1 Project objectives (work group objectives)
   4.2 Project environment analysis
   4.3 Opportunities and risks (risk analysis)
   4.4 Project structure

5 Cost estimate
   5.1 Scope of the project
   5.2 Exempted services
   5.3 Effort and costs, personnel and budget
   5.4 Project duration, schedule (Gantt chart)

6 Further information
   6.1 Affected and interested parties
   6.2 General conditions
      6.2.1 Interfaces
      6.2.2 Classification into the IT-strategy, prioritization

7 Equipment

Fig. 12: Project Application 2.

Here a large extent of the contents from the project application can be reused as well, however the addition of the client's requirements are required.

From the practical experience remains to be stated that the project manager usually creates the order himself and the client only signs the same.

## 2.4 Projektorganisation

Die Projektorganisation beschreibt den formalen Rahmen der Organisation einer Behörde und die Einbettung des Projektes in diesen Rahmen. Grundsätzlich unterscheidet man vier Möglichkeiten der Projektorganisation. Daneben gibt es zahlreiche Mischformen.

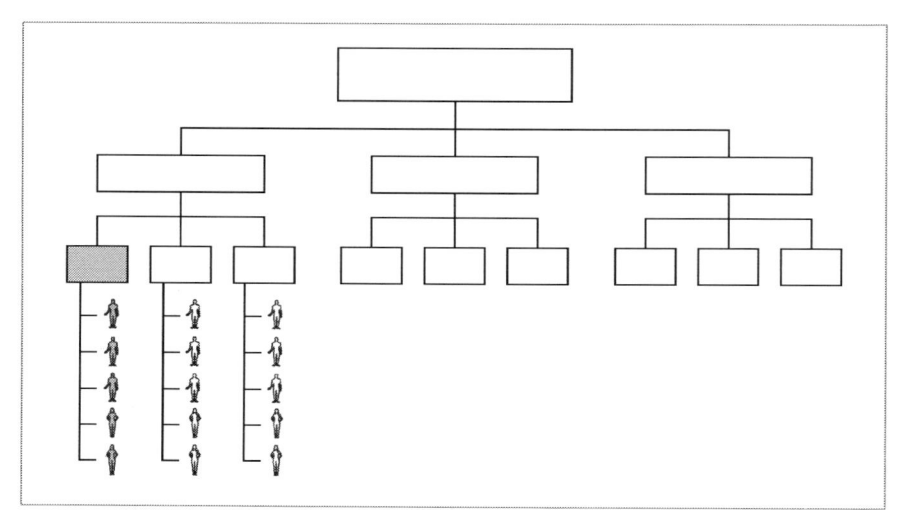

### 2.4.1 Linien-Projektorganisation

- Projektteam in der Linie setzt sich aus Mitarbeitern des Linienvorgesetzten und zugleich Projektleiters zusammen.
- Weitere, außerhalb der Linie stehende Personen werden nicht hinzugezogen.

Abb. 13: Linien-Projektorganisation.

| Vorteile | Nachteile |
| --- | --- |
| + Einheit der Leitung | – Doppelbeanspruchung des Projekt- und Abteilungsleiters |
| + Einheit des Auftragsempfangs | – nicht immer fachlich und qualitativ richtiges Personal verfügbar |
| + keine Personalversetzung | – schwieriger Ausgleich von Personalbelastungsspitzen |
| + geringer Koordinierungsaufwand | |

Tab. 2: Vor- und Nachteile der Linien-Projektorganisation.

## 2.4 Project Organization

The project organization describes the formal framework of an administrative body's organization and the project's integration in this context. Basically you have to distinguish four variations of project organization. In addition, there are numerous mixed forms.

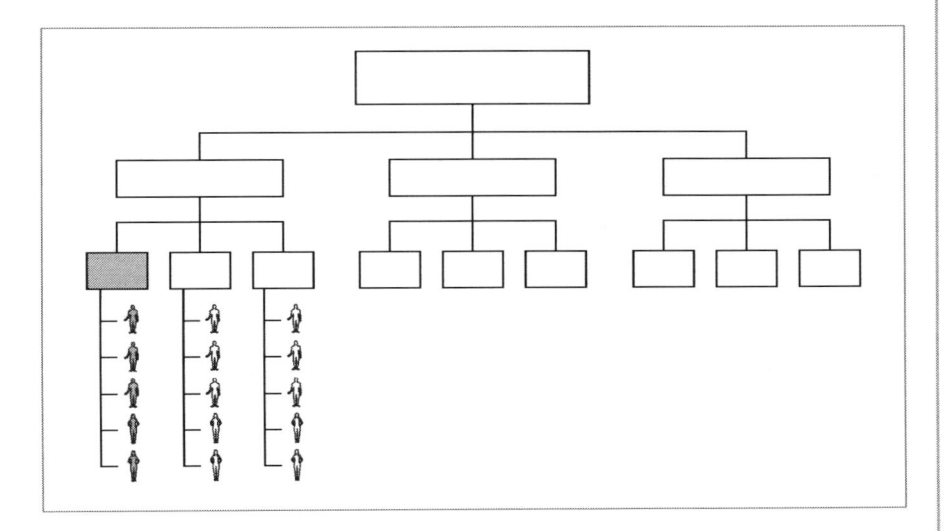

### 2.4.1 Linear Project Organization

- A linear project team consists of employees of the line manager and project manager both.
- Further persons, outside the linear relationship, are not involved.

Fig. 13: Linear Project Organization.

| Benefits | Disadvantages |
|---|---|
| + Cohesive management | – Dual demands on the project and division lead |
| + Single order receipt | – Technically and qualitatively suitable staff not always available |
| + No personnel movement | – Difficult to balance personnel load spikes |
| + Low coordination effort | |

Tab. 2: Benefits and Disadvantages Linear Project Organization.

## 2.4.2 Stabs- oder Einfluss-Projektorganisation

- Der Projektkoordinator erhält eine Stabsstelle und ist direkt der Geschäftsleitung angegliedert.
- Die Mitarbeiter verbleiben in der Linie.
- Projekt-Leiter hat keine Weisungsbefugnis gegenüber der Linie, sondern ist nur Koordinator mit Vorschlagsrecht.
- Die Stabsstelle ist für die Informationssammlung, Entscheidungsvorbereitung und Berichterstattung verantwortlich.

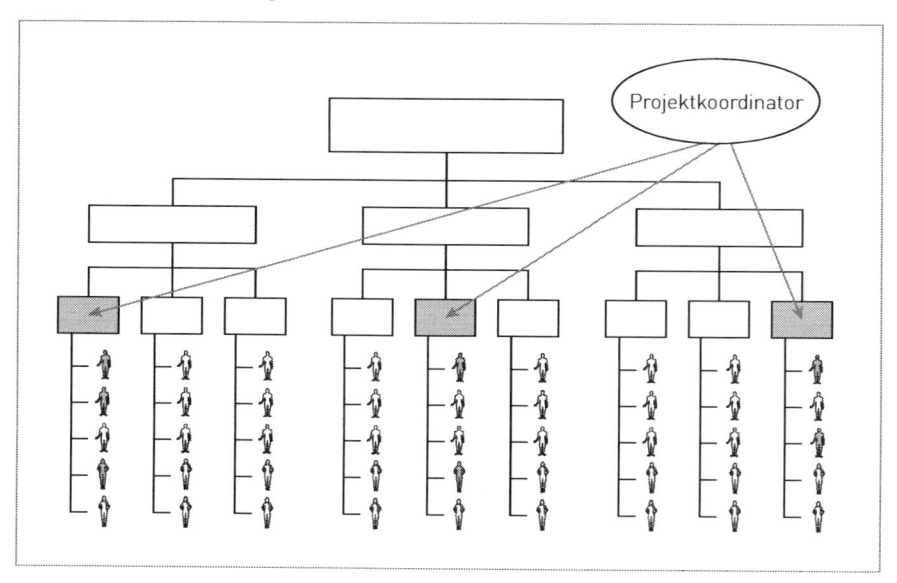

Abb. 14: Stabs-/Einfluss-Projektorganisation.

| Vorteile | Nachteile |
| --- | --- |
| + geringe organisatorische Veränderungen | – mangelndes Verantwortungsgefühl |
| + hohe Flexibilität beim Personaleinsatz | – fehlender Teamgeist |
| + schnell zu realisieren | – langsame Reaktionsgeschwindigkeit bei Störungen |
| + fachlich hohe Ausstattung durch Koordination der Fachabteilungen | – hohe Konfliktgefahr |
| + Nähe zur Dienststellenleitung (Entscheidungsinstanz und Machtorgan) | – fehlende Autorität des Projektleiters |
|  | – hoher Aufwand für die Dienststellenleitung |
|  | – Störungen müssen direkt von dieser Stelle bereinigt werden |

Tab. 3: Vor- und Nachteile der Stabs-/Einfluss-Projektorganisation.

## 2.4.2 Staff or Influence Project Organization

- The project coordinator is placed in a staff position and reports directly to management.
- The employees report linear as before.
- Project leader has no authority over the linear aligned employees, and is only coordinator with a right of suggestion.
- The staff position is responsible for information gathering, decision making preparation and reporting.

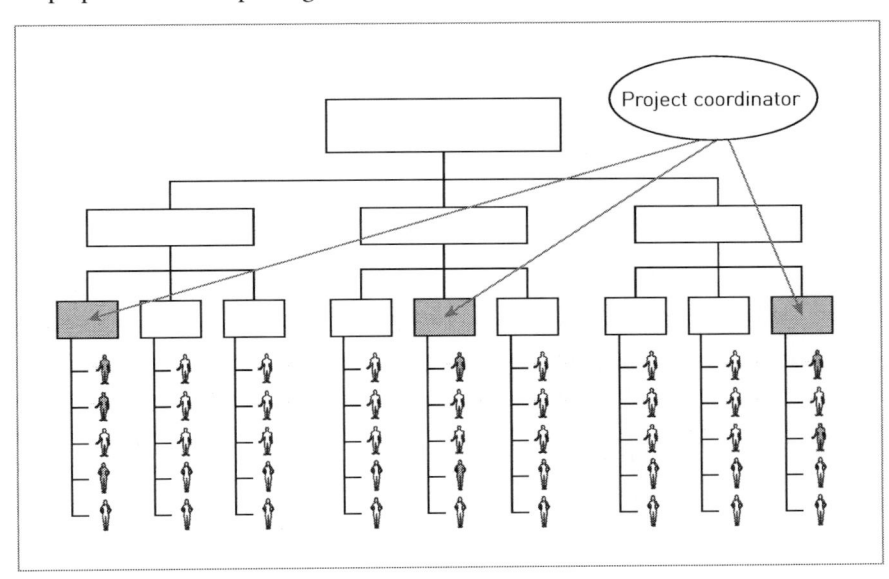

Fig. 14: Staff/Influence-Project Organization.

| Benefits | Disadvantages |
| --- | --- |
| + Low organizational impact | – Lack of feeling of responsible |
| + High flexibility in human resource management | – Lacking team spirit |
| + Fast to implement | – Slow response time in the event of problems |
| + Technically high equipment by coordination of the departments | – High risk of conflict |
| + Proximity to management (decision-making body and seat of power) | – Lacking authority of the project manager |
|  | – High expense for management |
|  | – Problems will have to be corrected directly from this location |

Tab. 3: Benefits and Disadvantages Staff/Influence Project Organization.

### 2.4.3 Reine Projektorganisation

- Ein Projektteam wird für die Dauer des Projekts gebildet.
- Die Teammitglieder sind aus der Linie herausgelöst und arbeiten ausschließlich für die Ziele des Projekts.
- Der Projektleiter hat die fachliche Projekt- und die Führungsverantwortung.
- Nach Beendigung des Projekts kehren alle Beteiligten wieder in ihre Linienfunktion zurück und werden aus dem Projekt entlassen.

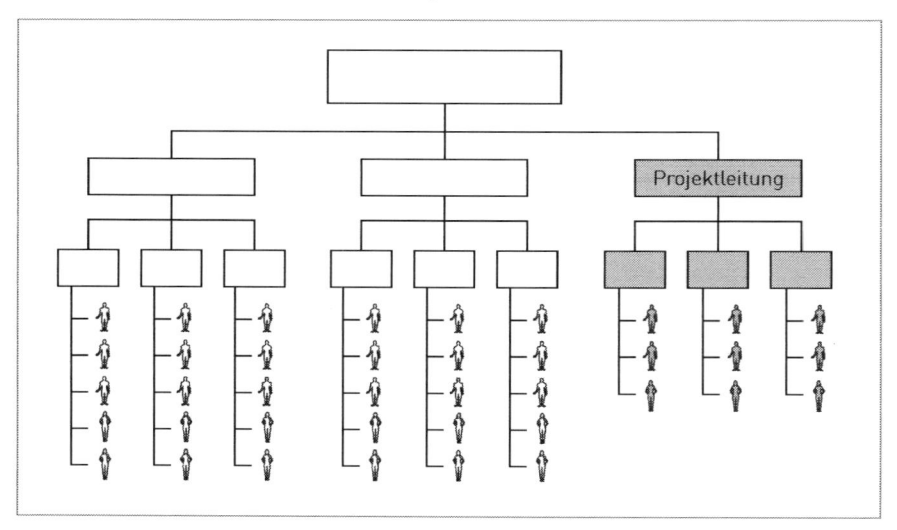

Abb. 15: Reine Projektorganisation.

| Vorteile | Nachteile |
| --- | --- |
| + große Kompetenz des Projektleiters | – großer organisatorischer Aufwand |
| + eindeutige Weisungsbefugnis | – hoher Personaleinsatz |
| + kurze Informationswege | – hohe Kosten |
| + optimale Ausrichtung aller Ressourcen auf das Projektziel | – Probleme der Projektmitarbeiter, zum Beispiel bei der Rückkehr in die Linie nach Projektende |
| + schnelle Reaktion auf Störungen | – u. U. großer Wissensverlust beim Ausscheiden von Projektmitgliedern |
| + Transparenz bei Aufgabenverteilung und Verantwortung | |
| + zielgerichtete Zusammenarbeit im Team | |
| + geringer Koordinierungsaufwand in den Fachabteilungen | |
| + hohe Identifikation mit dem Projekt | |

Tab. 4: Vor- und Nachteile der reinen Projektorganisation.

### 2.4.3 Pure Project Organization

- A project team is formed for the duration of the project.
- The team members are removed from the line and work exclusively for the objectives of the project.
- The project manager has the technical and managerial responsibility of the project.
- The completion of the project all parties return to their line management function and are dismissed from the project.

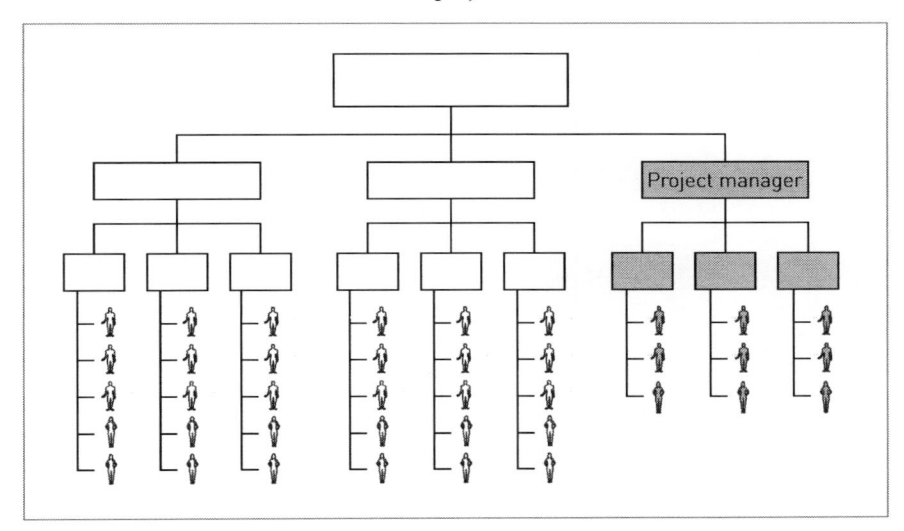

Fig. 15: Pure Project Organization.

| Advantages | Disadvantages |
| --- | --- |
| + Great expertise of the project manager | – large organizational effort |
| + unambiguous direction authority | – High demands on staffing levels |
| + Short information paths | – High costs |
| + Optimal orientation of all resources on the project objective | – Problems of project employees, such as at the time of their return to the line after the end of the project |
| + Fast response to problems | – Maybe great loss of knowledge on termination of project team members |
| + Transparency in allocation of tasks and responsibility | |
| + Targeted cooperation in team context | |
| + Low coordination effort in the individual departments | |
| + High level of identification with the project | |

Tab. 4: Benefits and Disadvantages Pure Project Organization.

## 2.4.4 Matrix-Projektorganisation

- Der Projektleiter wird aus der Linie ausgegliedert.
- Die Mitarbeiter verbleiben in der Linie und sind ihren Linienvorgesetzten weiterhin unterstellt.
- Der Projektleiter hat zusätzliche projektbezogene Weisungsbefugnisse (zeitlich befristetes Mehrliniensystem).
- Der Projektleiter ist für die Zielvorgabe und die zeitlichen Vorgaben verantwortlich, wobei der Linienvorgesetzte bestimmt, von wem und wie die Projektaufgabe durchgeführt wird.

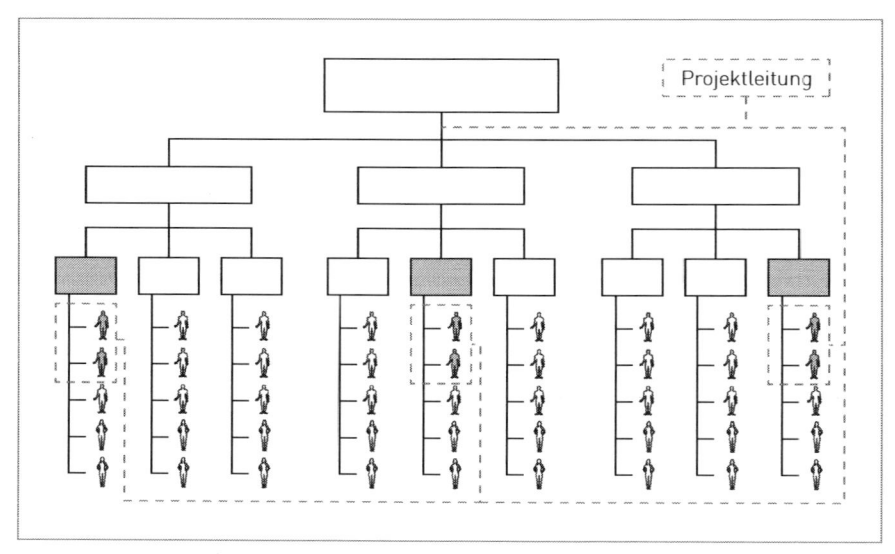

Abb. 16: Matrix-Projektorganisation.

| Vorteile | Nachteile |
| --- | --- |
| + Projektverantwortung durch Projektleiter | – Mitarbeiter als „Diener zweier Herren" |
| + hohe Identifikation des Projektleiters mit dem Projekt | – schwierige Teamentwicklung |
| + flexibler Personaleinsatz | – schwierige Kompetenzabgrenzung zwischen Linie und Projektleiter |
| + größeres Sicherheitsgefühl der Mitarbeiter | – hohe Anforderungen an Kommunikation und Information |
| + gute Weiterbildungsmöglichkeiten | – „Wettbewerb" um Ressourcen |
|  | – vorgesetztes Gremium wird häufig beansprucht |

Tab. 5: Vor- und Nachteile der Matrix-Projektorganisation.

## 2.4.4 Matrix Project Organization

- The project leader is spun off from the line.
- The employees will remain in the line and continue to report to the line manager.
- The project manager has additional project-related authority (temporary multi-chain system).
- The project manager is responsible for the objective statement and the schedule constraints while the line manager determines, by whom and how the project objectives will be performed.

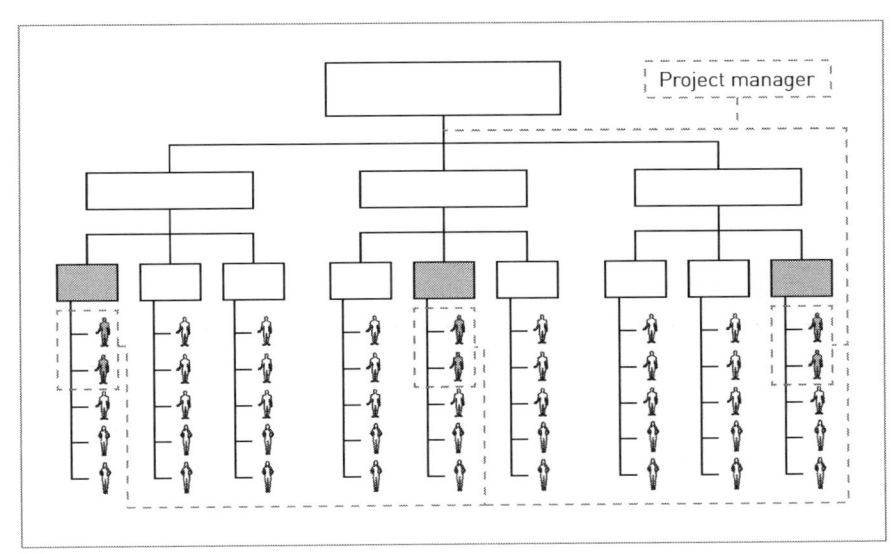

Fig. 16: Matrix Project Organization.

| Benefits | Disadvantages |
| --- | --- |
| + Project responsibility of the project manager | – Employees as "servant of two masters" |
| + High degree of identification of the project manager and the project | – Difficult team development |
| + Flexible staffing | – Difficult delineation of responsibilities between the line and project manager |
| + Greater feeling of security of employees | – High demands on communication and information |
| + Good training opportunities | – "Competition" for resources |
|  | – Frequent use of supervisory panel |

Tab. 5: Benefits and Disadvantages Matrix Project Organization.

## 2.4.5 Wechsel der Organisationsform

Es ist durchaus denkbar und sinnvoll, dass während eines Projektes die Organisationsform wechselt.

So empfiehlt es sich beispielsweise, in der Definitions- und Planungsphase, mit einer Matrix-Projektorganisation zu arbeiten, da man damit auf ein breit gefächertes Fachwissen zurückgreifen kann. Geht es dann in die Realisierungsphase, so sind die Vorteile einer reinen Projektorganisation nicht von der Hand zu weisen, da man mit einem speziellen Team die vorher geplanten Arbeitsschritte durchführen kann.

## 2.5 Übersicht Organisationsformen

Zum vereinfachten Gesamtüberblick werden die bereits betrachteten Organisationsformen in der folgenden Tabelle zusammengefasst:

| Aufgabenstellung | Organisationsform | | | |
|---|---|---|---|---|
| | Linien- | Stabs- | Reine | Matrix- |
| | Projektorganisation | | | |
| Produktentwicklung | | | ✓ | |
| vertriebsorientiertes Großprojekt | | | ✓ | |
| bereichsinterne Verfahrensentwicklung | ✓ | | | |
| bereichsübergreifende Verfahrensentwicklung | | | | ✓ |
| Entwicklung mit Fremdfirmen | | ✓ | | |
| kurze Entwicklungszeit (< 1 Jahr) | ✓ | | | |
| lange Entwicklungszeit (> 1 Jahr) | | | ✓ | |
| fester Terminrahmen | ✓ | | ✓ | |
| Projekt mit geringem Umfang | ✓ | | | |
| Projekt mittlerer Größe | | ✓ | | ✓ |
| großes Entwicklungsvolumen | | | ✓ | |
| hohes Projektrisiko | | ✓ | ✓ | |
| anteiliger Ressourcenzugriff | | | | ✓ |
| Ähnlichkeit mit anderen Entwicklungsaktivitäten | | | | ✓ |
| eindeutige Aufgabenteilung | | ✓ | | |
| klar abgegrenztes Thema | ✓ | | | |
| hoher Grad an Interdisziplinarität | | | | ✓ |

Abb. 17: Projektorganisationsformen.

## 2.4.5 Change of the Type of Organization

It is quite conceivable and appropriate that the organizational form changes during the project.

It is recommendable to work in the definition and planning phase with a matrix project organization since it can rely on a broad expertise. In the implementation phase the pure project organization is not to be dismissed out of hand, as it will have a dedicated team, which can perform the preplanned operations.

## 2.5 Overview Organizational Forms

For a simplified overview the organizational forms already discussed are summarized in the table below:

| Objectives | Organizational Structure | | | |
|---|---|---|---|---|
| | Line | Staff | Pure | Matrix |
| | | Project organization | | |
| Product development | | | ✓ | |
| Sales oriented major project | | | ✓ | |
| Divisional level process development | ✓ | | | |
| Cross-functional process development | | | | ✓ |
| Development with third parties | | ✓ | | |
| Short development schedule (<1 year) | ✓ | | | |
| Long development schedule (>1 year) | | | ✓ | |
| Fixed schedule | ✓ | | ✓ | |
| Small scale project | ✓ | | | |
| Medium sized project | | ✓ | | ✓ |
| Large development volume | | | ✓ | |
| High project risk | | ✓ | ✓ | |
| Pro-rata resource access | | | | ✓ |
| Similarity to other development activities | | | | ✓ |
| Clear division of responsibilities | | ✓ | | |
| Clearly defined topic | ✓ | | | |
| High degree of interdisciplinary approach | | | | ✓ |

Fig. 17: Project Organization Forms.

**Aufgaben zur Selbstkontrolle**

2.1 Erläutern Sie, welche Schritte im Rahmen einer Vorstudie/Aufgabenanalyse erledigt werden sollten und wozu diese Schritte dienen.

2.2 Welche Elemente sollte das sog. Lastenheft enthalten?

2.3 Erläutern Sie die vier Formen der Projektorganisation und diskutieren Sie, wann welche Form sinnvoll ist.

**Tasks for Progress Review**

*2.1   Explain what steps as part of a preliminary study/analysis should be done and for what these steps are used.*

*2.2   What elements should be contained in the so-called requirement specifications?*

*2.3   Explain the four forms of project organization and discuss when each of the forms is useful.*

# 3 Definitionsphase

## 3.1 Projekt-Start-up oder Kick-off

Der *„Projekt-Start-up"* (PSU), auch Kick-off genannt, ist die erste Projekt-Statussitzung und findet zum offiziellen Beginn eines Projektes statt.

Hier lernen sich die Mitarbeiter des Projektes kennen und werden über alle bereits bekannten Projektdaten informiert.

Wurde der Auftrag ohne vorherigen Vorhabensantrag direkt erteilt, so ist die erste Aufgabe des Projektteams, eine Aufgabenanalyse zu erarbeiten. Ansonsten wurde diese Analyse schon im Rahmen des Antragsverfahrens erstellt und kann hier allenfalls noch einmal vorgestellt oder überprüft werden, dies insbesondere dann, wenn die Mitglieder des Projektteams an der Erstellung der Aufgabenanalyse nicht mitgewirkt haben. Der Auftraggeber oder ein maßgeblicher Vertreter sollte hierbei zugegen sein.

Nachfolgende Punkte sollen beim Projekt-Start-up geklärt werden.

### 3.1.1 Aufgaben des Auftraggebers/Entscheiders

Der Auftraggeber ist der kleinste gemeinsame Nenner aller am Projekt beteiligten Stellen. Er besitzt Entscheidungsbefugnis über alle Projektbeteiligten. Seine Aufgaben in der Definitionsphase sind:

- Projektauftrag (auch Lastenheft genannt) erstellen
- Budget und Personal festlegen und sicherstellen
- Projektleiter ernennen und unterstützen
- Unterstützung bei der Zieldefinition
- Pflichtenheft und Projektpläne abnehmen
- Statusberichte prüfen
- Phasenergebnisse prüfen und genehmigen
- Projektergebnis abnehmen

# 3 Definition Phase

## 3.1 Project Start-Up or Kick Off

The *"project start-up"* (PSU), also known as kick-off, is the first project status meeting and takes place at the official start of the project.

Here the employees of the project will get to know each other and will be briefed on all project data known so far.

If the order was issued directly without a prior project application the first task of the project team is to work out a job task analysis. Otherwise this analysis was created as part of the application process and can only be presented or checked once again, particularly, if the members of the project team not had participated in the creation of the analysis. The client or a relevant representative should be present.

The following points should be clarified during the project start-up.

### 3.1.1 Tasks of the Client / Decision Maker

The client is the lowest common denominator of all departments involved in the project. It has decision-making power over all project participants. His tasks in the definition phase are:

- Create project order (also called specifications)
- Determine and secure budget and personnel
- Appoint and support project manager
- Support in the definition of objectives
- Accept functional specifications and project plans
- Check status reports
- Review and approve phase results
- Accept project results

### 3.1.2 Anforderungen an den Projektleiter

Der Projektleiter untersteht der Weisung des Auftraggebers / Entscheiders und muss direkt an ihn berichten. Die Anforderungen, die an einen Projektleiter gestellt werden, sind:

**Fachliche Kompetenz:**

- Sachkenntnis
- Führungstechniken
- Methoden und Techniken der Projektarbeit

**Soziale Kompetenz:**

- Kommunikation
- Motivation
- Konflikte lösen

### 3.1.3 Die Aufgaben des Projektleiters sind

- Projektteam aufstellen
- Pflichtenheft erstellen
- Projektziele definieren
- Controlling
- Einsatz von effizienten Arbeits- und Entscheidungstechniken
- Projektteam zusammenführen
- Konflikte im Projektteam schlichten und für zielgerichtete Zusammenarbeit sorgen
- Informationspflicht gegenüber den Projektbeteiligten

### 3.1.4 Befugnisse des Projektleiters

- projektbezogene Anordnungsbefugnisse, entsprechend der gewählten Form der Aufbauorganisation (Linien-, Stabs-, reine und Matrixorganisation)
- eingeschränkte Verhandlungsbefugnisse mit Fremdfirmen unter Beachtung der Ausschreibungs- und Vergaberichtlinien
- Mitspracherecht bei der Benennung der Projektteammitglieder
- Vorschlagsrecht bei erforderlichen Fortbildungsmaßnahmen
- Entscheidungsrecht bei Alternativenauswahl
- direktes Kommunikationsrecht mit Projektbeteiligten
- Einberufung von Projektausschusssitzungen

## 3.1.2 Requirements for the Project Manager

The project manager is under the instruction of the client/decision maker and reports directly to same. The requirements to be met by a project manager are:

**Technical competence:**

- Expertise
- Leadership qualities
- Methods and techniques of project work

**Social competence:**

- Communication
- Motivation
- Resolve conflicts

## 3.1.3 The Tasks of the Project Manager Are:

- Establish project team
- Draft specifications
- Define project objectives
- Cost control
- Use of efficient labor and decision techniques
- Form the project team
- Deconflict the project team and ensure targeted cooperation
- Duty to keep the project participants informed

## 3.1.4 Competencies of the Project Leader

- Project-related authority, according to the chosen form of organizational structure (line, bar, pure and matrix organization)
- Limited negotiation authority with contractors in accordance with the tendering and procurement directives
- Co-determination rights in the appointment of the project team members
- Nomination rights for necessary training
- Decision making power in the selection of alternatives
- Right of direct communication with project stakeholders
- Convening of project steering committee meetings

### 3.1.5 Anforderungen an das Projektteam

> Ein Team ist eine Arbeitsgruppe, in der direkt kommuniziert wird, deren Mitglieder ergänzende Fähigkeiten und Funktionen aufweisen und die über einen stark ausgeprägten Gemeinschaftssinn verfügen sollten.

Nicht selten scheitern Projekte, weil der menschliche Aspekt vom Projektleiter zu sehr vernachlässigt wird und weil die Teammitglieder nicht zueinander finden. In so einem Fall ist eine produktive Arbeit unmöglich. Deshalb sind an die Teammitglieder folgende Anforderungen zu stellen (siehe dazu auch Kapitel 7 „Teamentwicklung"):

- fachliche Kompetenz
- soziale Kompetenz (Teamfähigkeit)
- nicht Arbeitnehmer, sondern Auftragnehmer
- selbstverantwortlich für Aufgabenerfüllung
- Flexibilität, um kreative Problemlösungen zu entwickeln
- hohes Abstraktionsvermögen, Fähigkeit zu ganzheitlichem, vernetztem Denken
- Teamgröße (7–20) als Grundlage der Kommunikationsbeziehungen

### 3.1.6 Festlegung der Aufbau- und Ablauforganisation

- Wer macht was?
- Wer hat welche Funktionen, Rechte, Pflichten?
- Informationsfluss des Projektleiters zum Auftraggeber, Team, Gremien u. a.
- Abwicklungs-Richtlinien
- Festlegung des Umgangs mit Änderungen im Projekt (Konfigurationsmanagement)
- Kommunikationswege
- Projekt-Dokumentation
- Festlegung von Terminen regelmäßiger Projekt-Statussitzungen (PSS)
- Festlegung der zu verwendenden Hilfsmittel, Schablonen, Checklisten etc.

## 3.1.5 Requirements of the Project Team

> A team is a working group, with direct communications, whose members have complementary skills and capabilities and exhibit a strong sense of community.

Projects often fail because the project manager overlooks the human aspect and the team members do not find each other. In such a case productive work is almost impossible. Therefore the following requirements are to be met by the team members (also see chapter 7 on the topic "Team building"):

- Technical competence
- Social skills (teamwork)
- Not employees but contractors
- Personally responsible for meeting objectives
- Flexibility to develop creative problem solutions
- High ability to grasp abstract concepts, capability for holistic, networked thinking
- Team size (7–20) as the basis of the communication relationships

## 3.1.6 Definition of the Organizational and Operational Structure

- Who does what
- Who has which functions, rights, obligations
- Information flow of the project manager to the client, team, panels, etc.
- Process guidelines
- Definition of the handling changes in the project (configuration management)
- Communication channels
- Project documentation
- Definition of deadlines for regular project status meetings (PSM)
- Determination of which tools, templates, checklists, etc. to use.

**Notizen**

### 3.1.7 Erstellung

- eines groben Terminplanes
- einer groben Risikoanalyse
- eines Qualitätssicherungsplanes

## 3.2 Werkzeuge in der Definitionsphase

Innerhalb der Definitionsphase stehen verschiedene Werkzeuge zur Festlegung der Rahmenbedingungen zur Verfügung.

### 3.2.1 Planungsplan

- Aufgliederung der Planungsphase in die erforderlichen und zu erstellenden Projektpläne
- Schätzung des jeweiligen Zeitbedarfs für die planerischen Teilaufgaben
- Festlegung der Zuständigkeiten

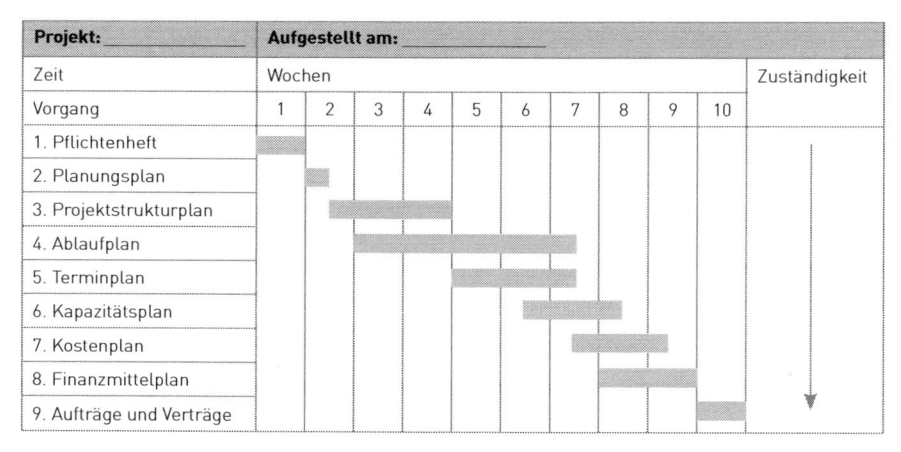

| Projekt: | Aufgestellt am: | | | | | | | | | | |
|---|---|---|---|---|---|---|---|---|---|---|---|
| Zeit | Wochen | | | | | | | | | | Zuständigkeit |
| Vorgang | 1 | 2 | 3 | 4 | 5 | 6 | 7 | 8 | 9 | 10 | |
| 1. Pflichtenheft | | | | | | | | | | | |
| 2. Planungsplan | | | | | | | | | | | |
| 3. Projektstrukturplan | | | | | | | | | | | |
| 4. Ablaufplan | | | | | | | | | | | |
| 5. Terminplan | | | | | | | | | | | |
| 6. Kapazitätsplan | | | | | | | | | | | |
| 7. Kostenplan | | | | | | | | | | | |
| 8. Finanzmittelplan | | | | | | | | | | | |
| 9. Aufträge und Verträge | | | | | | | | | | | |

Abb. 18: Planungsplan.

### 3.2.2 Zieldefinition – Projektziele und Zielstrukturplan

Die Zieldefinition bildet die Vorstufe zum Projektstrukturplan. Erst wenn die Ziele der Projektarbeit hinreichend definiert sind, darf in die nächste Phase der Projektarbeit, die Planungsphase, übergegangen werden. Wird dies nicht beachtet, fällt man, wie die Praxis gezeigt hat, immer wieder in die (Ziel-)Definitionsphase zurück und dreht sich mit der Projektarbeit im Kreis.

## 3.1.7 Creation

- Of a rough schedule
- Of a rough risk analysis
- Of a quality assurance plan

## 3.2 Tools in the Definition Phase

There are several tools available within the definition phase for defining the framework conditions.

### 3.2.1 Design Plan

- Breakdown of the planning phase in the required and to be drafted project plans
- Estimate of the time required for the planning subtasks
- Determination of responsibilities

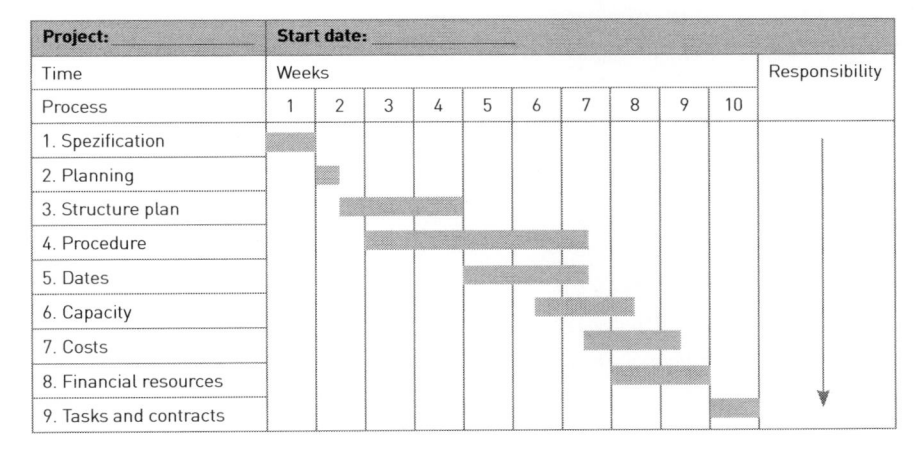

| Project: | Start date: | | | | | | | | | | |
|---|---|---|---|---|---|---|---|---|---|---|---|
| Time | Weeks | | | | | | | | | | Responsibility |
| Process | 1 | 2 | 3 | 4 | 5 | 6 | 7 | 8 | 9 | 10 | |
| 1. Spezification | | | | | | | | | | | |
| 2. Planning | | | | | | | | | | | |
| 3. Structure plan | | | | | | | | | | | |
| 4. Procedure | | | | | | | | | | | |
| 5. Dates | | | | | | | | | | | |
| 6. Capacity | | | | | | | | | | | |
| 7. Costs | | | | | | | | | | | |
| 8. Financial resources | | | | | | | | | | | |
| 9. Tasks and contracts | | | | | | | | | | | |

Fig. 18: Design Plan.

### 3.2.2 Objective Definition – Project Objectives and Target Structure Plan

The target objective definition is the precursor to the work breakdown structure. Only when the objectives of the project are sufficiently well defined may the project work proceed to the next phase: the project-planning phase. If this is not observed, the project will continually revert, as has been shown in practice, back to the (target) definition phase with the project work will turn in a circle.

> Ziele sind vorausgedachte Ergebnisse der Arbeit. Klare, eindeutige, erreichbare und von allen Projektbeteiligten akzeptierte Ziele und Zwischenziele müssen vorhanden sein. Sie sind die Basis aller Aktivitäten.

**Anforderungen an Ziele:**

- Ergebnis (Qualität, Quantität)
- Termin (Zeit)
- messbar
- Rahmenbedingungen
- Verantwortlichkeiten
- kontrollierbar
- schriftlich festgehalten
- lösungsneutral

Auch Nicht-Ziele sollten definiert werden, um eine klare Abgrenzung der Projektziele zu erreichen.

> **Hilfsfragen für die Kontrolle der formulierten Ziele:**
> - Woran merken wir, dass wir die Ziele erreicht haben?
> - Können wir die Aufgaben und Tätigkeiten genau bestimmen, um das Ziel zu erreichen?
> - Kann das Projektziel von uns oder anderen unterschiedlich interpretiert werden?
> - Woran messen wir den Erfolg?

Projekte sind immer in eine Umwelt eingebettet, die aus verschiedenen Institutionen und Personen besteht:

> Objectives are imagined results of the work. Clear, unambiguous, achievable objectives as well as intermediate objectives accepted by all project participants must exist. They are the foundation of all activities.

**Requirements for Objectives:**

- Result (quality, quantity)
- Schedule (time)
- Measurable
- General conditions
- Responsibilities
- Controllable
- Documented in writing
- Neutral to the outcome

Also non-objectives should be defined to achieve a clear delineation of the project objectives.

> **Review Questions for the Control of the Formulated Objectives:**
>
> - How do we realize that we have met our objective?
> - Can we determine exactly the tasks and activities to achieve the objective?
> - Can the project objective be interpreted in different ways either by others or us?
> - How will we measure success?

Projects are always embedded in an environment, which is made up of various institutions and people:

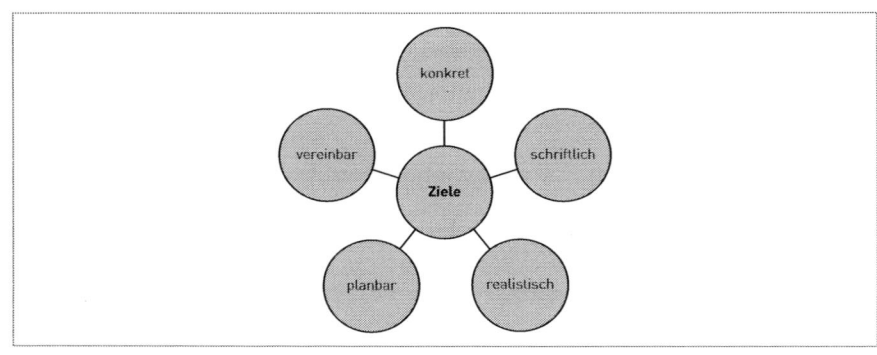

Abb. 19: Ziele.

*Zielarten*

Innerhalb der Projektziele werden sechs Zielarten unterschieden.

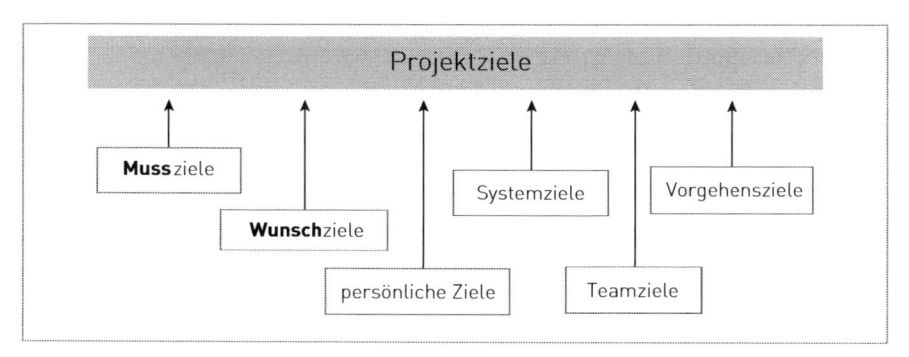

Abb. 20: Zielarten.

**Mussziele**

- müssen unbedingt erreicht werden und
- bilden die Kriterien für Lösungsalternativen (Lösung muss Mussziel erfüllen).
- In dieser Gruppe sind die kritischen Ziele zu suchen.
- sind klar formuliert oder quantifiziert, damit sie später zweifelsfrei überprüfbar sind, sonst ist hier Potenzial für Streit bei Lösungsbeurteilung über Grad der Zielerreichung.

**Wunschziele**

- Erreichen ist positiv, aber nicht unbedingt zu 100 % erforderlich.
- sind keine Voraussetzung zur Erfüllung des Projektergebnisses,
- sollten dennoch beachtet werden, da sie für die Lösung wertsteigernd sein können und
- können sowohl qualitativ (objektive Beurteilung schwierig) als auch quantitativ sein.

**Systemziele**

- Sie enthalten die Muss- und Wunschziele und weisen auf das Projektergebnis hin.

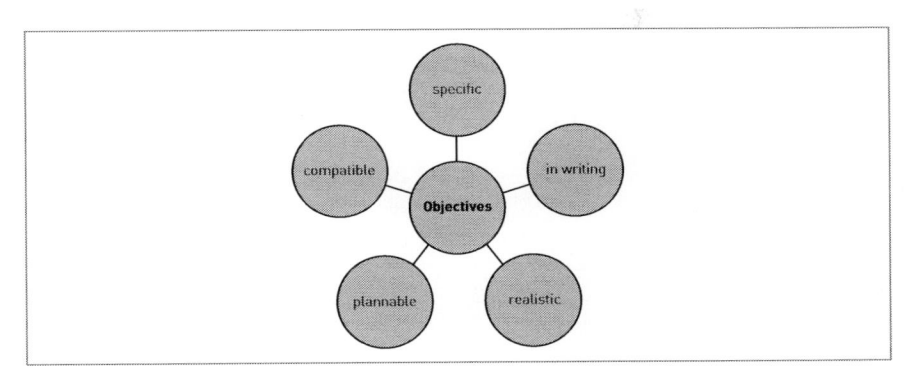

Fig. 19: Objectives.

*Type of Objectives*

Within the project objectives six different types exist.

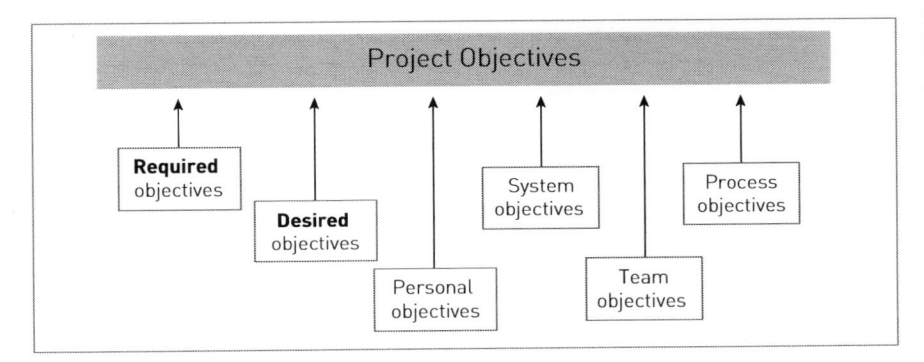

Fig. 20: Objective Types.

**Required Objectives**

- Must absolutely be achieved
- Form the criteria for alternative solutions (solution must meet the must objective)
- Within this group are the to be found the critical objectives
- Clearly formulated or quantified, so that they are later verifiable, otherwise there is potential for dispute when judging the solution or the degree of achievement.

**Desired Objectives**

- Achievement is positive, but not necessarily required at 100%
- Not a requirement for achievement of the project result
- Should be considered nevertheless, as they can add value to the solution
- Can be either qualitative (objective assessment difficult), or quantitative

**System objectives**

- They contain the required and desired objectives and indicate the result of the project.

**Vorgehensziele**

- Wie wird vorgegangen, um das Projektergebnis zu erreichen?

**Teamziele**

- Wie gehen wir als Team an die gestellten Aufgaben heran?
- Vereinbarte „Spielregeln"

**Persönliche Ziele**

- Kennt Projektleiter die persönlichen Ziele seiner Mitarbeiter?
- Sie sind immer vorhanden.

*Zielstrukturplan*

Ein Hilfsmittel, um Projektziele hinreichend zu definieren, stellt der Zielstrukturplan dar. Damit werden die Ziele in einer vertikalen Hierarchie vom Grobziel zum operational ausformulierten Ziel herunter gebrochen. Erst wenn auf der untersten Ebene alle Anforderungen an Ziele erfüllt sind, ist der Zielstrukturplan hinreichend ausgestaltet. Hinsichtlich der Planbarkeit kann man hier allerdings Abstriche vornehmen, da die Termine, zu denen das eine oder andere Ziel erreicht werden muss, erst im Rahmen der Planungsphase festgelegt werden. Es kann vorkommen, dass unter Umständen die in der Definitionsphase festgelegten Ziele in der Planungs- oder insbesondere in der Realisierungsphase angepasst oder geändert werden müssen.

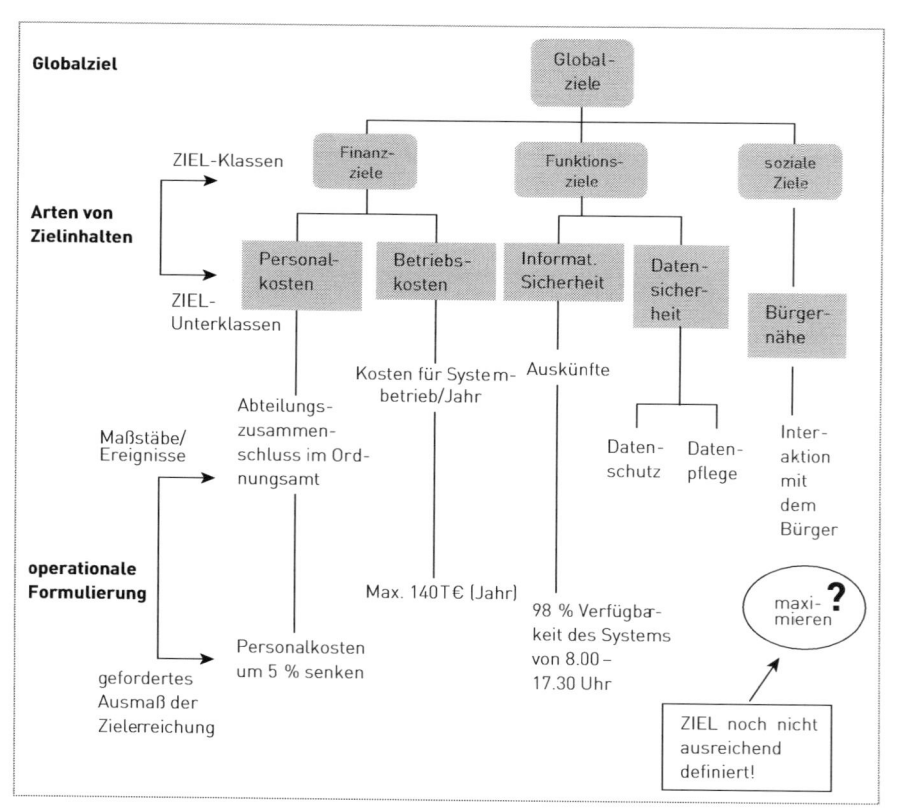

Abb. 21: Zielstrukturplan.

**Process Objectives**

- Which is the process to achieve the result of the project?

**Team Objectives**

- How do we as a team approach the tasks?
- Agreed "rules of the game"

**Personal Objectives**

- Does the project manager know the personal objectives of his employees?
- They always exist.

*Target Structure Plan*

The target structure plan is a tool to define project objectives sufficiently. With it the objectives are broken down in a vertical hierarchy from a draft objective to an operationally formulated objective. The target structure plan is only sufficiently detailed when at the lowest level all requirements to be met by the objectives are described. With regards to the planability concessions have to be made, since the milestone by which the one or the other objective must be reached can only be determined in the context of the planning phase. It may be that in some circumstances the objectives worked out in the definition phase must be adapted or changed in the planning or specially during the implementation phase.

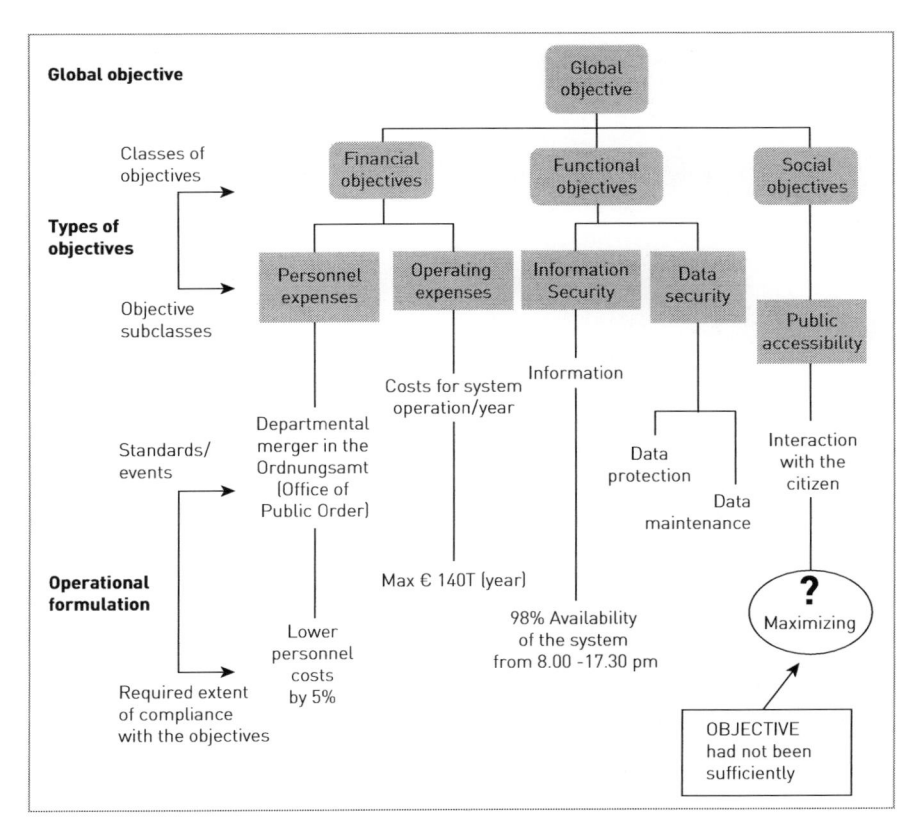

Fig. 21: Target Structure Plan.

### 3.2.3 Pflichtenheft

In der Definitionsphase wird vom Projektleiter eine Erstfassung des Pflichtenheftes erstellt, um die Vorgaben und Anforderungen des Auftraggebers zu erfassen und umsetzen zu können. Dieses muss nach folgendem Muster gegliedert sein:

1 *Projektbeschreibung*
   1.1 *Projektname*
   1.2 *Hintergrund*
   1.3 *Projektziele*
      1.3.1 *Ausformulierung der Projektziele*
      1.3.2 *Nicht-Ziele*

2 *Projektorganisation*
   2.1 *Aufbauorganisation*
      2.1.1 *Projektleiter*
      2.1.2 *Betroffene Organisationseinheiten und personelle Besetzung (Projektteam)*
      2.1.3 *Externe Projektbeteiligte*
   2.2 *Ablauforganisation*
   2.3 *PM-Regelungen (Projektmanagement)*
   2.4 *SE-Regelungen (Systemerstellung)*
   2.5 *KM-Regelungen (Konfigurationsmanagement)*
   2.6 *QS-Regelungen (Qualitätssicherung)*

3 *Projektleistungen*
   3.1 *Aktivitäten und Produkte*
      3.1.1 *Projektstrukturplan*
      3.1.2 *Beschreibung der Arbeitspakete*
      3.1.3 *Projektablaufplan*
      3.1.4 *Projektressourcenplan*
      3.1.5 *Projektkostenplan*
      3.1.6 *Projektfinanzplan*
      3.1.7 *Meilensteine*
   3.2 *Ausgeschlossene Leistungen*

4 *Rahmenbedingungen*
   4.1 *Termine*
   4.2 *Personal*
   4.3 *Budget*
   4.4 *Sonstige Ressourcen*
   4.5 *Einzuhaltende Standards*
   4.6 *Schnittstellen*

5 *Risiken und Maßnahmen*

6 *Sonstige Regelungen und Hinweise*

7 *Anlagen*

Abb. 22: Pflichtenheft.

### 3.2.3 Performance Specifications

In the definition phase the project manager drafts a first version of the performance specification to document and to capture the specifications and requirements of the client. This must be structured as per the following example:

---

1 *Project description*
   *1.1 Project name*
   *1.2 Background*
   *1.3 Project objectives*
      *1.3.1 Formulation of project objectives*
      *1.3.2 Non-objectives*

2 *Project organization*
   *2.1 Organizational structure*
      *2.1.1 Project manager*
      *2.1.2 Affected organizational units and staffing (project team)*
      *2.1.3 External stakeholders*
   *2.2 Process organization*
   *2.3 PM provisions (project management)*
   *2.4 SC provisions (system creation)*
   *2.5 CM provisions (configuration management)*
   *2.6 QA provisions (quality assurance)*

3 *Project deliverables*
   *3.1 Activities and products*
      *3.1.1 Work breakdown structure*
      *3.1.2 Description of the work packages*
      *3.1.3 Project schedule*
      *3.1.4 Project resource plan*
      *3.1.5 Project budget*
      *3.1.6 Project financial plan*
      *3.1.7 Milestones*
   *3.2 Exempted services*

4 *General Conditions*
   *4.1 Schedule*
   *4.2 Personnel*
   *4.3 Budget*
   *4.4 Other resources*
   *4.5 Standards to be observed*
   *4.6 Interfaces*

5 *Risks and measures*

6 *Other provisions and instructions*

7 *Equipment*

---

Fig. 22: Performance Specifications.

**Notizen**

In der Definitionsphase werden die in Ziffer 3.1 des Pflichtenheftes genannten Gliederungspunkte noch nicht mit Inhalten versehen – dies geschieht erst in der Planungsphase.

**Aufgaben zur Selbstkontrolle**

*3.1   Welche Punkte sollten beim Projekt-Start-up definiert werden?*

*3.2   Welchen Anforderungen sollten Projektziele genügen? Weshalb ist dies so wichtig?*

The structural elements referred to in Section 3.1 of the specifications are not being populated during the definition phase – this is done only during the planning stages.

**Tasks for Progress Review**

*3.1   What items should be defined during the project start-up?*

*3.2   What requirements should the project objectives meet? Why is this so important?*

## 4 Planungsphase

Der Erfolg eines Projektes hängt direkt von der Qualität der Planung ab. Ein Vergleich der Projektabwicklung zweier Projekte mit unterschiedlich ausführlicher Planungsphase zeigt, dass eine gute Planung wegen der Fehlervermeidung die Gesamtprojektlaufzeit deutlich verkürzen kann.

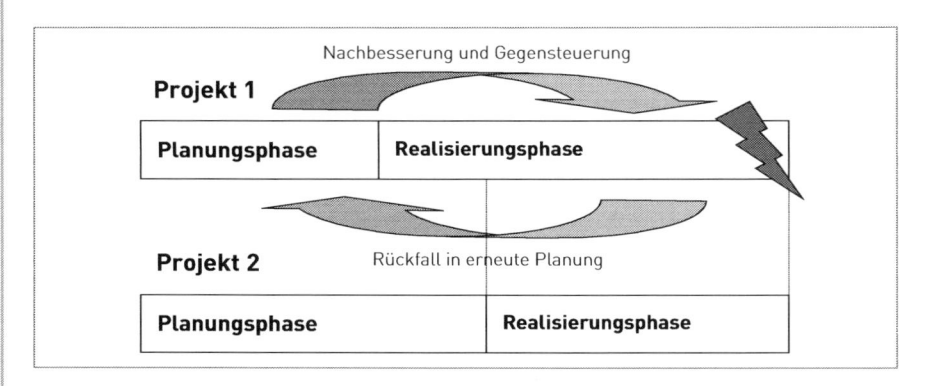

Abb. 23: Planungsphasen.

**Wesentliche Ergebnisse einer guten Planung sind:**

- sichere Aussagen zum Projektablauf
- Ermittlung von kritischen Faktoren im Projektablauf zur Verminderung des Projektrisikos
- Ermöglichung des zielgerichteten Einsatzes aller Projektressourcen
- Basis zur effizienten Projektsteuerung

Die Planung eines Projektes kann in die Grob- und Fein- oder Detailplanung unterteilt werden.

### 4.1 Grobplanung

In die Grobplanung gehören:

- Teilprojekte / Teilaufgaben
- Strukturierung des Projektablaufs
- Ressourcenabschätzung
- Kostenschätzung
- Aufgabenverteilung
- Meilensteine und Termine

# 4 Planning Phase

The project's success depends directly on the quality of the planning. A comparison of two projects with a differently executed planning phase project 2 shows that good planning can significantly shorten the overall project schedule, due to an avoidance of problems.

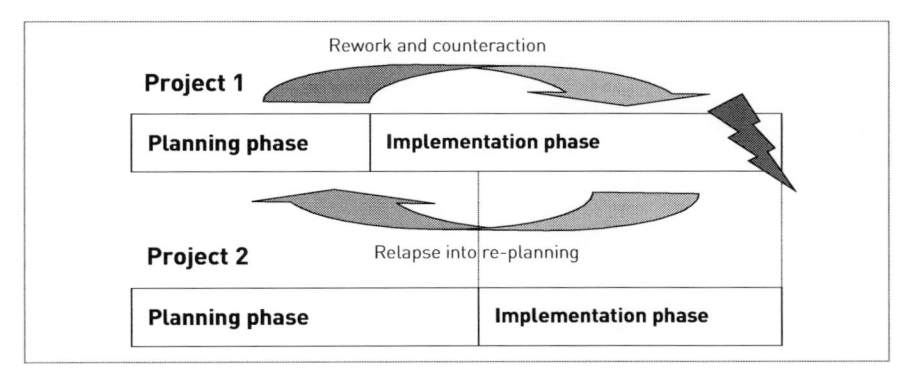

Fig. 23: Graphic Planning Stages.

**Main Results of Good Planning Are:**

- Reliable statements to the project schedule
- Identification of critical factors in the project schedule to reduce the project risk
- Permit the targeted use of all project resources
- Basis for efficient project management

The planning of a project will be divided into rough and fine or detailed planning.

## 4.1 Rough Planning

In the rough plan belong:

- Subprojects / subtasks
- Structuring of the project schedule
- Resource assessment
- Cost estimate
- Division of responsibilities
- Milestones and schedule

## 4.2 Fein- oder Detailplanung

In dieser Planungsphase werden die Ergebnisse der Grobplanung präzisiert und mit weiteren Methoden planerisch erfasst:

- detaillierte Kostenplanung
- detaillierte Abschätzung des Zeitaufwandes
- detaillierte Ressourcenplanung

## 4.3 Erforderliche Projektpläne in der Übersicht

### a) Projektstrukturplan (PSP)

- Zerlegung des Projekts in einzelne abgrenzbare Tätigkeiten, um eine Übersicht aller Aktivitäten zu erhalten (Teilprojekte – Teilaufgaben – Arbeitspakete)
- Ordnung der Einzelvorgänge zu einer hierarchischen Struktur

### b) Projektablaufplan (PAP)

- Festlegung einer logischen zeitlichen Reihenfolge der einzelnen Arbeitspakete
- Festlegung parallel abarbeitbarer Arbeitspakete

### c) Aktivitätenliste / Balkendiagramm / Netzplan

- Ergänzung des Projektablaufplans um die Zeitkomponente Projektterminplan
- Ermittlung des Anfangs- und Endtermins für jedes Arbeitspaket sowie des Verantwortlichen
- alternative Darstellung mittels tabellarischer Liste oder Balkendiagramm

### d) Ressourcenplan

- Ermittlung des benötigten Personals und der benötigten Betriebsmittel
- Darstellung als zeitbezogene Gesamtübersicht aller erforderlichen Kapazitäten während der Projektlaufzeit
- Darstellung der Verfügbarkeit von Ressourcen zum geplanten Ablaufzeitpunkt

### e) Kostenplan

- Ermittlung der Kosten je Arbeitspaket
- Darstellung als Gesamtübersicht über die Projektlaufzeit

### f) Finanzplan

- Planung der Finanzmittel im vorgesehenen Zeitpunkt des Projektverlaufs

## 4.2 Fine or Detailed Planning

In this planning phase the results of the outline planning will be clarified and documented with further planning techniques:

- Detailed cost planning
- Detailed estimate of the time
- Detailed resource planning

## 4.3 Necessary Project Plans in the Overview

**a) Work Breakdown Structure (WBS)**

- Disassembly of the project in the separately identifiable activities, in order to obtain an overview of all activities (subprojects – tasks – work packages)
- Arranging of the individual processes into a hierarchical structure

**b) Project Schedule (PS)**

- Defining a logical chronological order of the individual work packages
- Defining parallel workable packages

**c) Activities List / Gantt Chart / Network Plan**

- Completion of the project schedule by the time component of the project milestone plan
- Determination of the start and end date for each work package, as well as the responsible individual
- Alternative representation via tabular list or Gantt chart

**d) Resource Plan**

- Determination of the required staff and the amount of materials required
- Representation as a time-based overview of all necessary capacities during the project period
- Display of the availability of resources at the scheduled milestone

**e) Cost Plan**

- Calculation of the cost per work package
- Representation as a general overview of the project schedule

**f) Financial Plan**

- Planning of the funding provided for milestone of the project

## 4.4 Projektpläne als Beispiel

### 4.4.1 Projektstrukturplan

Der Projektstrukturplan (PSP) wird auf der Grundlage des Zielstrukturplanes erstellt. Dazu werden Arbeitspakete (AP) als kleinste Einheit im Strukturplan definiert, mit denen das jeweilige Ziel erreicht wird. Die Arbeitspakete wiederum können in einzelne Vorgänge untergliedert werden. Die Aufschlüsselung Projekt(ziel) – Teilprojekt – Teilaufgabe – Arbeitspaket erfolgt durch das Projektteam und die Aufschlüsselung der Arbeitspakete in Vorgänge erfolgt durch den/die für die Erledigung des Arbeitspaketes zuständigen Auftragnehmer.

Ein Arbeitspaket gilt dann als „geschnürt", wenn das Projektteam eine weitere Untergliederung für nicht mehr sinnvoll hält.

Man unterscheidet:

* objektorientierter Strukturplan
* funktionsorientierter Strukturplan
* gemischt orientierter Strukturplan

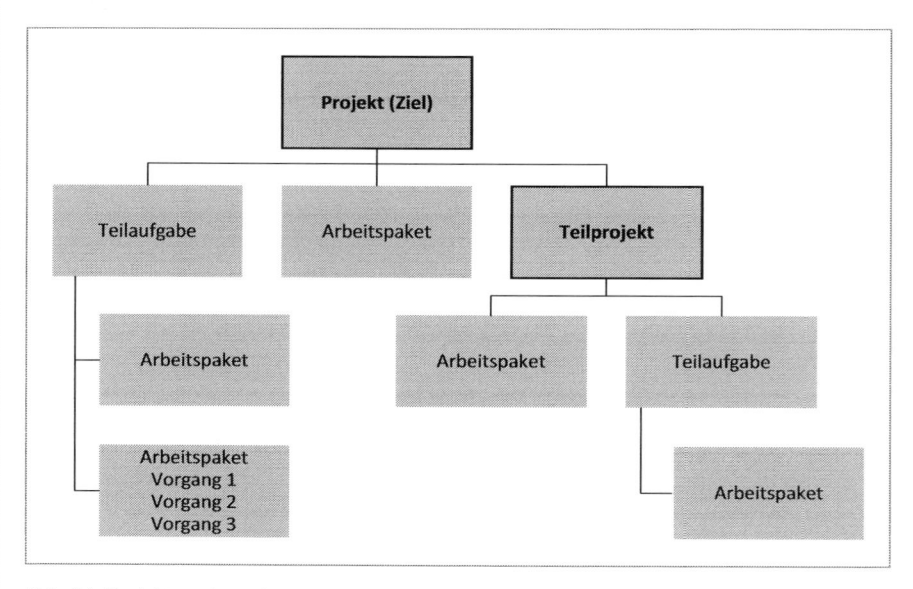

Abb. 24: Projektstrukturplan.

## 4.4 Project Plans as an Example

### 4.4.1 Work Breakdown Structure

The work breakdown structure (WBS) will be created on the basis of the target structure plan. To do this work packages (WP) are defined as the smallest unit in the work breakdown, with which each objective is achieved. The work packages, in turn, can be broken down into individual activities. The breakdown project (objective) – subproject – subtask – work package is performed by the project team and the contractor responsible for the execution of the work package carries out the breakdown of the work packages in processes.

A work package will then be considered as a "package", when the project team no longer considers a further breakdown as useful.

A distinction is made between:

- Object-oriented WBS chart
- Functionally-oriented WBS chart
- Mixed-oriented WBS chart

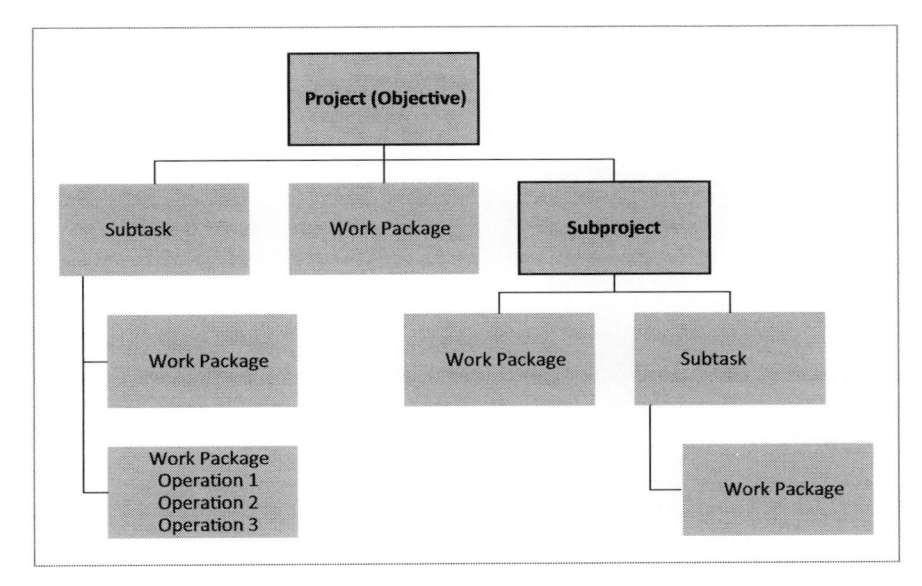

Fig. 24: Work Breakdown Structure.

Unter **Teilprojekt** wird hier eine Aufgabenstellung im Projekt verstanden, die für sich gesehen wieder in Teilaufgaben und Arbeitspakete untergliedert werden muss und die ein eigenes Projektmanagement erfordert – es gelten ebenfalls die Bedingungen eines Projektes. Bei sehr großen Projekten kann es erforderlich werden, Teilprojekte auf mehreren Hierarchieebenen zu gliedern.

**Teilaufgabe** ist die Summe von zusammengehörigen Arbeitspaketen.

**Arbeitspakete** stellen die untersten, nicht weiter aufgelösten Elemente der Projektstruktur dar (siehe DIN 69901).

Jetzt kann mit der Erstellung des Projektstrukturplanes begonnen werden. Zur Sicherheit sollte nochmals geprüft werden, ob alle Voraussetzungen erfüllt sind.

**Checkliste für den Start[2]**

- ✓ Sind Projektantrag und Projektfreigabe ordnungsgemäß abgeschlossen?
- ✓ Sind die Ziele des Projekts ausreichend definiert?
- ✓ Entspricht die Organisationsform den Anforderungen des Projekts?
- ✓ Sind die notwendigen Kompetenzen des Projektleiters festgelegt?
- ✓ Ist das Projektteam festgelegt?
- ✓ Sind alle Betroffenen über den Start des Projekts informiert?
- ✓ Ist die maximale Laufzeit für das Projekt vorgegeben?
- ✓ Stehen die maximalen Budgetwerte fest?
- ✓ Sind Berichts- und Informationswege festgelegt?
- ✓ Gibt es Überschneidungen mit anderen Projekten?

Sind alle Fragen geklärt, kann mit der Strukturierung des Projekts begonnen werden.

---

2  Vgl. M. Gröger, H. Schelle; Grundlagen Projektmanagement CBT-Programm; Bayerische Akademie für Verwaltungsmanagement GmbH / BStMI.

As **subproject** here is understood a task in the project, which again must be broken down into subtasks and work packages and requires its own project management – it is equally subject to the conditions of the project. For very large projects, it may be necessary to divide subprojects on multiple hierarchical levels.

**Subtask** is the sum of related work packages.

**Work packages** are the lowest, not further resolved items of the project structure (cf. DIN 69901).

The creation of the work break down structure can now be started. To be on the safe side it should be re-examined whether all the conditions are met.

**Checklist for the Start[2]**
- ✓ Are project application and project sign-off properly concluded?
- ✓ Are the objectives of the project adequately defined?
- ✓ Does the organizational form meet the requirements of the project?
- ✓ Are the necessary skills of the project manager defined?
- ✓ The project team is established?
- ✓ Are all the parties concerned informed about the start of the project?
- ✓ Is the maximum duration for the project set?
- ✓ Are the maximum budget values available?
- ✓ Are reporting and information channels set?
- ✓ Is there any overlap with other projects?

If all the issues are resolved, the structuring of the project can be started.

---

2  Cf. M. Gröger, H. Schelle; Grundlagen Projektmanagement CBT-Programm; Bayerische Akademie für Verwaltungsmanagement GmbH / BStMI.

**Sechs wichtige Regeln für die Arbeit am Projektstrukturplan[3]**

- Für jedes Arbeitspaket ist nur ein Verantwortlicher zuständig.
- Bei phasenorientiertem Projektmanagement sollte ein Arbeitspaket eindeutig einer Phase zugeordnet sein.
- Aufgaben, die extern vergeben werden, sind als Teilaufgaben oder Arbeitspakete auszuweisen.
- Die Leistung, die aus einem Arbeitspaket hervorgeht, muss von den Leistungen anderer Arbeitspakete klar abgrenzbar sein. Nur so wird eine wirksame Planung und Kontrolle erreicht.
- Die geplante Zeitdauer pro Arbeitspaket sollte – verglichen mit der Projektdauer – nicht zu groß sein. Der Grund: Der Terminverzug wird zu spät erkannt, Maßnahmen zur Gegensteuerung greifen nicht mehr. (Diese Regel gilt nicht für Arbeitspakete, die über den gesamten Projektzeitraum geplant sind zum Beispiel laufende Aufgaben wie Terminüberwachung).
- Der Kostenplanwert pro Arbeitspaket darf nicht zu klein sein, weil sich sonst die projektbezogene Kostensteuerung erschwert. Eine eindeutige Regelung über den richtigen Kostenplanwert gibt es nicht.

*Arbeitspaket*

In einem Arbeitspaket (AP) werden in der Regel alle Vorgänge eines Projektes, die sachlich eine Einheit bilden, zusammengefasst. Arbeitspakete werden in einer kleinen organisatorischen Einheit erledigt; dies kann entweder durch einen einzelnen Mitarbeiter beziehungsweise einen Teil des Projektteams oder auch durch einen externen Auftragnehmer erfolgen.

Die einzelnen Arbeitspakete müssen so klar wie möglich voneinander abgegrenzt werden und es ist ein eindeutig definiertes Ergebnis festzulegen. Der Auftragnehmer ist für die Erreichung des Ergebnisses, die Einhaltung der kalkulierten Kosten und für die termingerechte Erledigung verantwortlich.

---

3   Vgl. M. Gröger, H. Schelle: Grundlagen Projektmanagement CBT-Programm; Bayerische Akademie für Verwaltungsmanagement GmbH/BStMI und H. Schelle: Projektmanagement, Erfolgspotenziale in der Verwaltung. In: Modernes Verwaltungsmanagement, hrsg. von der Bayerischen Verwaltungsschule; Fortbildung & Praxis; Bd. 5; 1996, S. 204.

> **Six Important Rules for the Work on the Work Breakdown Structure[3]**
>
> - For each work package only one person is responsible.
> - In phase orientated project management a work package should be associated clearly with one phase
> - Tasks that are outsourced must be disclosed as subtasks or work packages
> - The performance resulting of a work package must clearly differentiate from the performance of other work packages. Only this way an effective planning and control is achieved
> - The planned amount of time per work package should be compared with the project duration – not be too large
> - The reason: if a delay is detected too late, measures to counteract this are no longer appropriate. (This rule does not apply to work packages, which are planned for the entire project; e. g. ongoing tasks such as schedule monitoring).
> - The cost plan value per work package must not be too small, because otherwise the project-related cost control becomes more difficult. A unique value of the correct cost plan value does not exist.

*Work Package*

In a work package (WP) usually all activities of a project are combined, which form a de facto unity. Work packages are handled in a small organizational unit; this can be achieved either by an individual employee or a part of the project team or by an external contractor.

The individual work packages must be as clearly as possible differentiated from each other and a clearly defined outcome needs to be specified. The contractor is responsible for the achievement of the result, the compliance within the calculated costs and responsible for the timely completion.

---

[3] Cf. M. Gröger, H. Schelle: Grundlagen Projektmanagement CBT-Programm; Bayerische Akademie für Verwaltungsmanagement GmbH / BStMI – H. Schelle: Projektmanagement, Erfolgspotentiale in der Verwaltung. In: Modernes Verwaltungsmanagement, hrsg. von der Bayerischen Verwaltungsschule; Fortbildung & Praxis; Bd. 5; 1996, P. 204.

Arbeitspakete müssen demnach

- ein konkretes Ergebnis beinhalten,
- in Aufwand und Mengen kalkulierbar sein,
- klare Schnittstellen haben und
- eine geregelte organisatorische Zuständigkeit vorweisen.

Es ist unumgänglich, Arbeitspakete in schriftlicher Form zu vergeben. Dazu kann ein Formular verwendet werden, wie es nachfolgend vorgeschlagen wird:

| **Arbeitspaketbeschreibung** | Blatt-Nr. / von: |
|---|---|
| Vorhaben / Projekt: | Projektstrukturplan-Nr. (PSP-Code) (Ordnungsnummer) |
| AP-Titel:<br>AP-Beginn (Datum):<br>AP-Ende (Datum):<br>AP-Verantwortlicher: | Bearbeiter:<br>Tel.- / CNP-Nr.:<br>Ausgabedatum: |
| 1. Leistungsbeschreibung (ggf. Zusatzblatt) ||
| 2. Anzuwendende Produkte / Dokumente (genaue Bezeichnung) ||
| 3. Erforderliche Zulieferungen (z. B. Ergebnisse anderer Arbeitspakete)<br>    Lieferant:    Lieferdatum: ||
| 4. AP-Ziele (aus Zieldefinition / Zielstrukturplan) ||
| 5. AP-Genehmigung<br>Besonderheiten:<br>Bemerkungen:<br>Auftraggeber:    Datum, (Name) Unterschrift ||
| 6. Anlagen<br>☐ Terminplan<br>☐ Kostenplan<br>☐ Sonstiges: ||

Abb. 25: Arbeitspaketbeschreibung.

Work packages must therefore

- Include a concrete result
- Be calculable in expenses and quantities
- Have clear interfaces and
- A defined organizational competence

It is essential to issue work packages in written form. A form can be used to do this, as is proposed below:

| **Work Package Description** | Sheet No. / from: |
|---|---|
| Plan / Project: | Work breakdown structure No. (WBS-Code) (Serial Number) |
| WP title: <br> WP Start (date): <br> WP end (date): <br> WP responsible person: | Initiator: <br> Tel.- / CNP-No: <br> Issue date: |
| 1. Statement of work (if necessary addl. sheet) ||
| 2. Applicable products / documents (exact name) ||
| 3. Required prerequisites (e.g. results of other work packages) <br><br> Supplier:                               Delivery date: ||
| 4. WP-objectives (from objectives definition / Work Breakdown Structure) ||
| 5. WP-approval <br><br> Special notes: <br> Comments: <br> Client:         Date (name) signature ||
| 6. Attachment <br> ☐ Schedule <br> ☐ Budget <br> ☐ Misc.: ||

Fig. 25: Work Package Description.

*Gliederungsvorschläge für die Strukturplanung*

Ein Gliederungssystem bei der Strukturplanung ist von großer Bedeutung, weil

- die einzelnen Elemente der Strukturplanung eindeutig identifiziert werden können,
- die Kontrolle und Steuerung dadurch erleichtert wird und
- dadurch Übersichtlichkeit gewonnen wird.

Es werden folgende Gliederungssysteme vorgeschlagen:

- Umfangreiches und stark zergliedertes Projekt:

| Projekt | Teilprojekt | Teilaufgabe | (Teil-Teilaufgabe) | Arbeitspaket |
|---|---|---|---|---|
| ↓ | ↓ | ↓ | ↓ | ↓ |
| ABCD[4]- | AA- | 01- | 01- | 01 |

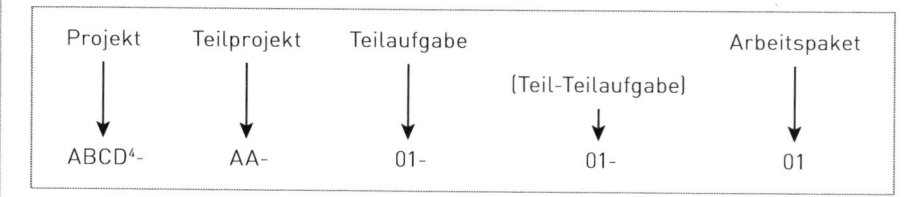

Hierarchieebenen, die nicht gegeben sind, werden mit „0" gekennzeichnet. Ein Arbeitspaket, das beispielsweise auf oberster Ebene, also direkt unter dem Projektziel, zu erledigen ist, erhält zum Beispiel folgende Gliederung: ABCD-00-00-01.

Bei diesem System ist neben der Zugehörigkeit und der Gliederungsebene auch noch die Art des Gliederungspunktes zu ersehen (Teilprojekt – Teilaufgabe – Teil-Teilaufgabe – Arbeitspaket).

Dieses System ist flexibel einzusetzen, da keine stark kategorisierende Elementhierarchie aufgebaut werden muss.

- Weniger stark zergliedertes Projekt:

| Projekt | 1. Ebene | 2. Ebene | 3. Ebene |
|---|---|---|---|
| ↓ | ↓ | ↓ | ↓ |
| 0 | 10 | 101 | 1011 |

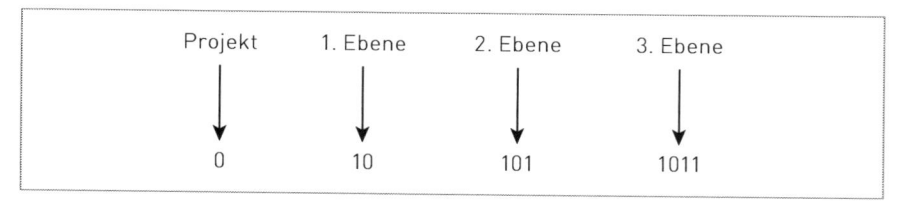

Bei diesem Gliederungssystem sind nur die Zugehörigkeit und die Gliederungsebene zu ersehen. Die Art des Gliederungspunktes kann hieraus nicht geschlossen werden. Es erfordert eine starke und streng hierarchisch aufgebaute Kategorisierung von oben nach unten, wenn man die Art des Gliederungspunktes ersehen will.

---

4  Anstatt „ABCD" ist das Projektkürzel einzusetzen.

*For Proposed Classification the Work Break Down Structure*

A classification system is of great importance in structural planning because

- The individual elements of the structural planning can be clearly identified
- This makes it easier to control and
- Clarity is obtained

The following classification systems are proposed:

- Substantial and highly disparate project:

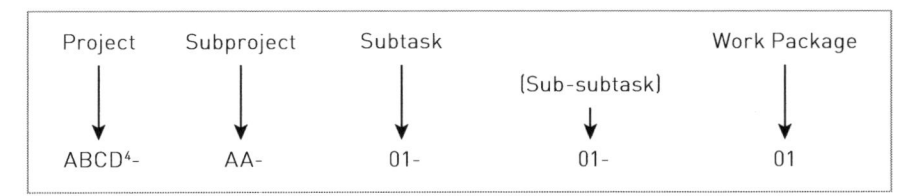

| Project | Subproject | Subtask | (Sub-subtask) | Work Package |
|---------|------------|---------|---------------|--------------|
| ↓ | ↓ | ↓ | ↓ | ↓ |
| ABCD[4]- | AA- | 01- | 01- | 01 |

Hierarchy levels, which do not exist, are indicated with "0". A work package, which is for example at the top-level, and therefore directly under the project objective, takes on the following structure: ABCD-00-00-01

This system is in addition to the membership and the level as well as the type of the structure element to see (Subproject – Subtask – Sub-subtask – work package)

This system is flexible, since highly categorized element hierarchy must not be established.

- Less disparate project:

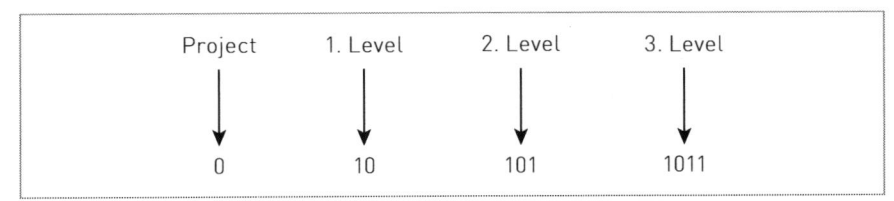

| Project | 1. Level | 2. Level | 3. Level |
|---------|----------|----------|----------|
| ↓ | ↓ | ↓ | ↓ |
| 0 | 10 | 101 | 1011 |

In this structural system only the membership and the level are to be seen. The nature of the structural element cannot be deducted. It requires a strong and strictly hierarchical categorization from top to bottom, if you want to see the type of structural element.

---

[4] Instead of "ABCD" the project abbreviation is to be used.

*Abbildung der Projektstruktur in einer EDV-Projektbibliothek*

Im Rahmen der Bearbeitung eines Projekts ist es aus Gründen der eindeutigen Zuordnung von Dokumenten sinnvoll, den Projektstrukturplan in einer Explorer-Struktur[5] zentral auf einem Server anzulegen, um eine Projektbibliothek zu schaffen, in deren einzelnen Ordnern die Mitarbeiter später alle Dokumente abspeichern und abrufen können.

Dabei sollten die einzelnen Ordner mit der eindeutigen Ordnungsnummer (PSP-Code) aus dem Gliederungssystem bezeichnet werden, damit aus Gründen der Übersichtlichkeit später die Dokumente und sonstigen Dateien leicht gefunden werden können.

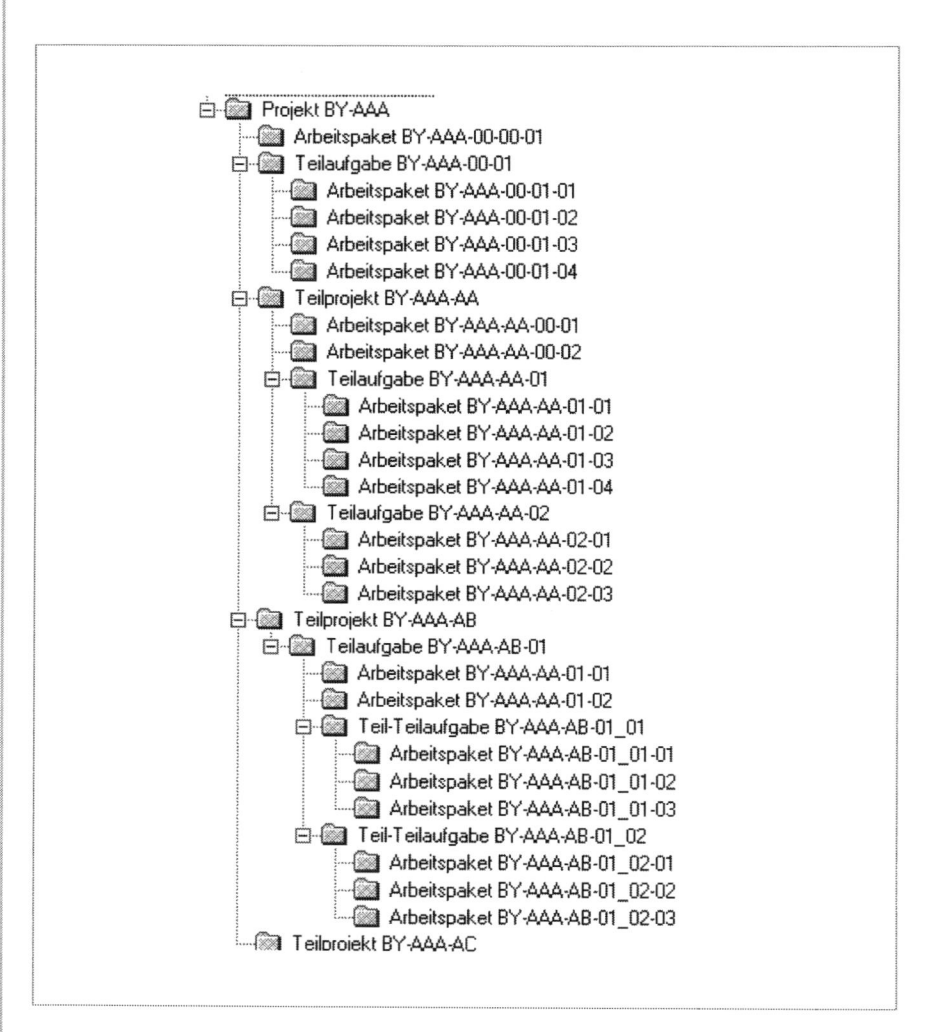

```
Projekt BY-AAA
   Arbeitspaket BY-AAA-00-00-01
   Teilaufgabe BY-AAA-00-01
      Arbeitspaket BY-AAA-00-01-01
      Arbeitspaket BY-AAA-00-01-02
      Arbeitspaket BY-AAA-00-01-03
      Arbeitspaket BY-AAA-00-01-04
   Teilprojekt BY-AAA-AA
      Arbeitspaket BY-AAA-AA-00-01
      Arbeitspaket BY-AAA-AA-00-02
      Teilaufgabe BY-AAA-AA-01
         Arbeitspaket BY-AAA-AA-01-01
         Arbeitspaket BY-AAA-AA-01-02
         Arbeitspaket BY-AAA-AA-01-03
         Arbeitspaket BY-AAA-AA-01-04
      Teilaufgabe BY-AAA-AA-02
         Arbeitspaket BY-AAA-AA-02-01
         Arbeitspaket BY-AAA-AA-02-02
         Arbeitspaket BY-AAA-AA-02-03
   Teilprojekt BY-AAA-AB
      Teilaufgabe BY-AAA-AB-01
         Arbeitspaket BY-AAA-AA-01-01
         Arbeitspaket BY-AAA-AA-01-02
         Teil-Teilaufgabe BY-AAA-AB-01_01
            Arbeitspaket BY-AAA-AB-01_01-01
            Arbeitspaket BY-AAA-AB-01_01-02
            Arbeitspaket BY-AAA-AB-01_01-03
         Teil-Teilaufgabe BY-AAA-AB-01_02
            Arbeitspaket BY-AAA-AB-01_02-01
            Arbeitspaket BY-AAA-AB-01_02-02
            Arbeitspaket BY-AAA-AB-01_02-03
   Teilprojekt BY-AAA-AC
```

Abb. 26: Projektstruktur EDV-Projektbibliothek (Screenshot Ordnerstruktur Windows).

---

5    Die Explorer-Struktur zeigt den Projektstrukturplan um „90° nach rechts gedreht".

*Figure the Project Structure in a Computer Project Library*

In the context of the processing of a project for reasons of clear allocation of documents it is recommended to save the work breakdown structure depicted[5] in an image centrally on a server in order to create a project library in which employees can save and retrieve all documents later in their individual folders.

Individual folders should be labeled with the unique serial number (WBS) code from the work break down schedule for reasons of clarity, so that later documents and other files can easily be found.

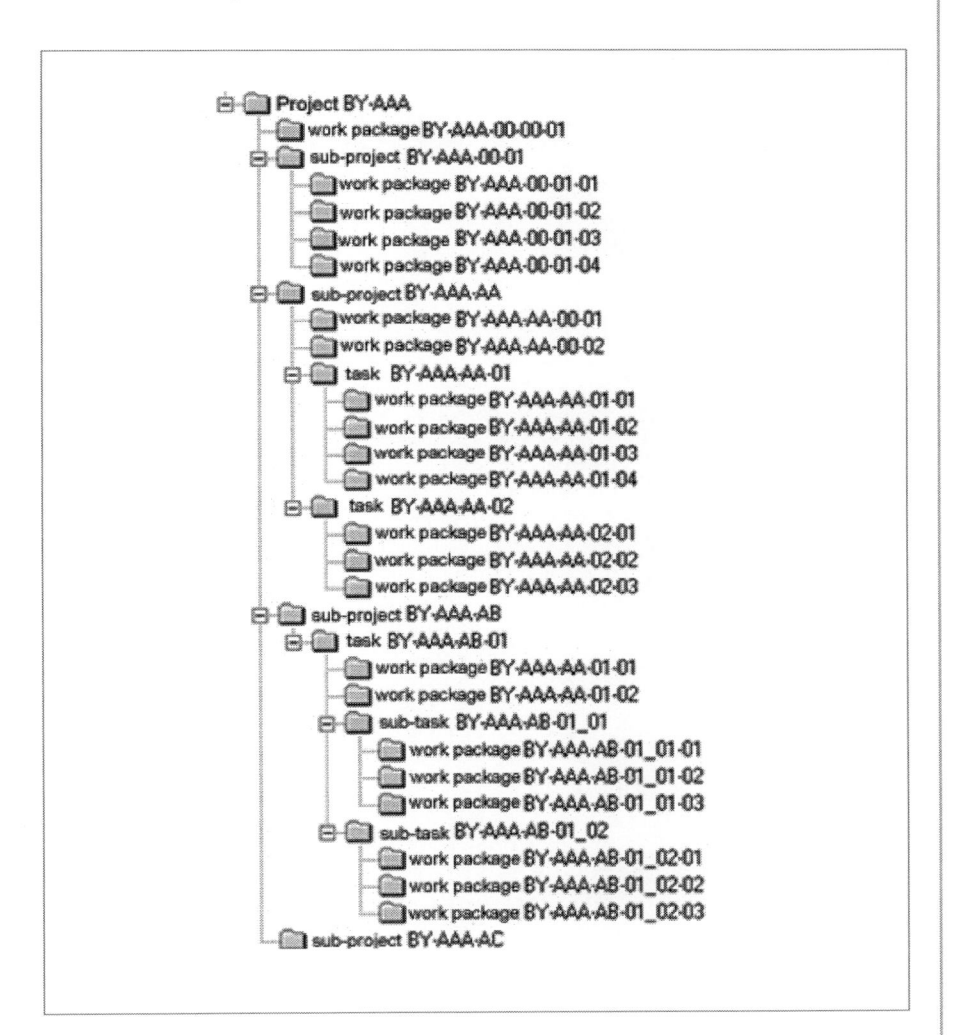

```
Project BY-AAA
    work package BY-AAA-00-00-01
    sub-project BY-AAA-00-01
        work package BY-AAA-00-01-01
        work package BY-AAA-00-01-02
        work package BY-AAA-00-01-03
        work package BY-AAA-00-01-04
    sub-project BY-AAA-AA
        work package BY-AAA-AA-00-01
        work package BY-AAA-AA-00-02
        task BY-AAA-AA-01
            work package BY-AAA-AA-01-01
            work package BY-AAA-AA-01-02
            work package BY-AAA-AA-01-03
            work package BY-AAA-AA-01-04
        task BY-AAA-AA-02
            work package BY-AAA-AA-02-01
            work package BY-AAA-AA-02-02
            work package BY-AAA-AA-02-03
    sub-project BY-AAA-AB
        task BY-AAA-AB-01
            work package BY-AAA-AA-01-01
            work package BY-AAA-AA-01-02
            sub-task BY-AAA-AB-01_01
                work package BY-AAA-AB-01_01-01
                work package BY-AAA-AB-01_01-02
                work package BY-AAA-AB-01_01-03
            sub-task BY-AAA-AB-01_02
                work package BY-AAA-AB-01_02-01
                work package BY-AAA-AB-01_02-02
                work package BY-AAA-AB-01_02-03
    sub-project BY-AAA-AC
```

Fig. 26: Project Structure IT-Project Library (Screenshot Windows File Structure).

---

5   The explorer structure shows the work breakdown structure "turned to the right by 90".

Abbildung 26 soll die Explorer-Struktur an einem Beispiel verdeutlichen. Gezeigt werden von links nach rechts vorgehend fünf Hierarchieebenen innerhalb eines Projekts mit den Strukturelementen Projekt, Teilprojekt, Teilaufgabe, Teil-Teilaufgabe und Arbeitspaket.

Aus Gründen der Übersichtlichkeit sind in dem Beispiel die Strukturelemente mit „Teilprojekt", „Teilaufgabe", „Arbeitspaket" benannt.

### 4.4.2 Projektablaufplan

Nach Erstellung des Projektstrukturplanes wird der Projektablaufplan gefertigt.

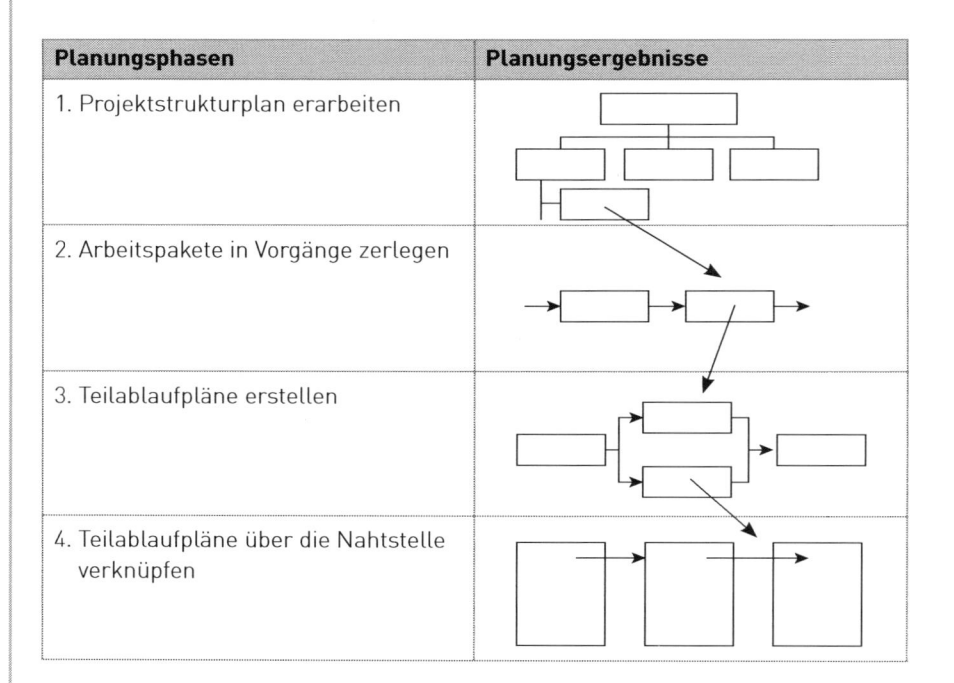

| Planungsphasen | Planungsergebnisse |
|---|---|
| 1. Projektstrukturplan erarbeiten | |
| 2. Arbeitspakete in Vorgänge zerlegen | |
| 3. Teilablaufpläne erstellen | |
| 4. Teilablaufpläne über die Nahtstelle verknüpfen | |

Abb. 27: Projektablaufplan.

Für die Ablaufplanung stehen mehrere Methoden zur Verfügung. Bei kleineren Projekten genügt es, eine Vorgangs- bzw. Aktivitätenliste zu erstellen (siehe Abb. 28). Alternativ dazu kann die Planung der Abläufe im Projekt mittels eines Balkendiagrammes (siehe Abb. 29) erfolgen. Handelt es sich aber um ein großes Projekt mit vielen Abhängigkeiten der einzelnen Vorgänge, so ist die Netzplantechnik die beste Methode zur Ablaufplanung.

Figure 26 depicts an example of the explorer structure. Shown from left to right are five hierarchical levels within a project with the structure elements project, subproject, subtask, sub-subtask and work package.

For reasons of clarity the structure elements in the example are labeled "subproject", "task", "work package".

### 4.4.2 Project Schedule

After the creation of the work break down structure the project schedule is created.

| Planning Phase | Planning Results |
|---|---|
| 1. Work out a project structure | |
| 2. Cut processes into working packages | |
| 3. Create sub-schedules | |
| 4. Link sub-schedules | |

Fig. 27: Project Schedule.

There are several methods that can be used for scheduling. For smaller projects, it is sufficient to create an activity or activities list (cf. Fig. 28). Alternatively, the processes in the project can be planned via a Gantt chart (cf. Fig. 29). If this is a big project with many dependencies of the various activities, the best method for scheduling is a critical path analysis.

| Vorgang Nr. | Vor- gänger | Priorität A B C | Vorgang | delegiert an | Beginn | Dauer |
|---|---|---|---|---|---|---|
| | | | Was? | Wer? | Wann? | Wie lange? |

Abb. 28: Vorgangs-/Aktivitätenliste.

| Projekt: | Aufgestellt am: | | | | | | | | | | |
|---|---|---|---|---|---|---|---|---|---|---|---|
| Zeit | Wochen | | | | | | | | | | Zuständigkeit |
| Vorgang | 1 | 2 | 3 | 4 | 5 | 6 | 7 | 8 | 9 | 10 | |
| 1. Aktivität | | | | | | | | | | | |
| 2. Aktivität | | | | | | | | | | | |
| 3. Aktivität | | | | | | | | | | | |
| 4. Aktivität | | | | | | | | | | | |
| 5. Aktivität | | | | | | | | | | | |
| 6. Aktivität | | | | | | | | | | | |
| 7. Aktivität | | | | | | | | | | | |
| 8. Aktivität | | | | | | | | | | | |
| 9. Aktivität | | | | | | | | | | | |
| 10. Aktivität | | | | | | | | | | | |

Abb. 29: Balkendiagramm.

| Vorteile | Nachteile |
|---|---|
| + leichte Lesbarkeit und Überschaubarkeit | – Abhängigkeiten von Aktivitäten können schlecht dargestellt werden |

Tab. 6: Vor- und Nachteile Balkendiagramm.

*Netzplan*

**Definition Netzplantechnik und Netzplan nach DIN 69901[6]:**

„Die Netzplantechnik umfasst Verfahren zur Projektplanung und -steuerung. Der Netzplan ist die graphische Darstellung von Ablaufstrukturen, die die logische und zeitliche Aufeinanderfolge von Vorgängen veranschaulichen."

Die Netzplantechnik (NPT) ist generell für jedes Projekt geeignet, unabhängig von Größe, Art und Dauer. Mit ihrer Hilfe lassen sich Aufwendungen und Einsatzmittel im Projekt planen und kontrollieren. Sie erfordert einen relativ hohen Schulungsaufwand und genaue Kenntnisse der Erstellungsregeln. Ändern sich die Gegebenheiten

---

6  Vgl. Deutsches Institut für Normung (2009), DIN 69901.

| Pred. No | Prede-cessor | Priority A B C | Opera-tion | Delegat-ed to | Start | Duration |
|---|---|---|---|---|---|---|
|  |  |  | What? | Who? | When? | How long? |

Fig. 28: Process/Activity list.

| Project: | Start Date: | | | | | | | | | | |
|---|---|---|---|---|---|---|---|---|---|---|---|
| Time | Weeks | | | | | | | | | | Responsibility |
| Process | 1 | 2 | 3 | 4 | 5 | 6 | 7 | 8 | 9 | 10 | |
| 1. Activity | | | | | | | | | | | |
| 2. Activity | | | | | | | | | | | |
| 3. Activity | | | | | | | | | | | |
| 4. Activity | | | | | | | | | | | |
| 5. Activity | | | | | | | | | | | |
| 6. Activity | | | | | | | | | | | |
| 7. Activity | | | | | | | | | | | |
| 8. Activity | | | | | | | | | | | |
| 9. Activity | | | | | | | | | | | |
| 10. Activity | | | | | | | | | | | |

Fig. 29: Gantt chart.

| Benefits | Disadvantages |
|---|---|
| + Easy legibility and visibility | − Dependencies of activities are displayed poorly |

Tab. 6: Benefits and Disadvantages Gantt-Chart.

*Activity Network*

**Definition critical path analysis and activity network according to DIN 69901[6]:**

> "The critical path analysis includes procedures for project planning and control. The network is the graphical representation of process structures that illustrate the logical and chronological sequence of activities."

The critical path analysis (CPA) is generally suitable for every project, regardless of size, type and duration. With its help it is possible to plan and control expenses and the resources available in the project. It requires a relatively high training effort and detailed knowledge of the creation rules. If the circumstances change in the course of a project, it is time-consuming to change the existing activity plan – maybe all activity nodes need to be changed, which are sequential to the changed network nodes.

---

6  Cf. Deutsches Institut für Normung (2009), DIN 69901.

im Verlauf eines Projektes, so ist es aufwändig, den vorhandenen Netzplan zu ändern – es müssen unter Umständen sämtliche Netzknoten geändert werden, die im Anschluss an den geänderten Netzknoten folgen.

Bei kleineren Projekten stellt sich die Frage, ob sich der Aufwand eines Netzplanes lohnt und ob man nicht aus Gründen der Einfachheit auf die Balkendiagrammtechnik oder die Erstellung einer Vorgangsliste zurückgreift. EDV-Programme, wie zum Beispiel das bei der Projektarbeit häufig eingesetzte MS-Project, ermöglichen es, die grafische Ablaufplanung wahlweise als Balkendiagramm (Gantt[7]) oder als Netzplan (PERT[8]) anzeigen zu lassen.

| Vorteile | Nachteile |
| --- | --- |
| + exaktes und detailliertes Durchdenken des gesamten Projektes mit allen beteiligten Stellen | – hoher Aufwand bei der Darstellung des Projektablaufes |
| + Auskunft, welche Vorgänge in welcher Reihenfolge zur Fertigstellung eines Projektes durchzuführen sind (zeitliche und sachlogische Abhängigkeiten) | – großer Änderungsaufwand bei manueller Anwendung |
| + erleichtert die Projektkontrolle | – Schulungsaufwand erforderlich |
| + transparenter Projektablauf, zeigt Entscheidungskonsequenzen auf | |
| + schneller Überblick über Arbeits- und Zeitaufwand | |
| + sicheres Terminieren der Vorgänge und des Materialbedarfs | |
| + zeigt Zeitreserven/-mängel auf | |
| + EDV-Unterstützung möglich | |

Tab. 7: Vor- und Nachteile Netzplan.

Ein Netzplan besteht aus **formalen** und **strukturellen** Elementen:

| Formale Elemente | |
| --- | --- |
| Pfeile | gerichtete Verbindungen zwischen zwei Knoten |
| Knoten | Verknüpfungspunkte (Kreise/Rechtecke) |

Tab. 8: Elemente des Netzplanes.

---

7  Gantt = Alternative Bezeichnung.
8  PERT = Program Evaluation and Review Technique.

For smaller projects, the question arises as to whether the cost of an activity plan is efficient and whether for reasons of simplicity the bar chart technology or an activity list would be sufficient. EDP (Electronic Data Processing) programs, such as the often in project work used MS-project allow the graphical scheduling to be shown either as a bar chart (Gantt[7]) or a network (PERT[8]).

| Benefits | Disadvantages |
|---|---|
| + Accurate and detailed analysis of the entire project with all the interested parties | – High cost for the presentation of the project schedule |
| + Information, which operations are to be performed in which order to completion of the project (temporal and logical sequence of dependencies) | – High modification effort in case of manual application |
| + Simplifies the project control | – Training is necessary |
| + Transparent project development, shows decision matrix | |
| + Quick overview of work and time effort | |
| + Reliable scheduling of activities and material requisition | |
| + Shows scheduling buffer/deficiencies | |
| + EDP support possible | |

Tab. 7: Benefits and Disadvantages Activity Network.

An activity schedule consists of **formal** and **structural** elements:

| Formale Elements | |
|---|---|
| Arrows | Pointed connections between two nodes addressed |
| Nodes | Junction points (circles/rectangles) |

Tab. 8: Elements Activity Network.

---

7 Bar chart = Alternative name for Gantt chart.
8 PERT = Program Evaluation and Review Technique.

| Strukturelle Elemente | |
|---|---|
| Vorgang | Abschnitt des Projektablaufes mit definiertem Anfang und definiertem Ende; gekennzeichnet durch Benennung der Aufgabe und der Zeitdauer |
| Anordungsbeziehung (AOB) | kennzeichnet die Abhängigkeit zwischen Ereignissen oder zwischen Vorgängen. Es wird unterschieden zwischen:<br>1. logische AOB ohne Zeitangabe<br>2. logisch-zeitliche AOB mit Zeitangabe |
| Ereignis | Eintreten eines definierten Zustandes (jeder Vorgang beginnt und endet mit einem Ereignis) |

Tab. 8 (Fortsetzung): Elemente des Netzplanes.

Bei der Netzplantechnik im Projektmanagement werden Knoten als Darstellungsform für Vorgänge (Vorgangs-Knotennetzplan) oder auch für Ereignisse (Ereignis-Knotennetzplan) verwendet. Die Anordnungsbeziehungen werden durch Pfeile dargestellt, wobei die Pfeilspitzen jeweils auf die nachfolgenden Vorgänge weisen.

Beispiel für einen Netzplanknoten:

| Nr. | FA | FE |
|---|---|---|
| | Bezeichnung | |
| | SA | SE |
| Dauer | Puffer | |

Abb. 30: Netzplanknoten.

Wenn alle Vorgänge in ihrem logisch-zeitlichen Ablauf festgelegt sind, können für jeden Vorgang folgende Termine errechnet werden:

FA: frühester Anfang
FE: frühestes Ende
SA: spätester Anfang
SE: spätestes Ende
GP: Gesamtpuffer
FP: freier Puffer

| Structural Elements | |
|---|---|
| Operation | Section of the project schedule with a defined start and a defined end; marked by naming the task and the duration |
| Ordered relationship (OR) | Signifies the dependencies between events or between processes There is a distinction between:<br>1. Untimed logical OR<br>2. Logical timed OR with time indication |
| Event | Occurrence of a defined condition (each process begins and ends with an event) |

Tab. 8 (Continuation): Elements Activity Network.

Nodes are used in the critical path analysis in project management as a representation for operations (process node activity plan) or also for events (event node activity plan). Arrows represent the ordered relationships, where the arrowheads point to the subsequent operations.

Example of an activity plan node:

| Nr. | FA | FE |
|---|---|---|
| | Name | |
| | SA | SE |
| Duration | Buffer | |

Fig. 30: Activity Plan Node.

If all of the operations are determined by their logical timing, can for each operation the following milestones be calculated:

FA: Earliest possible start
FE: Earliest possible finish
SA: Latest possible start
SE: Latest possible finish
GP: Total Float and the
FP: Free float

**Vorwärtsrechnung** (Anfangstermin festlegen, Endtermin berechnen):
Mit der Vorwärtsrechnung werden die frühesten Anfangs- und Endzeiten (FA und FE) der einzelnen Vorgänge errechnet. Hierbei wird Schritt für Schritt folgendermaßen vorgegangen:

- Der Beginn des ersten Arbeitspaketes (AP) wird gleich Null gesetzt und die geplante Dauer addiert.
- Beginn + Dauer des ersten AP = FE
- FE des ersten AP = FA des zweiten AP
- FA des AP + Dauer = FE

Bei parallel zu erledigenden Arbeitspaketen ist als FA für das nachfolgende AP der FE des AP mit der längsten Dauer anzusetzen.

**Rückwärtsrechnung** (Endtermin festlegen, Anfangstermin berechnen):
Mit der Rückwärtsrechnung werden für die einzelnen Vorgänge die spätesten Anfangs- und Endzeiten (SA und SE) ermittelt. Die Vorgehensweise ist folgendermaßen:

- FE des letzten AP = SE (alternativ das gesetzte Projektende)
- SA des letzten AP = SE der vorausgehenden AP
- SE – Dauer = SA

| Pufferberechnung | |
|---|---|
| Gesamtpuffer (GP) | Der Gesamtpuffer eines AP sagt aus, inwieweit sich dieses verzögern kann, ohne dass dies Auswirkungen auf die Dauer des Gesamtprojekts hat.<br>**Formel:** GP = SE – FE oder GP = SA – FA |
| freier Puffer (FP) | Der freie Puffer eines Arbeitspaketes gibt an, inwieweit sich dieses verschieben kann, ohne dass sich dies auf den nachfolgenden Knoten auswirkt.<br>**Formel:** FP = FA – FE |
| kritischer Pfad | Arbeitspakete, die den geringsten Puffer oder keinen Puffer haben, sind besonders zu kennzeichnen. Der Weg durch das Netz über diese Arbeitspakete wird als kritischer Pfad bezeichnet. Verzögern sich die Arbeitspakete auf diesem Weg, so hat dies Auswirkungen auf die Gesamtdauer des Projekts. |
| Meilensteine | Meilensteine sind Netzknoten mit der Dauer 0. |

Tab. 9: Pufferberechnung.

**Forward calculation** (set starting date, calculate finish date):
The forward calculation calculates the earliest start date (FA) and the finish dates (FE) of the individual processes. This is a step-by-step explanation:

- The beginning of the first work package (AP) is set equal to zero and the planned duration is added.
- Start + duration of the first AP = FE
- FE of the first AP = FA of the second AP
- FA of the AP + duration = FE

For work packages, which are to be accomplished in parallel, the FA is to be set for the subsequent AP the FE of the AP with the longest duration.

**Reverse calculation** (set finish date calculate start date):
The latest start (SA) and finish times (SE) are calculated for the individual processes with the reverse calculation. The procedure is as follows:

- FE of the last AP = SE (alternatively the set end of the project)
- SA of the last AP = SE of the preceding AP
- SE – Duration = SA

| Float Time Calculation | |
|---|---|
| Total Float (GP) | The total float of a WP indicates how much this can be delayed without affecting the duration of the entire project. <br> **Formula:** GP = SE – FE oder GP = SA – FA |
| Free Float | The free float of a work package indicates to which extent this can be delayed without affecting the subsequent node. <br> **Formula:** FP = FA – FE |
| Critical Path | Work packages, which have the lowest float or no float at all, are specially marked. The path through the network over these work packages is known as the critical path. In this way the work packages are delayed, so this has effects on the total duration of the project. |
| Milestones | Milestones are nodes with the duration of 0. |

Tab. 9: Float Time Calculation.

## Anordnungsbeziehungen

Im Vorgangsknoten-Netzplan werden fünf Anordnungsbeziehungen unterschieden und durch entsprechende Pfeile ausgedrückt:

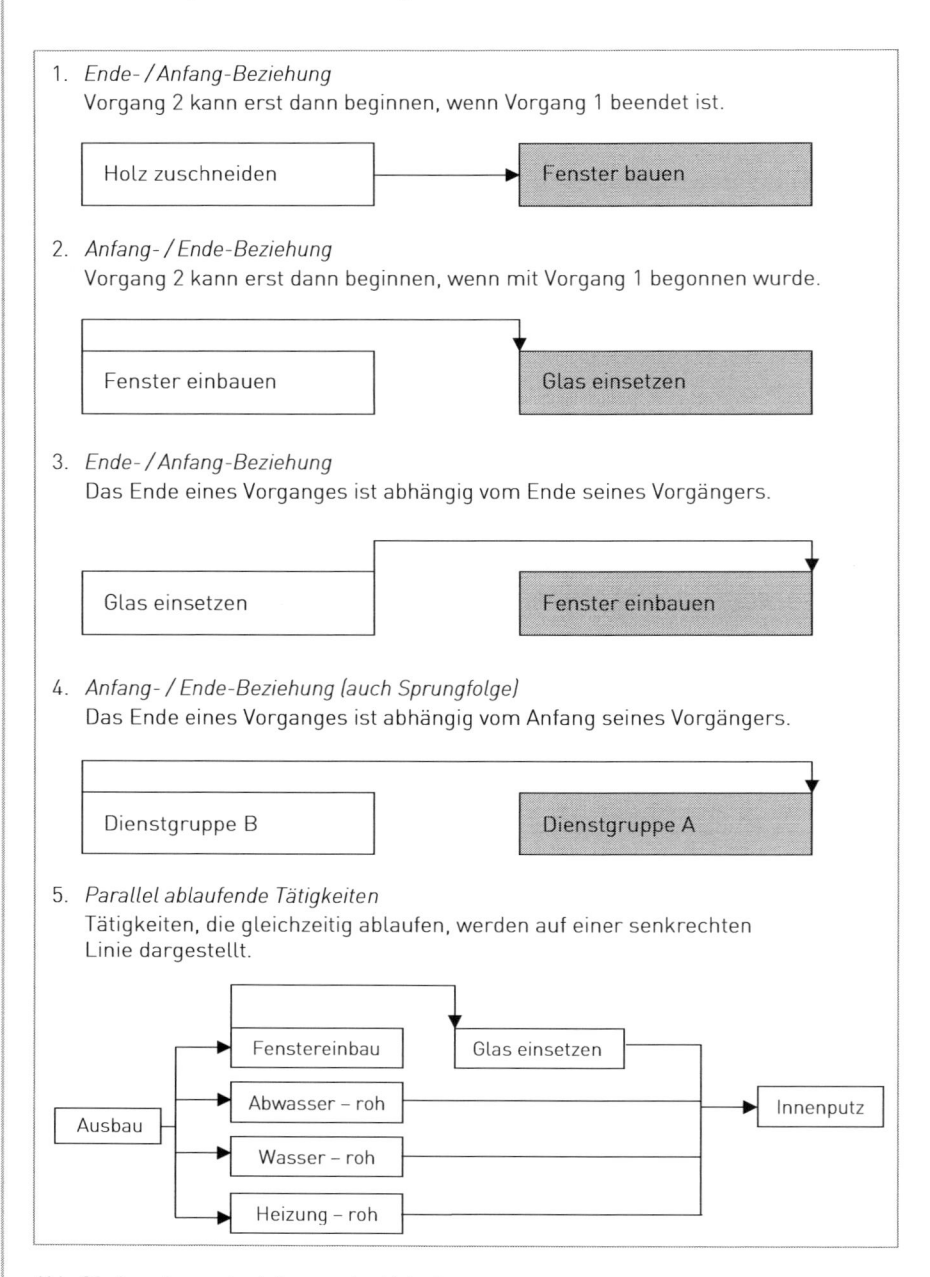

1. *Ende- / Anfang-Beziehung*
   Vorgang 2 kann erst dann beginnen, wenn Vorgang 1 beendet ist.

   Holz zuschneiden → Fenster bauen

2. *Anfang- / Ende-Beziehung*
   Vorgang 2 kann erst dann beginnen, wenn mit Vorgang 1 begonnen wurde.

   Fenster einbauen → Glas einsetzen

3. *Ende- / Anfang-Beziehung*
   Das Ende eines Vorganges ist abhängig vom Ende seines Vorgängers.

   Glas einsetzen → Fenster einbauen

4. *Anfang- / Ende-Beziehung (auch Sprungfolge)*
   Das Ende eines Vorganges ist abhängig vom Anfang seines Vorgängers.

   Dienstgruppe B → Dienstgruppe A

5. *Parallel ablaufende Tätigkeiten*
   Tätigkeiten, die gleichzeitig ablaufen, werden auf einer senkrechten Linie dargestellt.

   Ausbau → Fenstereinbau → Glas einsetzen → Innenputz
   Ausbau → Abwasser – roh → Innenputz
   Ausbau → Wasser – roh
   Ausbau → Heizung – roh

Abb. 31: Anordnungsbeziehungen im Netzplan.

**Ordered Relationships**

In the preceding node activity plan four ordered relationships are differentiated and expressed by corresponding arrows:

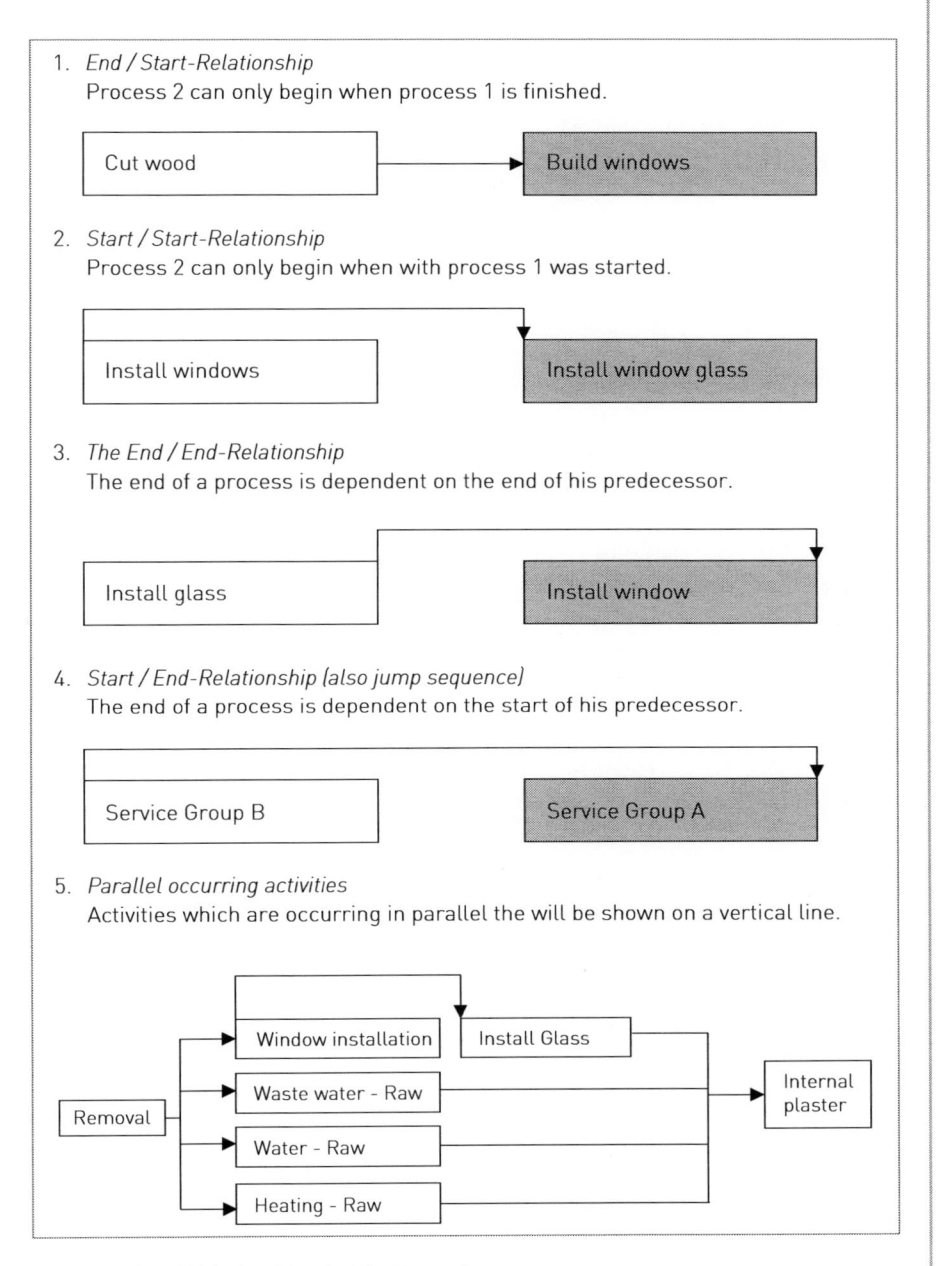

1. *End / Start-Relationship*
   Process 2 can only begin when process 1 is finished.

   Cut wood → Build windows

2. *Start / Start-Relationship*
   Process 2 can only begin when with process 1 was started.

   Install windows → Install window glass

3. *The End / End-Relationship*
   The end of a process is dependent on the end of his predecessor.

   Install glass → Install window

4. *Start / End-Relationship (also jump sequence)*
   The end of a process is dependent on the start of his predecessor.

   Service Group B → Service Group A

5. *Parallel occurring activities*
   Activities which are occurring in parallel the will be shown on a vertical line.

   Removal → Window installation → Install Glass → Internal plaster
   Removal → Waste water - Raw
   Removal → Water - Raw
   Removal → Heating - Raw

Fig. 31: Ordered Relationships Activity Network.

### 4.4.3 Personal- / Ressourcenplanung

Ausgehend vom Projektstrukturplan und den dort definierten Arbeitspaketen als kleinster Einheit wird die Personal-, Sachmittel- und Werkzeugplanung vorgenommen. Die zentralen Fragen sind hier wer, wann, wie viel und wie lange. Aus dieser Planung lassen sich auch die Kosten eines Projektes relativ leicht ableiten, da man nur mit überschaubaren Größen rechnen muss.

Die Ressourcenplanung lässt sich auf zwei Arten darstellen (Listentechnik):

- in Form einer um die benötigten Ressourcen erweiterte Vorgangs- oder Aktivitätenliste oder
- mittels eines Arbeitskräfte-Bedarfsplanes.

| Tag | Fachkraft Anzahl | Einsatzort | Fachkraft Anzahl | Einsatzort | ... |
|---|---|---|---|---|---|
|  |  |  |  |  |  |

Abb. 32: Personalplanung Listentechnik.

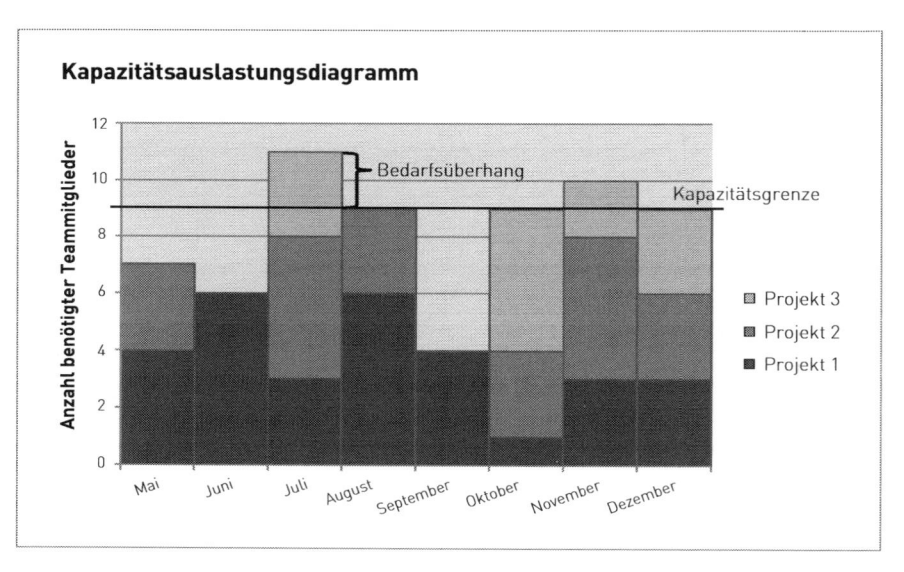

Abb. 33: Kapazitätsauslastungsdiagramm.

### 4.4.3 Staff/Resource Planning

Based on the work breakdown structure, and the work packages defined in it the smallest unit executed is the personnel, material and tool planning. The central issues here are who, when, how much, and for how long. From this planning the cost of the project can also be derived relatively easily, because only manageable variables need to be calculated.

There are two ways to depict the resource planning (list technique):

* In the form of a process or activities list extended by the required resources;
* In the form of a personnel requirement plan.

| Day | Skilled employee number | Location | Skilled employee number | Location | ... |
|---|---|---|---|---|---|
|  |  |  |  |  |  |

Fig. 32: Personnel Planning List Technique.

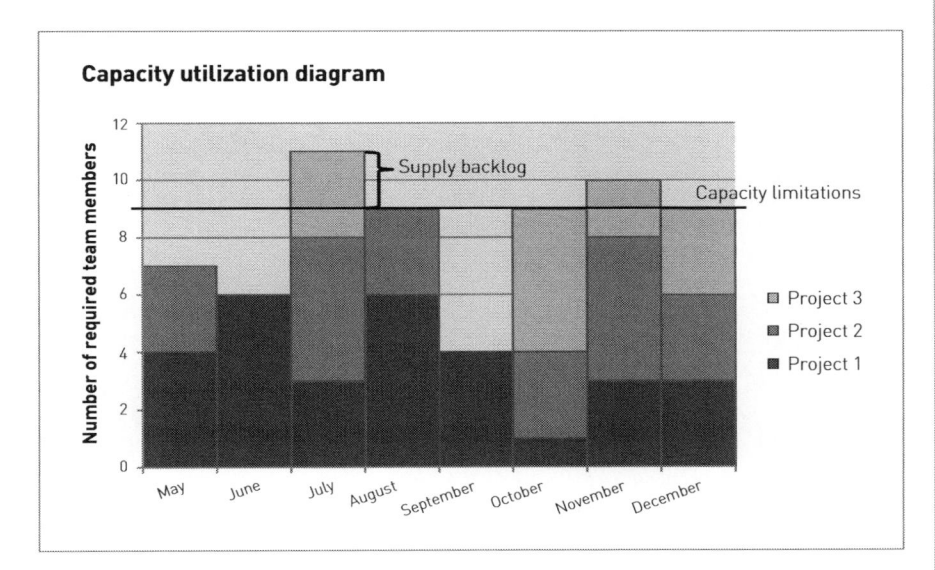

Fig. 33: Capacity Utilization Diagram.

**Checkliste für Ressourcenplanung**[9]

- ✓ Welche Qualifikation wird für das Arbeitspaket benötigt?
- ✓ Ist diese Qualifikation in der eigenen bzw. in einer anderen Dienststelle vorhanden oder muss das Arbeitspaket an Externe vergeben werden?
- ✓ Falls eine Personengruppe eingesetzt wird: Haben alle Mitglieder die gleichen Qualifikationen? Wenn nein, worin unterscheiden sie sich hinsichtlich ihrer Qualifikation?
- ✓ Haben die Mitglieder bereits Teamerfahrung?
- ✓ Welche Maschinen, Materialien, Arbeitsmittel, Räume werden gebraucht?
- ✓ Sind die aufgelisteten Sachmittel auch wirklich nötig? Auf welche kann verzichtet werden?
- ✓ Gibt es Sachmittel, die erst beschafft werden müssen? Wenn ja: Welche?
- ✓ Auf welche Sachmittel kann notfalls ausgewichen werden, damit die Liste der erforderlichen Mittel komplett ist?
- ✓ Stehen die Ressourcen für die gesamte Zeitdauer, die für das Arbeitspaket notwendig ist, bereit oder können sie nur zeitweise genutzt werden?

### 4.4.4 Kostenplanung

Die Ermittlung der Kosten für das gesamte Projekt erfolgt auf der Grundlage der im Projektstrukturplan aufgeführten Arbeitspakete als überschaubare Einheiten.

Da die Kostenermittlung gerade bei Projekten mit hohem Neuheitsgrad äußerst schwierig ist, kann man die Kostenermittlung mit sogenannten Schätzrunden durchführen. Dazu treffen sich mehrere Experten, die nicht zwangsläufig dem Projektteam angehören müssen und geben ihre Kostenschätzung für die Erledigung des Arbeitspaketes ab. Bei stark abweichenden Schätzungen begründet jeweils der Experte mit der höchsten und der niedrigsten Kosteneinschätzung seine Entscheidung. Nach der anschließenden Diskussion erfolgt eine erneute Kostenschätzung. Aus den Schätzungen wird nun der Mittelwert gebildet und als geplante Kosten für das Arbeitspaket angesetzt.

---

9 Vgl. M. Gröger, H. Schelle; Grundlagen Projektmanagement CBT-Programm; Bayerische Akademie für Verwaltungsmanagement GmbH / BStMI; in Anlehnung an: Ewert, W. u. a.: Handbuch Projektmanagement Öffentliche Dienste: Grundlagen, Praxisbeispiele und Handlungsanleitungen für die Verwaltungsreform durch Projektarbeit. Sachbuchverlag Kellner, Bremen, Boston 1996.

**Checklist for the Resource Planning**[9]

- ✓ What qualifications will be required for the work package?
- ✓ Is this qualification in the own or in another department present or does the work package have to be assigned to a third party?
- ✓ If a group is used: Do all members have the same qualifications? If not, how do they differ in terms of their qualifications?
- ✓ Do the members have already team experience?
- ✓ What machines, materials, equipment, rooms will be needed?
- ✓ Are the listed materials really necessary? Which can be eliminated?
- ✓ There are materials, which first have to be procured? If yes: Which?
- ✓ Which materials can be substituted if necessary, so that the list of necessary resources is complete?
- ✓ Are the resources, which are required for the work package, available for the entire duration or can they only be used temporarily?

## 4.4.4 Cost Planning

The determination of the costs for the entire project is based on the work packages as manageable units listed in the work breakdown structure.

As the cost determination for projects with a high degree of innovation is extremely difficult, the cost determination can be performed with so-called round table estimates. For this several experts, which do not necessarily belong to the project team meet and arrive at cost estimates for the execution of the work package. The experts with the highest and the lowest estimate will have to defend their decision if the estimates deviate largely from each other. After the ensuing discussion, renewed cost estimates are provided. From the ensuing estimates of the mean value is calculated and used as the planned costs for the work package.

---

9   Cf.. M. Gröger, H. Schelle; Grundlagen Projektmanagement CBT-Programm; Bayerische Akademie für Verwaltungsmanagement GmbH / BStMI; closely modeled after Ewert, W. and others: Manual Project Management Public Services: Grundlagen, Praxisbeispiele und Handlungsanleitungen für die Verwaltungsreform durch Projektarbeit. Sachbuchverlag Kellner, Bremen, Boston 1996.

An Stelle der gemeinsamen Schätzrunde kann man die Experten die Kosten für ein Arbeitspaket auch unabhängig voneinander schätzen lassen, ohne dass der eine Experte von der Schätzung des anderen weiß. Auch hier wird dann aus allen Schätzungen der Mittelwert gebildet und als geplante Kosten für die Erledigung des Arbeitspaketes angesetzt.

**Kostenstellen**

Nachfolgend sind exemplarisch Kostenstellen bei der Durchführung eines Projektes dargestellt.

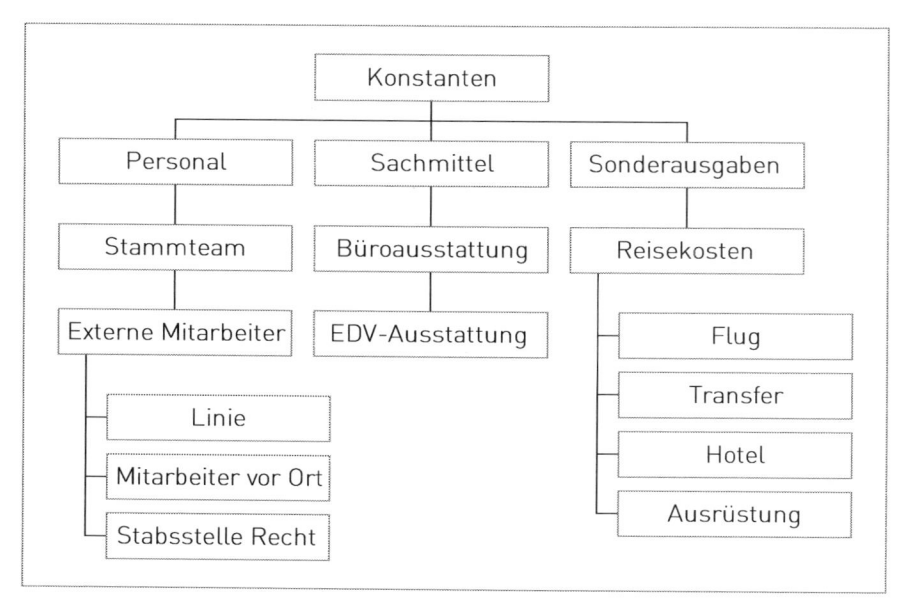

```
                            Konstanten
          ┌────────────────────┼────────────────────┐
       Personal            Sachmittel          Sonderausgaben
          │                    │                    │
       Stammteam          Büroausstattung       Reisekosten
          │                    │                    │
   Externe Mitarbeiter     EDV-Ausstattung      ┌── Flug
          │                                     ├── Transfer
          ├── Linie                             ├── Hotel
          ├── Mitarbeiter vor Ort               └── Ausrüstung
          └── Stabsstelle Recht
```

Abb. 34: Kostenstellen.

**Kostentableau**

Sowohl die geplanten als auch die bei der Projektdurchführung tatsächlich entstandenen Kosten können in einem Kostentableau nach dem folgenden Muster eingetragen werden.

| Kosten / Arbeitspakete | Personal | Sach- und Betriebsmittel | Sonderausgaben | **Summe** |
|---|---|---|---|---|
| Arbeitspaket 1 | | | | |
| Arbeitspaket 2 | | | | |
| Arbeitspaket 3 | | | | |
| ... | | | | |
| **Summe** | | | | |

Abb. 35: Kostentableau.

In place of the communal round table estimate the experts can prepare the cost estimate for a work package also independently of one another, without one expert knowing the estimate of the others. Here, too, a mean value is calculated from all the estimates and used as planned costs for the execution of the work package

**Cost Centers**

The following are exemplary cost centers for the implementation of a project.

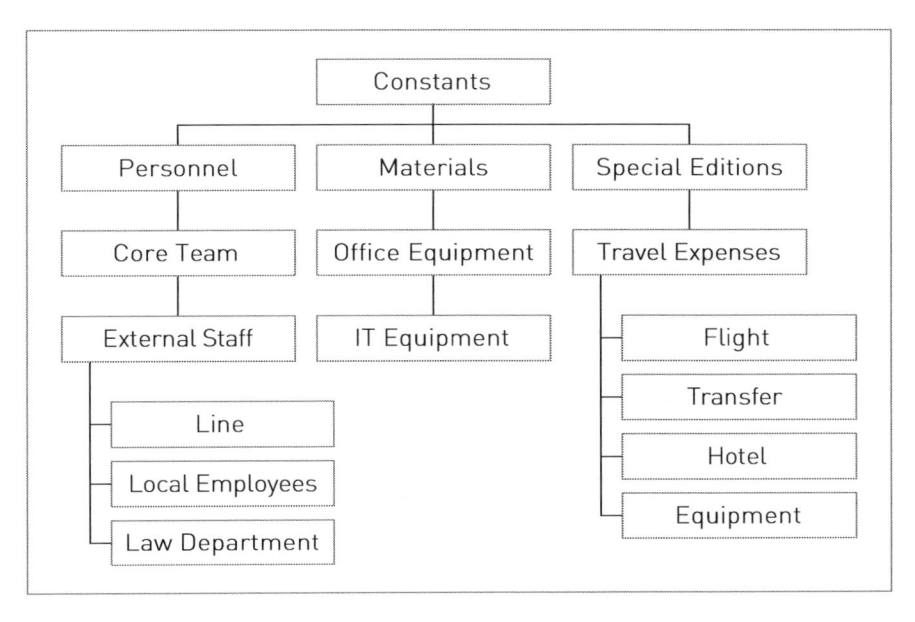

Fig. 34: Cost Centers.

**Cost Tables**

Both the planned as well as the actual costs incurred during the project can be entered in a cost table according to the following pattern.

| Costs / Work packages | Personnel | Equipment and resources | Extraordinary expenses | **Total** |
|---|---|---|---|---|
| Work packages 1 | | | | |
| Work packages 2 | | | | |
| Work packages 3 | | | | |
| ... | | | | |
| **Total** | | | | |

Fig. 35: Cost Tables.

## 4.4.5 EVA – Earned-Value-Analyse

Die Earned-Value-Analyse (EVA) ist ein Instrument des Earned-Value-Managements. Sie ist eine Controllingmethode, mit deren Hilfe ohne großen Aufwand ein objektives Bild des Projektstatuses und der weiteren Entwicklung geliefert werden kann. Mit den Kennzahlen der EVA können Budget, Terminplan, Ressourcen und Risiken eines Projekts analysiert und greifbar gemacht werden. Durch die Earned-Value-Analyse lassen sich Kostenabweichungen schnell erkennen, wodurch die Einhaltung des Projektbudgets gesteuert werden kann. Termine lassen sich anhand des Vergleichs zwischen Fertigstellungsgrad und -plan überwachen. Die Teammitglieder erlangen einen Überblick, welcher Aufwand je Arbeitspaket zu leisten ist und wie viel Zeit dafür zur Verfügung steht.

### 4.4.5.1 Grundvoraussetzungen

Die wichtigste Grundvoraussetzung ist, dass eine ausführliche Projektplanung vorliegt, die einen detaillierten Projektstrukturplan mit eindeutigen, budgetierten Arbeitspaketen beinhaltet. Eine weitere Voraussetzung ist ein vollständiger Projektablaufplan, um eine umfassende Terminplanung vornehmen zu können. Ziel dieser Terminplanung ist es, den Verlauf der Projektkosten über die gesamte Projektlaufzeit darstellen und erfassen zu können. Diese zwei Grundvoraussetzungen der Planung dienen als Planbasis, weshalb ein regelmäßiger Soll- / Ist-Vergleich durchgeführt werden muss. Eine Fortschrittsverfolgung ist nur auf einer fundierten Basis möglich. Für die Earned-Value-Analyse werden zudem folgende Elemente vorausgesetzt:

**Projektstruktur**
Es muss eine ausführliche und inhaltliche Aufteilung des gesamten Projekts in Teilprojekte, Arbeitspakete und Einzelaufgaben vorhanden sein, um einen Projektstrukturplan erstellen zu können.

**Netzplan**
Aus den einzelnen Elementen des Projektstrukturplans wird ein Projektablaufplan erstellt, der die Terminplanung des Ablaufes ermöglicht.

**Terminplan**
Mit Hilfe des Netzstrukturplans werden den einzelnen Elementen des Projekts die zur Umsetzung notwendigen Aufwände und Ressourcen zugeteilt. Die benötigte Zeit der Realisierung lässt sich über die vorhandenen Kapazitäten der Ressourcen errechnen.

**Basisplan und Cost Baseline**
Erst wird der erstellte Projektplan als Basisplan für die Earned-Value-Analyse genehmigt. Hieraus lassen sich die Plankosten pro Zeiteinheit, die Cost Baseline, zur Fortschrittsverfolgung festlegen.

**Projektfortschrittskontrolle**
Bei der Projektfortschrittskontrolle wird die Planbasis mit der Realität verglichen (Ist-Werte).

## 4.4.5 EVA – Earned Value Analysis

The earned value analysis (EVA) is an instrument of the earned value management. It is a cost control method, which helps without a great deal of effort to deliver an objective picture of the project status and the further development. With the key performance indicators of the EVA budget, schedule, resources, and risks of a project can be analyzed and made tangible. The earned value can quickly identify analysis cost variances through which compliance with the project budget can be controlled. Milestones can be monitored by the comparison between planned and actual percentage of completion. The team members gain an overview how much effort is required for each work package and how much time is available for same.

### 4.4.5.1 Basic Requirements

The most important precondition is that detailed project planning, which consists of a detailed work breakdown structure with clear, budgeted work packages exists. A further prerequisite is a complete project schedule to enable a comprehensive scheduling, the aim of this scheduling is to project and record the cost during the entire project duration. These two essential elements of the plan are used as a basis for planning, based on which a regular target/actual comparison must be performed. Progress tracking is only possible on a well-founded basis. For the earned value analysis the following items are also prerequisites:

**Project Structure**
There must be a detailed breakdown of the entire project into subprojects, work packages and individual tasks to be able to create a work breakdown structure.

**Activity Network**
From the individual elements of the work breakdown structure a project schedule is created, which enables the scheduling of the process.

**Schedule**
With the help of the activity network structure the individual elements of the project are allocated the necessary outlay and resources for the implementation of the project. The required time for the implementation can be calculated by the existing capacities of the resources.

**Baseline and Cost Baseline**
First the generated project plan is approved as a baseline for the earned value analysis. From this the planned cost per time unit and the cost baseline for tracking can be determined.

**Project Progress Review**
For the project progress review the planning basis is compared with reality (actual values).

### 4.4.5.2 Kennzahlen

**Basiswerte**

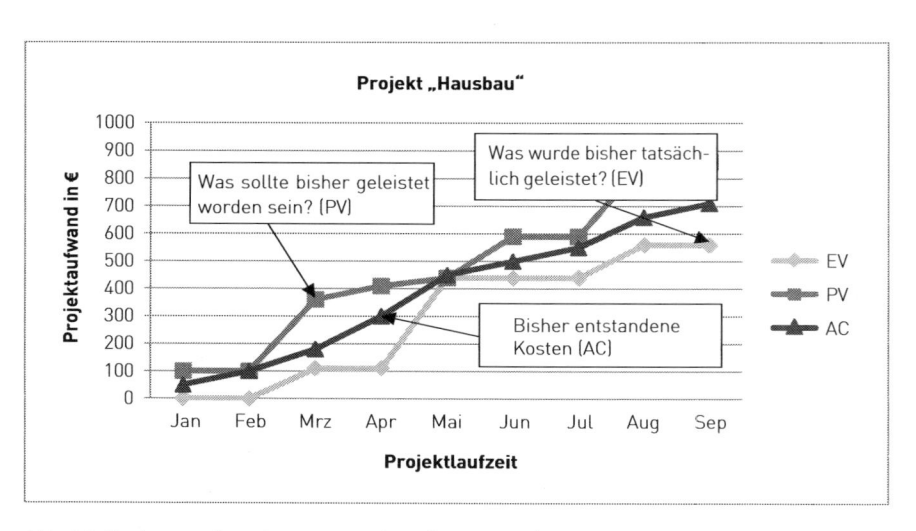

**Projekt „Hausbau"**

[Diagramm: Projektaufwand in € (0–1000) über Projektlaufzeit (Jan–Sep) mit den Kurven EV, PV und AC. Beschriftungen: „Was sollte bisher geleistet worden sein? (PV)", „Was wurde bisher tatsächlich geleistet? (EV)", „Bisher entstandene Kosten (AC)".]

Abb. 36: Basiswerte (vgl. Zyzik, Armin (2004), Teil 4, S.1).

**Planned Value (PV):** Mit dieser Basisgröße wird der Budget- und Kostenverlauf über den gesamten Projektzeitraum dargestellt; sie entspricht dem Kostenplan des Projekts. Der Planned Value zeigt die Entwicklung der (kumulierten) Projektkosten über die Laufzeit des Projekts. Mit seiner Hilfe wird die Frage „Was sollte geleistet worden sein?" beantwortet.

*Beispiel: Bis März soll das Fensterglas in die Fensterrahmen eingesetzt werden.*

**Actual Cost (AC):** Der tatsächliche Kostenverlauf wird durch die Actual Cost aufgezeigt; sie wird durch die aktuellen Kosten in Bezug auf bestimmte Arbeitspakete in einem gegebenen Betrachtungszeitraum dargestellt. Durch die Actual Cost kann die Frage „Was hat das Projekt bisher gekostet?" beantwortet werden.

*Beispiel: Bis März sind für das Anfertigen der Fensterrahmen Kosten von 80 € entstanden. Das Fertigen der Fenstergläser kostete insgesamt 100 €.*

**Earned Value (EV):** Die dritte Basisgröße errechnet sich aus dem Projektfertigstellungsgrad x Projektbudget. Wichtig ist hierbei, dass nur die Arbeitspakete des Projekts in die Berechnung mit einbezogen werden, die zu 100 % abgeschlossen sind. Durch den Earned Value wird die Frage „Welche Leistung wurde tatsächlich erbracht" geklärt.

*Beispiel: Bis März wurden die Fensterrahmen und Gläser fertiggestellt.*

**Buchungssystematik:** Es werden ausschließlich Arbeitspakete gebucht, die zu 100 % erledigt sind. Ihnen wird genau die Höhe ihres Planungsaufwands (Planned Value) zugeteilt. Hieraus folgt, dass der Planned Value und der Earned Value stufenartig ansteigen, während die Ist-Kosten kontinuierlich wachsen.

### 4.4.5.2 Key Performance Indicators

**Base Values**

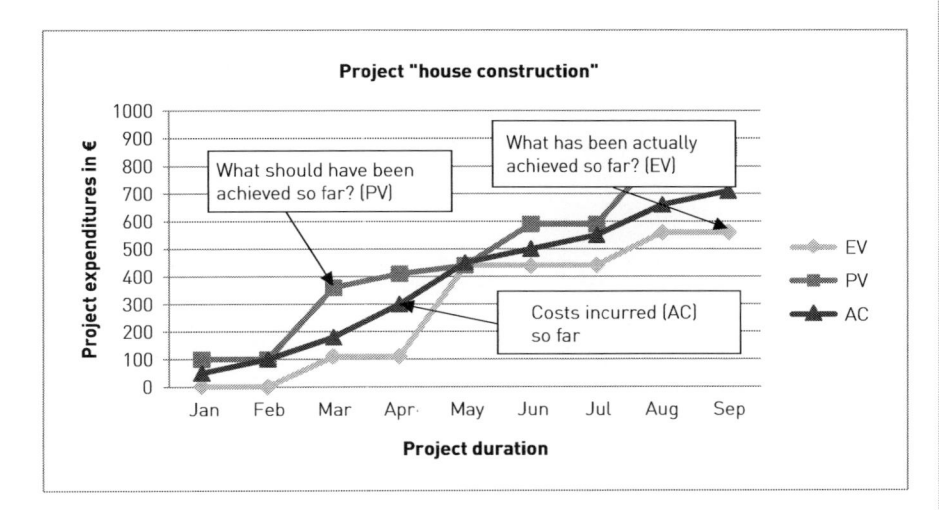

Fig. 36: Base Values (cf. Zyzik, Armin (2004), part 4, p. 1).

**Planned Value (PV):** With this yardstick the budget and expenses development is shown for the entire project, it corresponds to the costs plan of the project. The planned value shows the development of the (accumulated) project costs over the lifetime of the project. With its help, the question: "What should have been achieved?" has been answered.

*Example: Until March, the window glass in the window frames needs to be inserted.*

**Actual Cost (AC):** The actual cost history is shown by the actual cost; it is depicted by the actual costs, in relation to certain work packages, in a given time period. Through the actual cost, the question "What has the project cost us to date?" can be answered.

*Example: Until March the costs of Euro 80 have been incurred for the manufacture of window frames. The manufacturing of the window glasses cost a total Euro 100.*

**Earned Value (EV):** The third base variable is calculated from the project completion progress x project budget. Here it is important that only the work packages of the project be included in the calculation are 100% complete. Through the earned value the question, which performance has actually been achieved, can be answered.

*Example: Until March the window frames and glasses have been completed.*

**Posting Method:** Exclusively work packages, which are the 100% completed are posted. Exactly the amount of their planning effort (planned value) is allocated to them. It follows therefore that the planned value and the earned value increase incrementally, while the actual cost grow continuously.

| Planned Value (PV) | Actual Cost (AC) | Earned Value (EV) |
|---|---|---|
| Was soll geleistet worden sein? | Was hat das Projekt bisher gekostet? | Welche Leistung wurde tatsächlich erbracht? |

Tab. 10: Übersicht Basiswerte.

*Variances und Indices*

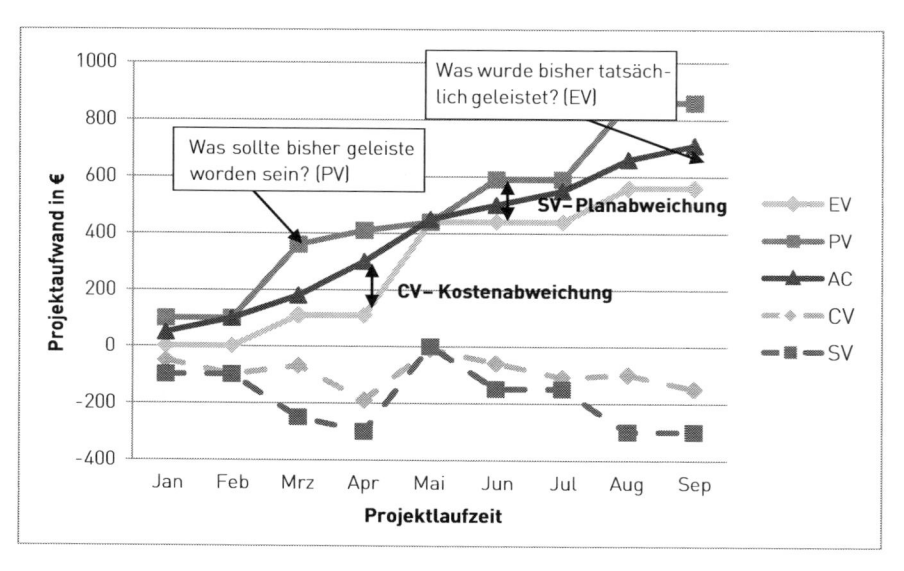

Abb. 37: Variances und Indices (vgl. Zyzik, Armin (2004), Teil 5, S. 1).

**Cost Variance (CV):** Mit der Cost Variance wird die Abweichung von Earned Value und den tatsächlich anfallenden Kosten (Actual Cost) berechnet. Die Formel hierfür lautet: CV = EV– AC. Ist die Kostenabweichung größer als 0, wurde weniger Budget benötigt als veranschlagt, liegt sie unter 0, wurde mehr ausgegeben als geplant.

*Beispiel: Im März verzögert sich die Anfertigung der Fenster, da die Gläser nicht richtig zugeschnitten wurden. Es fallen Mehrkosten für das zusätzliche Zuschneiden an.*
$CV_{April} = EV_{April} - AC_{April} = 110 - 300 = -190$

**Schedule Variance (SV):** Durch die Schedule Variance wird errechnet, inwieweit eine absolute Abweichung zwischen Earned Value und Plankosten stattgefunden hat. Dies wird über die Formel SV = EV– PV deutlich gemacht. Bei einer Planabweichung über 0, wurde bereits mehr erledigt als ursprünglich geplant. Beträgt die Differenz einen Wert kleiner 0, wurde weniger Punkte erfüllt als vorgesehen.

*Beispiel: Durch die Verzögerung wurde der geplante Fertigstellungsgrad nicht erreicht, auch der geplante Projektablauf verschiebt sich.*
$SV_{April} = EV_{April} - PV_{April} = 110 - 410 = -300$

| Planned Value (PV) | Actual Cost (AC) | Earned Value (EV) |
|---|---|---|
| What should have been achieved? | What the project has cost to date? | What is the performance actually achieved? |

Tab. 10: Overview Base Values.

*Variances und Indices*

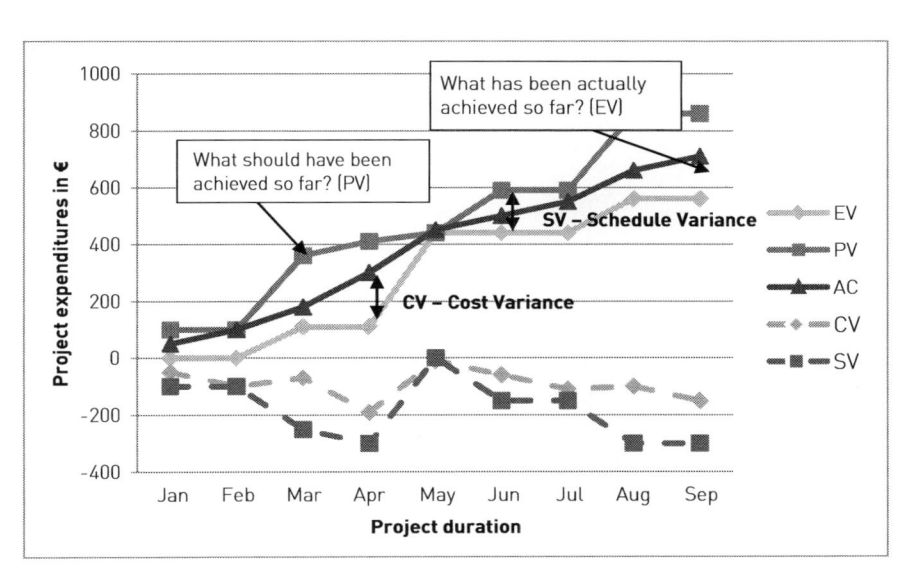

Fig. 37: Variances and Indices (cf. Zyzik, Armin (2004), Teil 5, S. 1).

**Cost Variance (CV):** With the cost variance is the deviation between earned value and the actual costs is calculated. The formula for this is: CV = EV− AC. If the cost variance is greater than 0 less budget was required than estimated if it is less than 0, more was spent than planned.

*Example: In March the manufacture of the window was delayed, as the glass was not cut correctly. There are additional costs for the additional cutting.*
$CV_{April} = EV_{April} - AC_{April} = 110 - 300 = -190$

**Schedule Variance (SV):** How much of an absolute deviation between earned value and planned costs has occurred is calculated through the schedule variance. This will clarified by the formula SV= EV−PV. When the schedule variance is greater than 0 more has already been completed than originally planned. If the difference is a value less than 0, fewer milestones than expected have been met.

*Example: By the delay the planned percent complete was not achieved, also the planned project is delayed.*
$SV_{April} = EV_{April} - PV_{April} = 110 - 410 = -300$

| Cost Variance | Schedule Variance |
|---|---|
| CV = EV − AC | SV = EV − PV |
| CV < 0 ⇧ | SV > 0 ⇧ |
| CV > 0 ⇩ | SV < 0 ⇩ |

Tab. 11: Übersicht Basiswerte.

**Cost Performance Index (CPI):** Anhand dieser kostenbezogenen Kennzahl wird das Verhältnis zwischen Earned Value und Actual Cost dargestellt. Beträgt das Ergebnis einen Wert über 1, sind die Ausgaben geringer, liegt der Wert unter 1, sind die Ausgaben höher als geplant.

*Beispiel: Da die Gesamtkosten der Fensterglasscheiben gestiegen sind, verringert sich die Kosteneffizienz.* $CPI_{April} = EV_{April} / AC_{April} = 110/300 = 0{,}367$

**Schedule Performance Index (SPI):** Mit Hilfe der Gegenüberstellung von Earned Value und Planned Value wird der Schedule Performance Index dargestellt. Liegt dieser Wert über 0, schreiten die Ergebnisse schneller voran als geplant, liegt er unter 0, langsamer.

*Beispiel: Die Fertigstellung der Fenster verzögert sich aus oben genannten Gründen, wodurch sich das gesamte Projekt in die Länge zieht.*
$SPI_{April} = EV_{April} / PV_{April} = 110/410 = 0{,}268$

| Cost Performance Index | Schedule Performance Index |
|---|---|
| CPI = EV / AC | SPI = EV / PV |
| CPI > 1 ⇧ | SPI > 0 ⇧ |
| CPI < 1 ⇩ | SPI < 0 ⇩ |

Tab. 12: Übersicht Indices.

*Kostenprognose*

Unter Zuhilfenahme des Cost Performance Index kann eine Kostenprognose vorgenommen werden; hierfür werden benötigt:

**Budget at Completion (BAC):** Bezeichnet das ursprünglich geplante Projektbudget.

**Estimate at Completion (EAC):** Dieser Wert beschreibt die Ist-Kosten bei Projektende. Hierbei wird anhand von Earned Value, Planned Value und Cost Performance Index eine Kostenprognose erstellt. Die Formel hierfür lautet:
EAC = AC + (BAC − EV) / CPI

*Beispiel: Das vorher festgelegte Projektbudget bleibt unverändert, es beträgt 860 €. Da sich aber der Einbau der Fenster verzögert, kommt es zu einer negativen Auswirkung auf die weiteren Werte, woraus eine Erhöhung der tatsächlich erwarte-*

| Cost Variance | Schedule Variance |
|---|---|
| CV = EV − AC | SV = EV − PV |
| CV < 0 ⇧<br>CV > 0 ⇩ | SV > 0 ⇧<br>SV < 0 ⇩ |

Tab. 11: Overview Base Values.

**Cost Performance Index (CPI):** The relationship between earned value and actual cost is showed based on this cost-related performance indicator. If the result is a value greater than 1, the expenditures are below the plan, if the value is less than 1 the expenditures are higher than planned.

*Example: Since the total cost of the window glass panes has increased, the cost-effectiveness is reduced.* $CPI_{April} = EV_{April} / AC_{April} = 110/300 = 0{,}367$

**Schedule Performance Index (SPI):** The schedule performance index is shown with the help of the comparison between earned value and planned value. If this value exceeds 0 the results are progressing faster than planned, if it is below 0 slower.

*Example: The completion of the windows is delayed for the reasons mentioned above, which extends the performance period of the entire project.*
$SPI_{April} = EV_{April} / PV_{April} = 110/410 = 0{,}268$

| Cost Performance Index | Schedule Performance Index |
|---|---|
| CPI = EV / AC | SPI = EV / PV |
| CPI > 1 ⇧<br>CPI < 1 ⇩ | SPI > 0 ⇧<br>SPI < 0 ⇩ |

Tab. 12: Overview Indices.

*Cost Forecast*

Using the cost performance index a cost forecast can be projected, for this the following is required:

**Budget at Completion (BAC):** Refers to the originally planned project budget.

**Estimate at Completion (EAC):** This value describes the actual costs at the end of the project. A cost forecast will be created based on earned value and planned value and the cost performance index. The formula for this is:
EAC = AC + (BAC − EV) / CPI

*Example: The previously defined project budget remains unchanged, it is €860. However, since the installation of the windows is delayed a negative effect is applied to the following values, resulting in an increase of the actually expected costs at the end of the project.*
$EAC_{April} = AC_{April} + (BAC − EV_{April}) / CPI_{April} = 300 + (860 − 110)/(110/300) = 2.343{,}60$

ten Kosten zu Projektende resultiert. $EAC_{April} = AC_{April} + (BAC - EV_{April})/CPI_{April}$ = 300 + (860 – 110)/(110/300) = 2.343,60

**Estimate to Completion (ETC):** Hiermit wird der geschätzte restliche Aufwand, der noch bis zur Beendigung des Projektes nötigt ist, errechnet. Die Formel setzt sich aus der Differenz zwischen den Ist-Kosten um Projektende und der Actual Cost zusammen: ETC = EAC – AC

*Beispiel: Noch zu erbringender Aufwand des Projektes „Hausbau":*
$ETC_{April} = EAC_{April} - AC_{April}$ = 2.343,60 – 300 = 2.043,60

**Variance at Completion (VAC):** Aus der Differenz des ursprünglich geplanten und des vorhergesagten Budgets lässt sich die prognostizierte Budgetabweichung berechnen. Liegt dieser Wert über 1, entstehen wahrscheinlich geringere Kosten, liegt der Wert unter 1, wahrscheinlich höhere Kosten als erwartet. Die Formel hierfür lautet: VAC = BAC – EAC

*Beispiel: Prognostizierte Budgetabweichung des Projektes „Hausbau":*
$VAC_{April} = BAC - EAC_{April}$ = 860 – 2.343,60 = -1.483,60

| Estimate at Completion | Estimate to Completion | Variance at Completion |
|---|---|---|
| EAC = AC + (BAC – EV) / CPI | ETC = EAC – AC | VAC = BAC – EAC |
| | | VAC > 1 ⇧<br>VAC < 1 ⇩ |

Tab. 13: Übersicht Kostenprognose.

*Laufzeitprognose*

Unter Zuhilfenahme des Schedule Performance Index (SPI) kann eine Laufzeitprognose vorgenommen werden. Hierfür werden benötigt:

**Plan at Completion (PAC):** Bezeichnet das ursprünglich geplante Projektende.

**Plan at Start (PAS):** Bezeichnet den ursprünglich geplanten Projektstart.

**Time Now (TN):** Bezeichnet den aktuellen Berichtszeitpunkt, beziehungsweise einen Stichtag.

**Time at Completion (TAC):** Dieser Wert sagt den Fertigstellungszeitpunkt des Projektes voraus. Die Formel hierfür lautet: TAC = PAS + (PAC-PAS) / SPI

*Bespiel: Der Start des Hausbaus wurde für Januar angesetzt und sollte im September beendet sein, also 9 Monate dauern. Durch die Verzögerung im Einbau verschiebt sich auch der Fertigstellungszeitpunkt. TAC = 01.01.2075 + (01.09.2075 – 01.01.2075)/0,268 = 01.01.2075 + 33,58 Monate = 2 Jahre 9,6 Monate = 15.09.2077*

**Estimate to Completion (ETC):** The estimated remaining effort, which is still required to the completion of the project, is calculated with this. The formula is composed of the difference between the actual cost and the actual cost at the end of the project: ETC = EAC – AC

*Example: Still to be provided cost of the project "house construction":*
$ETC_{April} = EAC_{April} - AC_{April} = 2.343{,}60 - 300 = 2.043{,}60$

**Variance at Completion (VAC):** The forecast budget variance can be calculated from the difference between the original planned and of the predicted budget. If this value exceeds 1 it is likely to have lower costs, if the value is less than 1 will probably cost more than expected. The formula for this is: VAC = BAC – EAC

*Example: forecast budget deviation of the project "house construction":*
$VAC_{April} = BAC - EAC_{April} = 860 - 2.343{,}60 = -1.483{,}60$

| Estimate at Completion | Estimate to Completion | Variance at Completion |
|---|---|---|
| EAC = AC + (BAC – EV) / CPI | ETC = EAC – AC | VAC = BAC – EAC |
|  |  | VAC > 1  ⇧ <br> VAC < 1  ⇩ |

Tab. 13: Overview Cost Forecast.

*Forecast Schedule*

A forecast schedule can be created using the schedule performance index (SPI); for this will be required:

**Plan at Completion (PAC):** Refers to the originally planned end of the project.

**Plan at Start (PAS):** Refers to the originally planned project start.

**Time Now (TN):** The current reporting date, or a fixed date.

**Time at Completion (TAC):** This value states the completion date of the project. The formula for this is: TAC = PAS + (PAC-PAS) / SPI

*Example: The start of the house construction was scheduled for January and should have been completed in September, i. e. the duration was 9 months. Due to the delay in the installation the date of completion slides as well. TAC = 01.01.2075 + (01.09.2075 – 01.01.2075) / 0,268 = 01.01.2075 + 33,58 months = 2 years 9,6 months = 15.09.2077*

**Delay at Completion (DAC):** Aus der Differenz des ursprünglich geplanten und des vorhergesagten Projektendes lässt sich die prognostizierte Terminabweichung berechnen. Liegt dieser Wert unter 0, liegt das Projektende hinter dem eigentlichen Endtermin, liegt der Wert über 0, vor dem eigentlichen Endtermin. Die Formel hierfür lautet: DAC = PAC – TAC

*Beispiel: DAC = PAC – TAC = 01.09.2075 – 15.09.2077 < 0*

**Estimate Time to Completion (ETTC):** Durch die Differenz zwischen dem Wert der Time at Completion und dem Wert Time Now wird die vorausgesagte Restlaufzeit vom Stichtag bis zum Ende des Projekts (ETTC) berechnet. Die Formel ist: ETTC = TAC – TN

*Beispiel: ETTC = TAC – $TN_{April}$ = 15.09.2077 – 01.04.2075 = 2 Jahre 5 Monate 14 Tage*

| Time at Completion | Delay at Completion | Estimate Time to Completion |
|---|---|---|
| TAC = PAS + (PAC – PAS)/SPI | DAC = PAC – TAC | ETTC = TAC – TN |
| | DAC > 0  ⇧<br>DAC < 0  ⇩ | |

Tab. 14: Übersicht Laufzeitprognose.

**Aufgaben zur Selbstkontrolle**

*4.1  Weshalb ist eine sorgfältige Projektplanung notwendig?*

*4.2  Nennen Sie die sechs erforderlichen Projektpläne und beschreiben Sie zwei dieser Pläne ausführlich.*

**Delay at Completion (DAC):** The predicted schedule variance can be calculated from the difference between the original planned and the predicted project end date. If the number is less than 0 the end of the project is behind the actual finish date, if the value is greater than 0 before the actual finish date. The formula for this is: DAC = PAC – TAC

*Example: DAC = PAC – TAC = 01.09.2075 – 15.09.2077 < 0*

**Estimate Time to Completion (ETTC):** The predicted remaining schedule is calculated from the fixed date to the end of the project (ETTC) by the difference between of the value of the time at completion, and the value of time now. The formula is: ETTC = TAC – TN

*Example: ETTC = TAC – $TN_{April}$ = 15.09.2077 – 01.04.2075 = 2 years 5 months 14 days*

| Time at Completion | Delay at Completion | Estimate Time to Completion |
|---|---|---|
| TAC = PAS + (PAC – PAS)/SPI | DAC = PAC – TAC | ETTC = TAC – TN |
|  | DAC > 0 ⇧<br>DAC < 0 ⇩ |  |

Tab. 14: Overview Forecast Schedule.

**Tasks for Progress Review**

*4.1    Why is careful project planning necessary?*

*4.2    Name the six necessary project plans and describe two of these plans in detail.*

## 5 Realisierungsphase

### 5.1 Projektsteuerung / Controlling

#### 5.1.1 Controlling – Begriff

Controlling wird häufig mit dem deutschen Begriff „Kontrolle" übersetzt und im Sprachgebrauch auch entsprechend verwendet. Die Übersetzung erfasst den Sinngehalt dieses Fremdwortes nur ungenügend.

> Mit Controlling meint man die Prozessüberwachung und -lenkung zu einem vorgegebenen oder optimierten Ergebnis. Controlling beinhaltet eine Mixtur aus Führungskonzepten, betrieblichen Funktionen, Techniken und Werkzeugen.

Man unterscheidet zwischen internem Controlling, das beispielsweise ein Dienststellenleiter für seinen eigenen Einflussbereich durchführt, und externem Controlling, das zum Beispiel von einem unabhängigen Gutachter- und Beratergremium durchgeführt wird.

Nachstehend ist das Regelkreismodell mit den Grundfunktionen des Controllings dargestellt.

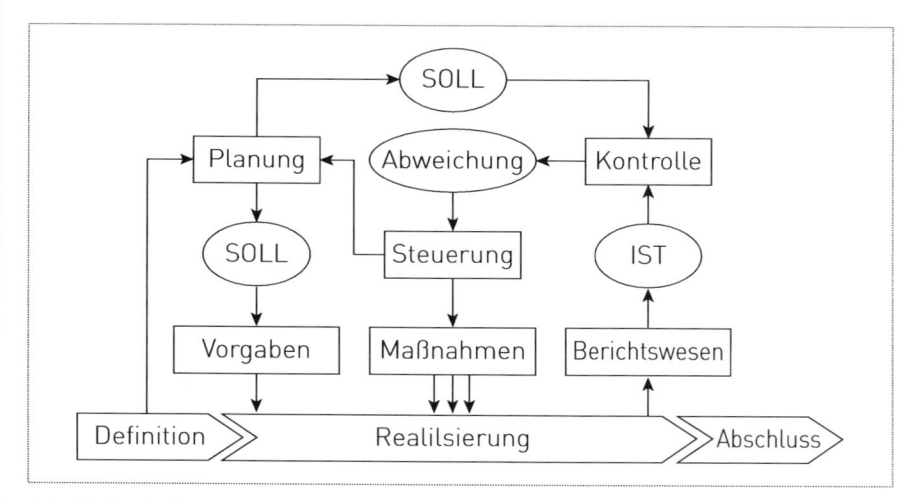

Abb. 38: Controlling.

# 5 Implementation Phase

## 5.1 Project Management / Cost Control

### 5.1.1 Cost Control – Concept

Controlling is often translated with the German word "control" and used accordingly. The translation captures the meaning of this foreign word insufficiently.

> The German word "Controlling" refers to the English cost control and therefore the German "Controlling" means the process of monitoring and steering to a specified or optimized result. "Controlling" [German] is a mix of management concepts, corporate functions, techniques and tools.

There is a difference between internal "controlling" which, for example, a chief of the office performs for his own sphere of influence and external controlling, which will be performed for example by an independent expert and advisory board.

Below is a control loop model shown with the basic functions of "controlling".

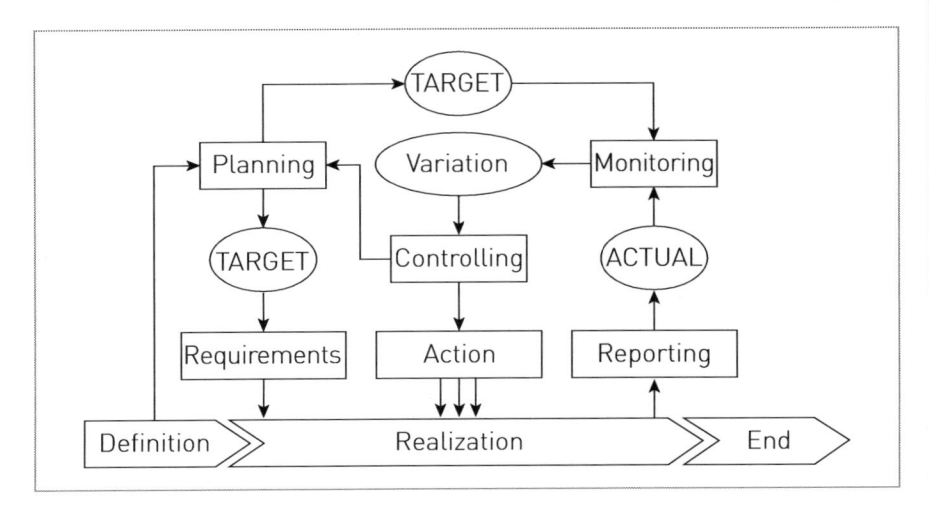

Fig. 38: Controlling.

## 5.1.2 Grundregeln

Die Projektmanagementpraxis hat gezeigt, dass es wichtig ist, Probleme möglichst frühzeitig zu erkennen. Voraussetzung dafür ist, dass die zu erledigenden Aufgaben definiert sind. Die Projektsteuerung ist die Hauptaufgabe des Projektleiters und des Projektteams in der Realisierungsphase, das heißt eine konsequente Fortführung der Planung in der Ausführungsphase. Im Controlling wird nun Geplantes mit dem Tatsächlichen verglichen, die Basis hierfür bildet die Meilensteinanalyse oder der Projektplan.

## 5.1.3 Systematik des Projektcontrollings

Nachfolgend soll verdeutlicht werden, wie mit Hilfe der einzelnen Schritte der Projektcontrolling-Systematik ein Weg zur Steuerung des Projektes entwickelt werden kann:

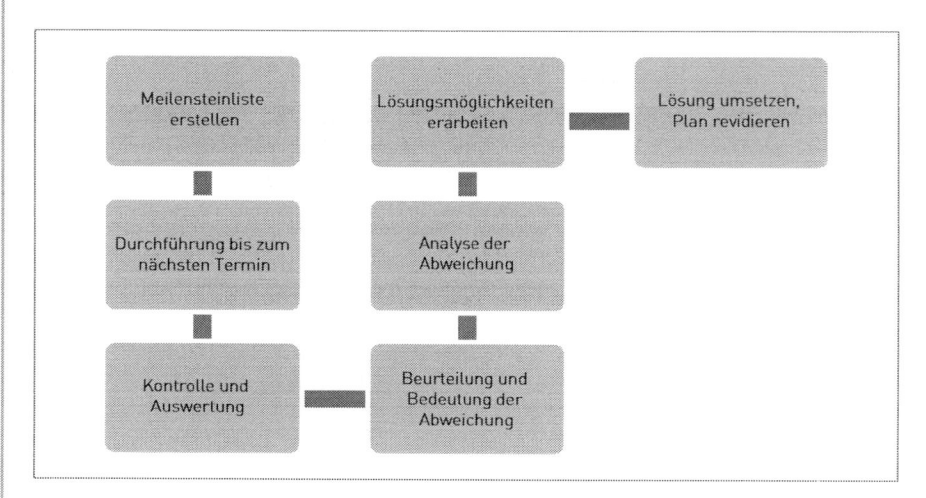

Abb. 39: Systematik des Projektcontrollings.

## 5.1.2 General Rules

Experience in project management has shown that it is important to identify problems as early as possible. The prerequisite for this is that the tasks to be performed are defined. Project management is the main task of the project leader and project team in the implementation phase, that is to say a logical continuation of the planning in the execution phase. In "Controlling" the "planned" is compared with the "actual", the basis for this is the milestone analysis or the project plan.

## 5.1.3 Classification of Project Controlling

The diagram below helps to develop a means to control the project by clarifying the individual steps of the project controlling approach:

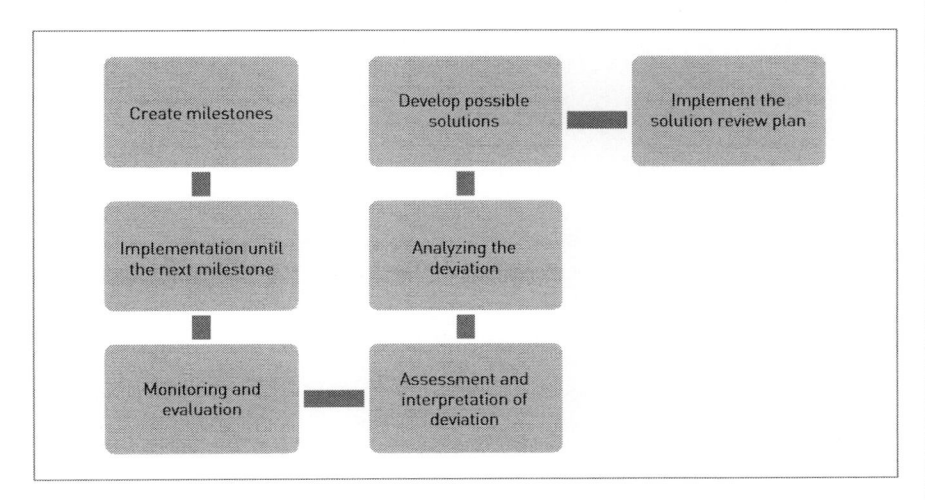

Fig. 39: Classification of Project Controlling.

**Hilfsfragen:**

- Gibt es Abweichungen?
- Wo treten Abweichungen auf? Kosten? Zeit? Qualität?
- Welchen Einfluss hat die Abweichung?
- Warum trat die Abweichung auf?
- Was können wir tun?
- Welche Auswirkung hat die Steuerung auf die anderen Faktoren?
- Was werden wir konkret tun?
    - Projekt weiterführen?
    - Mit abgeänderter Zielsetzung weiterführen?
    - Projekt abbrechen?

### 5.1.4 Qualitätssicherung

Qualität ist die Beschaffenheit eines Produkts/Dienstleistung/Projektergebnisses zur Erfüllung von Kundenwünschen.

Die Qualitätssicherung soll im Rahmen eines Projekts einerseits dazu beitragen, die **Kundenzufriedenheit** zu erreichen, beziehungsweise zu steigern, und andererseits soll sie einen Beitrag zur **Fehlervermeidung** und **wirtschaftlichen Producterstellung** leisten.

**Review Questions:**

- Are there deviations?
- Where do the deviations occur? Costs? Time? Quality?
- What effect does the deviation have?
- Why did the deviation occur?
- What can we do?
- What effect has the control on the other factors?
- What exactly will we do?
  - Continue the project?
  - Continue with a modified objective?
  - Cancel the project?

## 5.1.4 Quality Assurance

Quality is the nature of the product/service/project result for the fulfillment of customer re-quirements.

The quality assurance in the context of a project contributes **to achieve or increase customer satisfaction**, and, on the other hand contributes to **error prevention** and **economic product creation**.

**Hilfsfragen:**

- Welche Qualitätsstandards bestehen?
- Wer ist verantwortlich?
- Welche Prüfverfahren sind implementiert?
- Welche Fehler könnten in den einzelnen Phasen auftreten (Risiken)?
- Wie könnten Fehler im Voraus vermieden werden?
- Welche Auswirkungen haben die Fehler?
- Gibt es Abweichungen?
- Wie kann gegengesteuert werden?

### 5.1.5 Meilenstein-Trendanalyse

Meilensteine sind Zeitpunkt-Betrachtungen definierter Ereignisse bzw. definierter Ergebnisse.

Die Meilenstein-Trendanalyse kann als Frühwarnsystem verwendet werden; sie dient zur einfachen und übersichtlichen Methode zur Erkennung von Terminabweichungen. Bei der Meilenstein-Trendanalyse werden Meilenstein-Termine und -Ereignisse definiert, welche periodisch überprüft werden sollen. Tritt eine Verzögerung oder Terminverschiebung ein, wird der neue Termin abgeschätzt. Alle Meilensteine werden in einem Terminchart festgehalten, Abweichungen sind zu kommentieren und Auswirkungen sowie mögliche Korrekturmaßnahmen anzugeben.

**Review Questions:**

- What quality standards exist?
- Who is responsible?
- What testing procedures are implemented?
- What errors could occur in the individual phases (risks)?
- How could the errors be avoided in advance?
- What are the consequences of the errors?
- Are there deviations?
- What can be done to stem this process?

## 5.1.5 Milestone Trend Analysis

Milestones are point in time views of defined events or defined results.

The milestone trend analysis can be used as an early warning system; it serves as a simple and straightforward method for the detection of event discrepancies. For the milestone trend analysis milestone dates and events are defined, which are reviewed periodically. If there is a delay or rescheduling of a milestone, a new milestone will be estimated. All milestones are recorded in a milestone chart, deviations are to be commented and impact as well as possible corrective action is to be annotated.

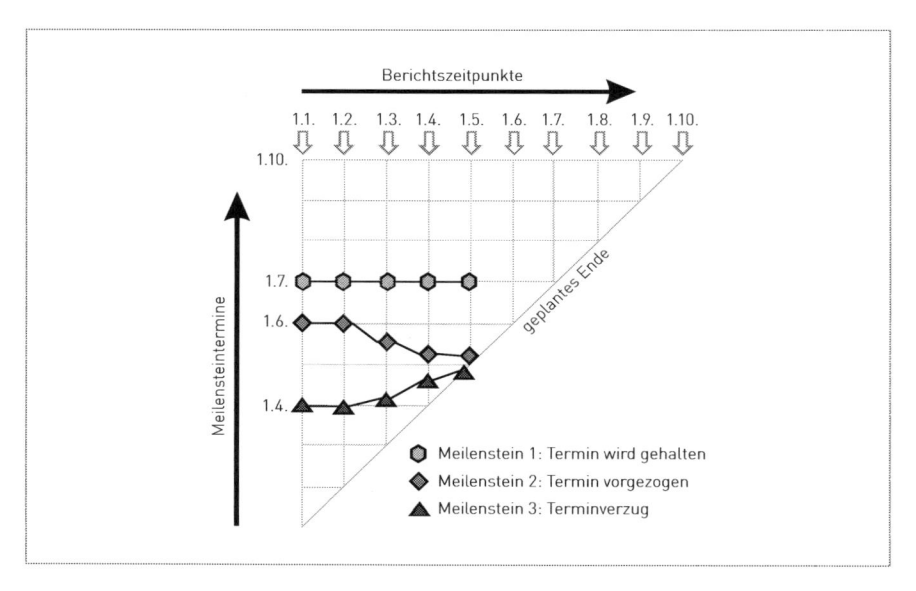

Abb. 40: Meilenstein-Trendanalyse.

## 5.2 Projektstatussitzung

Ein wesentliches Instrument der Projektsteuerung sind Projektsitzungen. Sie dienen nicht nur dem Projektabgleich, sondern weisen sehr frühzeitig auf Abweichungen vom „Soll" hin. Auf Störungen im Projektverlauf kann demzufolge zeitgerecht reagiert werden.

Eine wesentliche Aufgabe von Projektsitzungen ist der Informationsaustausch der Projektbeteiligten untereinander sowie zwischen Sitzungsbeteiligten aus Gremien und eventuell anderen Projekten.

### 5.2.1 Arten von Sitzungen

**Regelmäßige Statussitzung (Jour Fixe)**
Dabei handelt es sich um fest vereinbarte Termine zur Lagebesprechung, Problemlösung etc. (Monatsbesprechung, Freitagssitzung).

**Startup-Sitzung (auch Kick-off)**
Mit dieser Sitzung erfolgt die Begründung des Projektes.

**Ereignisorientierte Statussitzung**
Die Projektgruppe kommt wegen unerwarteter Ereignisse zusammen (Störfall, Krisensitzung etc.).

**Phasenentscheidungssitzung**
Zusammenkommen eines Entscheidungsgremiums über den Abschluss und den Start von Projektphasen nach dem Phasenplan.

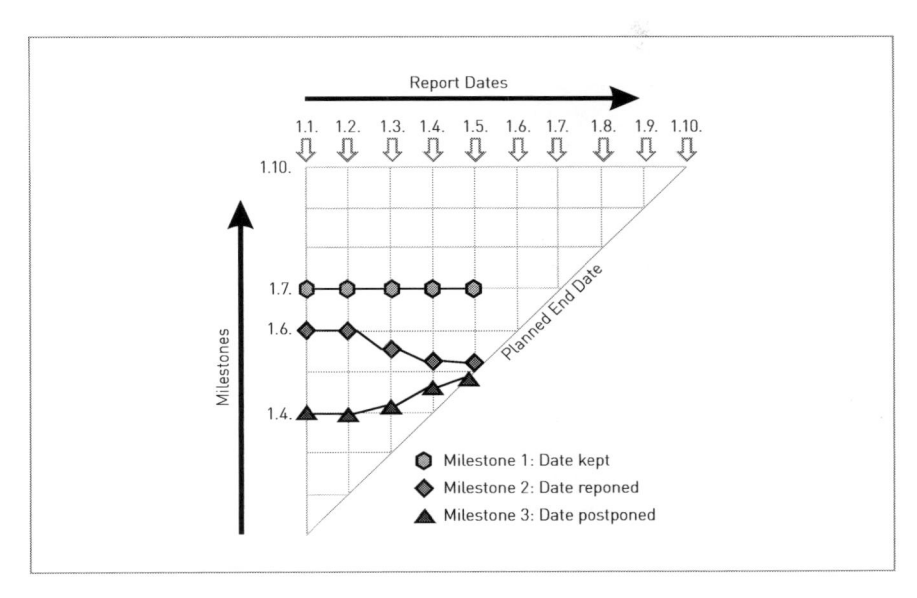

Fig. 40: Milestone Trend Analysis.

## 5.2 Project Progress Review

An essential instrument of project control is project reviews. They serve not only as project review, but indicate early any deviations from the "should-be status". As a result any problem in the course of the project can be responded to in a timely manner.

An essential task of project reviews is the exchange of information between the project participants with each other, as well as between review participants from panels and possibly other projects.

### 5.2.1 Type of Reviews

**Regular Status Review (Jour Fixe)**
These are fixed dates for reviews, problem solving, etc. (monthly review, Friday meetings).

**Startup Meeting (also Kick Off)**
With this session the justification of the project is provided.

**Event-Driven Progress Meeting**
The project group meets due to unexpected events (incident, crisis meeting, etc. ).

**Phase Decision-Making Meeting**
A decision-making body will meet at the conclusion and the start of project phases according to the phase plan.

**Ergebnisorientierte Sitzungen**
Diese Sitzungen dienen der Vorstellung von Teilergebnissen, Feststellung des Erreichens von Meilensteinen; es handelt sich grundsätzlich um eine Informationssitzung, um die Projektbeteiligten auf einen einheitlichen Wissensstand zu bringen.

**Ereignisorientierte Sitzungen**
Sitzungen, bei denen in der Regel aktuelle Probleme im Projektverlauf erörtert werden und bei denen Entscheidungen über das weitere Vorgehen getroffen werden müssen.

**Abschluss-Sitzung**
Hierbei handelt es sich um die formelle Beendigung des Projektes und Abnahme des Ergebnisses durch den Auftraggeber.

### 5.2.2 Was soll bei Projektsitzungen beachtet werden?

(gilt auch allgemein für Besprechungen)

| Vorbereitung |
|---|
| Tagesordnung rechtzeitig vorher festlegen und an Teilnehmer versenden (Besprechungsziele) |
| Vertreterregelung für Sitzungsteilnehmer grundsätzlich nicht zulassen |
| Arbeitsaufträge an Teilnehmer rechtzeitig erteilen |
| mehrtägige Sitzungen vorsehen |
| geeigneten Raum buchen (Größe, Einrichtung, Medien, Werkzeuge etc.) |
| für Pausenbetreuung sorgen |
| Moderator einsetzen |
| Protokollführer bestimmen |
| Agenda zu Sitzungsbeginn aufstellen |
| Teilnehmerunterlagen vorbereiten und ggf. vorher versenden |
| **Ablauf** |
| keine Sitzung/Besprechung ohne Agenda |
| als „TOP 1" immer allgemeine Informationen/Neuigkeiten abfragen |
| Präsentation von Arbeitsergebnissen |
| für zielgerichtete Diskussionen und Gespräche sorgen |
| Besprechungsergebnisse zusammenfassen |
| Besprechungsergebnisse kategorisieren |
| keine Sitzung/Besprechung ohne Protokoll |

Tab. 15: Projektsitzung.

**Results Oriented Meetings**
These meetings are used for the presentation of partial results, determination of the achievement of milestones; this is basically a briefing session, to get the project participants on the same playing field.

**Event-Driven Meetings**
At event-driven meetings usually current problems in the course of the project are discussed and decisions must be made on how to proceed further.

**Completion Meeting**
This is the formal completion of the project and acceptance of the result by the client.

## 5.2.2 What Is Important to Note in Project Meetings?

(This also applies for general meetings)

| Preparation |
|---|
| Set agenda and send to participants ahead of time (meeting objectives) |
| Do not allow by principle deputy rules for participants |
| Provide work orders to participants in good time |
| Plan multi-day sessions |
| Book a suitable room (size, furniture, media, tools, etc.) |
| Ensure refreshments during the breaks |
| Use a moderator |
| Nominate a note taker to keep the protocol |
| Issue the meeting agenda in the beginning |
| Prepare and send hand-outs ahead of time if necessary |
| **Schedule** |
| No session/meeting without agenda |
| As a "Top 1" always query general information/news |
| Presentation of work results |
| Ensure focused discussions and conversations |
| Summarize discussion results |
| Categorize discussion results |
| No session/meeting without protocol |

Tab. 15: Project Meeting.

**Aufgaben zur Selbstkontrolle**

5.1 Welche Ziele verfolgt die Qualitätssicherung beim Projektmanagement?

5.2 Erläutern Sie, zwischen welchen Arten von Sitzungen man unterscheidet.

5.3 Was sollte man bei Projektsitzungen beachten? Warum sind diese Aspekte wichtig?

**Tasks for Progress Review**

*5.1   What are the objectives of the quality assurance in project management?*

*5.2   Discuss the different types of meetings, which exist.*

*5.3   What you should note in project meetings? Why are these issues important?*

## 6 Abschlussphase

In der Projektabschlussphase wird das Projektergebnis präsentiert und vom Auftraggeber abgenommen. Um den Abschluss eines Projektes durchführen zu können, muss vorher ein Ende definiert worden sein. Zuletzt werden das Projekt und die dazugehörige Projektgruppe (Projektleiter und Projektteam) aufgelöst.

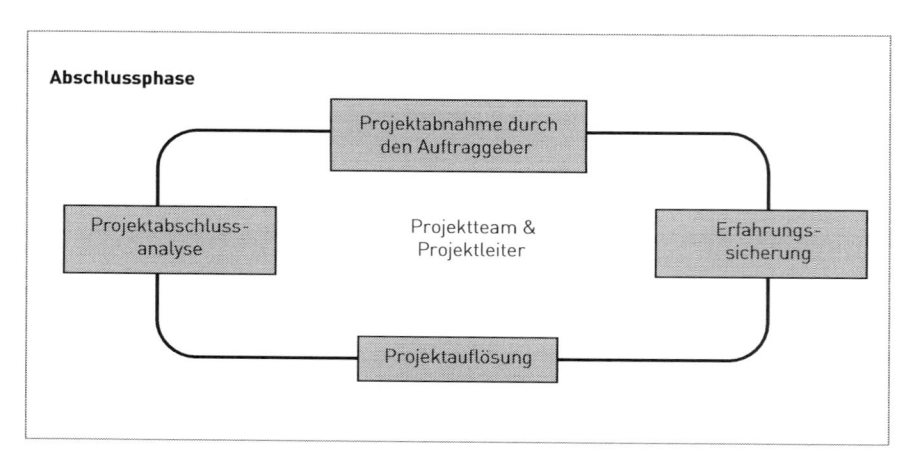

Abb. 41: Projektabschlussphase.

**Während der Abschlussphase hat der Projektleiter folgende Aufgaben zu erfüllen:**

- Abnahmebedingungen definieren
- Abschlussbericht erstellen
- Abschlusssitzung mit Auftraggeber durchführen
- Feedback der Projektmitglieder einholen
- Realisierungsverantwortliche einbeziehen
- Leistung der Projektmitglieder würdigen
- Reintegration der Projektbeteiligten vorbereiten
- Erfahrungen dokumentieren
- Abschlussfest mit Projektgruppe

Sind die definierten Zielpunkte erreicht, werden die Projektergebnisse und die gemachten Erfahrungen schriftlich festgehalten. Ein solcher Abschlussbericht dient der Gegenüberstellung des geplanten und des tatsächlichen Ergebnisses. Der Projektabschlussbericht ist ebenfalls nach DIN 69901 geregelt[10]. Neben dem Vergleich von Terminen, Kosten, Aufwänden und Zielen werden auch Hindernisse und deren Lösungen sowie konstruktive Kritiken notiert. Eine Analyse von Stärken und

---

10 Vgl. Deutsches Institut für Normung (2009), DIN 69901.

## 6 Final Phase

During the final phase of the project the project results are presented and accepted by the client. To carry out the completion of a project the completion must have been previously defined. Last, the project and the associated project group (project manager and project team) will be disbanded.

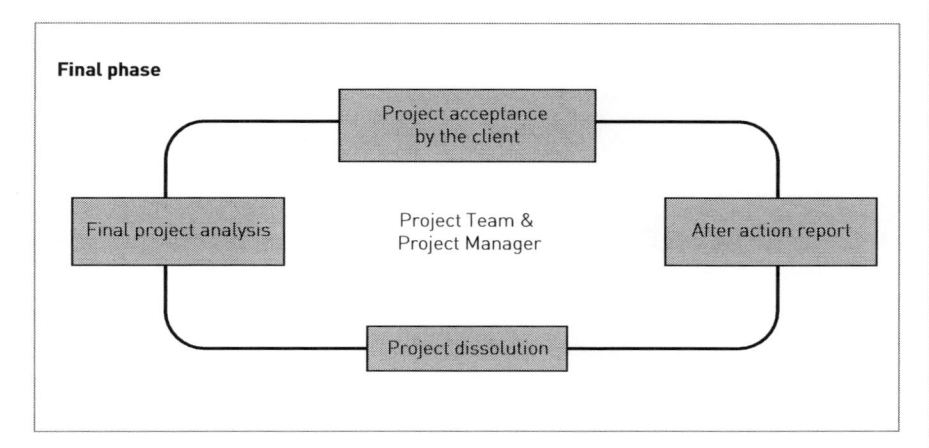

Fig. 41: Final Project Phase.

**During the final phase, the project manager must perform the following tasks:**

- Define acceptance conditions
- Create final report
- Perform final meeting with the client
- Obtain feedback from the project members
- Involve individuals in charge of implementation
- Recognize the performance of the project members
- Prepare the reintegration of the project participants
- Document the experiences
- Final party with project group

When the defined goals are achieved, the project results and experiences are documented in writing. Such a final report is used for comparison of the planned and the actual outcome. The project completion report is also regulated according to DIN 69901[10]. In addition to the comparison of dates, costs, expenses and objectives, also obstacles and their solutions, as well as constructive criticisms are noted. An analysis of strengths and weaknesses is recommended. Provided the project objectives were not achieved, the reasons for this are to be documented. When appropriate, a list of

---

10  Cf. German Institute for Standardisation (2009), DIN 69901.

Schwächen ist empfehlenswert. Wurden im Projekt vorgesehene Ziele nicht erreicht, sind die Gründe hierfür zu vermerken. Gegebenenfalls ist eine Liste mit noch offenen Punkten zu erstellen und festzulegen, wer für die Erledigung zuständig ist. Alle Abschlussberichte sollten gesammelt werden und auch für andere Projektteams als Wissenspool zugänglich sein. Nachfolgende Tabelle stellt die wichtigen Punkte eines Abschlussberichtes dar.

| | |
|---|---|
| **Empfänger** | – Auftraggeber<br>– Projektteam<br>– Eventuell weitere Personen |
| **Inhalt** | – Vergleich der geplanten Termine, Kosten, Aufwände, Ziele mit den tatsächlichen Termine, Kosten, Aufwände und Ziele (Soll-/Ist-Vergleich)<br>– Besondere Problemstellungen/Ereignisse und Lösungen<br>– Darstellung gesammelter Erfahrungen |
| **Unterzeichner** | – Projektleiter<br>– Auftraggeber |

Tab. 16: Inhalte eines Abschlussberichts (vgl. Patzka, Rattay (2004), S. 394).

Auch bei abgebrochenen und nicht beendeten Projekten ist es von besonderer Bedeutung einen Abschlussbericht zu erstellen, um die gemachten Erfahrungen zu dokumentieren und nutzen zu können. Hierbei sind auch die Gründe für das nicht Beenden oder Abbrechen darzustellen und zu untersuchen.

Zur offiziellen Beendigung des Projekts wird eine Abschlusssitzung mit dem Auftraggeber durchgeführt, an der sowohl der Projektleiter als auch das Projektteam teilnimmt. Es ist wichtig, hierbei die Ergebnisse und Prozesse kritisch zu analysieren und zu bewerten. Neben der Sicherstellung gesammelter Erfahrungen werden auch die Leistungen des Projektteams gewürdigt.

Je nach Umfang und Dauer der Projektarbeit ist es erforderlich, die Teammitglieder wieder in das normale Alltagsgeschäft zu reintegrieren. Daher ist es wichtig ein Projekt auch auf emotionaler Ebene, beispielsweise mit einem Abschlussfest zu beenden und das Team aufzulösen (siehe hierzu auch Kapitel „Teamentwicklung").

open issues is to be drafted and to determine the responsible person for the execution. All final reports should be collected and be made available for other project teams as part of a knowledge pool. The following table summarizes the important points of a final report.

| **Recipient** | – Client<br>– Project team<br>– Potentially further persons |
|---|---|
| **Contents** | – Comparison of the planned milestones, costs, expenses, goals with the actual dates, costs, expenses, and objectives (target/actual comparison)<br>– Special problems/events and solutions<br>– After action report |
| **Signatories** | – Project manager<br>– Client |

Tab. 16: Contents of the Final Report (cf. Patzka, Rattay (2004), p. 394).

Specially in abandoned and not completed projects it is of particular importance to produce a final report to document and draw benefit from the experience. The reasons for non-completion or the cancellation of the project should be documented and discussed.

To officially end the project a final review is performed with the client, in which both the project manager and the project team participates. It is important during this review to critically analyze and evaluate the results and processes. In addition to documenting the experience gained the performance of the project team will be recognized.

Depending on the scope and duration of the project work, it may be necessary to reintegrate the team members into the day-to-day business operations. It is therefore important to close the project on an emotional level and disband the team, for example, with a final party. See also the chapter 7 on the subject of team development.

**Notizen**

**Aufgaben zur Selbstkontrolle**

6.1  *Wozu dient die Projektabschlussphase?*

6.2  *Welche sind die Aufgaben des Projektleiters innerhalb der Abschlussphase?*

**Tasks for Progress Review**

6.1  What is the purpose of the project completion phase?

6.2  What are the tasks of the project manager within the final phase?

# 7 Teamentwicklung

Zu beachten ist, dass es sich bei dem Projektteam um ein Team auf Zeit handelt. Es ist nicht von Anfang an arbeitsfähig, sondern entwickelt sich erst allmählich. Im Prinzip ist ein Teamentwicklungsprozess zwar einmalig, doch sind gewisse Gesetzmäßigkeiten erkennbar. Es liegt eine klare Transparenz hinsichtlich Projektklarheit, Aufgabenverteilung, Rollen und organisatorischer Einordnung des Projekts vor.

```
            Projektaufgabe
               /\
              /  \
             /    \
            /      \
         ich ------> wir
```

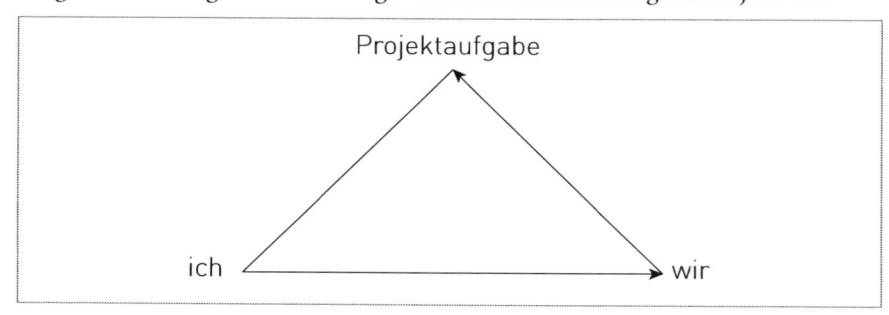

Abb. 42: Auswirkungsbeziehungen im Projekt.

Die Teamentwicklung selbst ist ein stetiger Veränderungs- und Wachstumsprozess, denn bei einem Projektteam handelt es sich um eine Gruppe von Individuen, die auf ein gemeinsames Ziel oder eine gemeinsame Aufgabe fokussiert ist. Dieser Teamentwicklungsprozess benötigt Zeit, Verantwortlichkeit und gegebenenfalls die Stimulierung eines weiteren Entwicklungsfortschritts. Daher ist es die Aufgabe des Teamleiters, entwicklungsfördernde Bedingungen aufzubauen und zu pflegen.

**Phasen der Teamentwicklung** (abgrenzbare Entwicklungsphasen)

**Phase 1: Anfangsphase der Gruppen-Konstituierung:**

Teamstruktur ist durch hohe Unsicherheit gekennzeichnet.
*Aufgabe des Teamleiters: Sorge dafür, dass jeder seinen Platz findet.*

**Phase 2: Phase der Turbulenz, Konflikte, Konkurrenz:**

*Aufgabe des Teamleiters: Krisen und Konflikte sind zu erwarten und ein gutes Zeichen für Teamentwicklung.*

**Phase 3: Phase der Einigung auf Spielregeln, Etablierung von Normen:**

Gegenseitige Unterstützung und Zusammenhalt bildet sich aus.
*Aufgabe des Teamleiters: Klarheit des Auftrages, der Aufgaben und der Zielsetzung überprüfen; Kommunikationsregeln vorschlagen.*

**Phase 4: Funktionale Teamstruktur zur Aufgabenerfüllung:**

Probleme sind weitgehend gelöst und entschärft, konstruktive Aufgabenbewältigung ist möglich.
*Aufgaben des Teamleiters: Moderation des Teamprozesses und der Themenbearbeitung als vorrangige Aufgabe betrachten.*

# 7 Team Development

It is important to note that the project team is a team for a finite period of time. It is not capable of work from the beginning, but only gradually develops into a team. While in principle a team development process is unique, it is nevertheless subject to certain regularities. A clear transparency with respect to project clarity, allocation of responsibilities, roles and organizational classification of the project exists.

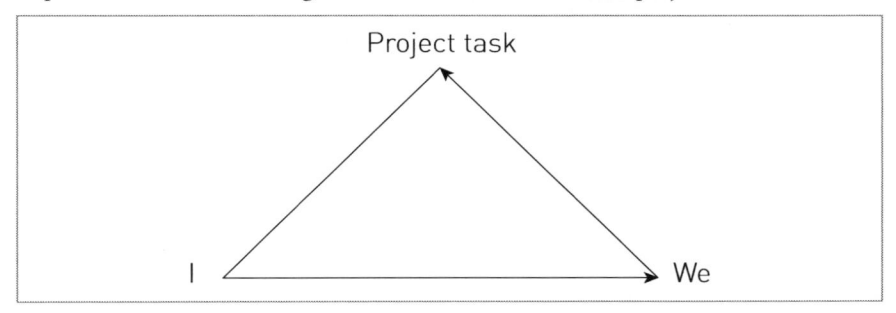

Fig. 42: Impact of Relationships in the Project.

The team development itself is a constant change and growth process, because a project team is a group of individuals, with a common goal or a common task. This team development process requires time, responsibility and, where appropriate, the stimulation of a further development progress. It is therefore the task of the team leader to establish and maintain conditions which further the development of the team.

**Stages of Team Development** (definable stages)

**Phase 1: Initial stage of team building:**

Team structure is characterized by high level of uncertainty
*Task for group control: Ensure that everyone finds his or her seat*

**Phase 2: Phase of turbulence, conflict, competition:**

*Task for group control: Crises and conflicts are to be expected and are a good sign for team development*

**Phase 3: Phase of agreement on rules, establishment of standards:**

Mutual support and cohesion is formed
*Task for group control: Review the clarity of the order, the tasks, and objectives; Propose rules of communication*

**Phase 4: Functional team structure for performance of tasks:**

Problems are resolved to the extent possible and defused, constructive task performance is possible
*Tasks for group control: Regard the moderation of the team process and the topic processing as a priority task*

**Notizen**

**1. Phase: Orientierung**
höflich
unpersönlich
gespannt
vorsichtig

**2. Phase: Kampf**
unterschwellige Konflikte
Konfrontationen
Cliquenbildung
mühsames Vorwärtskommen
Gefühl der Ausweglosigkeit

**Teamentwicklung**

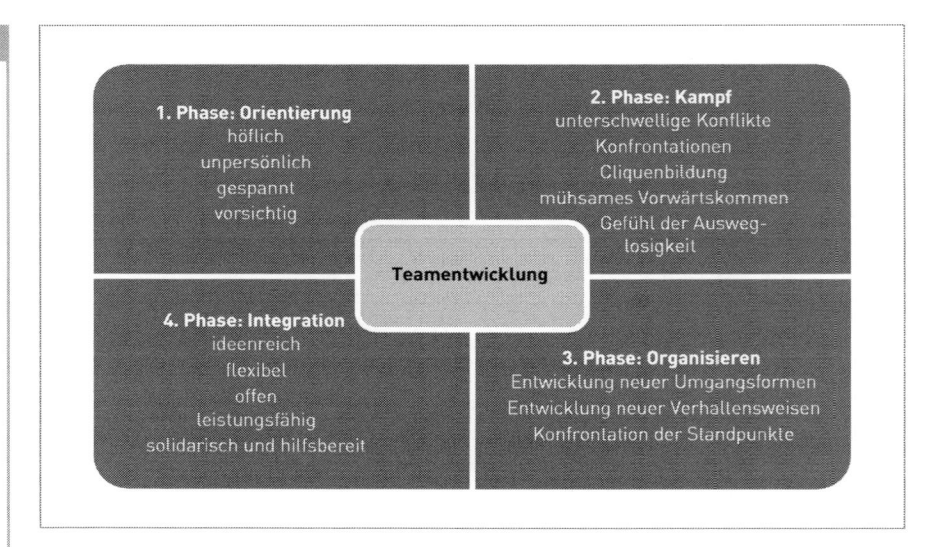

**4. Phase: Integration**
ideenreich
flexibel
offen
leistungsfähig
solidarisch und hilfsbereit

**3. Phase: Organisieren**
Entwicklung neuer Umgangsformen
Entwicklung neuer Verhaltensweisen
Konfrontation der Standpunkte

Abb. 43: Teamentwicklung.

**Aufgaben zur Selbstkontrolle**

*7.1 Beschreiben Sie die Phasen der Teambildung.*

**Team Development**

| 1 Orientation Phase | 2 Combative Phase |
| --- | --- |
| Polite | Subliminal conflicts |
| Impersonal | Confrontations |
| Tense | Forming of cliques |
| Cautious | Laborious progress |
| | Feeling of hopelessness |
| **4 Integration Phase** | **3 Organization Phase** |
| Imaginative | Development of new manners |
| Flexible | Development of new behavior |
| Open | Confrontation of positions |
| Powerful | |
| Solidarity and helpfulness | |

Fig. 43: Team Development.

**Tasks for Progress Review**

*7.1 Describe the stages of team building.*

# 8 Projektmanagementmethoden

## 8.1 Klassisches Projektmanagement

Grundsätzlich stehen bei jedem Projekt drei Parameter im Mittelpunkt: Ziele, Kosten und Termine. In der klassischen Vorgehensweise werden als erstes die Ziele des Projekts festgelegt, die unter Einsatz verfügbarer Ressourcen zu bestimmten Terminen erreicht werden sollen. Dementsprechend werden nach dem Setzen eines Ziels Ressourcen- und Zeitpläne erstellt. Nun kann es bei der Umsetzung dieser Pläne dazu kommen, dass gegebene Ziele nicht mit dem vorhandenen Budget an Ressourcen und Zeit erreicht werden können. Tritt dieser Fall ein, werden als erstes diese zwei Komponenten verändert. Von der Änderung des Projektumfangs und somit der Ziele wird im klassischen Projektmanagement weitestmöglich abgesehen. Dies ist der Punkt, an den das agile Projektmanagement ansetzt.

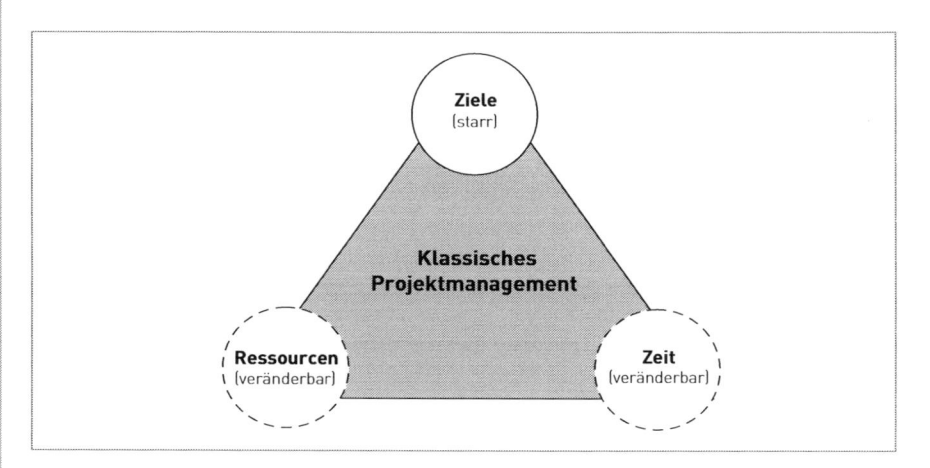

Abb. 44: Klassisches Projektmanagement (vgl. Wagener; Ziller (2012), S. 166).

## 8.2 Agiles Projektmanagement

Die Bezeichnung „Agiles Projektmanagement" wird überwiegend in der Softwareentwicklung verwendet und formt dort einen Oberbegriff zu Entwicklungsmodellen wie Scrum oder Extreme Programming, die von der traditionellen, starren Vorgehensweise absehen und eine dynamischere, flexiblere Herangehensweise zur Problemlösung zulassen. Im agilen Manifest[11] wird der Basisgedanke aller agilen Modelle sinngemäß wie folgt beschrieben:

a) Der Mensch ist wichtiger als der Prozess.
b) Das entstehende Produkt ist wichtiger als eine umfassende Dokumentation.
c) Die Kooperation mit dem Kunden ist wichtiger als Vertragsverhandlungen.
d) Im laufenden Entstehungsprozess Änderungen am Produkt vorzunehmen ist wichtiger als die strikte Verfolgung eines Plans.

---

[11] Verfasst von Beck, Kent et al. (2001).

# 8 Project Management Methodologies

## 8.1 Classic Project Management

In principle, three parameters are at the heart of every project: objectives, costs, and milestones. In the classic approach first the objectives of the project are established, which are to be achieved at specific dates with the use of available resources. Accordingly, after setting of the objective target resource plans and schedules are created. During the implementation of these plans, it can happen that provided goals couldn't be achieved within the existing budget resources and time. If this occurs, these two components are the first to be changed. In the classic project management the changing of the scope of the project and therefore the objectives will be avoided as much as possible. This is the point at which the agile project management approach starts.

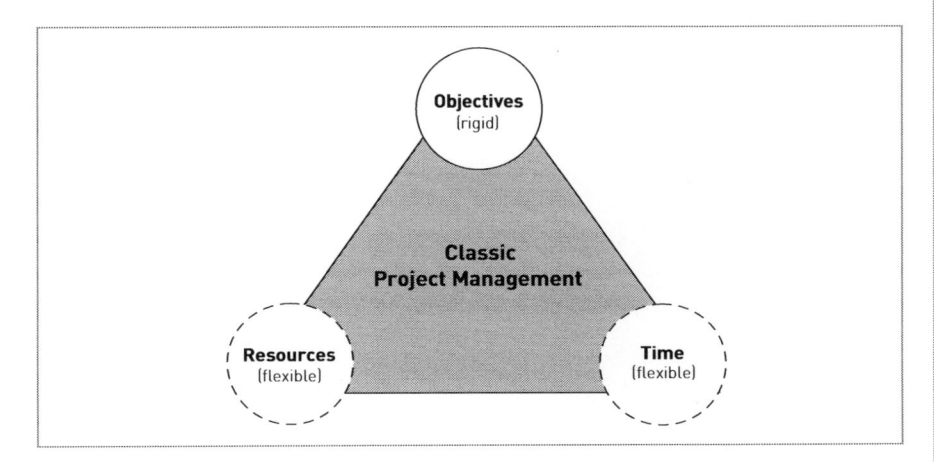

Fig. 44: Classic Project Management (cf. Wagener; Ziller (2012), p. 166).

## 8.2 Agile Project Management

The term "Agile Project Management" is used mainly in the software development models and forms a generic term for developmental models such as Scrum or Extreme Programming, which allow a departure from a traditional, rigid approach towards a more dynamic, more flexible approach to problem solving. In the Agile Manifesto[11] the underlying thought for all agile models is described as follows:

a) The human being is more important than the process
b) The final product is more important than a comprehensive documentation
c) The cooperation with the customer is more important than contract negotiations
d) Is more important to make changes to the product in the current development process than to strictly follow a plan

---

11  Written by Beck, Kent et al (2001).

Bei den agilen Projektmanagement-Methoden wird an erster Stelle der Projektumfang verändert. Die zur Verfügung gestellten Ressourcen (Kosten) und der gegebene Zeitrahmen bleiben möglichst unangetastet.

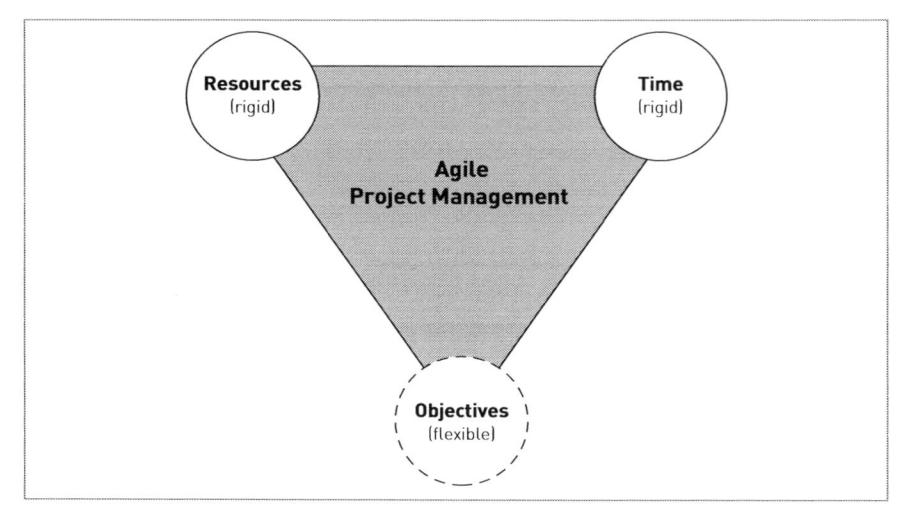

Abb. 45: Agiles Projektmanagement (vgl. Wagener; Ziller (2012), S. 169).

Im Folgenden sollen die klassische Projektmanagementmethode Prince2 und die agile Projektmanagementmethode Scrum näher betrachtet werden.

## 8.3 Prince2

Prince2 (Projects in Controlled Environments) ist eine Projektmanagementmethode, die auf den Prozess an sich ausgerichtet ist und frei an beinah jede Art von Projekt angepasst werden kann. Neben Scrum gehört Prince2 zu den weltweit führenden Projektmanagementmethoden.

Eine Besonderheit von Prince2 ist es, dass diese Methode unabhängig von Art und Größe des Unternehmens / des Projektes universell eingesetzt werden kann. Des Weiteren werden bei Prince2 Management und Facharbeiten voneinander getrennt.

Es sind die Aufgaben des Projektmanagers, die Reihenfolge der Vorgänge, die benötigten Ressourcen zur Umsetzung zu planen und die Realisierung dieser Planung zu überwachen.

Jedes Projekt besteht aus sechs Variablen, die bei der Steuerung durch den Projektmanager berücksichtigt werden müssen: **Kosten, Umfang, Zeitrahmen, Risiko, Qualität, Nutzen.**

Zur Steuerung dieser Bereiche stellt Prince2 dem Projektmanager jeweils sieben Themen und Prozesse, die im Folgenden näher erläutert werden, zur Verfügung.

In the agile project management methods, the project scope will be changed first. The available resources (cost) and the given period remain untouched as far as possible.

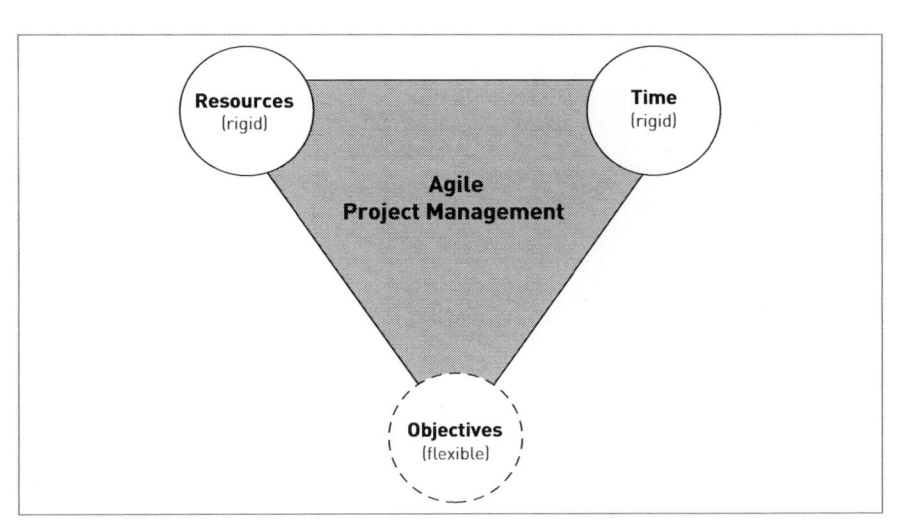

Fig. 45: Agile Project Management (cf. Wagener; Ziller (2012), p. 169).

In the following section, the classic project management method Prince2 and agile project management method Scrum will be examined in more detail.

## 8.3   Prince2

Prince2 is a project management method, which is focused on the process itself and freely adaptable to almost any type of project. In addition to the below described method "Scrum" Prince2 belongs to one of the world's leading project management methodologies.

A special feature of Prince2 is that this method can be used universally regardless of the type and size of the company / project. In addition, Prince2 separates management and skilled work from each other.

It is the task of the project manager to monitor the order of the processes, to plan the resources required, and to monitor the implementation of the plan.

Each project consists of six variables, which the project manager considers for the control. These six variables are: **cost, scope, period, risk, quality, benefit.**

To control these areas Prince2 provides the project manager seven topics and processes, which are explained in more detail below.

Neben den wiederum sieben Grundprinzipien und der Anpassungsmöglichkeit in das jeweilige Projektumfeld stellen diese die vier Bestandteile der Prince2-Methode dar: Projektumfeld, Themen, Prozesse und Grundprinzipien.

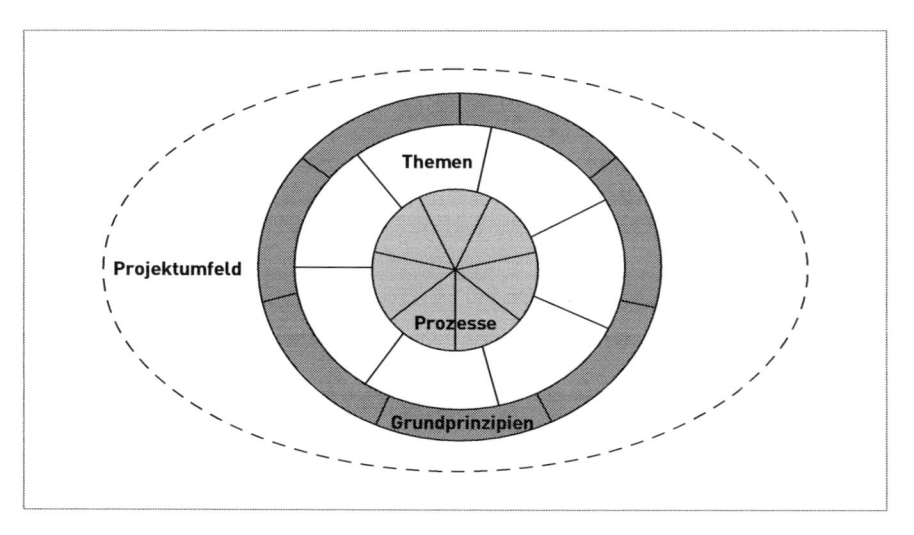

Abb. 46: Modell Prince2 (vgl. OGC (2009), S. 6).

*Grundprinzipien*

Die sieben Grundprinzipien bilden eine feste Basis und den Kern der Methode. Daher dürfen diese Grundprinzipien auch bei der Anpassung der universellen Methode an unterschiedliche Projekte nicht verändert werden.

**Fortlaufende geschäftliche Rechtfertigung**
Der Grund für die Umsetzung des Projektes muss von Anfang bis Ende durchgängig gegeben sein. Die fortlaufende geschäftliche Rechtfertigung muss in einem Business Case dokumentiert werden.

**Lernen aus Erfahrung**
Vor dem Projektstart sind Erfahrungen aus früheren und ähnlichen Projekten aufzuarbeiten. Während des Projekts werden fortlaufende Erfahrungswerte in Berichten und Reviews dokumentiert, stets mit dem Ziel möglichst viele Erfahrungen noch im laufenden Projekt umzusetzen. Nach Abschluss des Projekts werden die gesammelten und dokumentierten Erfahrungen weitergegeben.

In addition to the seven basic principles in turn and their adaptability in the respective project environment, these four components represent the Prince2 method.

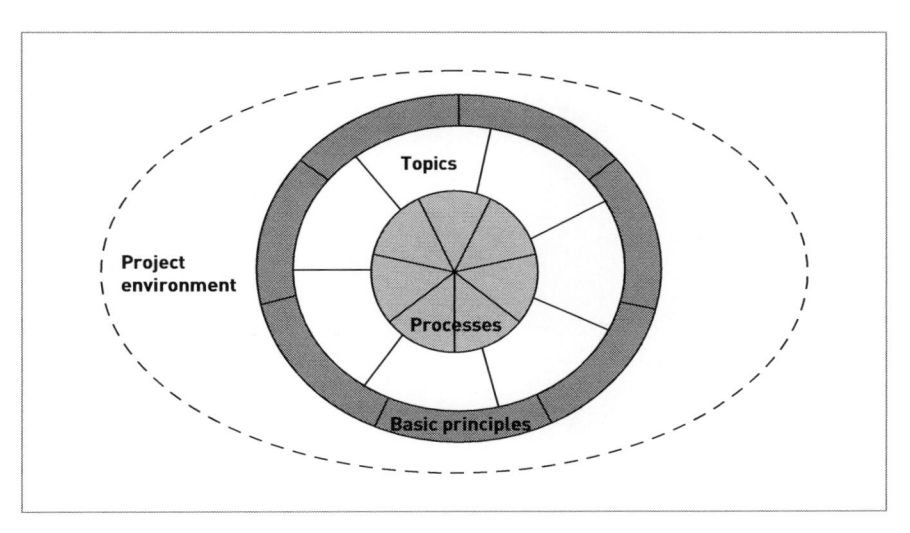

Fig. 46: Modell Prince2 (cf. OGC (2009), p. 6).

*Basic Principles*

The seven basic principles provide a solid base and the core of the method. These basic principles may therefore not be changed, even when adapting the universal method to different projects.

**Ongoing Business Justification**
The reason for the implementation of the project must be maintained consistently from the beginning to the end. The ongoing business justification must be documented in a business case.

**Learn from Experience**
Prior to the start of the project, experience from previous and similar projects has to be analyzed. During the project, ongoing experience is documented in reports and reviews, always with the aim to transfer as much experience as possible in the course of the current project. After completion of the project, the experience gathered and documented will be passed on.

### Definierte Rollen und Verantwortlichkeiten
Es sind drei unterschiedliche Rollen und Verantwortlichkeiten festgelegt.

| Rolle | Verantwortlichkeit |
|---|---|
| Vertreter geschäftlicher Interessen | Zielsetzung und Investition |
| Benutzer | Projektprodukte nutzen |
| Lieferanten | Ressourcen/Fachkenntnisse |

Tab. 17: Rolle und Verantwortlichkeiten Prince2.

### Steuern über Managementphasen
Ein Projekt kann in mehrere Phasen unterteilt werden. Diese Phasen dienen zur Planung, Überwachung und Steuerung.

### Steuern nach dem Ausnahmeprinzip
Es werden klare Verantwortlichkeiten für das Lenken, Managen und Liefern innerhalb des Projektes festgelegt. Dazu sind das Delegieren bestimmter Befugnisse sowie das Einrichten von Steuerungsmitteln und die Bereitstellung von Sicherungsmechanismen notwendig. Führungskräfte sollen dadurch ohne Kontrollverluste zeitlich entlastet werden.

### Produktorientierung
Die Projekte sollen nach dem Prinzip der Ergebnisorientierung durchgeführt werden. Das Ergebnis eines Projekts ist ein Produkt oder mehrere Produkte.

### Anpassen an Projektumgebung
Das Grundprinzip, die Methode an die Projektumgebung anzupassen, soll dazu dienen, auf die unterschiedlichen Umgebungen eingehen zu können und ihr damit entsprechend gerecht werden zu können.

*Themen*

Die sieben Themen sind Punkte, die bei der Umsetzung des Projekts stets berücksichtigt werden müssen. Sie dienen als Werkzeug zur Umsetzung der Grundprinzipien.

### Business Case
Mit dem Business Case soll die Frage nach dem Warum beantwortet werden. Dabei soll dargelegt werden, ob das Projekt realisierbar und lohnend ist. Der Business Case stellt den Investitionsnutzen und den Nutzen des Projekts dar. Zielsetzung ist es, die Überzeugung des Lenkungsausschusses und der Stakeholder zu sichern.

### Organisation
Dieses Thema soll darlegen, wer welche Zuständigkeiten, Rollen und Verantwortlichkeiten innerhalb des Projekts übernimmt. Innerhalb von Prince2 sind vier Managementebenen festgelegt. Diese vier Ebenen sind das Unternehmens- oder Programmmanagement, die Ebene Lenken, die Ebene Managen und die Ebene Liefern.

**Defined Roles and Responsibilities**
Three different roles and responsibilities are defined.

| Role | Responsibility |
| --- | --- |
| Representative of commercial interests | Objectives and investment |
| User | Use project products |
| Suppliers | Resources/expertise |

Tab. 17: Roles and Responsibilities Prince2.

**Control Through Management Phases**
A project can be divided into several phases. These phases are used for planning, monitoring, and control.

**Control by Exception**
Clear responsibilities for steering, manage and deliver within the project are stated. To this end, the delegation of certain powers, as well as the setting of control mechanisms and the provision of safeguards is necessary. Managers should be relieved of time-consuming duties without loss of control.

**Product Orientation**
The projects should be carried out according to the principle of results orientation. The result of a project is a product or multiple products.

**Adaption to Project Environment**
The basic principle is to adapt the method the project environment serves to address the different environments and to meet the needs of the method accordingly.

*Topics*

The seven topics are points, which always need to be considered in the implementation of the project. They serve as a tool for the implementation of the basic principles.

**Business Case**
With the business case the underlying question of "why" should be answered. It should be discussed whether the project is feasible and worthwhile. The business case represents the investment value and the benefits of the project. Objective is to secure the conviction of the steering committee and the stakeholders.

**Organization**
This topic should demonstrate who carries which competencies, roles and responsibilities within the project. Within Prince2 four management levels are defined. These four levels are the "corporate or program management", the level "steering", the level "managing" and the level "delivery".

```
┌─────────────────────────────────────────────────┐
│         Unternehmens- oder Programmmanagement    │
│  ┌──────┬──────────────────────────────────────┐│
│  │ P    │   Lenken - Lenkungsausschuss         ││
│  │ r    ├──────────────────────────────────────┤│
│  │ o... │   Managen - Projektmanager           ││
│  │      ├──────────────────────────────────────┤│
│  │      │   Liefern - Teammanager              ││
│  └──────┴──────────────────────────────────────┘│
└─────────────────────────────────────────────────┘
```

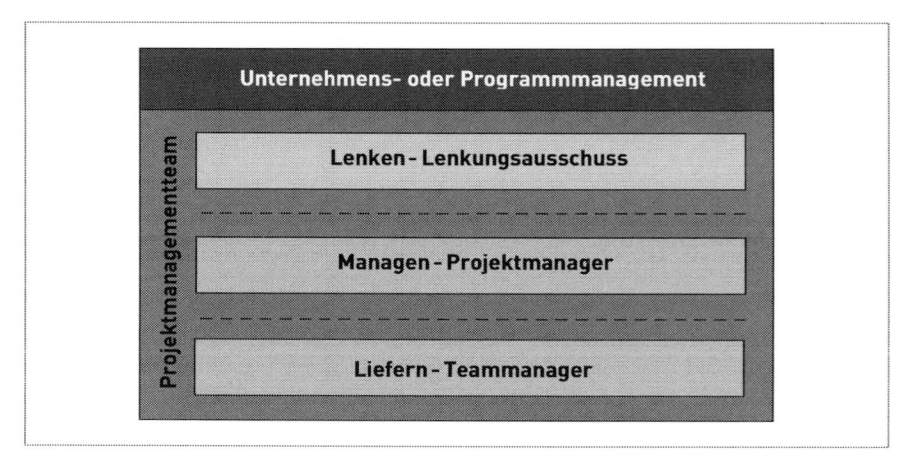

Abb. 47: Managementaufbau Prince2 (vgl. OGC (2009), S. 37).

Das Unternehmensmanagement gibt das Projekt in Auftrag und legt den Spielraum für den Lenkungsausschuss fest. Der Lenkungsausschuss (die Managementebene Lenken) trägt die Verantwortung für den Projekterfolg. Der Projektmanager (die Managementebene Managen) ist verantwortlich dafür, die sechs gegebenen Dimensionen Zeit, Kosten, Qualität, Umfang, Risiken, Nutzen einzuhalten und das geforderte Ziel zu erreichen. Der Teammanager (die Managementebene Liefern) ist zuständig, die geforderten Produkte innerhalb des gegebenen Zeit- und Kostenrahmens zu erstellen.

**Qualität**
Hier findet die Ausarbeitung einer ersten Idee bis hin zu konkreten Qualitätskriterien statt, um die Frage nach dem Was zu klären.

**Pläne**
Bei diesem Thema steht die Beantwortung dreier Fragen im Zentrum: Wie? Wie viel? Wann?

Das Thema der Qualität wird ergänzt, einzelne Schritte werden beschrieben. Die weitergegebenen Informationen werden an die Bedürfnisse der Teammitglieder angepasst. Pläne dienen auch als Anleitung für Kommunikation und Steuerung.

**Risiken**
Es wird festgehalten, was ist, wenn ein bestimmter Fall eintritt. Zudem kann durch das Risikomanagement das Prinzip der fortlaufenden geschäftlichen Rechtfertigung gesichert werden.

**Änderungen**
Diese dienen zur Beseitigung von Problemen und Qualitätsänderungen. Dieses Thema liefert eine Antwort auf die Frage „was sind die Auswirkungen von ...?"

**Fortschritt**
Bei diesem Thema steht wiederum die Beantwortung dreier Fragen im Zentrum: Wo stehen wir jetzt? Wohin gehen wir? Sollen wir weiter machen?

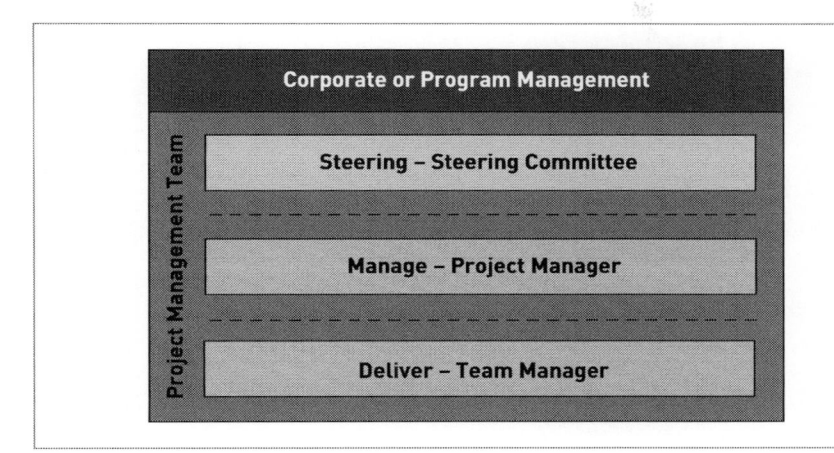

Fig. 47: Management structure Prince2 (cf. OGC (2009), p. 37).

The business management orders the project and sets the scope for the steering committee. The steering committee (the management level "steering") is responsible for the project's success. The project manager (the management level "managing") is responsible for managing the six provided dimensions time, cost, quality, scope, risks, benefits and to achieve the required objectives. The team manager (the management level "delivery") is responsible for creating the demanded products within the given time and budget.

**Quality**
Here the drafting of a first idea up to the level of specific quality criteria takes place, in order to clarify the question of the what.

**Plans**
The heart of his topic is the answer to three questions: How? How much? When?

The issue of quality is complemented, individual steps are described. The information disclosed will be adapted to the needs of the team members. Plans also serve as a guide for communication and control.

**Risks**
It is documented what happens if a certain event occurs. In addition, the risk management can assure the principle of continuous business justification.

**Changes**
Serve to eliminate problems and adjust for quality changes. This topic provides an answer to the question "What are the effects of?"

**Progress**
The heart of this topic is the again the answer to three questions: Where are we now? Where are we going? Should we continue?

Es wird eine Kontrolle der Durchführbarkeit stattfinden und bewertet werden, ob das Projekt weiter verfolgt oder abgebrochen werden soll.

| Business Case | Organisation | Qualität | Pläne | Risiken | Änderungen | Fortschritt |
|---|---|---|---|---|---|---|
| Warum? | Wer? | Was? | Wie? | Was, wenn? | Was sind die Auswirkungen von ...? | Wo stehen wir jetzt? |
| | | | Wie viel? | | | Wohin gehen wir? |
| | | | Wann? | | | Sollen wir weiter machen? |

Tab. 18: Aufgaben Projektmanager Prince2.

*Prozesse*

Die sieben Prozesse dienen zur Vorbereitung und Durchführung eines Projekts. Sie sind notwendig, um ein Projekt erfolgreich zu lenken, zu managen und letztendlich das gewünschte Produkt zu liefern.

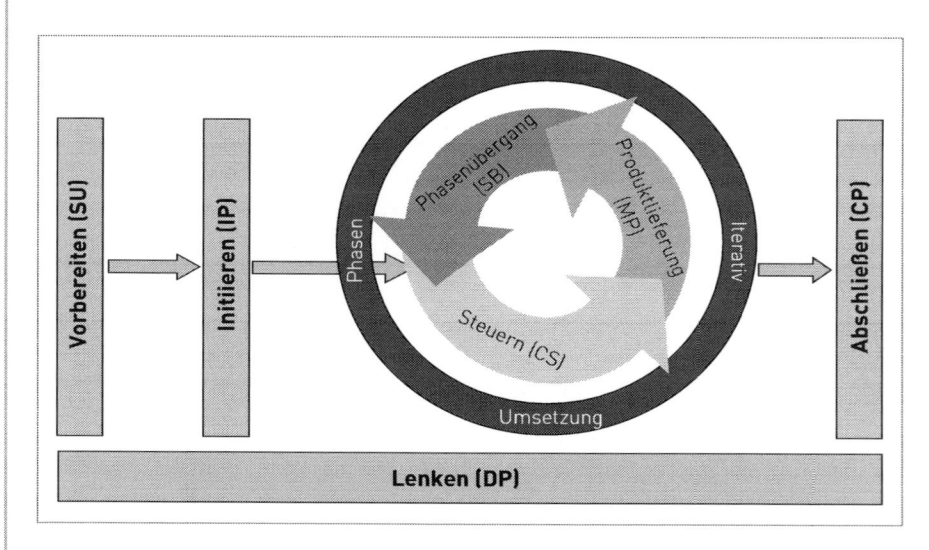

Abb. 48: Prozesse Prince2 (vgl. Ebel (2011), S. 88).

**Vorbereiten eines Projekts (SU – Starting Up a Project)**
In dieser Phase wird eine Projektidee zum konkreten Projektvorschlag entwickelt. Der Projektmanager sammelt alle notwendigen Informationen: Der Business Case wird erstellt, vorhandene Erfahrungen geprüft, Vorgehensweisen geplant, der Lenkungsausschuss zusammengesetzt, der Aufwand zur Initiierung des Projektes und Lösungsansätze festgelegt.

A control of the feasibility takes place and an assessment whether the project is to be pursued or abandoned?

| Business Case | Organization | Quality | Plans | Risks | Changes | Progress |
|---|---|---|---|---|---|---|
| Why? | Who? | What? | How? | What if? | What are the effects of…? | Where are we now? |
| | | | How much? | | | Where are we going? |
| | | | When? | | | Should we continue? |

Tab. 18: Tasks Project Manager Prince2.

*Processes*

The seven processes for the preparation and implementation of a project. They are necessary to successfully guide, manage, and ultimately to provide the desired product to a project.

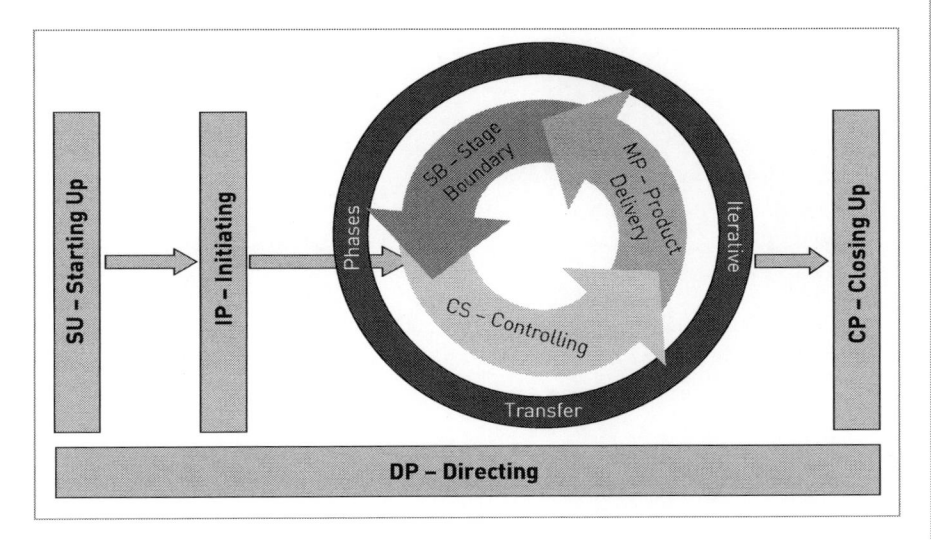

Fig. 48: Prince2 Processes (cf. Ebel (2011), p. 88).

**Starting Up a Project (SU)**
In this phase, a project idea is developed into a concrete project proposal. The project manager collects all the necessary information: the business case will be created, existing experiences checked, procedures planned, the steering committee assembled, the effort required to initiate the project and solution approaches determined.

### Initiieren eines Projekts (IP – Initiating a Project)
Hier findet der eigentliche Start des Projekts statt. Eine planmäßige Durchführung wird vorbereitet, Endprodukte und Ergebnisse definiert. Es findet die Planung des gesamten Projekts und die Anpassung der Projektmanagementmethodik statt.

### Lenken eines Projekts (DP – Directing a Project)
Diese Phase findet parallel zu den anderen Projektprozessen statt. Es werden die Aktivitäten des Lenkungsausschusses beschrieben. Es werden Genehmigungen erteilt und Anforderungen zur Projektinitiierung, zum Start, den weiteren Managementphasen, beim Auftreten von Problemen und zum Projektabschluss festgelegt.

### Steuern einer Phase (CS – Controlling a Stage)
Die tägliche Arbeit des Projektmanagers mit dem Ziel, das geforderte Produkt zu liefern, ist mit dem Prozess „Steuern einer Phase" abgedeckt. Der Projektmanager überwacht hierbei den Projektfortschritt, aktualisiert, kontrolliert Pläne und informiert Interessenvertreter über den aktuellen Stand.

### Managen der Produktlieferung (MP – Managing Product Delivery)
Es wird eine klare Trennung zwischen Projektmanagement und Produkterzeugung vorgenommen. Dies erfolgt durch eine Übergabe der Arbeitspakete vom Projektmanager an den Teammanager, der die Ausführung der Arbeitspakete steuert und so die Lieferung qualitätsgeprüfter Arbeitsergebnisse überwachen kann.

### Managen eines Phasenübergangs (SB – Managing a Stage Boundary)
Mit diesem Prozess wird der Übergang von einer Phase zur nächsten geregelt. Es sind Reviews zu erstellen, der Business Case sowie die Projektrisiken und der Projektplan sind zu aktualisieren. Der Projektmanager hat die Detailplanung der neuen Phase vorzulegen. Vom Lenkungsausschuss ist der Abschlussbericht der aktuellen Phase zu autorisieren, Dokumente und Pläne müssen von ihm aktualisiert werden. Des Weiteren wird das Budget für die neue Phase vom Lenkungsausschuss freigegeben. Zudem ist es dem Lenkungsausschuss möglich, an dieser Stelle Richtungsänderungen im Projekt vorzunehmen oder es abzubrechen.

### Abschließen eines Projekts (CP – Closing a Project)
Ziel des CP ist es, einen kontrollierten Projektabschluss zu leisten. Hierbei erfolgt die Abnahme des Produktes durch den Kunden beziehungsweise die Überführung des Produktes an den Betrieb. Die Projektdokumente werden zur Erfahrungssammlung übergeben und ein Projektabschlussbericht erstellt. Diese Vorgehensweise wird auch bei einem Projektabbruch beibehalten, wichtig ist hierbei besonders der Transfer gesammelter Erfahrungswerte.

**Initiating a Project (IP)**
Here the actual start of the project takes place. A planned implementation is being prepared; finished products and outcomes are being defined. The planning of the whole project and the adaptation to the project management methodology takes place.

**Directing a Project (DP)**
This phase will take place in parallel to the other project processes. It describes the activities of the steering committee. Approvals are being issued and requirements for project initiation, for the start, for further management phases, when problems occur and for the end of the project are being set.

**Controlling a Stage (CS)**
The day-to-day work of the project manager with the aim to provide the required product is covered with the process "Control a Stage" (phase). The project manager monitors the project progress, updates, controls plans, and informs stakeholders about the current status.

**Managing Product Delivery (MP)**
There is a clear separation between project management and product production sector. This is done by a handover of the work packages by the project manager to the team manager, who controls the execution of the work packages and monitors the delivery of quality assured work results.

**Managing a Stage Boundary (SB)**
This process regulates the transition from one stage to the next. Reviews are to be created, the business case, the project risks and the project plan should be updated. The project manager has to submit the detailed planning of the new phase. The steering committee authorizes the final report of the current phase, documents and the project manager must update plans. In addition, the budget for the new phase is approved by the steering committee. In addition, it is possible for the steering committee to make changes in direction of the project or to cancel it.

**Closing a Project (CP)**
The aim of the CP is to perform it a controlled project closure. With it occurs the acceptance of the product by the client and/or the transfer of the product to the company. The project documents are turned over to experience gathering and a project completion report is created. This approach will be also maintained in the case of a project cancellation; especially important is the transfer of collected experience.

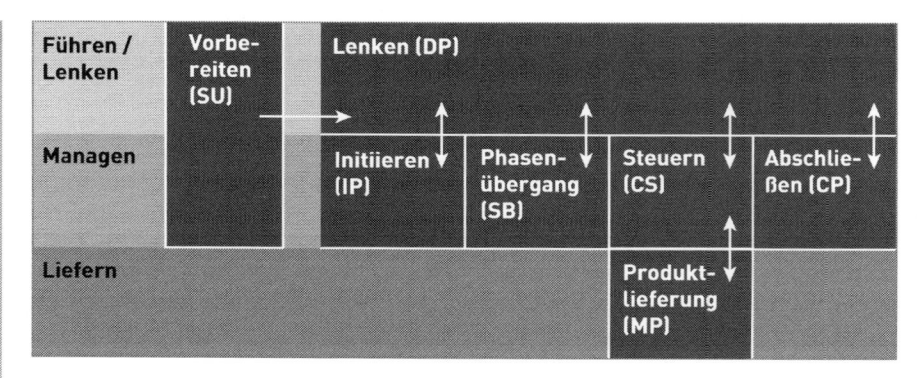

|  | Vorbereiten (SU) | Lenken (DP) | | | |
|---|---|---|---|---|---|
| **Führen / Lenken** | | | | | |
| **Managen** | | Initiieren (IP) | Phasenübergang (SB) | Steuern (CS) | Abschließen (CP) |
| **Liefern** | | | | Produktlieferung (MP) | |

Abb. 49: Überblick Prince2 (vgl. Wagener; Ziller (2012), S. 178).

*Projektumgebung*

Die Projektmanagementmethode Prince2 zeichnet sich durch ihre Unabhängigkeit von Art und Größe des Unternehmens / des Projektes aus. Die Themen und Prozesse können individuell und universell angepasst werden, lediglich die Grundprinzipien müssen durchgehend berücksichtigt und eingehalten werden.

**Themen:** Bei den Themen ist eine Anpassung in Bezug auf Umfang und Ausprägung möglich.

**Produktbeschreibungen für Managementprodukte:** Es besteht die Möglichkeit, verschiedene Managementprodukte zusammenzufassen.

**Rollenbeschreibungen:** Die verschiedenen Rollen lassen sich auf mindestens drei Personen reduzieren. Der Kunde kann gleichzeitig Benutzervertreter und Auftraggeber sein, der Projektmanager kann zusätzlich die Funktion des Teammanagers und der Projektunterstützung übernehmen. Zu diesen zwei Rollen wird noch ein Lieferantenvertreter benötigt.

**Prozesse:** Gegebenenfalls können mehrere Prozesse zu einem zusammengefasst werden. Zum Beispiel können die Vorbereitungsphase und das Initiieren eines Projektes in einem Prozess vorgenommen werden, wenn ein qualifiziertes und umfangreiches Projektmandat vorliegt.

Prince2 ist eine Projektmanagementmethode, die dank ihrer Flexibilität sowohl in Betrieben und Unternehmen verschiedener Größe als auch in öffentlichen, behördlichen Bereichen eingesetzt wird. Im Vergleich zu anderen Methoden ist die Ausbildung und Zertifizierung von Einzelpersonen in der Anwendung der Prince2-Methode relativ günstig und unkompliziert durchzuführen. Zudem ist Prince2 lizenzfrei nutzbar.

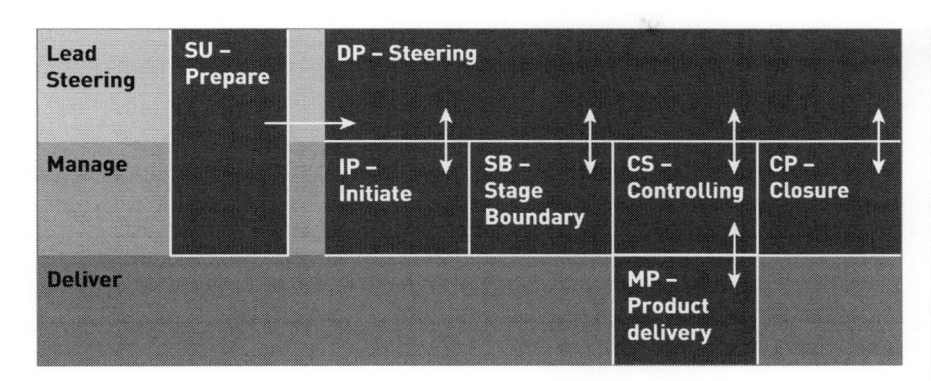

Fig. 49: Overview Prince2 (cf. Wagener; Ziller (2012), p. 178).

*Project Environment*

The project management method Prince2 is characterized by its independence of the kind and size of the company / project. The topics and processes can be adjusted individually and universally, only the basic principles must be taken into account and complied with throughout.

**Topics:** The subject can be adjusted in relation to scope and expression.

**Product Descriptions for Management Products:** It is possible to summarize several management products.

**Role Descriptions:** The various roles can be reduced to a minimum of three persons. The customer can also be user representative and client; the project manager can in addition assume the function of the team manager and project support. Additionally to these two roles a supplier' representative will be required.

**Processes:** Several processes may be merged. For example, the preparatory phase and initiating of a project can be merged into one process if a qualified and extensive project mandate exists.

Prince2 is a project management method, which, thanks to its flexibility is used both in businesses and organizations of different sizes, as well as in public, regulatory areas. In comparison with other methods, the training and certification of individuals in the application of the Prince2 method can be performed relatively easily and at low cost. Furthermore, Prince2 can be used without license.

| Vorteile | Nachteile |
|---|---|
| + nutzenorientierte und produktbasierte Methode | – Befugnisse der Projektmanager nur noch innerhalb von Phasentoleranzen (in Bezug auf Kosten, Nutzen, Umfang etc.) |
| + basiert auf sich als am besten bewiesenen Verfahren | – bei falscher Anpassung stark dokumentationslastig |
| + kontrollierter Start und Verlauf sowie kontrolliertes Ende | – Risikogrundsätze nicht richtig anzuwenden |
| + flexibel und anpassbar | – zusätzliche Investitionskosten durch Anpassung möglich |

Tab. 19: Vor- und Nachteile Prince2.

*Beispiel: Projekt „Hausbau" mit Prince2*

**a) Grundprinzipien** müssen erfüllt werden, sind nicht anpassbar

| | |
|---|---|
| **Fortlaufende geschäftliche Rechtfertigung** | Grund des Projektes „Hausbau": Wertanlage, eigene vier Wände |
| **Lernen aus Erfahrung** | Die Verzögerung durch falsch zugeschnittene Fensterglasscheiben wird dokumentiert, um bei einem eventuellen nächsten Hausbau oder einem ähnlichen Projekt wieder auf die Erfahrung zurückgreifen zu können. |
| **Rollen und Verantwortlichkeiten** | Vertreter geschäftlicher Interessen – Bauherren, Bank Benutzer – Bewohner Lieferanten – Bauunternehmen |
| **Steuern über Managementphasen** | 1. Phase – Bauplatzsuche 2. Phase – Spatenstich, Keller 3. Phase – 1. OG 4. Phase – 2. OG ... |
| **Steuern nach dem Ausnahmeprinzip** | verschiedene Zuständigkeiten für Bauherr A (Maurer, Landschaftsarchitekt etc.) und Bauherr B (Schreiner, Installateur etc.) |
| **Produktorientierung** | Das Ergebnis des Projektes (= Produkt) soll ein bezugsfertiges Haus sein. |
| **Anpassen an die Projektumgebung** | Der Umfang der Themen und Prozesse kann an das Projekt „Hausbau" angepasst werden. |

Tab. 20: Beispiel Prince2 – Grundprinzipien.

| Benefits | Disadvantages |
|---|---|
| + Value-focused and product-based method | – Powers of the project manager only within phase variances (in terms of costs, benefits, scope..) |
| + Is based on the most proven technique | – If incorrectly adapted a heavy document burden exists |
| + Controlled start and schedule, as well as a controlled end | – Risk principles cannot be applied correctly |
| + Flexible and adaptable | – Possible additional investment cost by adapting |

Tab. 19: Benefits and Disadvantages Prince2.

*Example: Project "house construction" with Prince2*

a) **Basic Principles** must be met, are not customizable

| Ongoing Business Justification | Reason of the project "house construction": investment, own four walls |
|---|---|
| Learn from Experience | The delay by incorrectly cut window glass panes is documented in order to reuse the experience in the case of a potential further construction, or a similar project experience. |
| Roles and Responsibilities | Representative business interests – builders, bank<br>User – inhabitants<br>Suppliers – building contractors |
| Control Through Management Phases | 1 Phase – searching for construction site<br>2 Phase – ground-breaking ceremony, basement<br>3 Phase – 1. 1st floor<br>4 Phase – 2. 1st floor<br>… |
| Control by Exception | Different responsibilities for client A (mason, landscape architect etc.) and client B (carpenter, plumber.) |
| Product Orientation | The result of the project (= product) should be a house ready for occupancy. |
| Adaption for the Project Environment | The scope of the topics and processes can be customized to the project "house construction". |

Tab. 20: Example Prince2 – basic principles.

**b) Themen** können angepasst werden, da das Projekt „Hausbau" jedoch sehr umfangreich ist, sind alle Themen sinnvoll und verwendbar

| | |
|---|---|
| **Business Case** | Warum? – Analyse das Projektvorhabens, Investitionsvorhaben, Nutzen des Projekts |
| **Organisation** | Wer? – Verteilung der Rollen |
| **Qualität** | Was? – Haus mit Keller, 1. OG, 2. OG, Garten, Fenster etc. |
| **Pläne** | Wie soll das fertige Projekt aussehen? Wie viel / welche Ressourcen werden benötigt? Wann soll welcher Arbeitsschritt durchgeführt werden? |
| **Risiken** | Was wenn…? hier wird ein Plan erstellt, wie potenziell eintretende Risiken behandelt werden sollen. zum Beispiel das Vorgehen, wenn die Farbe des Fußbodens anders aussieht als gedacht. |
| **Änderungen** | Wie wirken sich Änderungen auf das gesamte Projekt aus? – Wird das Laminat neu bestellt, verzögert sich der Ablaufplan. Andernfalls muss die farbliche Abweichung hingenommen werden. |
| **Fortschritt** | Wo stehen wir? – Startphase, Bauplatz gefunden<br>Wohin gehen wir? – Grundsteinlegung, Kellerbau<br>Sollen wir weiter machen? – Ja |

Tab. 21: Beispiel Prince2 – Themen.

**c) Prozesse** können angepasst werden, da das Projekt „Hausbau" jedoch sehr umfangreich ist, sind alle Prozesse sinnvoll und verwendbar

| | |
|---|---|
| **Vorbereiten (SU)** | Die Projektidee (Wertanlage) wird zu einen konkreten Projektvorschlag (Hausbau) weiter entwickelt, ein Business Case wird erstellt, Erfahrungen geprüft und die Vorgehensweise geplant. |
| **Initiieren (IP)** | Planung des gesamten Projekts, Anpassung der Projektmanagementmethodik (Themen und Prozesse). |
| **Lenken (DP)** | Die Aktivitäten des Lenkungsausschusses werden festgelegt. |
| **Steuern (CS)** | Der Projektmanager überwacht den Projektfortschritt, aktualisiert und kontrolliert Pläne. |
| **Managen Produktlieferung (MP)** | Der Projektmanager übergibt Arbeitspakete (zum Beispiel Kellerbau) an den Teammanager, dieser liefert ein Phasenergebnis. |
| **Managen Phasenübergang (SB)** | Wurde eine Phase abgeschlossen, wird dokumentiert, was gemacht wurde (Kellergeschoss gebaut), welche Herausforderungen auftraten (Wasserleitung für Pool musste gesondert angefertigt werden), wie diese Herausforderung gelöst wurde (Fachmann) und ob sich das auf den Projektablauf ausgewirkt hat (keine zeitliche Verzögerung). |
| **Abschließen (CP)** | Das fertige Projekt wird abgeschlossen, Erfahrungen dokumentiert und aufgearbeitet (auch bei Projektabbruch). |

Tab. 22: Beispiel Prince2 – Prozesse.

**b) Topics** can be adjusted because the project "building a house" is very extensive, however all topics are useful and usable

| | |
|---|---|
| **Business Case** | Why? – Analysis of the project undertaking, investment project, benefit of the project |
| **Organization** | Who? – Distribution of roles |
| **Quality** | What? – House with basement, 1. floor 2. floor, garden, window ... |
| **Plans** | How will the finished project look like? How much/what resources are required? When should each work segment be carried out? |
| **Risks** | What if ... ? Plan how potential risks will be treated, for example, if the color of the floor looks different from planned. |
| **Changes** | How do changes effect the entire project? – If the [floor] laminate is reordered, schedule is delayed. Otherwise, the color variation has to be accepted. |
| **Progress** | Where do we stand? – Start-up phase, building site found Where are we going? – Laying the foundation stone, basement construction Should we continue? – Yes |

Tab. 21: Example Prince2 – Subjects.

**c) Processes** can be adapted, however as the project "house construction" is very extensive, all processes are useful and usable

| | |
|---|---|
| **Preparing (SU)** | The project idea (investment) is further developed to a concrete project proposal (house construction), a business case is created, experiences tested and the procedure is planned. |
| **Initiate (IP)** | Planning of the whole project, adaptation of the project management methodology (topics and processes). |
| **Managing (DP)** | The activities of the steering committee will be established. |
| **Steering (CS)** | The project manager monitors the project progress, updates and monitors plans. |
| **Managing Product Delivery (MP)** | The project manager submits work packages (e. g. basement construction) to the team manager, who in turn provides a phase result. |
| **Managing a Stage Boundary (SB)** | It a phase has been completed, it will be documented, what has been done (the basement built), which challenges were encountered (water pipe for pool had to be manufactured separately), how was this task solved (expert), was there an effect on the project? (No time delay). |
| **Closure (CP)** | The finished project is completed, experience documented and processed (also in case of project cancellation). |

Tab. 22: Example Prince2 – Processes.

## 8.4 Scrum

Das Wort Scrum stammt ursprünglich aus dem Rugby und bezeichnet das Gedränge der Spieler zu Beginn eines Spiel-Neustarts. Dieses Wort ist auch Namensgeber einer agilen Projektmanagementmethode, in der täglich ein Zusammentreffen des Projektteams stattfindet (daily Scrum). Die Scrum-Methodik reduziert das Vorgehen des klassischen Projektmanagements, mit der Begründung, dass die Planung komplexer Systeme in der Realität meist nur mangelhaft umsetzbar ist.

Scrum ist ein empirisches, inkrementelles und iteratives System, das heißt, es beruht auf Erfahrungen, ist schrittweise aufeinander aufbauend und wiederholt sich ständig.

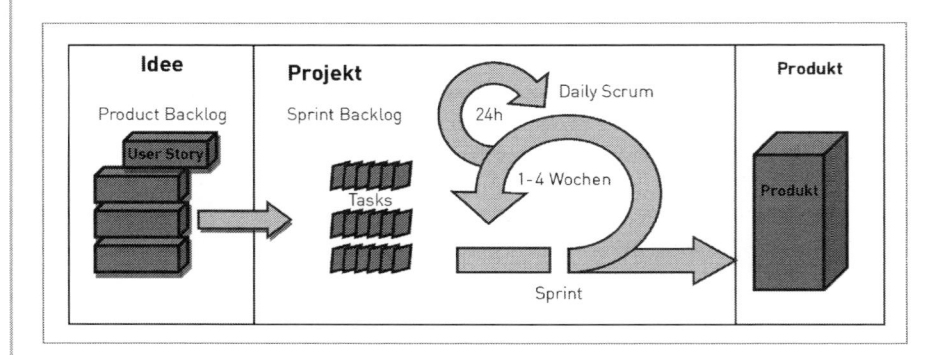

Abb. 50: Scrum-Prozess.

Die Komponenten des Vorgehensmodells „Scrum" lassen sich in drei Bereiche unterteilen. Diese umfassen Rollen, Zeremonien und Artefakte.

| Scrum | | | |
|---|---|---|---|
| Rollen | | Zeremonien | Artefakte |
| **Scrum Team** | **Externe** | | |
| Product Owner<br>Scrum Master<br>Entwicklerteam | Management<br>Costumer<br>User | Sprint Planning<br>Sprint Review<br>Daily Scrum | Product Backlog<br>Sprint Backlog<br>Burndown Chart |

Tab. 23: Scrum-Komponenten.

## 8.4 Scrum

The word Scrum originates from Rugby "Scrum", which refers to the huddle at the new start of a game. This term has also provided the name to an agile project management method in which the project team meets daily (daily Scrum). The Scrum method reduces the action of the classic project management, with the justification that the planning of complex systems in the real world usually provides inferior results.

Scrum is an empirical, incremental and iterative system, which means that it is based on experience, is step-by-step based on each other and is constantly repeated.

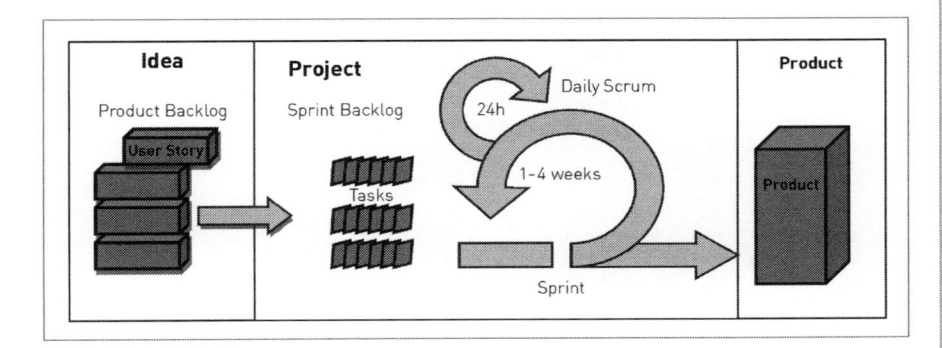

Fig. 50: Scrum-Process.

The components of the process model "Scrum" can be grouped into three categories, these include: roles, ceremonies and artifacts.

| Scrum | | | |
|---|---|---|---|
| Roles | | Ceremonies | Artifacts |
| Scrum team | External | | |
| Product owner<br>Scrum master<br>Development team | Management<br>Costumer<br>User | Sprint planning<br>Sprint review<br>Daily Scrum | Product backlog<br>Sprint backlog<br>Burndown chart |

Tab. 23: Scrum-Components.

## Rollen

Die unterschiedlichen Rollen lassen sich in das Scrum Team und in außenstehende Beteiligte einteilen. Im Scrum Team befinden sich der Product Owner, der Scrum Master und das Entwicklungsteam. Externe Beteiligte sind das Management, der Customer und der User.

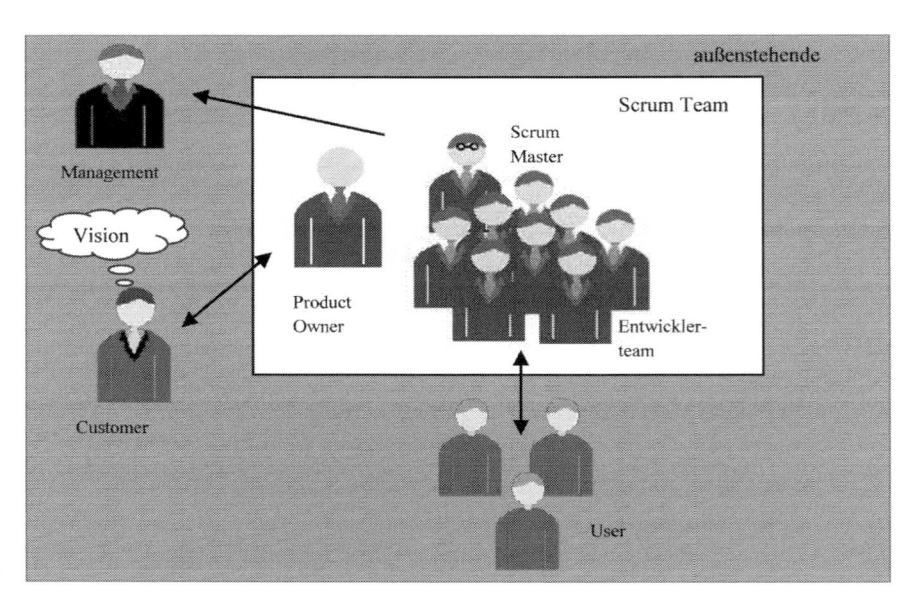

Abb. 51: Scrum-Rollen.

**Management**
Das Management legt die Rahmenbedingungen für das Projekt fest, es sorgt zum Beispiel für adäquate Räume und die richtigen Arbeitsmittel. Darüber hinaus ist es seine Aufgabe, den Scrum Master bei der Beseitigung von Hindernissen zu unterstützen.

**Customer**
Der Customer ist der Auftraggeber des Projekts, hierbei kann es sich um einen internen Auftraggeber (zum Beispiel eine Fachabteilung) oder um einen externen Kunden handeln. Der Customer steht für die Dauer des Projekts im engen Austausch mit dem Project Owner und gibt nach den ersten Sprints ein Feedback.

**User**
Der Customer kann der User, der Benutzer des Produkts, sein. Dieser Fall ist jedoch nicht immer gegeben. Es kann auch ein Customer ein Produkt erstellen lassen, das wiederum für seinen Kunden als eigentlicher User gedacht ist. Es ist empfehlenswert, ein Feedback des Users beim ersten Sprint Planning und bei der Sprint Review einzuholen.

**Product Owner**
Der Product Owner ist für die strategische Produktentwicklung zuständig, seine Aufgabe ist die Erstellung und Kommunikation einer klaren Produktvision. Weiter liegt es in seinem Aufgabenbereich, die einzelnen Produkteigenschaften festzulegen und zu priorisieren. Er ist dafür zuständig, die jeweiligen Sprint-Ergebnisse zu beurteilen

## Roles

The different roles can be divided into the Scrum team and external stakeholders. The Scrum team consists of the product owner, the Scrum master and the development team. External stakeholders are the management, the customer and the user.

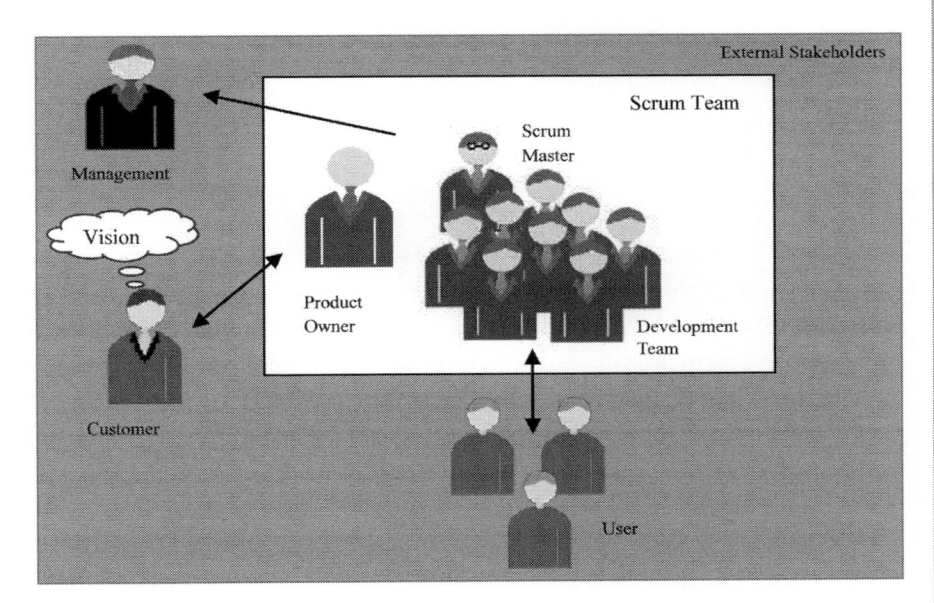

Fig. 51: Scrum-Roles.

**Management**
The management defines the framework for the project, provides for adequate rooms for example and the right equipment. In addition, it has the task to support the Scrum master by removing obstacles.

**Customer**
The customer is the sponsor of the project, this can be an internal client (for example, a specialist department) or an external customer. The customer stands for the duration of the project in close interaction with the project owner and provides feedback after the first sprint.

**User**
The customer can be the user of the product. However, this is not always the case. A customer can also create a product for his customers, who in turn are considered the actual user. It is recommended to obtain user feedback at the first sprint planning session and at the sprint review.

**Product Owner**
The product owner is responsible for the strategic product development, it is his task to create and communicate a clear product vision. It is further within his the scope of responsibilities to define and prioritize the individual product characteristics. He is responsible to assess the respective sprint results and to decide on the delivery, the functionality, as well as the costs. The product owner is in continuous contact with the customer.

und über den Auslieferungszeitpunkt, die Funktionalität sowie die Kosten zu entscheiden. Der Product Owner steht im fortlaufenden Kontakt mit dem Customer.

Der Product Owner legt im Product Backlog die Produkteigenschaften fest. In dieses Product Backlog werden von Product Owner und Entwicklungsteam auch sämtliche User Stories (Leistungsansprüche des Benutzers an das Produkt) eingetragen. Nach diesen User Stories entwirft und priorisiert der Product Owner die Produkteigenschaften.

**Scrum Master**
Im Idealfall wird der Scrum Master vom Entwicklerteam gewählt; er arbeitet eng mit dem Team zusammen, gehört jedoch nicht zu den eigentlichen Entwicklern dazu. Eine seiner Aufgaben ist es, zu beachtende Regeln innerhalb des Scrum-Prozesses aufzustellen und ihre Einhaltung zu überprüfen. Des Weiteren übernimmt er bei Meetings die Funktion des Moderators. Er beseitigt während des Prozesses auftretende (interne und externe) Störungen. Der Scrum Master stellt eine Führungskraft, aber keinen Vorgesetzten dar. Er ist vielmehr eine dienende Führungskraft.

Der Scrum Master verwendet das Impediment Backlog, um Hindernisse (impediments) zu dokumentieren.

**Entwicklungsteam**
Die Mitglieder des Entwicklungsteams bearbeiten mit dem Product Owner das Product Backlog. Sie schätzen den Umfang einer jeden User Story und des Umsetzens dieser Stories in einzelne Arbeitsschritte (Tasks). Eine jede Task soll ungefähr einen Tag Bearbeitung in Anspruch nehmen. Es ist die Aufgabe des Entwicklungsteams, die Lösung der Tasks in der vom Product Owner vorgegebenen Reihenfolge zu präsentieren, über die Anzahl der Tasks pro Sprint entscheiden sie jedoch selbst. Vereinbarte Qualitätsstandards sind stets einzuhalten.

| Product Owner | Scrum Master | Entwicklerteam |
|---|---|---|
| für das Was | für den Prozess | für das Wie |
| vertritt alle Interessengruppen außerhalb des Projektteams | Coach für die Anwendung von Scrum | Optimale Größe: 7 +/-2 |
| gibt die Vision vor | hilft dem Team (Beseitigung der organisatorischen Hindernisse) | interdisziplinär besetzt |
| formalisiert die Anforderungen im Product Backlog | schützt vor störenden Einflüssen und Versuchen der „Einmischung" | Alle Fähigkeiten, um das fertige Produkt zu erstellen, sind vorhanden |
| Anforderungen nach Geschäftswert priorisiert | arbeitet mit dem Product Owner zusammen und unterstützt bei der Priorisierung nach geschäftlichen Nutzen | muss die Vision des PO verstehen |

Tab. 24: Übersicht Product Owner, Scrum Master und Entwicklerteam.

The product owner sets the product properties in the product backlog. In this product backlog, the product owner and development team also document all the user stories (entitlements to performance of the product by the user). According to these user stories, the product owner designs and prioritizes the product properties.

**Scrum Master**
Ideally, the Scrum master is selected by the development team; he works closely with the team, but does not actually belong to the developers. One of his tasks is to establish rules to be observed within the Scrum process and to verify that they are met. Additionally he assumes the function of the moderator during meetings. He eliminates during the process problems that occur (internally and externally). The Scrum master is a leader, but not a manager. Rather he is a subordinate manager.

The Scrum master uses the impediment backlog to document obstacles (impediments.

**Development Team**
The members of the development team work on the product backlog with the product owner. They estimate the extent of each user story and the implementation of these stories in individual work steps (tasks). Each task should require approximately one day of processing. It is the task of the development team, to present the solution of the tasks in the order provided by the product owner, they decide themselves on the number of tasks per sprint. Agreed to quality standards must be observed at all times.

| Product Owner | Scrum Master | Development Team |
| --- | --- | --- |
| For the what | For the process | For the how |
| Represents all stakeholders outside the project team | Coach for the application of Scrum | Optimal size: 7 +/-2 |
| Provides the vision | Helps the team (removal of organizational barriers) | Interdisciplinary staffed |
| Formalizes the requirements in the product backlog | Protects against disruptive influences and attempts of "interference" | All of the necessary skills to create the finished product are available |
| Requirements prioritized according to business value | Working together with the product owner and support the prioritization according to business value | Must understand the vision of the PO |
| Changes in the product backlog are allowed | Cares for the support and recognition of the agile principles by all project participants | Organizes and manages himself |

Tab. 24: Overview Product Owner, Scrum Master and Development Team.

| Änderungen im Product Backlog sind erlaubt | sorgt für die Unterstützung und Anerkennung der agilen Prinzipien durch alle Projektbeteiligten | organisiert und verwaltet sich selbst |
|---|---|---|
| | | verpflichtet sich, vereinbarte Ziele zu erreichen |
| | | Jeder trägt mit seinem gesamten Wissen zum Erfolg bei (unabhängig von hierarchischer Position und formeller Qualifikation) |
| | | Vertrauenskultur: Es wird davon ausgegangen, dass jeder immer sein Bestes gibt |

Tab. 24 (Fortsetzung): Übersicht Product Owner, Scrum Master und Entwicklerteam.

## Zeremonien

**1. Sprint Planning Meeting**

Beim ersten Sprint Planning Meeting steht das Was im Vordergrund. Der Project Owner stellt die priorisierten User Stories aus seinem Product Backlog vor. Das Entwicklerteam hält die Ausführungen und Vorgaben des Project Owners schriftlich fest. Ist der User selbst anwesend, kann er erklären, was er wünscht. Als weiterer Punkt wird im ersten Sprint Planning Meeting festgelegt, welche Kriterien entscheidend sind, damit die Aufgabe am Ende des Sprints als erfüllt oder unfertig bewertet werden kann. Zusätzlich wird innerhalb des ersten Sprint Planning Meetings vom Entwicklerteam festgelegt, wie viele User Stories für den nächsten Sprint aufgenommen werden können.

Die Dauer des ersten Sprint Planning Meetings orientiert sich an der Länge der Sprint-Phase, man legt 60 Minuten Planung je Sprint-Woche fest.

**2. Sprint Planning Meeting**

Das zweite Sprint Planning Meeting findet im Idealfall am selben Tag statt wie das erste Sprint Planning Meeting. Anders als beim ersten Meeting geht es hierbei um das Wie der Umsetzung. Es werden die technischen Schritte geklärt. Beim zweiten Sprint Planning Meeting handelt es sich um ein vom Entwicklerteam eigenständig organisiertes Meeting. Die im Sprint zu behandelnden User Stories werden weiter in kleinere Tasks unterteilt. Eine Task sollte innerhalb eines Tages bearbeitet sein können. Die User Story und die dazugehörigen Tasks werden auf einem Task Board festgehalten und dargestellt.

|  |  | Undertakes to achieve agreed to objectives |
|---|---|---|
|  |  | Everyone contributes to the success with all his knowledge (regardless of hierarchical position and formal qualification) |
|  |  | Culture of trust: it is assumed that each always gives his best |

Tab. 24 (Continuation): Overview Product Owner, Scrum Master and Development Team.

## Ceremonies

**1. Sprint Planning Meeting**
During the first sprint planning meeting the what is in the foreground. The project owner introduces the prioritized user stories from the product backlog. The development team documents the statement and specifications of the project owners in writing. The user himself is present and can explain what he wants. As a further point, during the first sprint planning meeting is set which criteria are critical, so that the task at the end of the sprint can be assessed as met or unfinished. Additional within the first sprint planning meeting the developers set how many user stories can be included in the next sprint.

The duration of the first sprint planning meeting is based on the length of the sprint-phase, one sets 60 minutes planning per sprint week.

**2. Sprint Planning Meeting**
The second sprint planning meeting is ideally on the same day as the first sprint planning meeting. Unlike the first meeting, this is about the how of the implementation. The technical steps are being clarified. The second sprint planning meeting is a meeting organized independently by the developers themselves. The user stories, which will be discussed during the next sprint phase, will be further divided into smaller tasks. A task should be completed within a day. The user story and the associated tasks are recorded and displayed on a task board.

Auch die Dauer des zweiten Sprint Planning Meetings orientiert sich an der Länge der Sprint-Phase, man legt ebenfalls 60 Minuten Planung je Sprint-Woche fest.

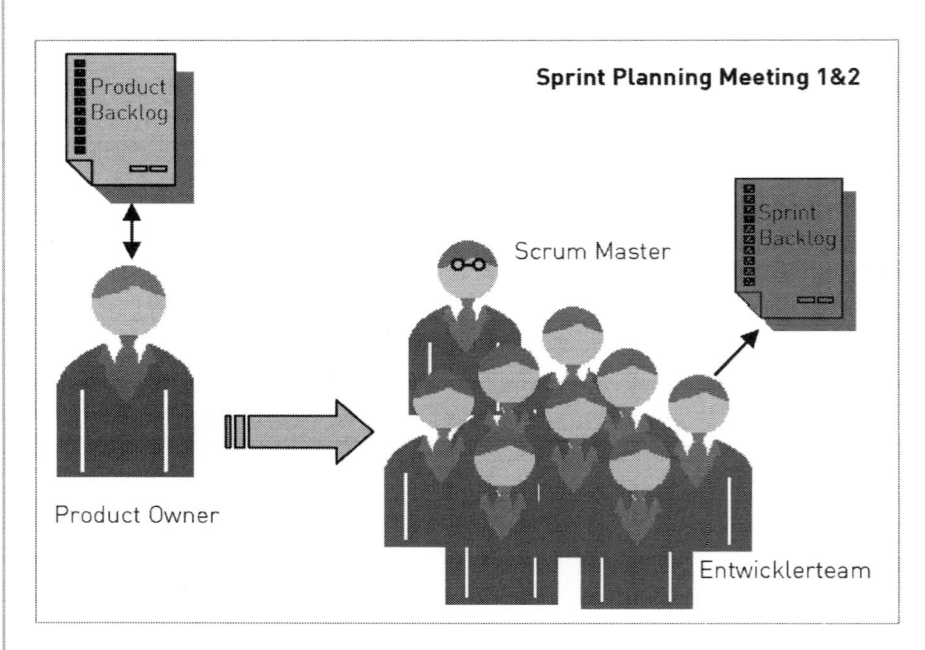

Abb. 52: Sprint Planning Meeting 1 & 2.

**Daily Scrum**
Jeden Tag wird zur selben Zeit ein 15-minütiges Scrum Meeting durchgeführt, am besten zu Beginn des Arbeitstages. Aufgrund der Kürze und um die Einhaltung der Zeit zu gewähren, empfiehlt es sich, diese Meetings im Stehen durchzuführen. Bei diesem Daily Scrum wird ein Überblick über den aktuellen Stand des Projektes gegeben. Jedes Entwicklungsteammitglied stellt mit Hilfe des Task Boards dar, was es seit dem letzten Daily Scrum erreicht hat, was bis zum nächsten geplant ist und was zur Realisierung dieses Zieles im Wege steht. Tasks, die sich als zu groß für einen Tag erweisen, werden moduliert und auf mehrere Teammitglieder aufgeteilt.

**Sprint**
Als Sprint wird die Phase zwischen erstem/zweitem Sprint Planning Meeting und der Fertigstellung der dort geplanten Funktionalitäten bezeichnet. Es handelt sich also um die Phase der Umsetzung der Tasks, somit der Realisierung der User Story, entlang vorher festgelegter Punkte. Während der Sprint-Phase trägt das Entwicklungsteam die Verantwortung das Ziel zu erreichen. Stellt das Team fest, dass die Erreichung des Sprint-Ziels unmöglich ist, darf der Product Owner den Sprint abbrechen. Es erfolgt dann keine Review, sondern gleich eine Retrospektive, danach wird mit dem nächsten ersten Sprint Planning Meeting begonnen. Die abgebrochene User Story wird vom Product Owner wieder in das Product Backlog aufgenommen und neu priorisiert.

Die Länge der Sprint-Phase soll innerhalb eines Projektes immer gleich sein und beträgt zwischen einer und maximal vier Wochen.

The duration of the second sprint planning meetings is based on the length of the sprint-phase, one also sets 60 minutes planning per sprint week.

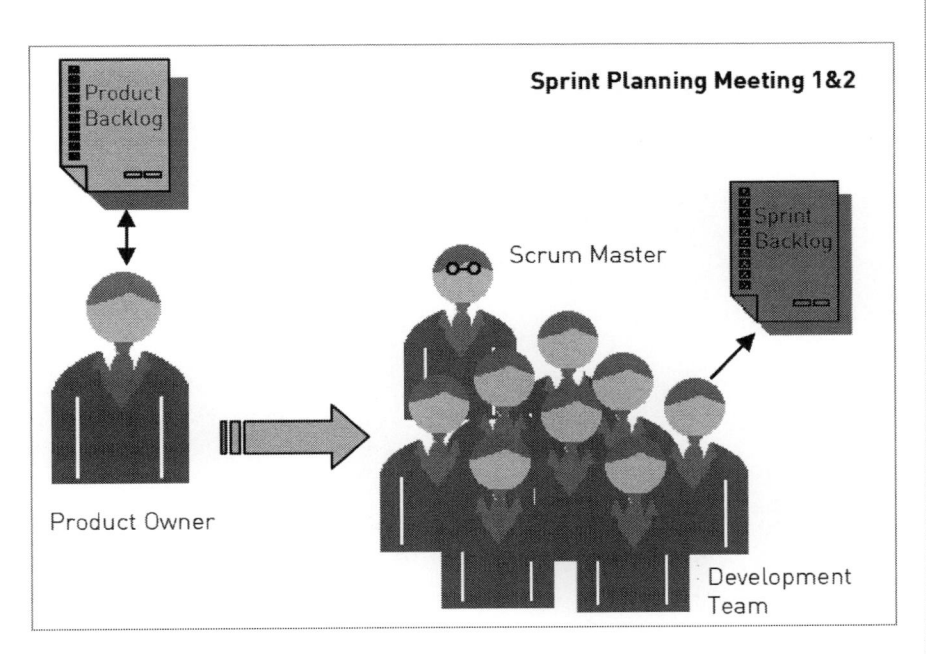

Fig. 52: Sprint Planning Meeting 1 & 2.

**Daily Scrum**
At the same time every day a 15-minute Scrum meeting is conducted, best at the beginning of the working day. Due to a shortness and in order to ensure compliance with the time, it is recommended that these meetings are conducted standing up. In this daily Scrum, an overview of the current status of the project is provided. Each development team standing member shows by using the task board what has been achieved since the last daily Scrum, and what is planned until the next planned Scrum and what stands in the way of the objective. Tasks, which are too large for a day, will be modulated and divided amongst several team members.

**Sprint**
Sprint is the name of the phase between first / second sprint planning meeting and the completion of the planned functionalities. It is therefore the phase of implementation of the tasks, thus the realization of the user story, along predetermined points. The development team bears the responsibility to reach the goal during the sprint-phase. If the team finds that the achievement of the sprint goal is impossible, the product owner may cancel the sprint. In that case, no review but a retrospective is conducted, and then the next first sprint planning meeting begins. The abandoned user story is put back into the product backlog and newly prioritized by the product owner.

The length of the sprint-phase within a project should always be the same and lasts between one and a maximum of four weeks.

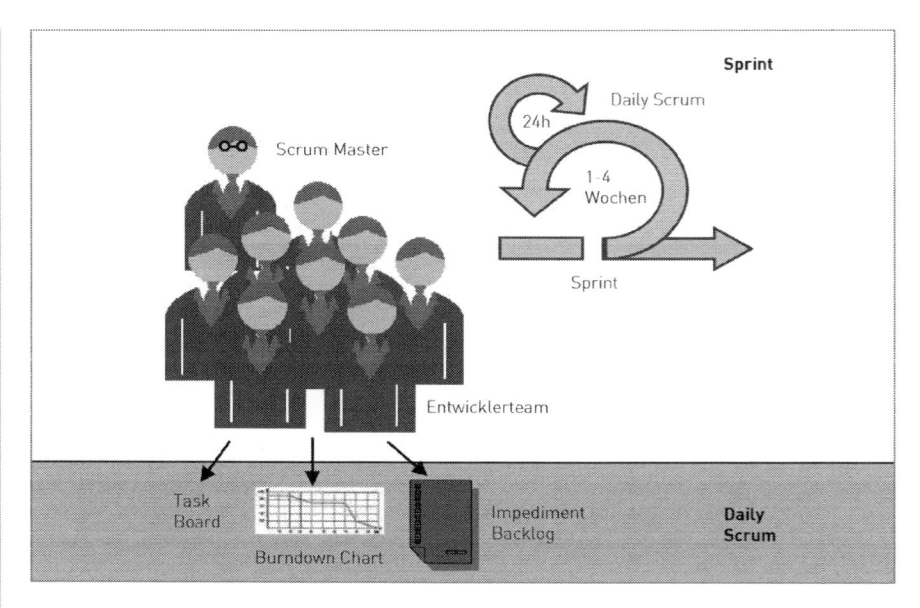

Abb. 53: Sprint & Daily Scrum.

**Sprint Review**
Die Sprint Review findet am Ende des Sprints statt. Das Entwicklungsteam stellt die Ergebnisse vor und überprüft anhand der vorher festgelegten Kriterien, ob das Ziel erreicht wurde. Auch der Product Owner bewertet das Ergebnis, Kompromisse werden nicht zugelassen. Ist eine User Story noch in Bearbeitung, wird sie wieder in das Product Backlog aufgenommen und vom Product Owner neu priorisiert.

Die Teilnahme des Users am Sprint Review ist besonders wichtig, um das bisher Erstellte zu testen. Der Scrum Master notiert mögliche neue Spezifikationen und leitet diese an den Project Owner weiter.

Die Sprint Review soll kürzer als 90 Minuten sein.

**Retrospektive**
Die Retrospektive wird zwischen Sprint Review und nächstem ersten Sprint Planning Meeting gehalten. Gegenstand dieses Meetings ist die Reflektion des Geleisteten und Aufarbeitung von Verbesserungsmaßnahmen. Hierfür eignet sich die Darstellung des letzten Sprints mit Hilfe eines Zeitstrahls. Danach wird auf separaten Flipcharts dargestellt, was gut verlief und was verbessert werden kann. Die verbesserungswürdigen Bereiche werden wiederum in teaminterne Punkte und externe Bereiche unterteilt. Anschließend werden beide nach Dringlichkeit sortiert. Der Scrum Master nimmt sich den externen Bereichen an, teaminterne Punkte werden auch vom Projektteam selbst gelöst.

Die Retrospektive soll eine Länge von 90 Minuten umfassen.

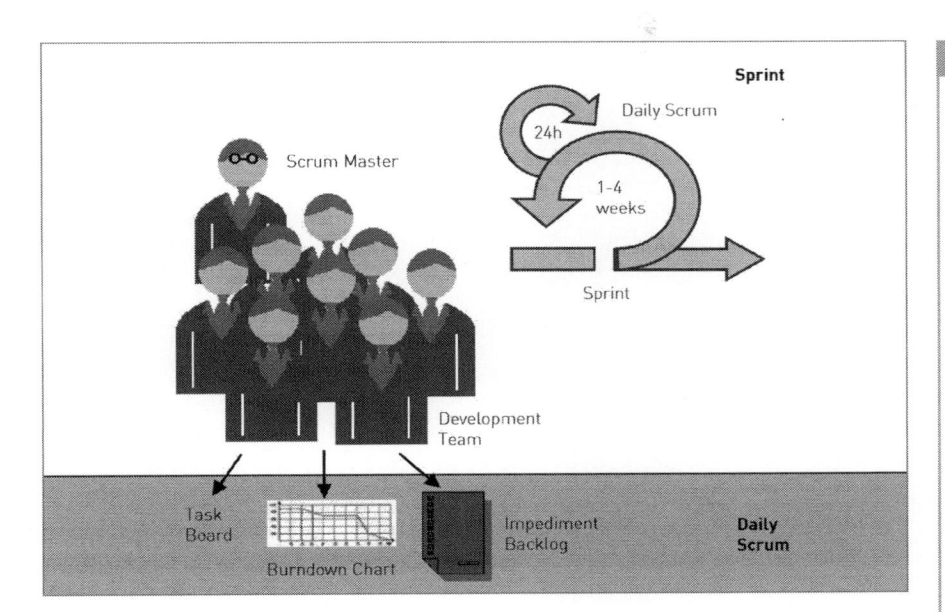

Fig. 53: Sprint & Daily Scrum.

**Sprint Review**
The sprint review takes place at the end of the sprint. The development team will present the results and validates if the target has been achieved by the previously defined criteria. Also the product owner evaluates the result, compromises are not allowed. If a user story is still in progress, it will be again included in the product backlog and re-prioritized by the product owner.

The participation of the user in the sprint review is particularly important in order to test all created until now. The Scrum master notes possible new specifications and forwards them to the project owner.

The sprint review should be shorter than 90 minutes.

**Retrospektive**
The retrospective will be held between sprint review and next first sprint planning meeting. The purpose of this meeting is the reflection of the achieved and discussion of improvement measures. For this the representation of the last sprint can used using a timeline. Later what was good and what could be improved will be shown on separate flip charts. The targeted areas are in turn divided into team internal points and external areas. Both are then sorted by urgency. The Scrum master will address the external areas the team internal points are resolved by the project team itself.

The retrospective should take about 90 minutes.

Abb. 54: Sprint Review & Retrospektive.

| 1. Sprint Planning Meeting | 2. Sprint Planning Meeting | Daily Scrum | Sprint Review | Retrospektive |
|---|---|---|---|---|
| Voraussetzung ist ein gepflegtes Product Backlog (PBL). Das heißt es sollte:<br>– existieren,<br>– nach Geschäftswert priorisiert sein und<br>– jeder Eintrag sollte ein Abnahmekriterium enthalten | Einträge des Sprint Backlogs werden in Aufgaben von maximal 1 Tag Aufwand aufgebrochen | täglich, stehend, < 15 min. | Präsentation und „Abnahme" der fertig gestellten Product-Backlog-Einträge | Was ist gut gelaufen?<br>Was kann verbessert werden?<br>Wer packt es an? |
| Das Team wählt so viele Einträge aus dem PBL aus, wie es denkt, im Sprint umsetzen zu können | Ziel für den Sprint wird erstellt | Was habe ich seit gestern erledigt?<br>Was mache ich bis morgen?<br>Was hindert mich/hat mich gehindert? | Überprüfung des Sprint-Zieles | |
| Product Owner steht für etwaige Rückfragen bereit | Termine für Sprint Review und das tägliche Statusmeeting werden ausgemacht | Das Team aktualisiert:<br>– Sprint Backlog<br>– Burndown Chart (Wie viele Aufgaben sind noch zu erledigen?)<br>– Liste der Hindernisse (Impediment Backlog) | Feedback der Beteiligten, evtl. neue Einträge im PBL | |

Tab. 25: Übersicht Zeremonien Scrum.

Fig. 54: Sprint Review & Retrospektive.

| 1. Sprint Planning Meeting | 2. Sprint Planning Meeting | Daily Scrum | Sprint Review | Retrospektive |
|---|---|---|---|---|
| A prerequisite is a well-maintained product backlog (PBL). i. e. it should<br>– exist<br>– be prioritized according to business value<br>– each entry should contain an acceptance criterion | Entries in the sprint backlog tasks are broken into a maximum of 1 day effort | Every day, standing, < 15 min | Presentation and "acceptance" of the finished product backlog entries | What went well?<br>What can be improved?<br>Who does it? |
| The team chooses as many entries from the PBL, as it feels to be able to implement during the sprint | The objective for the sprint is created | What have I achieved since yesterday?<br>What do I do until tomorrow?<br>What hindes me/has hindered me? | Review of the sprint objective | |
| Product owner is available for potential questions | Dates for sprint review and the daily status meeting will be identified | The team updates:<br>Sprint backlog burndown chart (how many tasks are still to be done?)<br>List of obstacles (impediment backlog) | Feedback from the participants, possibly new entries in the PBL | |

Tab. 25: Overview Scrum Ceremonies.

## Artefakte

**Product Backlog**

Das Product Backlog wird vom Product Owner bearbeitet. Hier werden die Anforderungen des zu entwickelnden Produktes in einer priorisierten Liste notiert. Die Gewichtung der Aufgaben wird anhand des wirtschaftlichen Nutzens, des Risikos und der Notwendigkeit festgelegt. Die Anforderungen an das Produkt sind stets benutzerorientiert, da sie anhand der aus Endbenutzersicht erstellten User Stories gesammelt werden. Die User Stories müssen mindestens die drei Fragen – Wer? Was? Wozu? – beantworten können. Ändert sich eine Anforderung im Laufe des Gesamtprozesses, so ändert sich diesbezüglich auch das Product Backlog.

**Sprint Backlog**

Das Sprint Backlog liefert eine Übersicht der zu erledigenden Aufgaben. Unterstützend kann hierzu ein Task Board verwendet werden. Das Task Board umfasst vier Spalten, in denen die Stories, Tasks to Do, der Work in Progress und erledigte Punkte (Done) dargestellt werden:

| Stories | Tasks to Do | Work in Progress | Done |
|---|---|---|---|
| A | a b c | b c | a |
| B | 1 2 3 | 3 | 1 2 |
| C | x y z | • x | |

Tab. 26: Taskboard.

War es unmöglich, eine Task innerhalb des dafür vorgesehenen Tages zu erledigen, wird diese mit einem Punkt markiert.

**Burndown Chart**

Anhand eines Burndown Charts werden die bereits geleistete Arbeit und die noch verbleibende dargestellt. Es werden das Sprint Burndown Chart, das Story Burndown Chart und das Release Burndown Chart unterschieden: Mit dem Sprint Burndown Chart wird die Erreichung des Sprint-Ziels in Bezug zu den einzelnen Tasks eines Sprints visualisiert. Auf der X-Achse ist der Zeitverlauf, auf der Y-Achse sind die offenen Tasks vermerkt.

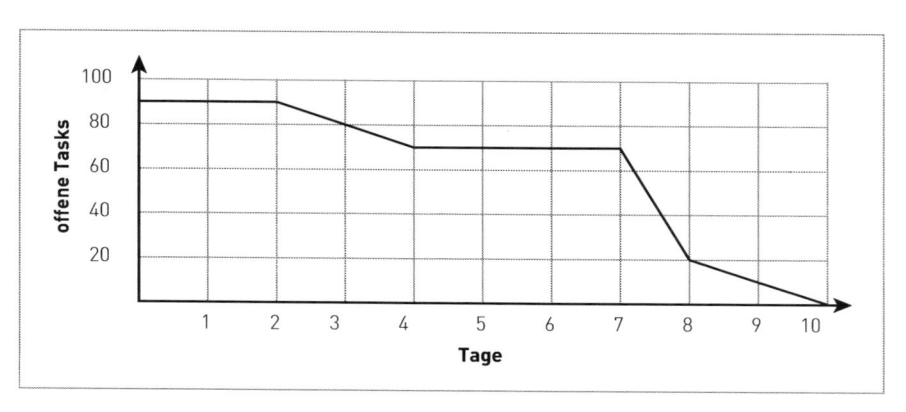

Abb. 55: Sprint Burndown Chart.

## Artifacts

### Product Backlog

The product owner processes the product backlog. Here the requirements of the product to be developed are noted in a prioritized list. The weighting of the tasks will be based on the economic benefits, the risk and the need. The product requirements are always based on user's intent, because they collected based on the user stories, which are created from the view of the end user. The user stories must at least be able to answer the three questions who? What? What do they do with it? If a request changes in the course of the overall process, this changes also the product backlog.

### Sprint Backlog

The sprint backlog provides an overview of the tasks to be accomplished. A task board can be used in support the task board consists of four columns in which the stories, tasks to do, the work in progress, and completed items (done) are shown:

| Stories | Tasks to Do | Work in Progress | Done |
|---|---|---|---|
| A | a b c | b c | a |
| B | 1 2 3 | 3 | 1 2 |
| C | x y z | • x | |

Tab. 26: Taskboard.

If it was impossible to complete a task within the designated day, it will be marked with a red dot.

### Burndown Chart

The burndown charts illustrate completed and remaining work. One differentiates between the sprint burndown chart, the story burndown chart and the release burndown chart:

The sprint burndown chart visualizes the achievement of the sprint objective in reference to the individual tasks of a sprint. On the X-axis is the time, on the Y-axis the open tasks are noted.

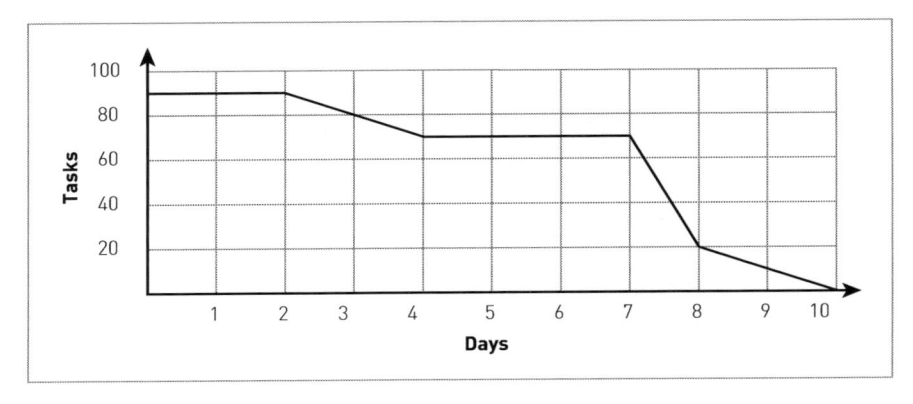

Fig. 55: Sprint Burndown Chart.

**Notizen**

Noch unbearbeitete User Stories werden auf dem Story Burndown Chart dargestellt. Der unterschiedliche Arbeitsumfang verschiedener User Stories wird durch variierende Punktgröße visualisiert. Auf der X-Achse ist die Dauer eines Sprints, auf der Y-Achse die Summe der verbleibenden User Story Points vermerkt.

Das Release Burndown Chart dient zur Darstellung des Gesamtprojektes, die X-Achse stellt die Sprints dar, die Y-Achse vermerkt die offenen User Stories.

**Impediment Backlog**
Im Impediment Backlog notiert der Scrum Master die aktuell auftretenden Hindernisse, wann sie zuerst eintraten und wann sie beseitigt wurden.

| Product Backlog | Sprint Backlog | Burndown Chart | Impediment Backlog |
|---|---|---|---|
| beinhaltet alle erwünschten Eigenschaften und Ergebnisse | beinhaltet Aufgaben zur Erreichung des Sprintziels | zeigt die verbleibenden Aufgaben eines Sprints | Hier werden Hindernisse vermerkt |
| Priorisierung durch den Product Owner (nach wirtschaftlichem Nutzen und Risiko) | Einträge, nach denen im Product Backlog gruppiert wird | wird täglich aktualisiert | kann zu neuen Aufgaben im Sprint Backlog führen |
| Änderungen jederzeit möglich | Organisationsbasis des Teams | steht im Idealfall am Ende des Sprints auf Null | wird vom Scrum Master gepflegt und verwaltet |
| kontinuierlich gepflegter Plan | Visualisierung auf Taskboard | | |

Tab. 27: Übersicht Artefakte Scrum.

Scrum ist eine einfach und schnell zu erlernende Projektmanagementmethode, für die aber bereits ein hohes Maß an Projekterfahrung vorhanden sein muss, um den anfallenden Aufgaben gerecht zu werden. Die Prozesse eines Projektes werden gut strukturiert dargestellt und die Flexibilität der Anforderungsumsetzung bietet eine dynamische Gestaltung. Dies kann aber wiederum auch zu einem Verlust des Gesamtüberblicks führen. Weitere Faktoren, welche die Verwendung der Scrum-Methode negativ beeinflussen können, sind mangelnd geregelte Zuständigkeiten und das Fehlen einer Führungsposition.

Yet unprocessed user stories are shown on the story burndown chart. The different scope of different user stories is visualized by varying dot size. On the X-axis is the duration of a sprint, on the Y-axis the sum of the remaining user story points is noted.

The release burndown chart is used for the representation of the overall project, the X-axis represents the sprints, and the Y-axis notes the open user stories.

**Impediment Backlog**
In the impediment backlog the Scrum master lists the current obstacles, when they first occurred and when they have been eliminated.

| Product Backlog | Sprint Backlog | Burndown Chart | Impediment Backlog |
|---|---|---|---|
| Includes all the desired properties and results | Includes tasks for the achievement of the sprint objective | Displays the remaining tasks of a sprint | Obstacles are noted here |
| Prioritization by the product owner (for economic benefit and risk) | Entries grouped according to those the product backlog | Will be updated on a daily basis | Can lead to new tasks in the sprint backlog |
| Changes are possible at any time | The organizational basis of the team | At the end of the sprint is ideally set to zero | Is maintained and managed by the Scrum master |
| Continuously maintained plan | Visualization on task board | | |

Tab. 27: Overview Scrum Artifacts.

Scrum is a simple and fast to learn project management method, for which a high level of project experience must be present in order to be able to meet the required tasks. The processes of a project are shown well structured and the flexibility of the requirements implementation offers a dynamic design. Which however lead to the loss of the overview. Other factors, which affect the use of the Scrum method negatively, are poorly defined competencies and the lack of a leadership position.

| Vorteile | Nachteile |
| --- | --- |
| + einfach und schnell zu erlernen | – hohes Maß an Projekterfahrung |
| + gut strukturierter Prozess | – Gesamtüberblick kann verloren gehen |
| + flexibel | – fehlende Führungsposition |
| + transparent | – ungeregelte Zuständigkeiten |
| + hoher Lernwert der Entwicklungsteammitglieder | |

Tab. 28: Vor- und Nachteile Scrum.

*Beispiel:*

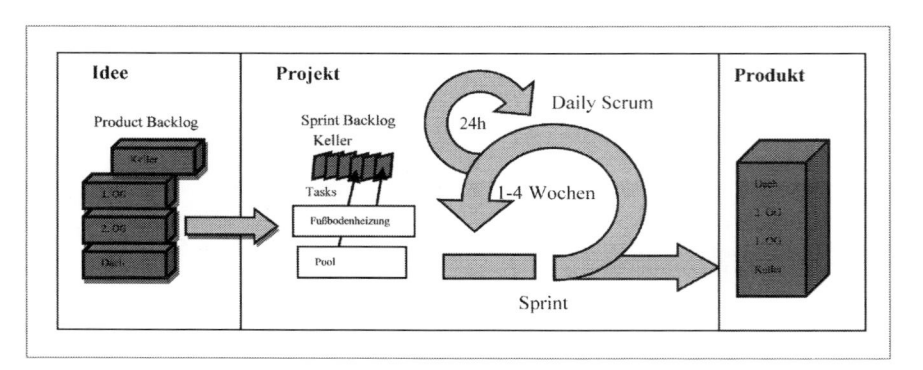

Abb. 56: Scrum-Beispiel-Projekt „Hausbau".

**Fragen zur Selbstkontrolle:**

8.1  Was sind die Unterschiede zwischen klassischem und agilem Projektmanagement?

8.2  Aus welchen Komponenten setzt sich das Projektmanagementmodell Prince2 zusammen?

8.3  Welche Rollen sind bei Prince2 anzutreffen?

8.4  Wie lässt sich Prince2 anpassen?

8.5  Aus welchen Komponenten setzt sich das Vorgehensmodell Scrum zusammen?

8.6  Welche Rollen sind im Scrum anzutreffen?

8.7  Was ist unter den Zeremonien zu verstehen?

8.8  Welche Artefakte werden verwendet?

| Benefits | Disadvantages |
|---|---|
| + Simple and easy to learn | – High level of project experience |
| + Well-structured process | – Overview can be lost |
| + Flexible | – Missing leadership |
| + Transparent | – Unclear competencies |
| + High value of learning of the development team members | |

Tab. 28: Benefits and Disadvantages Scrum.

*Example:*

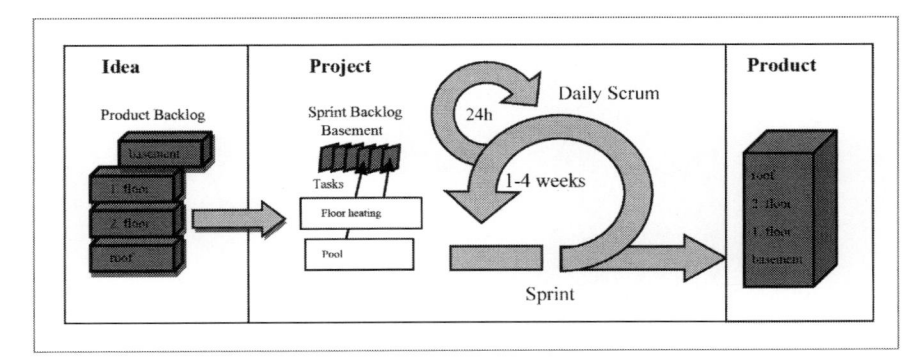

Fig. 56: Scrum Example Project "House Construction".

**Tasks for Progress Review:**

*8.1   What are the differences between classical and agile project management?*

*8.2   Which are the components of the project management model Prince2?*

*8.3   What roles can be found in Prince2?*

*8.4   How can Prince2 be adapted?*

*8.5   Which components are included in the process model Scrum?*

*8.6   What roles can be found in Scrum?*

*8.7   What means "ceremonies"?*

*8.8   What artifacts are used?*

## Notizen

Notes

# 9 Fallstudie

Das folgende Praxisbeispiel fasst die in diesem Werk behandelten Themen in einer konkreten Situation zusammen, um die Anwendung verständlich aufzuzeigen.

## 9.1 Ausgangssituation

In der betrachteten Organisation, die in sieben Abteilungen strukturiert ist, sind an fünf Standorten und einer Zentrale diverse operative und strategische Prozesse beherbergt. Die an der Zentrale angesiedelte Personalabteilung umfasst 14 Mitarbeiter, davon drei in der Personalentwicklung.

Ein Mitarbeiter der Personalentwicklung – Herr Mayer – hat die Idee, ein neues, integratives Personalentwicklungskonzept zu entwickeln und zu implementieren, da er im Rahmen der operativen Personalentwicklungen etliche Lücken im bestehenden Konzept feststellt.

Das vorliegende Beispiel beschreibt den Werdegang von der Projektidee bis hin zum Abschluss des Projektes.

### 9.1.1 Projekt und Abgrenzung zum Tagesgeschäft

Die Erstellung und Implementierung eines neuen Personalentwicklungskonzeptes stellt in der Personalabteilung ein Projekt dar: Eine neue, in dieser Form noch nicht vorhandene Situation wird in einem begrenzten Zeitraum mit begrenzten Ressourcen (Personal, Finanzen etc.) in einer eigenen Projektorganisation geschaffen. Das operative Personalgeschäft (Ermittlung von Personalentwicklungsbedarf, Planung, Durchführung und Nachbereitung/Evaluation von Personalentwicklungsmaßnahmen) grenzt sich von dieser Aufgabe deutlich ab.

### 9.1.2 Das magische Dreieck des Projektmanagements

Am vorliegenden Beispiel wird der Zusammenhang der Hauptfaktoren „Leistung/Qualität", „Termine" und „Kosten" deutlich.

Wenn beispielsweise das Projektbudget schlank ausfällt oder verschmälert wird, kann die Qualität des Konzeptes oder der Implementierung nur unter Terminverzug gehalten werden. Bei Veränderung des Endtermins (Zeitpunkt der Implementierung) ändern sich entweder die Qualität und/oder die Kosten des Projektes. Ähnlich verhält es sich mit Veränderungen an der Leistung/Qualität: Bei geringeren Anforderungen können kürzere Zeiten und/oder geringere Kosten anfallen.

# 9 Case Study

The following case study summarizes the topics addressed in this work in a specific situation, in order to show the application in an understandable way.

## 9.1 Initial Situation

Various operational and strategic processes are housed in the respective organization in five locations and a central operating center. The organization is structured in seven departments. The Human Resources department, which is based in the central operations center, includes 14 employees, three of them in the field of staff development.

A member of the staff of the human resources development – Mr. Mayer – has the idea to develop and implement a new, integrative concept for developing human resources, as he finds in the framework of the operational development some gaps in the existing concept.

The present example describes the development: From the project idea to the completion of the project.

### 9.1.1 Project and the Boundaries to the Day-to-Day Business

The creation and implementation of a new personnel development concept creates a project in the human resources department: A new, in this form, not yet existing situation in a limited period with limited resources (staff, finances, etc.) created in a separate project organization. The operational staffing business (identification of personnel development needs, planning, implementation and follow-up / evaluation of personnel development measures) differentiates significantly from this task.

### 9.1.2 The Magic Triangle of Project Management

In this example, the interaction of the main factors "performance / quality", "milestones" and "cost" is clarified.

For example, if the project budget is slight or gets reduced the quality of the concept or the implementation can only be kept with a delay. If the target date (date of the implementation) is changed either the quality and / or the cost of the project will equally change. Similarly, the situation changes when performance / quality is modified: for lesser requirements shorter times and / or lower cost may be incurred.

### 9.1.3 Phasenmodell

Das beschriebene Phasenmodell kann so zur Anwendung kommen, die Vorphase, Definitionsphase, Planungsphase, Realisierungsphase und Abschlussphase schließen jeweils mit einem Meilenstein ab.

## 9.2 Vorphase

Nachdem Herr Mayer mit dem Leiter der Personalabteilung seine Idee besprochen hat, entscheidet sich dieser nach ein paar Tagen Bedenkzeit dafür, dass erste Vorarbeiten durchgeführt werden können, damit das Projekt konkret werden kann.

### 9.2.1 Vorstudie

Zur Erstellung einer Vorstudie lädt Herr Mayer die beiden anderen Personalentwickler zu einem eintägigen Workshop ein. Herr Mayer nutzt einen organisationsinternen Moderator, der folgende abgestimmte Agenda an dem Tag unterbreitet.

---

**Integrative Personalentwicklung 2010 – Workshop-Agenda**
- *Ist-Zustand – Ziel-Zustand*
- *Zielbeschreibung*
- *wesentliche Arbeitsschritte zum Ziel-Zustand*
- *Meilensteine im Projekt*
- *Orte*
- *Rahmenbedingungen*
- *Projektabschlusskriterien*
- *Projektumfeld*
- *interessierte Parteien*
- *Projektrisiken*
- *Grobplanung: Arbeitspakete*
- *erste Ressourcenplanung*
- *erste Zeitplanung*
- *Entscheidungsvorbereitung: Start des Projektes*

---

Abb. 57: Projekt-Workshop.

Die beschriebenen Punkte werden innerhalb des Tagesworkshops bearbeitet. Nachfolgend werden einige Ergebnisse aus dem von Herrn Mayer verfassten Konzept dargestellt.

**Ziele**
Ein Ergebnisziel ist das Vorliegen eines integrativen Personalentwicklungskonzeptes, das die Bedarfe von Mitarbeitern und Führungskräften ebenso wie eine kurz-, mittel- und langfristige Planung der Personalentwicklung berücksichtigt. Ebenso ist es ein Ergebnisziel, dass das Konzept umgesetzt ist, das heißt operative Personalprozesse sich an dem Konzept orientieren.

## 9.1.3 Phase Model

The described phase model can be applied in this manner, the initial phase, definition phase, planning phase, implementation phase and final phase always conclude with a milestone.

## 9.2 Initial phase

After Mr. Mayer has discussed his idea with the head of the personnel department, the later provides his approval after a few days of a cooling-off period, to perform initial preparatory work, so that the project can be definitized.

### 9.2.1 Preliminary Study

To create a preliminary study Mr. Mayer invites the other two human resources developers to a one-day workshop. Mr. Mayer uses an organizational moderator, who submits the following coordinated agenda on the day of the workshop.

---

**Integrative Human Resources Development 2010 Workshop Agenda**
- *Status quo – target objective*
- *Target description*
- *Essential steps to target objective*
- *Milestones in the project*
- *Locations*
- *General Conditions*
- *Project completion criteria*
- *Project environment*
- *Interested parties*
- *Project risks*
- *Outline plan: work packages*
- *First resource planning*
- *First scheduling*

---

Fig. 57: Project Workshop.

The described items are processed within the one-day workshop; here you see some of the results from the written concept of Mr. Mayer.

**Objectives**
A target result is the existence of an integrative personnel development concept, which considers the requirements of employees and managers as well as a short, medium and long-term planning of personnel development. It is also a target that the concept is implemented, i. e. operational HR processes orientate themselves by the concept.

Vorgehensziele im Projekt sind systematisches Projektmanagement, Evaluation des Konzeptes, Partizipation aller Abteilungsleiter und einer Stichprobe von Mitarbeitern sowie die zielorientierte Zusammenarbeit des Projektteams.

| Meilensteine und grober Zeitplan | | |
|---|---|---|
| M090 | 14.07.2010 | Vorworkshop abgeschlossen |
| M091 | 19.07.2010 | Vorphase abgeschlossen |
| M092 | 19.07.2010 | Entscheidung pro Projekt |
| M093 | 09.08.2010 | Definitionsphase abgeschlossen |
| M094 | 13.09.2010 | Planungsphase abgeschlossen |
| M050 | 16.11.2010 | Konzept erstellt |
| M060 | 27.01.2011 | Konzept implementiert |
| M070 | 28.04.2011 | Konzept evaluiert |
| M089 | 28.04.2011 | Realisierungsphase abgeschlossen |
| M099 | 15.05.2011 | Projektabschluss |

Tab. 29: Fallbeispiel Meilensteine und Zeitplan.

**Wesentliche Teilaufgaben**

- Projektmanagement – verantwortlich: Hr. Mayer
- Konzepterstellung Workshop 1 Führungsebene – verantwortlich: Hr. Mayer
- Konzepterstellung Workshop 2 Mitarbeiter – verantwortlich: Hr. Mayer
- Konzepterstellung Workshop 3 Mix – verantwortlich: Hr. Mayer
- Implementierung Konzept – verantwortlich: Leiter Personalabteilung
- Evaluation Konzept – verantwortlich: Hr. Mayer

**Kernnutzen des Projekts**
Integrative Personalentwicklung berücksichtigt die Nachfrage sowohl von Mitarbeiterseite wie auch aus Führungssicht. Damit ist eine zielorientierte Personalentwicklung möglich, die zudem für eine höhere Mitarbeiterzufriedenheit sorgt.

**Projektabschlusskriterien**
Das Projekt kann abgeschlossen werden, wenn ein integratives Personalentwicklungskonzept vorliegt und mindestens 60 % der darin definierten Maßnahmen in die operative Personalarbeit integriert sind. Bei groben Unwägbarkeiten wird ein kontrollierter Projektabbruch durch den Projektleiter gemeinsam mit dem Personalleiter in die Wege geleitet.

Auch bei abgebrochenen und nicht beendeten Projekten ist es von besonderer Bedeutung einen Abschlussbericht zu erstellen, um die gemachten Erfahrungen zu dokumentieren und nutzen zu können.

Zur offiziellen Beendigung des Projekts wird eine Abschlusssitzung mit dem Auftraggeber durchgeführt, an der sowohl der Projektleiter als auch das Projektteam

Process targets of the project are systematic project management, evaluation of the concept, participation of all department heads and a representation of employees as well as the goal-oriented cooperation of the project team.

| Milestones and Outline Schedule | | |
|---|---|---|
| M090 | 14.07.2010 | Completed preliminary workshop |
| M091 | 19.07.2010 | Preparatory phase completed |
| M092 | 19.07.2010 | Decision per project |
| M093 | 09.08.2010 | Definition phase completed |
| M094 | 13.09.2010 | Planning phase completed |
| M050 | 16.11.2010 | Concept created |
| M060 | 27.01.2011 | Concept implemented |
| M070 | 28.04.2011 | Concept evaluated |
| M089 | 28.04.2011 | Implementation phase completed |
| M099 | 15.05.2011 | Project completion |

Tab. 29: Case Study Milestones and Outline Schedule.

**Essential Subtasks**

- Project management – responsible: Mr. Mayer
- Concept development workshop 1 senior management – responsible: Mr. Mayer
- Concept development workshop 2 employees – responsible: Mr. Mayer
- Concept development workshop 3 mix – responsible: Mr. Mayer
- Implementation concept – responsible: Human Resources director
- Evaluation concept – responsible: Mr. Mayer

**The Project Core Benefits**
Integrative personnel development takes into consideration the demand from both the employees as well as from management. With it a goal-oriented human resources development is possible, which also provides for a higher employee satisfaction.

**Project Completion Criteria**
The project can be completed, if there is an integrative concept for developing human resources and at least 60% of the defined measures are integrated in the operative HR work. In the event of gross uncertainties, the project manager together with the human resources managers initiates a controlled project cancellation.

For documentation purposes and further use the lessons learned also have to be written down in a final project report, even if the project was cancelled or not completed.

To give an official ending to the project a final meeting is held, in which both the project leader and the project team are participating. It is important to analyze and assess the results and processes. Together with consolidating the lessons learned, the performance of the team is honored.

teilnimmt. Es ist wichtig, hierbei die Ergebnisse und Prozesse zu analysieren und zu bewerten. Neben der Sicherstellung gesammelter Erfahrungen werden auch die Leistungen des Projektteams gewürdigt.

Je nach Umfang und Dauer der Projektarbeit ist es erforderlich, die Teammitglieder wieder in das normale Alltagsgeschäft zu reintegrieren. Daher ist es wichtig ein Projekt auch auf emotionaler Ebene, beispielsweise mit einem Abschlussfest, zu beenden und das Team aufzulösen. Siehe hierzu auch das Kapitel 7 zum Thema Teamentwicklung.

**Projektumfeld, Stakeholder**
Die Projektumfeldanalyse ergibt Folgendes:

| Interessens-gruppe | Nähe zum Projekt (1–3) | Einfluss auf das Projekt (1–3) | Prioritätsziffer (Nähe x Einfluss) |
|---|---|---|---|
| Geschäftsführung | 2 | 3 | 6 |
| Abteilungsleiter | 2 | 2 | 4 |
| Personalabteilung | 3 | 3 | 9 |
| Personalrat | 2 | 2 | 4 |
| Mitarbeiter allgemein | 1 | 1 | 1 |
| Mitarbeiter Personalabteilung | 3 | 2 | 6 |
| Projektleiter | 3 | 3 | 9 |
| Projektmitarbeiter | 3 | 3 | 9 |
| Kunden | 1 | 1 | 1 |
| Lieferanten | 1 | 1 | 1 |

Tab. 30: Fallbeispiel Projektumfeldanalyse.

Die Prioritätsziffer dient dem Projektleiter dazu, den Fokus auf die Interessensgruppen mit hoher Priorität zu lenken.

Als projektbeteiligte Stakeholder werden folgende Personengruppen identifiziert:

- Lenkungsausschuss Projekt (Geschäftsführung, Personalleitung, Projektleitung)
- Projektleiter
- Projektteam
- Projektmitarbeiter
- Betroffene des Projekts: Mitarbeiter

Die durchgeführte Risikoanalyse ergibt ein identisches Bild wie die in Kapitel 2.1 dargestellte Abbildung 6. Als stellvertretender Projektleiter wird die stellvertretende Personalleiterin, Frau Huber, eingesetzt.

Depending on the duration and scope of the project, it is necessary to reintegrate the team members back into normal day-to-day work. Therefore, it is also necessary to give a closure to the project on an emotional level and dissolve the team, for example, with a final celebration.

**Project Environment, Stakeholders**

The project environment analysis yields the following:

| Multi-Stakeholder Group | Proximity to the Project (1-3) | Influence on the Project (1-3) | Priority Index (Proximity x Influence) |
|---|---|---|---|
| Management | 2 | 3 | 6 |
| Department head | 2 | 2 | 4 |
| Human resources department | 3 | 3 | 9 |
| Works council | 2 | 2 | 4 |
| General staff | 1 | 1 | 1 |
| Employee human resources department | 3 | 2 | 6 |
| Project manager | 3 | 3 | 9 |
| Project co-workers | 3 | 3 | 9 |
| Customers | 1 | 1 | 1 |
| Suppliers | 1 | 1 | 1 |

Tab. 30: Case Study Project Environment Analysis.

The project manager to direct the focus of the interest groups with high priority uses the priority index.

The project stakeholders are identified in following personnel groups:

- Project steering committee (management, personnel management, project management)
- Project manager
- Project team
- Project team members
- Affected by the project: Employees

The performed risk analysis shows an identical as shown in chapter 2.1 of the TDR image. As deputy project manager the deputy human resources manager, Ms. Huber is appointed.

**Erste Projektstruktur**

Als Vorarbeit für einen ersten Projektstrukturplan dienen die wesentlichen Teilaufgaben.

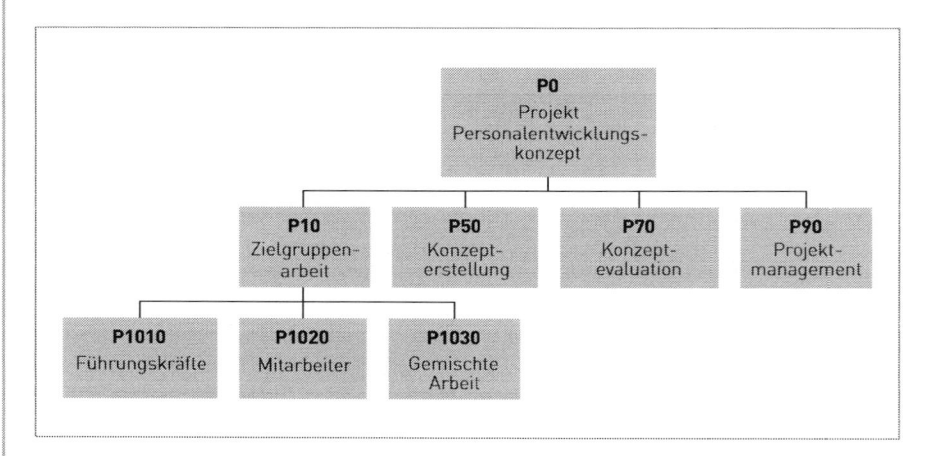

Abb. 58: Ressourcenplan.

**Ressourcenplan**

Die erste Projektstukturierung wird mit einer ersten Ressourcenplanung hinterlegt, die erfahrungsbasiert bottom-up erstellt wird.

| PSP-Code | Personen-Tage |
| --- | --- |
| P1010 | 24 |
| P1020 | 24 |
| P1030 | 24 |
| P50 | 10 |
| P70 | 10 |
| P90 | 10 |
| Summe Tage | 102 |

Tab. 31: Fallbeispiel Ressourcenplanung.

**Balkenplan**

Mittels Projektmanagementsoftware wird mit Eintrag der Meilensteine und der Inhalte des PSP ein Balkenplan erstellt.

**First Project Structure**

By way of preparation for a first work breakdown structure are the main subtasks.

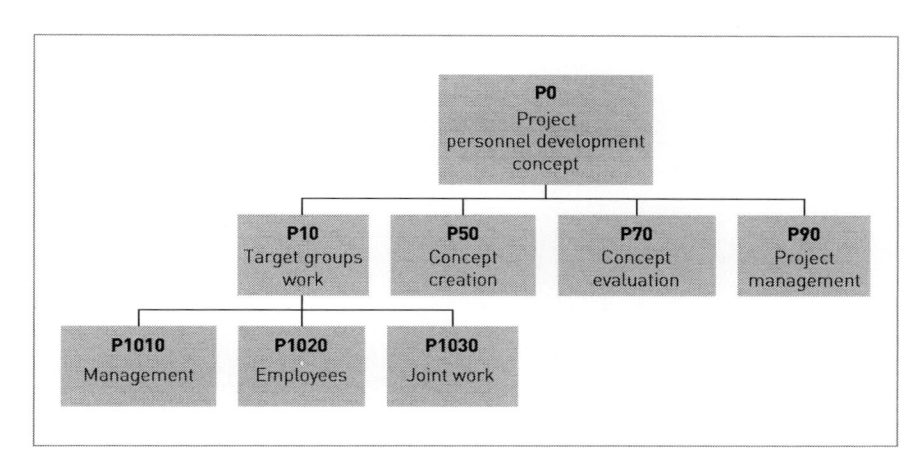

```
                    P0
                  Project
            personnel development
                  concept
    ┌──────────┬─────────┬─────────┐
    P10        P50       P70       P90
Target groups  Concept   Concept   Project
   work        creation  evaluation management
    │
 ┌──┼──┐
P1010 P1020 P1030
Management Employees Joint work
```

Fig. 58: Resource Plan.

**Resource Plan**

The first project structuring is deposited with a first resource planning; the bottom-up based on experience is created.

| PSP-Code | Man Days |
|---|---|
| P1010 | 24 |
| P1020 | 24 |
| P1030 | 24 |
| P50 | 10 |
| P70 | 10 |
| P90 | 10 |
| Total Days | 102 |

Tab. 31: Case Study Ressource Plan.

**Gantt Chart**

Using project management software, with the entry of the milestones and the contents of the PSP, a Gantt chart is created.

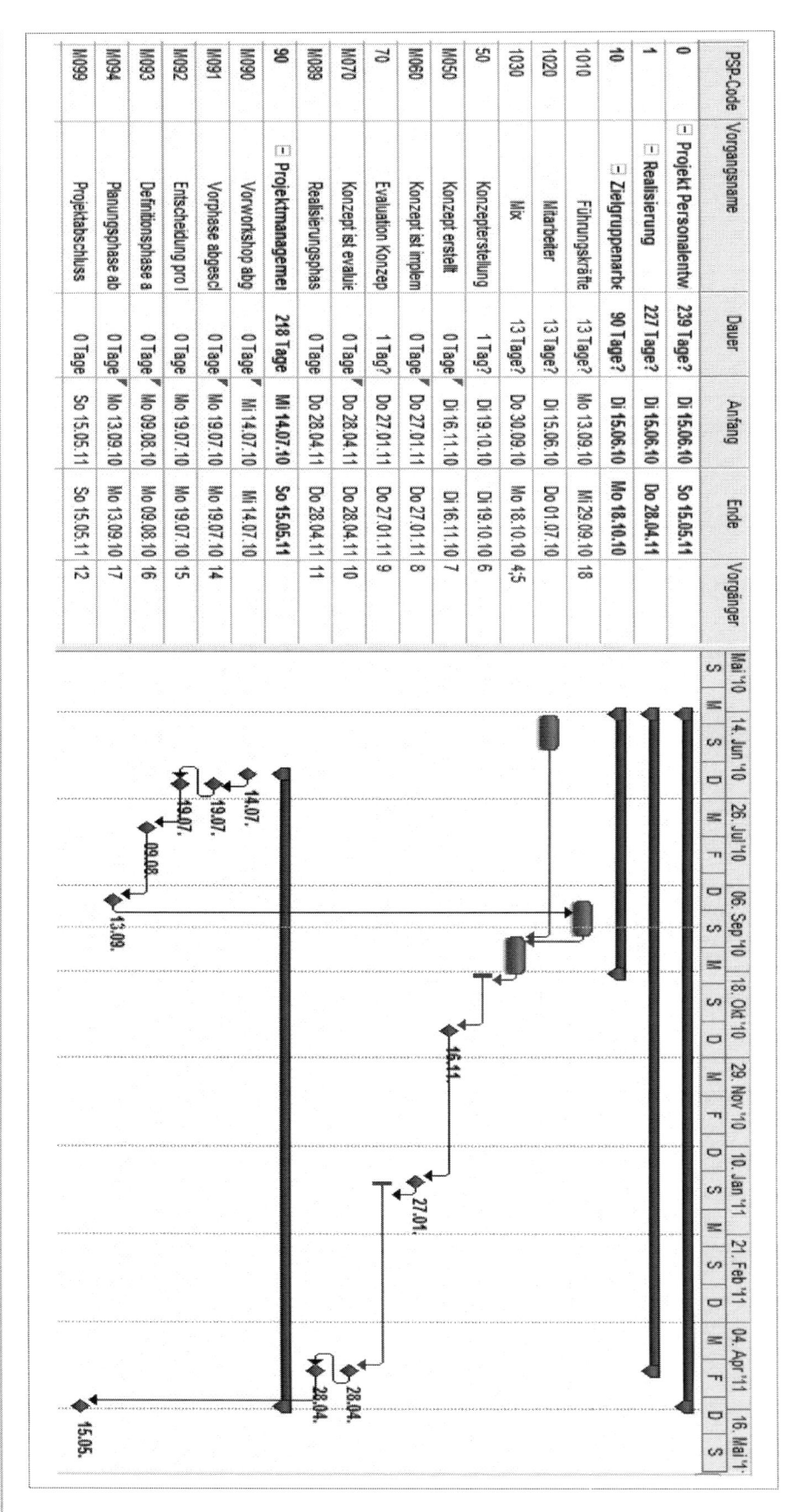

Abb. 59: Balkenplan (Screenshot MS-Project).

| PSP-Code | Name | Duration | Start | End | Previous |
|---|---|---|---|---|---|
| 0 | ⊟ personnel development | 239 days? | 15.06.10 | 15.05.11 | |
| 1 | ⊟ realisation | 224 days? | 15.06.10 | 28.04.11 | |
| 10 | ⊟ target-group work | 90 days? | 15.06.10 | 18.10.10 | |
| 1010 | executives | 13 days? | 13.09.10 | 29.09.10 | 18 |
| 1020 | co-workers | 13 days? | 15.08.10 | 01.07.10 | |
| 1030 | mix | 13 days? | 30.09.10 | 18.10.10 | 4,5 |
| 50 | concept prep. | 1 day? | 19.10.10 | 19.10.10 | 6 |
| M050 | concept ready | 0 days | 16.11.10 | 16.11.10 | 7 |
| M060 | implementation | 0 days | 27.01.11 | 27.01.11 | 8 |
| 70 | evaluation concept | 1 day? | 27.01.11 | 27.01.11 | 9 |
| M070 | evaluated | 0 days | 28.04.11 | 28.04.11 | 10 |
| M080 | realisation | 0 days | 28.04.11 | 28.04.11 | 11 |
| 90 | ⊟ project management | 218 days | 14.07.10 | 15.05.11 | |
| M091 | pre-workshop | 0 days | 14.07.10 | 14.07.10 | 14 |
| M092 | pre-phase | 0 days | 19.07.10 | 19.07.10 | 15 |
| M093 | decision | 0 days | 09.08.10 | 09.08.10 | 16 |
| M094 | defenition | 0 days | 13.09.10 | 13.09.10 | 17 |
| M099 | planning close-up | 0 days | 15.05.10 | 15.05.10 | 12 |

Fig. 59: Gantt Chart (Screenshot MS-Project).

## 9.2.2 Entscheidung

Mittels der ermittelten Parameter wird eine Entscheidung für oder gegen das Projekt herbeigeführt. Gemeinsam mit der Geschäftsführung, dem Personalleiter und dem Personalrat werden die Projekteckdaten besprochen, die weiteren Schritte und die Durchführung des Projekts eindeutig befürwortet.

## 9.2.3 Projektorganisation

Im Rahmen des Projektstarts wird eine Matrixorganisation für das Projekt festgelegt, da der Projektleiter Herr Mayer hierfür seine Position in der Personalabteilung nicht verlassen muss.

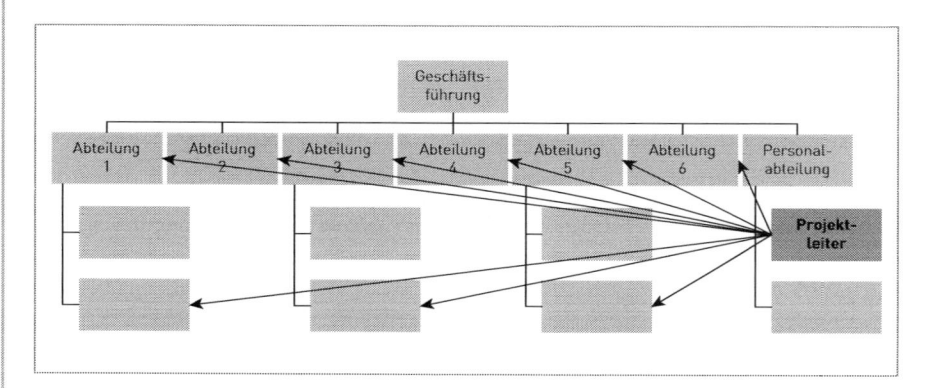

Abb. 60: Projektorganisation.

## 9.3 Definitionsphase

Im Folgenden ist es die Aufgabe des Projektleiters Herr Mayer, das Projekt voran zu bringen. Dazu startet er mit den notwendigen Festlegungen zum Projekt.

## 9.3.1 Projekt-Start-up

Im Rahmen einer Projekt-Start-up-Sitzung, die Herr Mayer als Kick-off-Meeting bezeichnet, bringt er sowohl die Geschäftsführung, den Personalleiter wie auch die stellvertretende Personalleiterin und die beiden Projektmitarbeiter im Projektteam an einen Tisch. Er verzichtet auf ausführliche Vorstellungsrunden, legt aber neben den relevanten Definitionen rund um das Projekt die Zusammenarbeit im Projektteam mittels „Spielregeln" fest.

Die Anwesenheit der Geschäftsführung der Organisation ist notwendig, um die wesentlichen Anforderungen dieser in Form eines Lastenhefts festzuhalten (bei internen Projekten wird das Lastenheft intern vorgegeben).

## 9.2.2 Decision

Using the identified parameters is a decision for or against the project is made. Together with the Management, the human resources director and the works council discussed the project key data, the further steps, and clearly support the implementation of the project.

## 9.2.3 Project Organization

In the framework of the project kick off, a matrix organization is set for the project, as the project manager Mr. Mayer does not need to leave his position in the human resource department for this purpose.

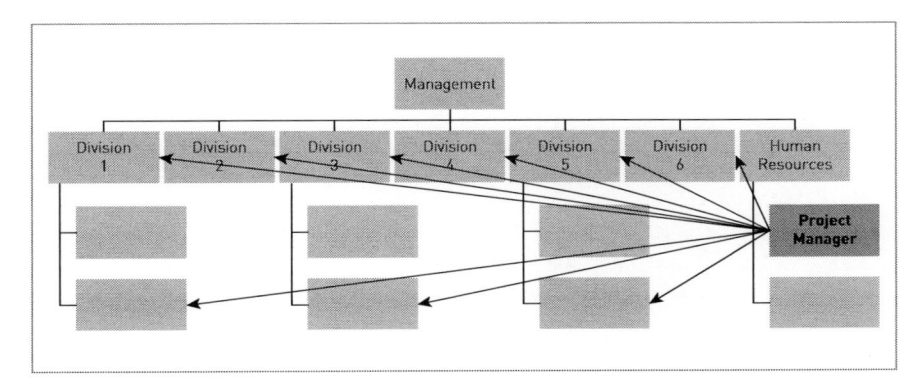

Fig. 60: Project Organization.

## 9.3 Definition Phase

In the following, it is the task of the project manager Mr. Mayer, to take the program forward. For this purpose, he starts with the necessary provisions for the project.

## 9.3.1 Project-Start-Up

In the context of a project-start-up meeting, which Mr. Mayer calls a kick-off-meeting, he brings both the management, the human resources director as well as the deputy human resources director and the two project team members included in the project team to the table. He forgoes detailed introductory rounds, but in addition to the relevant definitions concerning the project, he notes the rules for the cooperation in the project team.

The presence of the management of the organization is necessary to document their essential requirements in the form of specifications (for internal projects the specification is internally fixed).

### 9.3.2 Anforderungen an den Projektleiter und das Projektteam

Um die Anforderungen, aber auch die Befugnisse und Aufgaben des Projektleiters, der stellvertretenden Projektleiterin sowie der beiden Projektmitarbeiter zu klären, werden für alle „Projekt-Stellenbeschreibungen" erstellt.

Insbesondere die gute Kommunikation mit den Abteilungsleitern nach der internen Planung ist hier von hoher Bedeutung für das Projekt.

### 9.3.3 Verwendete Werkzeuge

Herr Mayer, der Projektleiter, setzt nach diesem Kick-off-Meeting verschiedene Werkzeuge ein, um das Projekt in der Realisierungsphase sicher steuern zu können.

**a) Planungsplan**
Als erstes erstellt Herr Mayer einen Plan, wann welche projektbezogenen Pläne erstellt sind. Hierbei legt er in seiner Zuständigkeit fest:

| Plan | Beschreibung Zeitfenster | Zeitpunkt Fertigstellung |
|---|---|---|
| Pflichtenheft | Kick-off-Meeting | 19.07.2010 |
| Planungsplan | nach Kick-off-Meeting | 23.07.2010 |
| Projektstrukturplan | | 16.08.2010 |
| Ablaufplan | | 30.08.2010 |
| Terminplan | | 30.08.2010 |
| Kapazitätsplan | | 03.09.2010 |
| Kostenplan | | 10.09.2010 |
| Finanzmittelplan | | 10.09.2010 |
| Aufträge und Verträge | | 13.09.2010 |

Tab. 32: Fallbeispiel Planungsplan.

### 9.3.2 Requirements for the Project Manager and the Project Team

To clarify the requirements, also the authority and duties of the project manager, the deputy project manager as well as of the two project team members' project job descriptions are created for all.

In particular, the good communication with the department heads after the internal planning is of high importance to the project.

### 9.3.3 Tools Used

Mr. Mayer, project manager, uses several tools after the kick-off-meeting to ensure control in the implementation phase.

**a) Design Plan**

First Mr. Mayer, creates a plan when which the project plans are created. With this he determines the competencies:

| Plan | Description Schedule | Completion Date Milestone |
|---|---|---|
| Performance specifications | Kick-off-meeting | 19.07.2010 |
| Design plan | After kick-off-meeting | 23.07.2010 |
| Work breakdown structure | | 16.08.2010 |
| Schedule | | 30.08.2010 |
| Schedule | | 30.08.2010 |
| Capacity plan | | 03.09.2010 |
| Budget | | 10.09.2010 |
| Financial means plan | | 10.09.2010 |
| Orders and contracts | | 13.09.2010 |

Tab. 32: Case Study Design Plan.

**b) Zielstrukturplan**

Folgende Ziele werden im Projektteam erarbeitet:

| Ziel | Ergebnisziel (E) / Vorgehensziel (V) | Mussziel (M) / Wunschziel (W) |
|---|---|---|
| Integratives Personsonalentwicklungskonzept liegt vor | E | M |
| Bedarfe von Mitarbeitern und Führungskräften sind im Konzept berücksichtigt | E | M |
| Kurz-, mittel- und langfristige Planung der Personalentwicklung ist im Konzept berücksichtigt | E | M |
| Konzept ist umgesetzt, Prozesse orientieren sich an dem Konzept | E | M |
| Systematisches Projektmanagement wird eingesetzt | V | W |
| Konzept wird im Projektverlauf evaluiert | V | M |
| Partizipation von Führungskräften und Mitarbeitern bei der Konzepterstellung | V | W |
| zielorientierte Zusammenarbeit des Projektteams | V | W |

Tab. 33: Fallbeispiel Zielstrukturplan.

**c) Pflichtenheft**

Herr Mayer fasst alle Erkenntnisse der bisherigen Arbeit in einem Pflichtenheft zusammen, das er der Geschäftsführung und dem Personalleiter als Antwort auf das gemeinsam erstellte Lastenheft vorlegt und die Freigabe dessen erteilen lässt. Damit erhält Herr Mayer die Rückmeldung, ob er den Auftrag bis ins Detail richtig verstanden hat oder ob in der Projektarbeit Anpassungen notwendig sind.

## 9.4 Planungsphase

Grundlegend für den Eintritt in die Planungsphase des Projekts ist die Freigabe der in der Definitionsphase erstellten Vorplanungen. Diese stellt die Grundlage für die weitere Planung von Herrn Mayer dar, sodass er diese präzisieren kann.

### 9.4.1 Grob- und Feinplanung

Im Projekt von Herrn Mayer sind bereits in den sehr frühen Phasen die meisten Arbeitsschritte der Grobplanung durch das Projektteam erledigt worden, sodass die Feinplanung im Fokus der Planungsarbeit steht. Insbesondere die im Folgenden dargestellten Pläne werden dabei von Herrn Mayers Projektteam detaillierter beschrieben und bieten damit eine solide Planungsgrundlage für das Projekt.

**b) Target Structure Plan**

The following objectives are developed in the project team:

| Objective | Results Objective (E) / Process Objective (V) | Required Objective (M) / Desired Objective (W) |
|---|---|---|
| Integrative personnel development concept is present | E | M |
| Requirements of employees and managers are taken into account in the concept | E | M |
| Short-, medium- and long-term planning of human resources development is taken into account in the concept | E | M |
| Concept is implemented; processes are based on the concept | E | M |
| Systematic project management is used | V | W |
| Concept will be evaluated in the course of the project | V | M |
| Participation of managers and employees in the conception | V | W |
| Goal-oriented cooperation of the project team | V | W |

Tab. 33: Case Study Target Structure Plan.

**c) Performance Specifications**

Mr. Mayer summarizes and releases all findings of the work done so far in a performance specification, which he provides to management and the Human Resources Director as a response to the jointly created specification. This gives Mr. Mayer the feedback whether he understood the job correctly in all details or whether adjustments in the project work are necessary.

## 9.4 Planning phase

The preliminary planning's release created in the definition phase is fundamental to the start of the planning phase of the project. This provides the basis for further planning by Mr. Mayer, so that he can clarify this.

### 9.4.1 Outline and Detail Planning

In the very early planning stages of Mr. Mayer's project the project team has completed steps for most of the work's outline plan, so that the detailed planning is the focus of the programming work. In particular, the following plans are described in more detail by Mr. Mayer's project team and provide a solid basis for planning for the project.

## 9.4.2 Projektpläne

Bei den abgebildeten Projektplänen handelt es sich um die wesentlichen Auszüge der Projektplanung, mit der diese nachvollziehbar wird.

**a) Projektstrukturplan**

Der in der Definitionsphase begonnene Projektstrukturplan wird nun detaillierter beschrieben. Die Nummerierung jedes Teilprojekts und Arbeitspakets (PSP-Code) ist von Herrn Mayer festgelegt worden.

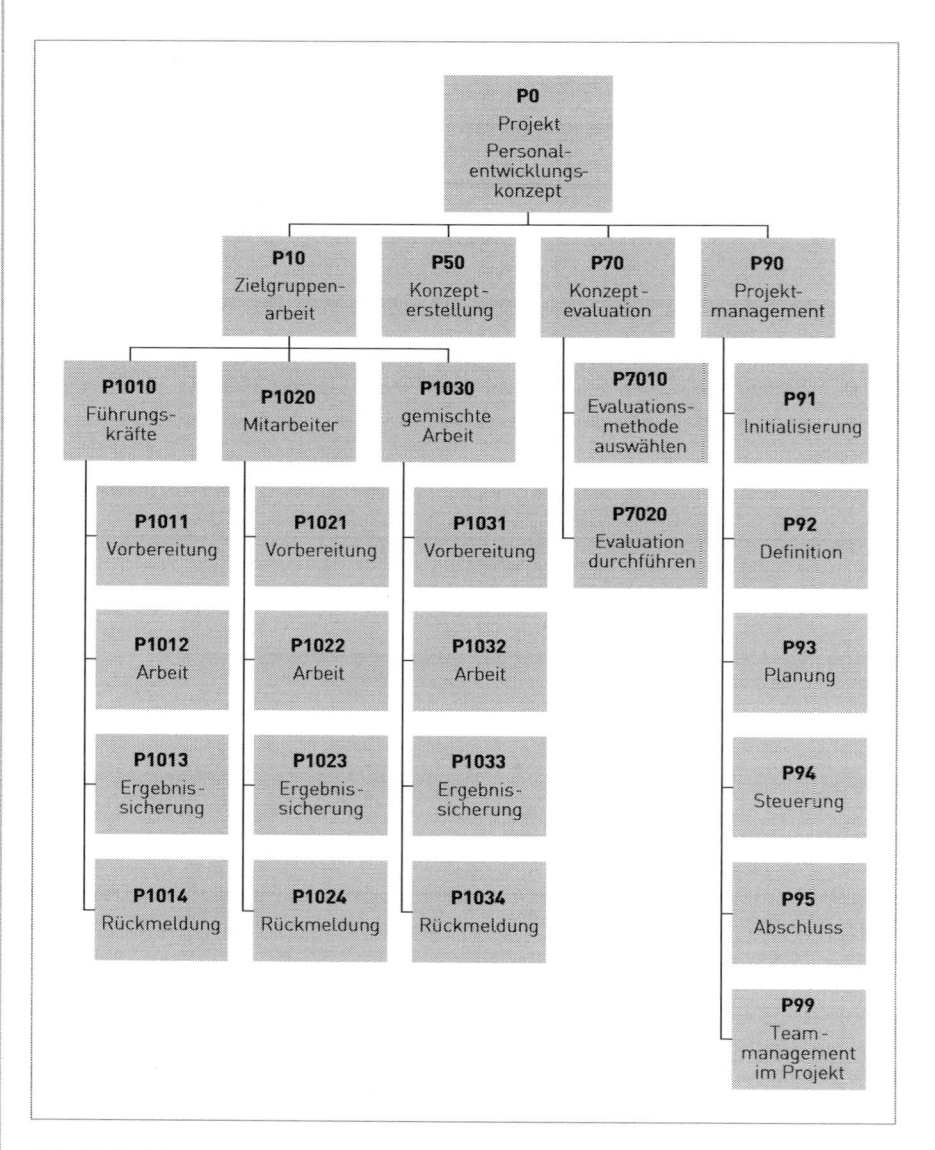

Abb. 61: Projektstrukturplan.

Der PSP stellt die Grundlage für die weitere Projektplanung dar.

## 9.4.2 Project Plans

Shown in the pictured project plans are the essential extracts from the project planning, which makes it possible to follow it.

**a) Work Breakdown Structure**

The work breakdown structure started in the definition phase is now described in more detail. Mr. Mayer has established the numbering of each subproject and work package (PSP) code.

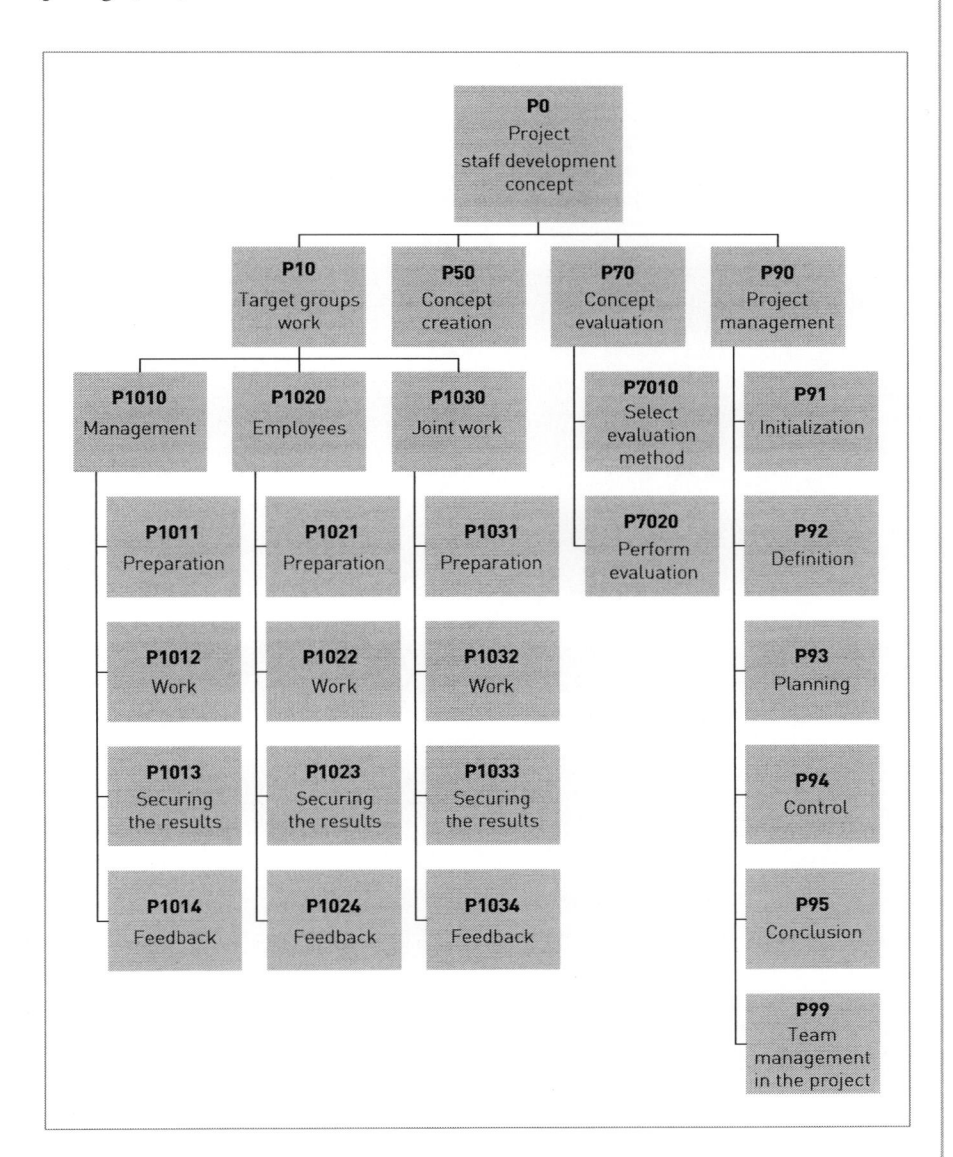

Fig. 61: Work Breakdown Structure.

The WBS provides the basis for the further project planning.

## b) Beispiel Arbeitspaketbeschreibung

Herr Mayer beschreibt alle Arbeitspakete im Projekt nach einer einheitlichen, organisationsinternen Vorlage, um den Arbeitspaketverantwortlichen klare Aufgaben zu übertragen. Das vorliegende Beispiel verdeutlicht, wie die Arbeitspakete beschrieben werden.

| Arbeitspaketformular | | | |
|---|---|---|---|
| **Datum** | 09.08.2010 | | |
| **Projekt** | Personalentwicklungskonzept neu | | |
| **Projektphase** | Realisierung | Zielgruppen-orientierung | AP 1012 |
| **Arbeitspaket-beschreibung** | Zielgruppenarbeit – Führungskräfte – Arbeit | | |
| **Ergebnis** | Bedarfe und Anforderungen der Führungskräfte werden in einem Workshop gesammelt und zusammengetragen. | | |
| **Aktivitäten** | Operative Workshopplanung, Workshopdurchführung, operative Nachbereitung. | | |
| **Voraussetzungen und notwendige Zulieferungen** | Projektplanung abgeschlossen | | |
| **Verantwortlicher** | Müller | **Stellvertretung** | Mayer |
| **Termin** | Mitte September | Anfang: 13.09.2010 | Geplantes Ende: 22.09.2010 |
| **beteiligte Mitarbeiter** | Projektteam, im Workshop Abteilungsleiter 1–7 | | |
| **Sonstiges** | Erkenntnisse in ein erstes Rohkonzept | **Kostenstelle** | 21 005 |

Abb. 62: Arbeitspaketbeschreibung.

## c) Projektablaufplan

Um einen einfachen Überblick zu erhalten, wird der Projektablaufplan in einer Projektmanagementsoftware auf Basis des Projektstrukturplans erstellt. Dabei kann einfach ein GANTT-Diagramm angezeigt werden.

## b) Example Work Package Description

Mr. Mayer describes all work packages in the project according to a uniform organizational template to assign clear tasks to the work package responsible individual. This example shows how the work packages will be described.

| Work Package Form | | | |
|---|---|---|---|
| **Date** | 09.08.2010 | | |
| **Project** | Human resources development concept new | | |
| **Project phase** | Implementation | Target-group orientation | AP 1012 |
| **Work package description** | Outreach work – Managers – Work | | |
| **Result** | Needs and requirements of the managers Collected and compiled in a workshop. | | |
| **Activities** | Operational workshop planning, workshop execution, operational follow-up. Project planning completed | | |
| **Conditions and necessary supplies** | | | |
| **Responsible person** | Müller | **Representation** | Mayer |
| **Date** | Mid-September | Start: 13.09.2010 | Planned end date: 22.09.2010 |
| **Involved staff** | Project team, in the workshop department heads 1-7 | | |
| **Miscellaneous** | Findings in a first draft concept | **Cost center** | 21 005 |

Fig. 62: Work Package Description.

## c) Project Schedule

In order to obtain a simple overview, the project schedule is created in a project management software based on the work breakdown structure. This can simply be displayed in a Gantt chart.

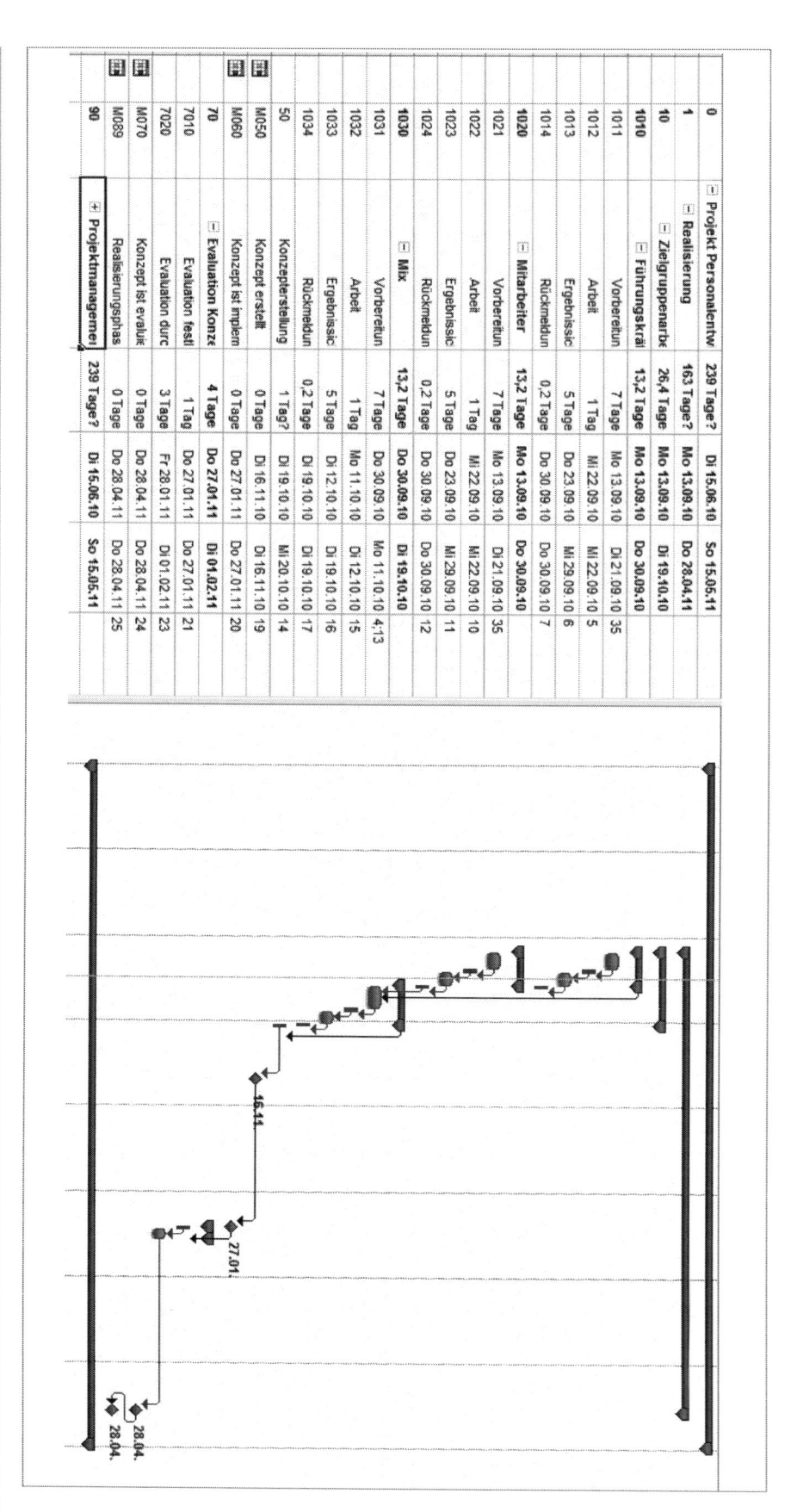

| Nr | | Vorgangsname | Dauer | Anfang | Ende | |
|---|---|---|---|---|---|---|
| 0 | ⊞ | Projekt Personalentw | 239 Tage? | Di 15.06.10 | So 15.05.11 | |
| 1 | ⊞ | Realisierung | 163 Tage? | Mo 13.09.10 | Do 28.04.11 | |
| 10 | ⊞ | Zielgruppenarb | 26,4 Tage | Mo 13.09.10 | Di 19.10.10 | |
| 1010 | ⊞ | Führungskräft | 13,2 Tage | Mo 13.09.10 | Do 30.09.10 | |
| 1011 | | Vorbereitun | 7 Tage | Mo 13.09.10 | Di 21.09.10 | 35 |
| 1012 | | Arbeit | 1 Tag | Mi 22.09.10 | Mi 22.09.10 | 5 |
| 1013 | | Ergebnissic | 5 Tage | Do 23.09.10 | Mi 29.09.10 | 6 |
| 1014 | | Rückmeldun | 0,2 Tage | Do 30.09.10 | Do 30.09.10 | 7 |
| 1020 | ⊞ | Mitarbeiter | 13,2 Tage | Mo 13.09.10 | Do 30.09.10 | |
| 1021 | | Vorbereitun | 7 Tage | Mo 13.09.10 | Di 21.09.10 | 35 |
| 1022 | | Arbeit | 1 Tag | Mi 22.09.10 | Mi 22.09.10 | 10 |
| 1023 | | Ergebnissic | 5 Tage | Do 23.09.10 | Mi 29.09.10 | 11 |
| 1024 | | Rückmeldun | 0,2 Tage | Do 30.09.10 | Do 30.09.10 | 12 |
| 1030 | ⊞ | Mix | 13,2 Tage | Do 30.09.10 | Di 19.10.10 | |
| 1031 | | Vorbereitun | 7 Tage | Do 30.09.10 | Mo 11.10.10 | 4;13 |
| 1032 | | Arbeit | 1 Tag | Mo 11.10.10 | Di 12.10.10 | 15 |
| 1033 | | Ergebnissic | 5 Tage | Di 12.10.10 | Di 19.10.10 | 16 |
| 1034 | | Rückmeldun | 0,2 Tage | Di 19.10.10 | Di 19.10.10 | 17 |
| 50 | ⊞ | Konzepterstellung | 1 Tag? | Di 19.10.10 | Mi 20.10.10 | 14 |
| M050 | | Konzept erstellt | 0 Tage | Di 16.11.10 | Di 16.11.10 | 19 |
| 70 | ⊞ | Evaluation Konzept | 4 Tage | Do 27.01.11 | Di 01.02.11 | |
| 7010 | | Evaluation festl | 1 Tag | Do 27.01.11 | Do 27.01.11 | 21 |
| M060 | | Konzept ist implem | 0 Tage | Do 27.01.11 | Do 27.01.11 | 20 |
| 7020 | | Evaluation durc | 3 Tage | Fr 28.01.11 | Di 01.02.11 | 23 |
| M070 | | Evaluation ist evaluie | 0 Tage | Do 28.04.11 | Do 28.04.11 | 24 |
| 90 | | Realisierungsphas | 0 Tage | Do 28.04.11 | Do 28.04.11 | 25 |
| M089 | | | | | | |
| | ⊞ | Projektmanageme | 239 Tage? | Di 15.06.10 | So 15.05.11 | |

Abb. 63: Projektablaufplan (Screenshot MS-Project).

| ID | | Task Name | Duration | Start | Finish | Pred |
|---|---|---|---|---|---|---|
| 0 | | Personnel Development | 239 days? | 15.06.10 | 15.05.11 | |
| 1 | | Realisation | 163 days? | 13.09.10 | 28.04.11 | |
| 10 | | Target-group work | 26,4 days | 13.09.10 | 19.10.10 | |
| 1010 | | Executives | 13,2 days | 13.09.10 | 30.09.10 | |
| 1011 | | Preparation | 7 days | 13.09.10 | 21.09.10 | 35 |
| 1012 | | Progress | 1 day | 22.09.10 | 22.09.10 | 5 |
| 1013 | | Results | 5 days | 23.09.10 | 29.09.10 | 6 |
| 1014 | | Evaluation | 0,2 days | 30.09.10 | 30.09.10 | 7 |
| 1020 | | Co-workers | 13,2 days | 13.09.10 | 30.09.10 | |
| 1021 | | Preparation | 7 days | 13.09.10 | 21.09.10 | 35 |
| 1022 | | Progress | 1 day | 22.09.10 | 22.09.10 | 10 |
| 1023 | | Results | 5 days | 23.09.10 | 29.09.10 | 11 |
| 1024 | | Evaluation | 0,2 days | 30.09.10 | 30.09.10 | 12 |
| 1030 | | Mix | 13,2 days | 30.09.10 | 19.10.10 | |
| 1031 | | Preparation | 7 days | 30.09.10 | 11.10.10 | 4,13 |
| 1032 | | Progress | 1 day | 12.10.10 | 12.10.10 | 15 |
| 1033 | | Results | 5 days | 12.10.10 | 19.10.10 | 16 |
| 1034 | | Evaluation | 0,2 days | 19.10.10 | 19.10.10 | 17 |
| 50 | | Prep. concept | 1 day? | 19.10.10 | 20.10.10 | 14 |
| 1050 | | Concept ready | 0 days | 16.11.10 | 16.11.10 | 19 |
| 1060 | | Concept implemented | 0 days | 27.01.11 | 27.01.11 | 20 |
| 70 | | Evaluation concept | 4 days | 27.01.11 | 01.02.11 | 21 |
| 7010 | | Create evaluation | 1 day | 27.01.11 | 27.01.11 | |
| 7020 | | Evaluate | 3 days | 28.01.11 | 01.02.11 | 23 |
| 1070 | | Evaluation done | 0 days | 28.04.11 | 28.04.11 | 24 |
| 1080 | | Realisation | 0 days | 28.04.11 | 28.04.11 | 25 |
| 90 | | Project Management | 239 days? | 15.06.10 | 15.05.11 | |

Fig. 63: Project Schedule (Screenshot MS-Project).

**d) Ressourcenplan**

Die einzelnen Arbeitspakete und Teilschritte werden nun mit Ressourcen beplant – Herr Mayer benötigt hierfür nur Personalressourcen und einen Raum für die Workshops. Durch die Ressourcenplanung mit einer Software erleichtert sich Herr Mayer die Lösung von Ressourcenkonflikten, da er die einzelnen Arbeitszeiten schnell im Überblick sehen kann.

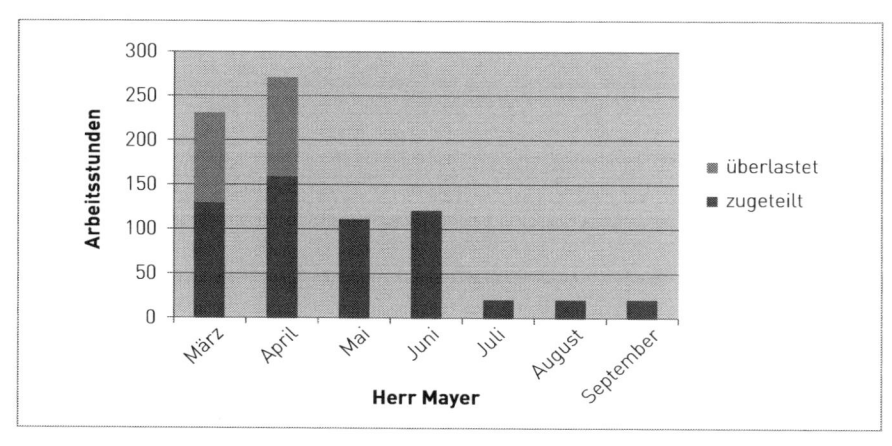

Abb. 64: Ressourcenplan.

**e) Kostenplan**

Herr Mayer hinterlegt die Arbeitsstunden der Mitarbeiter mit deren Lohn und erhält so einen Kostenplan – er hat einen Überblick über alle entstehenden Kosten des Projekts.

**f) Finanzplan**

Mit der Planung von Kosten kann Herr Mayer die zugehörige Finanzplanung erstellen, was im vorliegenden Projekt durch die Eingrenzung von benötigten Finanzmitteln auf Personalfinanzierung für ihn leicht wird – mit der Freigabe der Projektplanung durch die Geschäftsleitung hat Herr Mayer die Zusage für die Finanzierung.

## 9.5 Realisierungsphase

In der Realisierungsphase gehen die Arbeiten mit den Führungskräften und den Mitarbeitern in der Organisation richtig los. Herr Mayer muss nicht nur die projektinternen Mitarbeiter führen, sein Augenmerk muss auf der gesamten Organisation ruhen.

### 9.5.1 Projektcontrolling

Herr Mayer steuert das Projekt mit einfachen Leistungs-, Termin- und Kostenparametern. Kapitel 5.1.5 beschreibt mit der Meilensteintrendanalyse ein Steuerungsinstrument für die Termineinhaltung. Mittels Fertigstellungsgraden der Arbeitspakete, die vorher definiert werden (20 %-Statusschritte) werden die Leistungsparameter gesteuert, die Kostenstelle des Projekts (21 005) ermöglicht eine Kostensteuerung anfallender Kosten.

## d) Resource Plan

The individual work packages and sub-steps are now planned with resources – Mr. Mayer requires only human resources and a space for the workshops. Mr. Mayer simplifies the solution of conflicts over resources through a resource planning software, as he can see the individual working hours at a single glance.

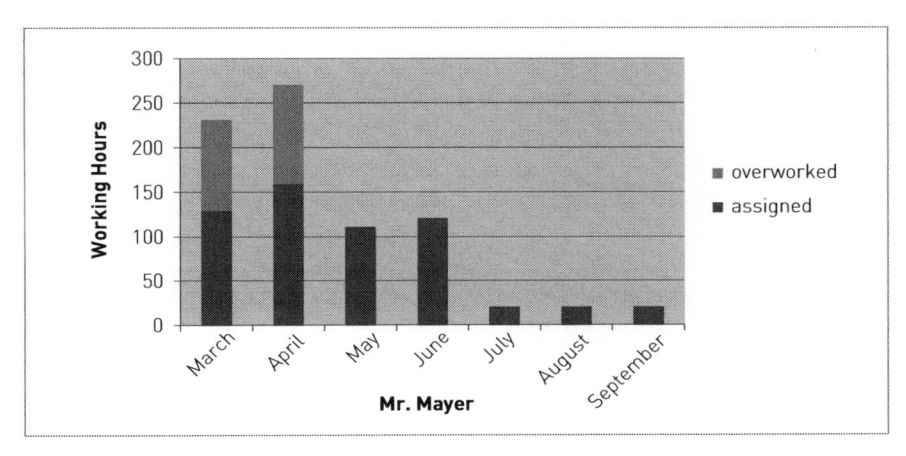

Fig. 64: Resource Plan.

## e) Budget

Mr. Mayer enters the working hours of the employees including the wages and gets a cost plan – he has an overview of all costs of the project.

## f) Financial Plan

By planning the costs Mr. Mayer can create of the associated financial planning, which becomes easy in the present project by the limitation of financial need to staff financing – with the release of project planning by the management Mr. Mayer has a commitment for the financing.

## 9.5 Implementation Phase

In the realization phase, work with the management and employees in the organization starts. Mr. Mayer not only leads the project internal employees, he also needs to pay attention to the overall organization.

### 9.5.1 Project Controlling

Mr. Mayer controls the project with simple performance, schedule and cost parameters. Chapter 5.2 describes the mile stone trend analysis instrument for the adherence to the schedule. Using percent complete types of work packages, which are previously defined (20%-status increments) the performance parameters are controlled, the cost center of the project (21 005) allows cost control of costs incurred.

## 9.5.2 Meilenstein-Trendanalyse

Für die Überwachung von Terminen nutzt Herr Mayer die bereits in der Projektdefinition festgelegten Meilensteine.

| Nr. | PSP-Code | Vorgangsname | Dauer | Anfang | Ende | Vor-gänger |
|---|---|---|---|---|---|---|
| 1 | 0 | Projekt Personalentwicklungskonzept | 235 Tage | 15.06.10 | 15.05.11 | |
| 2 | 1 | Realisierung | 227 Tage | 15.06.10 | 28.04.11 | |
| 13 | 90 | Projektmanagement | 218 Tage | 14.07.10 | 15.05.11 | |
| 14 | M090 | Vorworkshop abgeschlossen | 0 Tage | 14.07.10 | 14.07.10 | |
| 15 | M091 | Vorphase abgeschlossen | 0 Tage | 19.07.10 | 19.07.10 | 14 |
| 16 | M092 | Entscheidung pro Projekt | 0 Tage | 19.07.11 | 19.07.10 | 15 |
| 17 | M093 | Definitionsphase abgeschlossen | 0 Tage | 09.08.10 | 09.08.10 | 16 |
| 18 | M094 | Planungsphase abgeschlossen | 0 Tage | 13.09.10 | 13.09.10 | 17 |
| 8 | M050 | Konzept erstellt | 0 Tage | 16.11.10 | 16.11.10 | 7 |
| 9 | M060 | Konzept ist implementiert | 0 Tage | 27.01.11 | 27.01.11 | 8 |
| 11 | M070 | Konzept ist evaluiert | 0 Tage | 28.04.11 | 28.04.11 | 10 |
| 12 | M089 | Realisierungsphase abgeschlossen | 0 Tage | 28.04.11 | 28.04.11 | 11 |
| 19 | M099 | Projektabschluss | 0 Tage | 15.05.11 | 15.05.11 | 12 |

Tab. 34: Fallbeispiel Meilenstein-Trendanalyse.

Mit der Meilenstein-Trendanalyse kann Herr Mayer einen einfachen Überblick über den Projektfortschritt und dessen Termintreue erhalten – was ihm die Projektsteuerung erheblich erleichtert.

## 9.5.3 Qualitätssicherung

Zur Erreichung von Qualität bringt Herr Mayer viele Anforderungen von „Kundengruppen" in Form der Workshops mit Führungskräften, Mitarbeitern und im Mix in das Projekt ein, damit das neue Personalentwicklungskonzept diese Anforderungen neben den Vorgaben der Geschäftsführung und der Personalleitung erfüllen kann. Zur Validierung der Qualität wird noch als Projektbestandteil das Personalentwicklungskonzept mittels einfachen Instrumenten qualitativer Sozialforschung evaluiert.

## 9.5.2 Milestone Trend Analysis

For the monitoring of deadlines Mr. Mayer uses the milestones pre-defined in the project definition.

| No. | PSP code | Activity Name | Duration | Start | End | Prede-cessor |
|---|---|---|---|---|---|---|
| 1 | 0 | Project personnel development concept | 235 days | 15.06.10 | 15.05.11 | |
| 2 | 1 | Implementation | 227 days | 15.06.10 | 28.04.11 | |
| 13 | 90 | Project management | 218 days | 14.07.10 | 15.05.11 | |
| 14 | M090 | Completed preliminary workshop | 0 days | 14.07.10 | 14.07.10 | |
| 15 | M091 | Preparatory phase completed | 0 days | 19.07.10 | 19.07.10 | 14 |
| 16 | M092 | Preparatory phase completed | 0 days | 19.07.11 | 19.07.10 | 15 |
| 17 | M093 | Definition phase completed | 0 days | 09.08.10 | 09.08.10 | 16 |
| 18 | M094 | Planning phase completed | 0 days | 13.09.10 | 13.09.10 | 17 |
| 8 | M050 | Concept created | 0 days | 16.11.10 | 16.11.10 | 7 |
| 9 | M060 | Concept is implemented | 0 days | 27.01.11 | 27.01.11 | 8 |
| 11 | M070 | Concept is evaluated | 0 days | 28.04.11 | 28.04.11 | 10 |
| 12 | M089 | Implementation phase completed | 0 days | 28.04.11 | 28.04.11 | 11 |
| 19 | M099 | Project completion | 0 days | 15.05.11 | 15.05.11 | 12 |

Tab. 34: Case Study Milestone Trend Analysis.

With a milestone trend analysis Mr. Mayer can have a simple overview of the project progress and its adherence to deadlines – this facilitates the project control for him considerably.

## 9.5.3 Quality Assurance

To achieve quality, Mr. Mayer inserts many of the demands from "Customer Groups" to the project in the form of workshops with senior management, and employees, so that the new human resources development concept can meet these requirements in addition to the requirements of the management and the human resources manager. For the validation of the quality, the human resources development concept is evaluated as a project component using simple instruments of qualitative social research.

### 9.5.4 Projektstatussitzungen

Um regelmäßig über den Fortgang der Arbeitspakete unterrichtet zu sein, beruft Herr Mayer in vierwöchigem Abstand Projektstatussitzungen mit seinem Projektteam ein. Diese Jour-Fixe-Sitzungen geben ihm die notwendigen Informationen; die Dokumentation in geeigneten Ergebnisprotokollen sichern die Ergebnisse für den weiteren Projektverlauf.

Darüber hinaus beruft Herr Mayer gemeinsam mit seinem Projektteam bei Meilensteinerreichung eine Statussitzung mit dem Lenkungsausschuss ein, um diesen immer über den aktuellen Projektstand zu informieren.

## 9.6 Abschlussphase

Nachdem Herr Mayer mit seinem Projektteam das neue Personalentwicklungskonzept entwickelt, implementiert und evaluiert hat, ist das Projekt eigentlich beendet. Um dies auch in der Organisation angemessen abzubilden, fasst Herr Mayer mit seinem Projektteam die Ergebnisse zusammen und präsentiert dies dem Lenkungsausschuss (Geschäftsführung, Personalleitung, Projektleitung). Er übergibt die Ergebnisse und das Projekt und lässt sich durch den Auftraggeber entlasten, da dieser die Projektergebnisse wohlwollend und zufrieden annimmt. Herr Mayer schreibt mit seinem Projektteam einen kurzen, aber präzisen Abschlussbericht: Dieser gibt die Schritte des Projektmanagements wieder, geht aber auch auf die gute Zusammenarbeit mit der Geschäftsführung und den Abteilungsleitern sowie dem Personalrat als positive Erfahrungswerte ein. Als kritischer Punkt schreibt Herr Mayer die Ressourcenfreistellung der Mitarbeiter ein, die bei zukünftigen Projekten deutlicher durch die Geschäftsführung an die Abteilungsleiter kommuniziert werden muss. Damit sichert Herr Mayer die Erkenntnisse aus der Projektarbeit für weitere Projekte.

## 9.7 Teamentwicklung

Um mit seinem Projektteam eine zielführende Arbeitsweise aufrecht zu erhalten, sieht Herr Mayer stets auch die Teamarbeit als eine seiner Aufgaben als Projektleiter.

Er orientiert sich an den vier Phasen nach Tuckman: Zunächst vereinbart er mit seinem Projektteam die Regeln der Zusammenarbeit und bringt die Mitarbeiter durch eine gemeinsame Zielfindung (persönliche Ziele und Sachziele) zueinander. Durch gleichwertige Aufgabenverteilung der Arbeitspakete sowie regelmäßige Jour-Fixe-Meetings und persönliche Gespräche versucht er, keine Rivalitäten aufkommen zu lassen und alle Teammitarbeiter gemeinsam arbeitsfähig zu halten. Mit einem arbeitsfähigen Team, das in der Vorphase, Definitionsphase und Planungsphase seine Zusammenarbeit gefestigt hat, startet Herr Mayer in die Projektrealisierung. Hierbei werden die Projektteammitglieder auch im Unternehmen wahrgenommen und leisten hohe Präzision bei ihrer Arbeit. Um das Projektteam in der Abschlussphase aufzulösen, feiert Herr Mayer gemeinsam mit dem Team die erfolgreiche Projektdurchführung: Das gemeinsame Fest hat er bereits in die Projektkosten eingeplant.

### 9.5.4 Project Progress Meetings

In order to be regularly informed about the progress of the work packages Mr. Mayer convenes every four weeks project progress meetings with his project team. These regular jour fix meetings provide him with the necessary information, the documentation in appropriate summary proceedings back up the results for the further development of the project.

In addition, Mr. Mayer together with his project team convenes a progress meeting when milestones are reached a status meeting with the steering group to inform them about the current project status.

## 9.6 Final Phase

After Mr. Mayer develops, implements, and evaluates the new human resources development concept with his project team the project is actually completed. In order to illustrate this appropriately in the organization, Mr. Mayer summarizes the results with his project team and presents these to the steering committee (management, personnel management, project management). He turns the project results over to the client to the satisfaction of the same. Mr. Mayer writes with his project team a brief but precise final report: which outlines the steps of the project management; however, it also addresses the good cooperation with the management, the directors, and the staff committee as a positive experience. Mr. Mayer writes up as constructive criticism the chain of command for employees for future projects, which needs to be communicated more clearly by management of the company to the department heads. Mr. Mayer thus ensures the passing of the findings from the project for further projects.

## 9.7 Team Development

Mr. Mayer regards teamwork as one of his tasks as a project manager, this allows him to maintain an effective operation with his project team.

It is based on the four phases according to Tuckman's: first, he agrees with his project team the rules of engagement and brings the employees together through a common goal determination (personal goals and objectives). By equal distribution of responsibilities for the work packages as well as regular jour fix meetings and personal conversations, he tries preventing rivalries and maintains and all team members in a cooperative spirit. Mr. Mayer starts the project implementation with a working team that has strengthened its co-operation in the initial planning phase, the definition phase, and planning phase. Through this, the project team members are well regarded in the company and deliver high precision work quality. To dissolve the project team in the completion phase of the project, Mr. Mayer is celebrating the successful project implementation together with the team: he had already planned the cost of the celebration in the general project cost.

# 10 Lösungshinweise der Aufgaben zur Selbstkontrolle

1.1: Definieren Sie, wodurch ein Projekt gekennzeichnet ist.

Ein Projekt ist nach der DIN 69901 ein Vorhaben, das im Wesentlichen durch die Einmaligkeit der Bedingungen in ihrer Gesamtheit gekennzeichnet ist. Projekte sind Aufgaben mit besonderen Merkmalen. Projekte sind durch folgende Merkmale gekennzeichnet:

* Einmaligkeit
* klare Zielsetzung
* definierter(s) Anfang / Ende
* begrenzter Aufgabenumfang
* neu aufzubauendes System
* Veränderung des Status Quo
* Neuartigkeit
* Bruch mit etablierten Verfahren und Methoden
* Risiko bezüglich Ergebnis, Kosten und Zeitbedarf
* Komplexität
* spezielle Organisation
* Arbeiten außerhalb der Linie
* möglichst heterogene Mitarbeiterzusammensetzung
* begrenzte Mittel (zeitlich, finanziell, personell)
* besondere Größe und Bedeutung
* messbarer Erfolg
* mit außergewöhnlichen Kosten verbunden

1.2: Beschreiben Sie den Verlauf und die Inhalte der einzelnen Projektphasen.

*Vorphase*

* Beachtung der Regelungen aus dem Antragsmanagement für Projekte / sonstige Vorhaben
* Problembeschreibung durch Vorstudie / Aufgabenanalyse in einem Workshop
* Erarbeitung des Projektantrags
* Erteilung des Projektauftrages

# 10 Solutions for the Tasks for Progress Review

## 1.1: Define the Salient Characteristics of a Project.

A project is according to the DIN 69901 an undertaking, which is mainly defined through the uniqueness of the conditions in their entirety. Projects are tasks with special characteristics. Projects are identified by the following characteristics:

- Uniqueness
- Clear objectives
- Defined start / end
- Defined scope
- Newly-to-be-established system
- Departure from the status quo
- Novelty
- Departure from established procedures and methodology
- Risk of result, costs and time required
- Complexity
- Special organization
- Work outside the line
- Where possible a heterogeneous organizational participation
- Limited resources (time, financial, manpower)
- Special magnitude and importance
- Measurable success
- Associated with extraordinary costs

## 1.2: Describe the Course and the Content of the Individual Project Phases.

*Initial Phase*

- Compliance with the regulations from the application management for projects / other projects
- Problem description by preliminary study / task analysis in a workshop
- Development of the project application
- Issuing of the project mandate

*Definitionsphase*

- Projektgründung – Auftrag ist erteilt
- bei direkt erteilten Projektaufträgen Problemanalyse durch Aufgabenanalyse, ansonsten Überprüfung der Aufgabenanalyse aus der Vorphase
- Festlegung der Aufbauorganisation
- Regelung der Ablauforganisation
- Definition der Projektziele (Zielstrukturplan)
- Erstfassung des Pflichtenheftes
- Planungsplan (Planung der Planungsphase)

*Planungsphase*

- Projektstrukturplan – Bestimmung von Arbeitspaketen
- Aufgabenverteilung / Verantwortlichkeitsliste
- Ablaufplan als Aktivitätenliste, Balkenplan oder Netzplan
- gegebenenfalls Einteilung der Realisierungsphase in Ablaufphasen
- Meilensteine definieren
- Kapazitätsplan
- Terminplan
- Kostenplan
- Finanzplan
- Ergänzung des Pflichtenhefts mit den Plänen

*Realisierungsphase*

- Umsetzung der Projektpläne
- Kontrolle und Steuerung (Controlling)
- Qualitätssicherung
- gegebenenfalls Anpassung / Ergänzung der Projektziele
- Anpassung der Projektpläne im erforderlichen Umfang
- regelmäßige Information aller Betroffenen und Beteiligten
- Ergänzung des Pflichtenheftes mit den Produkten der Realisierungsphase

*Definition Phase*

- Project formation – order is issued
- Problem analysis by task analysis for directly issued project orders, otherwise check the task analysis from the initial phase
- Determination of the organizational structure
- Settling of the process management
- Definition of project objectives (target structure plan)
- First version of the specification
- Design plan (planning the planning phase)

*Planning Phase*

- Work Breakdown Structure – definition of work packages.
- Division of tasks / responsibility list
- Schedule as an activity list, Gantt chart, or network activities list
- Classification of the realization phase where appropriate in process phases
- Define milestones
- Capacity plan
- Schedule
- Budget
- Financial plan
- Completion of the specifications by adding the plans

*Implementation Phase*

- Implementation of the project plans
- Control and management (controlling)
- Quality assurance
- If necessary, adapt / supplement the project objectives
- Adjustment of the project plans in the required scope
- Regular information for all affected and interested parties
- Completion of the specification with the products of the implementation phase

*Abschlussphase*

- Präsentation des Projektergebnisses
- Abnahme des Projektergebnisses durch den Auftraggeber
- Sicherung des Projektergebnisses
- Abschlussbericht
- Auflösung des Projektes
- falls erforderlich Bestimmung einer Stelle zur Produktbetreuung

## 2.1: Erläutern Sie, welche Schritte im Rahmen einer Vorstudie / Aufgabenanalyse erledigt werden sollten und wozu diese Schritte dienen.

Das Instrument der Vorstudie / Aufgabenanalyse hilft dabei, den Projektantrag zu konkretisieren. Die Aufgabenanalyse hilft ebenso bei der Entscheidungsfindung, ob und wie diese Idee verwirklicht wird. Bei der Entscheidung, die Idee weiter zu verfolgen und außerhalb der allgemeinen Aufbauorganisation zu bearbeiten, gibt es zwei grundsätzliche Möglichkeiten dies zu tun: Entweder im Rahmen einer Arbeitsgruppe, unter Anlehnung an die Richtlinien zum Projektmanagement (nur ein Teil der Formalismen ist zu erfüllen), oder aber als Projekt nach den Richtlinien zum Projektmanagement. Hier sind grundsätzlich alle Regelungen zu beachten und zu erfüllen. Eine Anpassung an die tatsächlichen Erfordernisse ist mit Zustimmung des Auftraggebers möglich.

Wurde allerdings ein Projektauftrag / Lastenheft direkt durch den Auftraggeber erteilt, so dient die Aufgabenanalyse zur Konkretisierung dieses Auftrages und zur Klärung von noch offenen Fragen mit dem Auftraggeber. Bei einem Arbeitsgruppenauftrag gilt das gleiche.

### Vorstudie / Aufgabenanalyse im Rahmen eines Workshops

Die Vorstudie, oder Aufgabenanalyse, dient dazu, die Aufgabe, die sich durch ein (mögliches) Projekt ergibt, in ihrer Gesamtheit wahrzunehmen und zu beschreiben. Anstatt sich zu Anfang schon in Details zu verlieren, soll die Aufgabe aus allen denkbaren Blickwinkeln dargestellt und verstanden werden. Sie soll dem Bearbeiter ein Bild über die erforderlichen Tätigkeiten und Teilaufgaben liefern und ihm einen schnellen Einstieg in die Projektproblematik ermöglichen.

Die Fragen der Analyse nach dem WAS, WER, WO, WANN, WIE und WAS NICHT bilden einen „roten Faden", um den Projektrahmen festzulegen und ermöglichen dem Bearbeiter und dem Auftraggeber den Umfang des Vorhabens / Projektes zu erkennen.

*Final Phase*

- Presentation of the project result.
- Acceptance of the project result by the client
- Backing up of the project result
- Final report
- Dissolution of the project
- If necessary to determine a body for product support

## 2.1: Explain what steps as part of a preliminary study/analysis should be done and for what these steps are used.

The instrument of the preliminary study/analysis helps to clarify the project request. This task analysis helps in the decision-making, if and how this idea is put into practice. In the decision, to pursue the idea and to work it outside of the general organizational structure, there are two basic possibilities: either in the context of a working group, based on the guidelines for project management (only a part of the formal framework is met), or as a project, according to the guidelines for project management. In this case, principally all rules have to be observed and met. A customization to the actual requirements is possible with the consent of the client.

However, if a project mandate/specification is issued directly by the client, the task analysis is used toward the definition of this mandate and to clarify remaining questions with the client. The same shall apply in case of a work group order.

**Initial Study/Analysis in the Context of a Workshop**
The initial study, or task analysis, serves to get and describe a holistic view of the task, which results from a (potential) project. Instead of getting lost in the details at the beginning, the task should be viewed and understood from all possible angles. The aim is to provide the individual a picture of the required activities and subtasks and enable the project operator to get a quick start into the project objectives.

The questions of the analysis for the WHAT, WHO, WHERE, WHEN, HOW, and WHAT NOT constitute a common theme, in order to determine the scope of the project and allow the project operator and the client to recognize the scale of the undertaking/project.

## A] Problembeschreibung und anzustrebende Situation

### a) Hintergrundinformation

Dieser Abschnitt beschreibt den dienstlichen Aufgabenbereich des Auftraggebers und gibt an, warum das Projekt/Vorhaben für erforderlich gehalten wird. Hintergrund für ein Projekt/Vorhaben können zum Beispiel neue Tätigkeitsfelder, die Reaktion auf gesellschaftliche Veränderungen oder auch der Bedarf an Rationalisierungsmaßnahmen sein.

### b) Problembeschreibung (Ist-Stand)

Hier wird in einer informativen und knappen Weise die Problematik dargestellt, die durch die Umsetzung der Idee in Form eines Projektes oder sonstigen Vorhabens einer Lösung zugeführt werden soll.

Gefordert ist eine Untermauerung des Änderungsbedarfs durch die Nennung von Kenngrößen, wie zum Beispiel Ist-Aufwand, Informationsaufkommen, Kosten, Anzahl der beteiligten Mitarbeiter, Anzahl der Medienbrüche, unnötige Redundanzen usw.

Sofern es ähnliche Projekte oder Vorhaben gibt, die beabsichtigt, bereits begonnen oder abgeschlossen sind, sind diese hier zu nennen.

### c) Anzustrebende Situation

In diesem Kapitel fasst der Antragsteller alle Aspekte zusammen, welche die mit dem Vorhaben angestrebte künftige Situation beschreiben. Beschrieben werden auch die Aufbau- und Ablauforganisation sowie die bisherigen Arbeitsergebnisse, an denen Änderungen vorgenommen werden müssen. Auch die Form der Änderungen ist hier deutlich zu machen.

### d) Wesentliche Teilaufgaben

In welche Aufgabenblöcke als Teilaufgaben oder gar Teilprojekte ist die Aufgabe unterteilt? Werden Teilprojekte gebildet, so sind für diese unter einer Gesamtprojektleitung Teilprojektleiter zu bestimmen.

### e) Orte und Termine

Wo wird die Aufgabe gelöst? Seit wann besteht die Aufgabe? Ab wann wird das Vorhaben in Angriff genommen? Bis wann soll das Vorhaben beendet sein?

### f) Projektabschlusskriterien

Dieser Abschnitt identifiziert die wichtigsten Arbeitsergebnisse, damit das Projekt als erfolgreich abgeschlossen betrachtet werden kann. Sie sind vom Auftraggeber am Ende des Projektes abzunehmen. Es ist festzustellen, was das Projekt unbedingt erbringen muss und was als zusätzlich zwar wünschenswert, aber nicht zwingend erforderlich zu betrachten ist.

### g) Alternativen

Gibt es Alternativen? Warum hat man sich für die gewählte Alternative entschieden?

*A) Problem Description and Desired Results*

**a) Background Information**
This section describes the official mandate of the client and specifies why the project / undertaking is considered necessary. Background for a project / undertaking may for example, be new fields of activity, the response to social changes or the need for rationalization measures.

**b) Problem Description (Status Quo)**
Here the objectives are described in an informative and concise way, which should contribute to a solution by the implementation of the idea in the form of a project or another undertaking.

Required is a confirmation of the changes necessary by the definition of parameters, such as current expenditures, required information, cost, number of the employees involved, the changes of media format, avoiding unnecessary redundancy, etc.

If there are similar projects or undertakings, which are intended, have already begun, or are completed, these should be listed here.

**c) Target Situation**
In this chapter, the applicant summarizes all aspects of the project, which describe the target situation to be achieved by the project. Equally described are the organizational and operational structure, as well as the previous results, which have to be adapted. Also the form of the changes is to be specified clearly.

**d) Essential Sub-Tasks**
In what task units as subtasks or even as subprojects is the project divided? If subprojects will be created subproject managers need to be named below the main project management.

**e) Locations and Schedule**
Where will the problem be solved? Since when exists the task? When will the project be started? By when will the project be completed?

**f) Project Completion Criteria**
This section identifies the most important results, so that the project can be considered as successfully completed. The client accepts these at the end of the project. It is to be noted, which results are absolutely necessary and which are desirable, however not compulsory.

**g) Alternatives**
Are there alternatives? Why was the selected alternative chosen?

#### h) Rahmenbedingungen

Gibt es Einschränkungen oder Vorgaben, die auf die Arbeit an dem Vorhaben Einfluss haben? Hierzu zählen beispielsweise die anzuwendende Projektmethode, Prioritäten, Personal, Zeit, Technologie, Umgebung, Entscheidungszyklen, Werkzeuge und Techniken.

Eine wesentliche Rahmenbedingung bei Beschaffungsvorhaben stellt das Haushalts- und Vergaberecht dar. Die Durchführung eines Vergabeverfahrens hat stets Auswirkungen auf das Gesamtprojekt bezüglich Projektlaufzeit, formalen Zuständigkeiten und Vorgehensweisen, Projektrisiken und ggf. auf die Zusammensetzung der Projektgruppe. Deshalb wird dringend empfohlen, bereits im Vorfeld beziehungsweise in der Definitionsphase die zuständigen Spezialdienststellen zu kontaktieren.

Rahmenbedingungen können sich auch durch die Rechtsordnung, wie beispielsweise durch das Datenschutzrecht, ergeben.

Die Identifizierung von Rahmenbedingungen bestärkt das Management, diese zu kontrollieren, um den Erfolg sicherzustellen.

#### i) Verantwortung des Auftraggebers

Dem Auftraggeber muss nicht nur seine Verantwortung klar sein sondern auch die Rückwirkung auf den Projektverlauf und das Projektergebnis, wenn er dieser Verantwortung nicht gerecht wird. Dies bedeutet, dass der Auftraggeber das Projekt in jeder Hinsicht unterstützen und für das erforderliche Budget sorgen muss.

#### j) Annahmen

Annahmen beziehen sich beispielsweise auf vorgesehene Ergebnisse anderer Vorhaben, die ihrerseits aber Einfluss auf das Ergebnis des eigenen Projektes ausüben. Sie können sich auch auf die Erfüllung der oben genannten Regulierungsaufgaben beziehen. Eine derartige Annahme wäre beispielsweise, dass bis zum Abschluss des Projektes die dann erforderlichen technischen Voraussetzungen, die derzeit noch von einem anderen Projekt zu schaffen sind, auch tatsächlich erfüllt sind.

### B) Vorplanung und Analysen

#### a) Zielklärung – Zielhierarchie

Hier sind die sich aus den vorhergehenden Punkten im Teil A ergebenden wesentlichen Ziele „Was soll durch das Projekt erreicht werden?" zu nennen. Das Detaillieren der Projektziele wird in der Regel über mehrere Ebenen in Form einer Hierarchie durchgeführt. Das Oberziel wird dabei in mehrere sinnvolle Unterziele aufgespalten. Jedes Unterziel (Subziel) steht dabei zum Oberziel in einer Ziel-Mittel-Relation, d. h. das Unterziel ist das Mittel, das zur Erreichung des Oberziels beiträgt. Durch schrittweises Vorgehen werden immer weitere Ebenen gebildet.

Durch die Aufführung der einzelnen Projektziele soll eine umfassende Projektbetrachtung ermöglicht werden. Ein Projekt als Ganzes besteht aus kleineren, eng zusammenhängenden Zielen.

### h) General Conditions
Are there any restrictions or requirements, which impact on the work of the project? For example, this includes the applicable project method, priorities, staff, time, technology, environment, decision cycles, tools, and techniques.

An essential precondition for procurement is the budget and procurement law. The execution of a contract award procedure has always an impact on the overall project regarding project duration, formal responsibilities and procedures, project risks and, potentially, on the composition of the project group. It is strongly recommended to contact the competent special agencies early in the initial or definition phase. Basic conditions can result from the legal system, such as for example the Data Protection Law.

The identification of the environment encourages the management to control it, in order to ensure success.

### i) Responsibility of the Client
The client must not only be clear about his responsibility, but also on the impact of the development of the project and the result of the project, if he does not meet this responsibility. This means that the client is responsible for the project support and the necessary budget in every respect.

### j) Assumptions
Assumptions can, for example, refer to the results of other projects, which in turn influence the outcome of the own project. They can also refer to the fulfillment of the above-mentioned regulatory tasks. Such an assumption would, for example, that by the end of the project the then necessary technical conditions, which are still to be created by another project, will actually be in place.

## B) Pre-Planning and Analysis

### a) Objectives Statement – Objectives Hierarchy
Here the result from the previous points arising in the Part A essential objectives ("what should be achieved by the project?") are to be named. The detailing of the project objectives is usually performed in the form of a hierarchy with several levels. The overall objective is split into several meaningful sub-objectives. Each sub-objective fits to the overall objective in a goal-means relationship, i. e. , the sub-objective is the means, which contributes to achieve the main goal. Through an incremental approach, more and more levels will be created.

The listing of individual project objectives facilitates a comprehensive project overview. A project as a whole consists of smaller, closely related objectives.

These project objectives must be measurable and feasible in terms of quality and quantity. Additionally, content objectives may develop, such as organizational, personnel, and marketing objectives. Within the project processes are issues, such as cost, benefit, time, sales, etc., which can be defined as objectives to be achieved.

Diese Projektziele müssen in Bezug auf Qualität und Quantität messbar und durchführbar sein. Darüberhinaus können inhaltliche Zusatzziele auftreten, wie zum Beispiel Organisationsentwicklungsziele, Personalentwicklungsziele und Marketingziele. Innerhalb des Projektprozesses sind Punkte wie Kosten, Nutzen, Zeit, Umsatz u. a. als zu erreichende Ziele definierbar.

Eine weitergehende detaillierte Definition und Operationalisierung der Projektziele erfolgt nach Abschluss der Vorstudie/Aufgabenanalyse in einem weiteren Arbeitsschritt in der Definitionsphase.

**b) Projektumfeldanalyse (PUA)**
Projekte sind immer in ein Umfeld eingebettet (siehe Abb. 4), das aus verschiedenen Institutionen und Personen besteht. Positive und negative Projektinteressenten sind frühzeitig zu ermitteln, um bei eventuell später auftretenden Schwierigkeiten sofort reagieren zu können oder bereits zu Beginn des Projekts Förderer zu gewinnen und Hinderern den Wind aus den Segeln zu nehmen.

Einflüsse aus dem Projektumfeld berühren die Ziele und Erfolgsaussichten des Projektes und sind somit kritische Erfolgsfaktoren.

Um innerhalb eines Projektes alle betroffene Stakeholder zu identifizieren, wird die Projektumfeldanalyse (PUA) durchgeführt. Hierbei wird ein Projekt als ein System mit sozialen Strukturen betrachtet, wodurch eine Abgrenzung der Beteiligten im Projektumfeld möglich ist. Sie wird durchgeführt, um einerseits Betroffene zu Beteiligten zu machen, indem man sie in die Projektorganisation einbindet, und um andererseits Maßnahmen für kritische Beteiligte setzen zu können.

**Ziele der Projektumfeldanalyse sind:**

* Erkennung und Erfassung aller Randbedingungen und Einflussfaktoren für das Projekt
* Erfassung aller Interessensgruppen am Projekt (Stakeholder) und der Art ihrer Interessen
* Früherkennung von Projektrisiken
* Erkennung der Anknüpfungspunkte für die Einbettung des Projektes in das Unternehmen
* Erkennung von Chancen und Potenzialen
* Aufzeigen von Handlungsmöglichkeiten zur Beeinflussung des Projektumfeldes
* Dokumentation dieser Erkenntnisse für die Projektplanung

**c) Projektumfeldanalyse: Betroffene und Beteiligte der Projektorganisation**
Wer stellt die Instanzen des Projekts dar (welche Institutionen – Auftraggeber, Projektausschuss, der den Projektleiter stellende Verband, Mitglieder des Projektteams, Projekt-Geschäftsstelle)? Wer ist Projektbetroffener beziehungsweise Kunde (späterer Anwender des Projektergebnisses)?

A more detailed definition and operationalization of the project objectives is carried out after completion of the preliminary study / analysis in a further step in the definition phase.

**b) Project Environment Analysis (PEA)**
Projects are always rooted in an environment (cf. Fig. 4), which is formed by different institutions and persons. Positive and negative project leads need to be identified at an early stage, to be able to react immediately if later on difficulties arise or to obtain sponsors early in the project and to eliminate the objections of obstructionists.

Influences from the project environment touch on the objectives and prospects of success of the project and are therefore critical success factors.

To identify all affected stakeholders within a project a project environment analysis (PEA) is carried out. This is where a project is viewed as a system with social structures, which makes a distinction between the parties involved in the project context possible. The objective is to engage those affected to become involved in the project organization and initiate measures for critical stakeholders.

**Objectives of the Analysis of the Project Environment Are:**
- Recognition and documentation of all constraints and factors affecting the project
- Capturing of all stakeholders on the project and the nature of their interests
- Early detection of project risks
- Detection of the points of departure for the integration of the project in the company
- Detection of opportunities and potential
- Identify courses of action to influence the project environment
- Recording of these findings for the project planning

**c) Project Environment Analysis: Affected and Involved in the Project Organization**
Who represents the authorities of the project (which institutions – client, project steering committee, the association providing the project manager, members of the project team, project administration office? Who is affected by the project or customer (later on the user of the project result)?

### d) Projektrisikoanalyse

Da komplexe Projekte eine Vielzahl unbekannter Faktoren aufweisen, besteht eine wichtige Aufgabe der Projektleitung darin, in der Zukunft liegende Risiken vorauszusehen.

Das Risiko definiert sich durch die Eintrittswahrscheinlichkeit und die zu erwartende Schadenshöhe.

In der Projektrisikoanalyse sollen die Projektrisiken möglichst vollständig erfasst werden. Eine Orientierung am Projektstrukturplan und an der Projektumfeldanalyse fördert einerseits die Realisierung des Ziels der Vollständigkeit und sichert andererseits Konsistenz in der Projektdokumentation. Durch die Bestimmung von Projektrisiken werden gleichzeitig auch Maßnahmen zur Risikovermeidung und -vorsorge getroffen.

### e) Grobplanung der Projektstruktur (Projektstrukturplanung)

Hier sind zunächst die wesentlichen Maßnahmenbündel (= Arbeitspakete) zur Zielerreichung zu benennen, welche Produkte, Prozesse, und Anwendungen enthalten. Eine weitergehende Feinplanung der Projektstruktur ist erst nach Vorliegen einer mit dem Projektauftraggeber abgestimmten Zielhierarchie, nach Abschluss der Definitionsphase, möglich.

Die Darstellung der Maßnahmenbündel beinhaltet auch, welche externen Einflüsse und Entwicklungen zu berücksichtigen sind. Hierzu zählen zum Beispiel die Herstellung und Bedienung von Schnittstellen von bestehenden oder geplanten Systemen oder die Zusammenarbeit mit anderen Behörden und Organisationen.

Erforderliche Regulierungsaufgaben, wie beispielsweise die Einholung von Genehmigungen oder die Beschaffung bestimmter Hard- oder Software bestimmen die Maßnahmenbündel ebenso wie die Initialisierung von erforderlichen Vorschriften- und/oder Rechtsänderungen.

Baut das Projekt auf andere Vorhaben auf, so sind die Arbeitsergebnisse, die von dort zu liefern sind, hier zu beschreiben.

Der Projektstrukturplan (PSP) wird auf der Grundlage der Zielhierarchie erstellt. Dazu werden Arbeitspakete (AP) als kleinste Einheit im Strukturplan definiert, mit denen das jeweilige Ziel erreicht wird. Die Arbeitspakete wiederum können in einzelne Vorgänge untergliedert werden. Die Aufschlüsselung Projektziel – Teilprojekt – Teilaufgabe – Arbeitspaket erfolgt durch das Projektteam. Die Aufschlüsselung der Arbeitspakete in Vorgänge erfolgt durch den für die Erledigung des Arbeitspaketes zuständigen Auftragnehmer. Ein Arbeitspaket gilt dann als „geschnürt", wenn das Projektteam eine weitere Untergliederung für nicht mehr sinnvoll hält.

**Ziele der Strukturierung:**

- Schaffung von Transparenz
- Bildung von Teilprojekten und Arbeitspaketen

### d) Project Risk Assessment

Because complex projects have a number of unidentified factors, an important task of the project management is to predict future risks.

The "risk" is defined by the probability of their occurrence and the expected financial loss.

The project risks as far as possible are to be fully documented in the project risk assessment. An orientation on the work breakdown structure, and on the project environment analysis enhances the realization of the objective completeness and increases the consistency in the project documentation. By identifying the project risks at the same time risk prevention measures and precautions are being put in place.

### e) Outline of the Project Structure (Project Structure Planning)

Here are the essential packages of measures (=work packages) for the achievement are being identified, which contain products, processes, and applications. A more detailed planning of the project structure is only possible after the submission of the target hierarchy as agreed to with project sponsor and after the completion of the definition phase.

A presentation of the package of measures includes the type of external influences and developments, which are to be considered. These include, for example, the manufacture and operation interfaces of existing or planned systems or the co-operation with other authorities and organizations.

Required regulatory tasks, such as the collection of licenses or the procurement of hard or software determine the packages of measures as well as the initialization of the required regulations and/or legislative changes.

If the project is based on other projects, the results, which are to be provided by that project are to be described here.

The work breakdown structure (WBS) will be created on the basis of the target hierarchy. To do this work packages (WP) are defined as the smallest unit in the work breakdown, with which each objective is achieved. The work packages, in turn, can be broken down into individual activities. The breakdown of the project – subproject – subtask – work package is carried out by the project team. The breakdown of the work packages in operations is carried out by the contractor responsible for the execution of the work package. A work package will then be considered as a "package", when the project team does no longer consider a further breakdown for useful.

**Objectives of the Structure:**

- Creating transparency
- Formation of subprojects and work packages

### f) Ressourcenplan

Ausgehend vom Projektstrukturplan und den dort definierten Arbeitspaketen als kleinster Einheit wird die Personal-, Sachmittel- und Einsatzmittelplanung vorgenommen. Die zentralen Fragen sind hier: wer, wann, wie viel und wie lange. Aus dieser Planung lassen sich auch die Gesamtkosten eines Projektes relativ leicht ableiten, da man nur mit überschaubaren, d. h. gut schätzbaren Größen rechnen muss.

Die Planung der verfügbaren Ressourcen muss aus verschiedenen Gründen erfolgen. Erstens ist das Projektergebnis maßgeblich von den zur Verfügung stehenden Ressourcen abhängig und zweitens ist die wirtschaftliche Betrachtung für alle projektspezifischen Tätigkeiten relevant.

### g) Balkenplan

Der Balkenplan dient dazu, eine übersichtliche Darstellung der Terminplanung und der zeitlichen Lage der Arbeitspakete zu erhalten und ist in folgende Teilaufgaben untergliedert:

- Ermittlung der Zeiten für die einzelnen Aktivitäten
- Gesamtzeit für das Projekt
- Anfangs- und Endtermine
- kritische Pfade

### h) Stellungnahme des Strategischen Controlling (optional)

- Aussagen zur Strategieverträglichkeit
- Aussagen zur Portfolioverträglichkeit – gibt es bereits gleiche oder ähnliche Vorhaben / Projekte oder sind diese bereits beantragt?

### Entscheidung „Go" oder „No-Go"

Die Ergebnisse der durchgeführten Aufgabenanalyse bilden die Entscheidungsgrundlage zur Beantwortung der Fragen, ob das Projekt durchgeführt wird bzw. ob es unter den erörterten Gesichtspunkten überhaupt durchgeführt werden kann.

### f) Resource Plan

Based on the work breakdown structure, and the work packages defined as the smallest unit the planning of staff, material resources and supply is executed. The central issues here are: who, when, how much and for how long. From this planning the total cost of a project can be easily derived because only manageable, i. e. easily estimated variables are to be considered.

The planning of the available resources must be carried out for various reasons. First the result of the project largely depends on the resources available and, second, the economic view for all relevant project-specific activities is being considered.

### g) Gantt Chart

A Gantt chart is used to show a clear representation of the scheduling and the temporal location of the work packages and is divided into the following subtasks:

- Determination of the duration of the various activities
- Total time for the project
- Start and End dates
- Critical paths

### h) Position Statement of the Strategic Controlling Panel (Optional)

- Statements on strategy compatibility
- Statements on portfolio compatibility – are there identical or similar plans / projects or are these applied for?

### Decision "Go" or "No Go"

The results of the executed analysis form the basis for decision making, whether the project will be carried out or if, in light of the addressed objectives can be carried out at all.

## 2.2: Welche Elemente sollte das sog. Lastenheft enthalten?

1 Projekt (Arbeitsgruppe)
   1.1 Projektname (Arbeitsgruppenname)
   1.2 Hintergrund
   1.3 Auftragnehmer
       1.3.1 Projektleiter (Arbeitsgruppenleiter)
       1.3.2 Projektteam (Arbeitsgruppenmitglieder)
   1.4 Organisationsform (Aufbauorganisation)
   1.5 Projekt-Controlling-Stelle (entfällt bei Arbeitsgruppe)
   1.6 Projektausschuss (entfällt bei Arbeitsgruppe)

2 Problembeschreibung / Ist-Stand

3 Lösungsvorschlag / Alternativenauswahl

4 Nutzen
   4.1 Projektziele (Arbeitsgruppenziele)
   4.2 Projektumfeldanalyse
   4.3 Chancen und Risiken (Risikoanalyse)
   4.4 Projektstruktur

5 Aufwandsschätzung
   5.1 Umfang des Projektes
   5.2 ausgeschlossene Leistungen
   5.3 Aufwand und Kosten, Personal und Budget
   5.4 Projektdauer, Termine (Balkenplan)

6 weitere Informationen
   6.1 Betroffene und Beteiligte
   6.2 Rahmenbedingungen
       6.2.1 Schnittstellen
       6.2.2 Einordnung in die IT-Strategie, Priorisierung

7 Anlagen

Abb. 65: Projektantrag.

## 2.3: Erläutern Sie die vier Formen der Projektorganisation und diskutieren Sie, wann welche Form sinnvoll ist.

**Linien-Projektorganisation**
- Projektteam in der Linie setzt sich aus Mitarbeitern des Linienvorgesetzten und zugleich Projektleiters zusammen.
- Weitere, außerhalb der Linie stehende Personen werden nicht hinzugezogen.

## 2.2: What Elements Should Be Contained in the So-Called Requirement Specifications?

1 *Project (working group)*
   1.1 *Project name (workgroup name)*
   1.2 *Background*
   1.3 *Contractor*
      1.3.1 *Project manager (work group leader)*
      1.3.2 *Project team (work group member)*
   1.4 *Organizational structure (company organization)*
   1.5 *Project controlling body (not applicable for working group)*
   1.6 *Project steering committee (not applicable for working group)*

2 *Problem description (status quo)*

3 *Suggested solution / alternative selection*

4 *Benefit*
   4.1 *Project objectives (work group objectives)*
   4.2 *Project environment analysis*
   4.3 *Opportunities and risks (risk analysis)*
   4.4 *Project structure*

5 *Cost estimate*
   5.1 *Scope of the project*
   5.2 *Exempted services*
   5.3 *Effort and costs, personnel and budget*
   5.4 *Project duration, schedule (Gantt chart)*

6 *Further information*
   6.1 *Affected and interested parties*
   6.2 *General conditions*
      6.2.1 *Interfaces*
      6.2.2 *Classification into the IT-strategy, prioritization*

7 *Attachment*

Fig. 65: Project Application.

## 2.3: Explain the Four Forms of Project Organization and Discuss When Each of the Forms is Useful.

**Linear Project Organization**

- A linear project team consists of employees of the line manager and project manager both.

- Further persons, outside the linear relationship, are not involved.

| Vorteile | Nachteile |
| --- | --- |
| + Einheit der Leitung | – Doppelbeanspruchung des Projekt- und Abteilungsleiters |
| + Einheit des Auftragsempfangs | – nicht immer fachlich und qualitativ richtiges Personal verfügbar |
| + keine Personalversetzung | – schwieriger Ausgleich von Personalbelastungsspitzen |
| + geringer Koordinierungsaufwand | |

Tab. 35: Vor- und Nachteile der Linien-Projektorganisation.

**Stabs- oder Einfluss-Projektorganisation**

- Der Projektkoordinator erhält eine Stabsstelle und ist direkt der Geschäftsleitung angegliedert.
- Die Mitarbeiter verbleiben in der Linie.
- Projekt-„Leiter" hat keine Weisungsbefugnis gegenüber der Linie, sondern ist nur Koordinator mit Vorschlagsrecht.
- Die Stabsstelle ist für die Informationssammlung, Entscheidungsvorbereitung und Berichterstattung verantwortlich.

| Vorteile | Nachteile |
| --- | --- |
| + geringe organisatorische Veränderungen | – mangelndes Verantwortungsgefühl |
| + hohe Flexibilität beim Personaleinsatz | – fehlender Teamgeist |
| + schnell zu realisieren | – langsame Reaktionsgeschwindigkeit bei Störungen |
| + fachlich hohe Ausstattung durch Koordination der Fachabteilungen | – hohe Konfliktgefahr |
| + Nähe zur Dienststellenleitung (Entscheidungsinstanz und Machtorgan) | – fehlende Autorität des Projektleiters |
| | – hoher Aufwand für die Dienststellenleitung |

Tab. 36: Vor- und Nachteile der Stabs-/Einfluss-Projektorganisation.

| Benefits: | Disadvantages: |
|---|---|
| + Cohesive management | – Dual demands on the project and division lead |
| + Single order receipt | – Technically and qualitatively suitable staff not always available |
| + No personnel movement | – Difficult to balance personnel load spikes |
| + Low coordination effort | |

Tab. 35: Benefits and Disadvantages Linear Project Organization.

**Staff or Influence Project Organization**
- The project coordinator is placed in a staff position and reports directly to management.
- The employees report linear as before.
- Project leader has no authority over the linear aligned employees, and is only coordinator with a right of suggestion.
- The staff positions is responsible for information gathering, decision making preparation and reporting.

| Benefits: | Disadvantages: |
|---|---|
| + Low organizational impact | – Lack of feeling of responsible |
| + High flexibility in human resource management | – Lacking team spirit |
| + Fast to implement | – Slow response time in the event of problems |
| + Technically high equipment by coordination of the departments | – High risk of conflict |
| + Proximity to management (decision-making body and seat of power) | – Lacking authority of the project manager |
| | – High involvement for the managers – errors must be adjusted directly from this point |

Tab. 36: Benefits and Disadvantages Staff or Influence Project Organization.

**Reine Projektorganisation**

- Ein Projektteam wird für die Dauer des Projekts gebildet.
- Die Teammitglieder sind aus der Linie herausgelöst und arbeiten ausschließlich für die Ziele des Projekts.
- Der Projektleiter hat die fachliche Projektverantwortung und die Führungsverantwortung.
- Nach Beendigung des Projekts kehren alle Beteiligten wieder in ihre Linienfunktion zurück und werden aus dem Projekt entlassen.

| Vorteile | Nachteile |
|---|---|
| + große Kompetenz des Projektleiters | – großer organisatorischer Aufwand |
| + eindeutige Weisungsbefugnis | – hoher Personaleinsatz |
| + kurze Informationswege | – hohe Kosten |
| + optimale Ausrichtung aller Ressourcen auf das Projektziel | – Probleme der Projektmitarbeiter, zum Beispiel bei der Rückkehr in die Linie nach Projektende |
| + schnelle Reaktion auf Störungen | – u. U. großer Wissensverlust beim Ausscheiden von Projektmitgliedern |
| + Transparenz bei Aufgabenverteilung und Verantwortung | |
| + zielgerichtete Zusammenarbeit im Team | |
| + geringer Koordinierungsaufwand in den Fachabteilungen | |
| + hohe Identifikation mit dem Projekt | |

Tab. 37: Vor- und Nachteile der reinen Projektorganisation.

**Pure Project Organization**

- A project team is formed for the duration of the project.
- The team members are removed from the line and work exclusively for the objectives of the project.
- The project manager has the technical and managerial responsibility of the project.
- The completion of the project all parties return to their line management function and are dismissed from the project.

| Benefits: | Disadvantages: |
| --- | --- |
| + Great expertise of the project manager | − Large organizational effort |
| + Unambiguous direction authority | − High demands on staffing levels |
| + Short information paths | − High costs |
| + Optimal orientation of all resources on the project objective | − Problems of project employees, such as at the time of their return to the line after the end of the project |
| + Fast response to problems | − Maybe great loss of knowledge on termination of project team members |
| + Transparency in allocation of tasks and responsibility | |
| + Targeted cooperation in team context | |
| + Low coordination effort in the individual departments | |
| + High level of identification with the project | |

Tab. 37: Benefits and Disadvantages Pure Project Organization.

**Matrix-Projektorganisation**

- Der Projektleiter wird aus der Linie ausgegliedert.
- Die Mitarbeiter verbleiben in der Linie und sind ihren Linienvorgesetzten weiterhin unterstellt.
- Der Projektleiter hat zusätzliche projektbezogene Weisungsbefugnisse (zeitlich befristetes Mehrliniensystem).
- Der Projektleiter ist für die Zielvorgabe und die zeitlichen Vorgaben verantwortlich, wobei der Linienvorgesetzte bestimmt, von wem und wie die Projektaufgabe durchgeführt wird.

| Vorteile | Nachteile |
| --- | --- |
| + Projektverantwortung durch Projektleiter | − Mitarbeiter als „Diener zweier Herren" |
| + hohe Identifikation der Projektleiters mit dem Projekt | − schwierige Teamentwicklung |
| + flexibler Personaleinsatz | − schwierige Kompetenzabgrenzung zwischen Linie und Projektleiter |
| + größeres Sicherheitsgefühl der Mitarbeiter | − hohe Anforderungen an Kommunikation und Information |
| + gute Weiterbildungsmöglichkeiten | − „Wettbewerb" um Ressourcen |
|  | − vorgesetztes Gremium wird häufig beansprucht |

Tab. 38: Vor- und Nachteile der Matrix-Projektorganisation.

**Matrix Project Organization**

- The project leader is spun off from the line.
- The employees will remain in the line and continue to report to the line manager.
- The project manager has additional project-related authority (temporary multi chain system).
- The project manager is responsible for the objective statement and the schedule constraints while the line manager determines, by whom and how the project objectives will be performed.

| Benefits: | Disadvantages: |
|---|---|
| + Project responsibility of the project manager | – Employees as "servant of two masters" |
| + High degree of identification of the project manager and the project | – Difficult team development |
| + Flexible staffing | – Difficult delineation of responsibilities between the line and project manager |
| + Greater feeling of security of employees | – High demands on communication and information |
| + Good training opportunities | – "Competition" for resources |
|  | – Frequent use of supervisory panel |

Tab. 38: Benefits and Disadvantages Matrix Project Organization.

**Wechsel der Organisationsform**

Es ist durchaus denkbar und sinnvoll, dass während eines Projektes die Organisationsform wechselt. So empfiehlt es sich beispielsweise in der Definitions- und Planungsphase mit einer Matrix-Projektorganisation zu arbeiten, da man damit auf ein breit gefächertes Fachwissen zurückgreifen kann. Geht es dann in die Realisierungsphase, so ist die reine Projektorganisation nicht von der Hand zu weisen, da man mit einem speziellen Team die vorher geplanten Arbeitsschritte durchführen kann.

| Aufgabenstellung | Organisationsform | | | |
|---|---|---|---|---|
| | Linien- | Stabs- | Reine | Matrix- |
| | Projektorganisation | | | |
| Produktentwicklung | | | ✓ | |
| vertriebsorientiertes Großprojekt | | | ✓ | |
| bereichsinterne Verfahrensentwicklung | ✓ | | | |
| bereichsübergreifende Verfahrensentwicklung | | | | ✓ |
| Entwicklung mit Fremdfirmen | | ✓ | | |
| kurze Entwicklungszeit (<1 Jahr) | ✓ | | | |
| lange Entwicklungszeit (>1 Jahr) | | | ✓ | |
| fester Terminrahmen | ✓ | | ✓ | |
| Projekt mit geringem Umfang | ✓ | | | |
| Projekt mittlerer Größe | | ✓ | | ✓ |
| großes Entwicklungsvolumen | | | ✓ | |
| hohes Projektrisiko | | ✓ | ✓ | |
| anteiliger Ressourcenzugriff | | | | ✓ |
| Ähnlichkeit mit anderen Entwicklungsaktivitäten | | | | ✓ |
| eindeutige Aufgabenteilung | | ✓ | | |
| klar abgegrenztes Thema | ✓ | | | |
| hoher Grad an Interdisziplinarität | | | | ✓ |

Abb. 66: Projektorganisationsformen.

## Change of the Type of Organization

It is quite conceivable and appropriate that the organizational form changes during the project. It is recommendable to work in the definition and planning phase with a matrix project organization since it can rely on a broad expertise. In the implementation phase the pure project organization is not to be dismissed out of hand, as it will have a dedicated team, which can perform the preplanned operations.

| Objectives | Organizational Structure | | | |
| --- | --- | --- | --- | --- |
| | Line | Staff | Pure | Matrix |
| | Project organization | | | |
| Product development | | | ✓ | |
| Sales oriented major project | | | ✓ | |
| Divisional level process development | ✓ | | | |
| Cross-functional process development | | | | ✓ |
| Development with third parties | | ✓ | | |
| Short development schedule (<1 year) | ✓ | | | |
| Long development schedule (>1 year) | | | ✓ | |
| Fixed schedule | ✓ | | ✓ | |
| Small scale project | ✓ | | | |
| Medium sized project | | ✓ | | ✓ |
| Large development volume | | | ✓ | |
| High project risk | | ✓ | ✓ | |
| Pro rata resource access | | | | ✓ |
| Similarity to other development activities | | | | ✓ |
| Clear division of responsibilities | | ✓ | | |
| Clearly defined topic | ✓ | | | |
| High degree of interdisciplinary approach | | | | ✓ |

Fig. 66: Project Organization Forms.

## 3.1: Welche Punkte sollten beim Projekt-Start-up definiert werden?

**Aufgaben des Auftraggebers**
- Projektauftrag (auch Lastenheft genannt)
- Budget und Personal festlegen und sicherstellen
- Projektleiter ernennen und unterstützen
- Unterstützung bei der Zieldefinition
- Pflichtenheft und Projektpläne abnehmen
- Statusberichte prüfen
- Phasenergebnisse prüfen und genehmigen
- Projektergebnis abnehmen

**Aufgaben des Projektleiters**
- Projektteam aufstellen
- Pflichtenheft erstellen
- Projektziele definieren
- Controlling
- Einsatz von effizienten Arbeits- und Entscheidungstechniken
- Projektteam zusammenführen
- Konflikte im Projektteam schlichten und für zielgerichtete Zusammenarbeit sorgen
- Informationspflicht gegenüber den Projektbeteiligten

**Befugnisse des Projektleiters**
- projektbezogene Anordnungsbefugnisse, entsprechend der gewählten Form der Aufbauorganisation (Linien-, Stabs-, reine und Matrixorganisation)
- eingeschränkte Verhandlungsbefugnisse mit Fremdfirmen unter Beachtung der Ausschreibungs- und Vergaberichtlinien
- Mitspracherecht bei der Benennung der Projektteammitglieder
- Vorschlagsrecht bei erforderlichen Fortbildungsmaßnahmen
- Entscheidungsrecht bei Alternativenauswahl
- direktes Kommunikationsrecht mit Projektbeteiligten
- Einberufung von Projektausschusssitzungen

**Festlegung der Aufbau- und Ablauforganisation**
- Wer macht was?
- Wer hat welche Funktionen, Rechte, Pflichten?
- Informationsfluss des Projektleiters zum Auftraggeber, Team, Gremien u. a.
- Abwicklungs-Richtlinien

## 3.1: What Items Should be Defined During the Project Start-Up?

**Tasks of the Client**
- Project order (also called specifications)
- Determine and secure budget and personnel
- Appoint and support project manager
- Support in the definition of objectives
- Accept functional specifications and project plans
- Check status reports
- Review and approve phase results
- Accept project results

**Tasks of the Project Manager**
- Establish project team
- Drafting of specifications
- Define project objectives
- Cost control
- Use of efficient labor and decision techniques
- Form the project team
- Deconflict the project team and ensure targeted cooperation
- Duty to keep the project participants informed

**Competencies of the Project Leader**
- Project-related authority, according to the chosen form of organizational structure (line, bar, pure and matrix organization)
- Limited negotiation authority with contractors in accordance with the tendering and procurement directives
- Co-determination rights in the appointment of the project team members
- Nomination rights for necessary training
- Decision making power in the selection of alternatives
- Right of direct communication with project stakeholders
- Convening of project steering committee meetings

**Definition of the Organizational and Operational Structure**
- Who does what
- Who has which functions, rights, obligations
- Information flow of the project manager to the client, team, panels, etc.
- Process guidelines

- Festlegung des Umgangs mit Änderungen im Projekt (Konfigurationsmanagement)
- Kommunikationswege
- Projekt-Dokumentation
- Festlegung von Terminen regelmäßiger Projekt-Statussitzungen (PSS)
- Festlegung der zu verwendenden Hilfsmittel, Schablonen, Checklisten etc.

**Erstellung**
- eines groben Terminplanes
- einer groben Risikoanalyse
- eines Qualitätssicherungsplanes
- eines Planungsplanes (Planung der Planungsphase)
- eines PSU-Ergebnisprotokolls

### 3.2: Welchen Anforderungen sollten Projektziele genügen? Weshalb ist dies so wichtig?

**Zieldefinition – Projektziele und Zielstrukturplan**
Die Zieldefinition bildet die Vorstufe zum Projektstrukturplan. Erst wenn die Ziele der Projektarbeit hinreichend definiert sind, darf in die nächste Phase der Projektarbeit, die Planungsphase, übergegangen werden. Wird dies nicht beachtet, fällt man, wie die Praxis gezeigt hat, immer wieder in die (Ziel-)Definitionsphase zurück und dreht sich mit der Projektarbeit im Kreis.

**Definition**
Ziele sind vorausgedachte Ergebnisse der Arbeit.

Klare, eindeutige, erreichbare und von allen Projektbeteiligten akzeptierte Ziele und Zwischenziele müssen vorhanden sein. Sie sind die Basis aller Aktivitäten.

**Anforderungen an Ziele**
- Ergebnis (Qualität; Quantität)
- Termin (Zeit)
- messbar
- Rahmenbedingungen
- Verantwortlichkeiten
- kontrollierbar
- schriftlich festgehalten
- lösungsneutral

Auch Nicht-Ziele sollten definiert werden, um eine klare Abgrenzung der Projektziele zu erreichen.

- Definition of the handling changes in the project (configuration management)
- Communication channels
- Project documentation
- Definition of deadlines for regular project status meetings (PSM)
- Determination of which tools, templates, checklists, etc. to use

**Creation**
- of a rough schedule
- of a rough risk analysis
- of a quality assurance plan
- of a design plan (planning the planning phase)
- of a PSU performance statistics

## 3.2: What Requirements Should the Project Objectives Meet? Why Is This So Important?

**Objective Definition – Project Objectives and Target Structure Plan**
The target objective definition is the precursor to the work breakdown structure. Only when the objectives of the project are sufficiently well defined, may the project work proceed to the next phase: the project planning phase. If this is not observed, the project will continually revert, as has been shown in practice, back to the (target) definition phase with the project work will turn in a circle.

**Definition**
Objectives are imagined results of the work.

Clear, unambiguous, achievable objectives as well as intermediate objectives accepted by all project participants must exist. They are the foundation of all activities.

**Requirements for Objectives**
- Result (quality, quantity)
- Schedule (time)
- Measurable
- General conditions
- Responsibilities
- Controllable
- Documented in writing
- Neutral to the outcome

Also non-objectives should be defined to achieve a clear delineation of the project objectives.

### 4.1: Weshalb ist eine sorgfältige Projektplanung notwendig?

Eine sorgfältige Projektplanung stellt sicher, dass

- man sichere Aussagen zum Projektablauf treffen kann;
- kritische Faktoren im Projektablauf vorab ermittelt werden, um das Projektrisiko zu vermindern;
- alle Projektressourcen zielgerichtet eingesetzt werden können und
- man eine Basis zur effizienten Projektsteuerung hat.

### 4.2: Nennen Sie die sechs erforderlichen Projektpläne und beschreiben Sie zwei dieser Pläne ausführlich.

Die erforderlichen Projektpläne in der Übersicht:

**Projektstrukturplan (PSP)**
- Zerlegung des Projekts in einzelne abgrenzbare Tätigkeiten, um eine Übersicht aller Aktivitäten zu erhalten (Teilprojekte – Teilaufgaben – Arbeitspakete)
- Ordnung der Einzelvorgänge zu einer hierarchischen Struktur

**Projektablaufplan (PAP)**
- Festlegung einer logischen zeitlichen Reihenfolge der einzelnen Arbeitspakete
- Festlegung parallel abarbeitbarer Arbeitspakete

**Aktivitätenliste / Balkendiagramm / Netzplan**
- Ergänzung des Projektablaufplans um die Zeitkomponente Projektterminplan
- Ermittlung des Anfangs- und Endtermins für jedes Arbeitspaket sowie des Verantwortlichen
- alternative Darstellung mittels tabellarischer Liste oder Balkendiagramm

**Ressourcenplan**
- Ermittlung des benötigten Personals und der benötigten Betriebsmittel
- Darstellung als zeitbezogene Gesamtübersicht aller erforderlichen Kapazitäten während der Projektlaufzeit
- Darstellung der Verfügbarkeit von Ressourcen zum geplanten Ablaufzeitpunkt

**Kostenplan**
- Ermittlung der Kosten je Arbeitspaket
- Darstellung als Gesamtübersicht über die Projektlaufzeit

## 4.1: Why Is a Careful Project Planning Necessary?

A careful project planning ensures that

- you can make reliable statements about the project schedule.
- critical factors in the project schedule will be established in advance, in order to reduce the project risk.
- all project resources can be used purposefully and
- a basis for efficient project management exits.

## 4.2: Name the Six Necessary Project Plans and Describe Two of These Plans in Detail.

The required project plans in an overview

**Work Breakdown Structure (WBS)**
- Disassembly of the project in the separately identifiable activities, in order to obtain an overview of all activities (subprojects – tasks – work packages)
- Arranging of the individual processes into a hierarchical structure

**Project Schedule (PS)**
- Defining a logical chronological order of the individual work packages
- Defining parallel workable packages

**Activities List / Gantt Chart / Network Plan**
- Completion of the project schedule by the time component of the project milestone plan
- Determination of the start and end date for each work package, as well as the responsible individual
- Alternative representation via tabular list or Gantt chart

**Resource Plan**
- Determination of the required staff and the amount of materials required
- Representation as a time-based overview of all necessary capacities during the project period
- Display of the availability of resources at the scheduled milestone

**Budget**
- Calculation of the cost per work package
- Representation as a general overview of the project schedule

**Finanzplan**

- Planung der Finanzmittel im vorgesehenen Zeitpunkt des Projektverlaufs

*Ausführliche Beschreibung zweier Projektpläne: Kapitel 4.5 „Die Projektpläne als Beispiel".*

## 5.1: Welche Ziele verfolgt die Qualitätssicherung beim Projektmanagement?

Die Qualitätssicherung soll im Rahmen eines Projekts einerseits dazu beitragen, die **Kundenzufriedenheit** zu erreichen, beziehungsweise zu steigern, und andererseits soll sie einen Beitrag zur **Fehlervermeidung** und **wirtschaftlichen Produkterstellung** leisten.

## 5.2: Erläutern Sie, zwischen welchen Arten von Sitzungen man unterscheidet.

**Ereignisorientierte Statussitzung**
Die Projektgruppe kommt wegen unerwarteter Ereignisse zusammen (Störfall, Krisensitzung etc.).

**Startup-Sitzung (auch Kick-off)**
Mit dieser Sitzung erfolgt die Begründung des Projektes.

**Abschluss-Sitzung**
Hierbei handelt es sich um die formelle Beendigung des Projektes und Abnahme des Ergebnisses durch den Auftraggeber.

**Regelmäßige Statussitzung (Jour Fixe)**
Dabei handelt es sich um fest vereinbarte Termine zur Lagebesprechung, Problemlösung etc. (Monatsbesprechung, Freitagssitzung).

**Ergebnisorientierte Sitzungen**
Diese Sitzungen dienen der Vorstellung von Teilergebnissen, Feststellung des Erreichens von Meilensteinen; es handelt sich grundsätzlich um eine Informationssitzung, um die Projektbeteiligten auf einen einheitlichen Wissensstand zu bringen.

**Ereignisorientierte Sitzungen**
Sitzungen, bei denen in der Regel aktuelle Probleme im Projektverlauf erörtert werden und bei denen Entscheidungen über das weitere Vorgehen getroffen werden müssen.

**Phasenentscheidungssitzung**
Zusammenkommen eines Entscheidungsgremiums über den Abschluss und den Start von Projektphasen nach dem Phasenplan.

**Financial Plan**
- Planning of the funding provided for milestone of the project

*For detailed description of two project plans see chapter 4.5 "The project plans project plans as an example".*

## 5.1: What Are the Objectives of the Quality Assurance in Project Management?

The quality assurance in the context of a project contributes to achieve or increase customer satisfaction, and, on the other hand contributes to error prevention and economic product creation.

## 5.2: Discuss the different types of meetings, which exist

**Event-driven Progress Meeting**
The project group meets due to unexpected events (incident, crisis meeting, etc.).

**Startup Meeting (Also Kick Off)**
With this session the justification of the project is provided.

**Completion Meeting**
This is the formal completion of the project and acceptance of the result by the client.

**Regular Status Review (Jour Fixe)**
These are is fixed dates for reviews, problem solving, etc. (monthly review, Friday meetings).

**Results Oriented Meetings**
These meetings are used for the presentation of partial results, determination of the achievement of milestones; this is basically a briefing session, to get the project participants on the same playing field.

**Event Driven Meetings**
Meetings, where usually current problems in the course of the project are discussed and in which decisions must be made on how to proceed further.

**Phase Decision-Making Meeting**
A decision-making body will meet at the conclusion and the start of project phases according to the phase plan.

## 5.3: Was sollte man bei Projektsitzungen beachten? Warum sind diese Aspekte wichtig?

**Vorbereitung**

- Tagesordnung rechtzeitig vorher festlegen und an Teilnehmer versenden (Besprechungsziele)
- Vertreterregelung für Sitzungsteilnehmer grundsätzlich nicht zulassen
- Arbeitsaufträge an Teilnehmer rechtzeitig erteilen
- mehrtägige Sitzungen vorsehen
- geeigneten Raum buchen (Größe, Einrichtung, Medien, Werkzeuge etc.)
- für Pausenbetreuung sorgen
- Moderator einsetzen
- Protokollführer bestimmen
- Agenda zu Sitzungsbeginn
- Teilnehmerunterlagen vorbereiten und ggf. vorher versenden

Die hier genannten Aspekte der Vorbereitung sind wichtig, damit die Projektsitzung effektiv ablaufen kann. Ist den Teilnehmern vorher unklar, worum es in der Sitzung gehen soll, können sie sich nicht gezielt auf einzelne Themen vorbereiten und ggf. die erforderlichen Unterlagen zusammensuchen. Es ist wichtig, dass Entscheidungen nur im Beisein aller Teilnehmer getroffen werden, da alle Teilnehmer an deren Umsetzung mitwirken müssen. Der Einsatz eines Moderators ermöglicht ein klar strukturiertes Vorgehen und erhöht die Wahrscheinlichkeit eines konfliktfreien Ablaufs. Die Bestimmung eines Protokollführers sorgt erstens dafür, dass die Ergebnisse schriftlich fixiert werden, und zweitens dafür, dass alle übrigen Teilnehmer mit voller Aufmerksamkeit zuhören können. Auch die Rahmenbedingungen der Sitzung sind wichtig, um ungestört und effektiv arbeiten zu können.

**Ablauf**

- Als „TOP 1" immer allgemeine Informationen/Neuigkeiten abfragen
- Präsentation von Arbeitsergebnissen
- für zielgerichtete Diskussionen und Gespräche sorgen
- Besprechungsergebnisse zusammenfassen
- Besprechungsergebnisse kategorisieren

Das Abfragen von Neuigkeiten zu Beginn dient dazu, dass man diese in die Sitzung mit einbeziehen kann und alle Teilnehmer die Möglichkeit haben, als Erstes ihre wichtigsten Informationen mitzuteilen. Arbeitsergebnisse sollten für alle sichtbar präsentiert werden, damit alle den gleichen Ausgangsinformationsstand haben. Damit die Besprechung effektiv abläuft und sich nicht in unwichtigen Details verläuft, sollten die Gespräche stets zielgerichtet sein. Die gute und anschauliche Dokumentation der Ergebnisse ist wichtig, um sie allen Beteiligten zugänglich zu machen und immer wieder ins Gedächtnis zu rufen.

## 5.3: What You Should Note in Project Meetings? Why Are These Issues Important?

**Preparation**
- Set agenda and send to participants ahead of time (meeting objectives)
- Do not allow deputy rules for participants by principle
- Provide work orders to participants in good time
- Plan multi-day sessions
- Book a suitable room (size, furniture, media, tools, etc.)
- Ensure refreshments during the breaks
- Use a moderator
- Nominate a note taker to keep the protocol
- Issue the meeting agenda in the beginning
- Prepare and send hand-outs ahead of time if necessary

The above-mentioned aspects of the preparation are important, so that the project meeting can be carried out effectively. If the participants are unclear, about the purpose of the meeting, they cannot specifically prepare for individual subjects and, if necessary, research the required documents. It is important that decisions be made only in the presence of all participants, since all participants must participate in their implementation. The use of a moderator allows a clearly structured process and increases the likelihood of a conflict-free process. The nomination of a recorder for the protocol first ensures that the results are documented in written form, and secondly, that all other participants can listen while paying full attention. The general conditions of the meeting are equally important, to allow undisturbed and effective work.

**Schedule**
- As a "Top 1" always query general information / news
- Presentation of work results
- Ensure focused discussions and conversations
- Summarize discussion results
- Categorize discussion results

The querying of news at the beginning serves to incorporate these in the meeting and all participants will have the opportunity to communicate their most important information first. Results should be presented for all to see, so that all have the same ingoing level of information. So that the meeting progresses effectively and does not meander into unimportant details, the discussions should always be focused. The good and explanatory documentation of the results is important to make it available to all parties and to refocus everybody as necessary.

### 6.1: Wozu dient die Projektabschlussphase?

In der Projektabschlussphase wird das Projektergebnis präsentiert und vom Auftraggeber abgenommen. Um den Abschluss eines Projektes durchführen zu können, muss vorher ein Ende definiert worden sein. Zuletzt werden das Projekt und die dazugehörige Projektgruppe (Projektleiter und Projektteam) aufgelöst.

### 6.2: Welche sind die Aufgaben des Projektleiters innerhalb der Abschlussphase?

- Abnahmebedingungen definieren
- Abschlussbericht erstellen
- Abschlusssitzung mit Auftraggeber durchführen
- Feedback der Projektmitglieder einholen
- Realisierungsverantwortliche einbeziehen
- Leistung der Projektmitglieder würdigen
- Reintegration der Projektbeteiligten vorbereiten
- Erfahrungen dokumentieren
- Abschlussfest mit Projektgruppe

### 7: Beschreiben Sie die Phasen der Teamentwicklung.

**1. Anfangsphase der Gruppen-Konstituierung**

Teamstruktur ist durch hohe Unsicherheit gekennzeichnet.
*Aufgabe für Steuerung: Sorge dafür, dass jeder seinen Platz findet.*

**2. Phase der Turbulenz, Konflikte, Konkurrenz**

*Aufgabe für Steuerung: Krisen und Konflikte sind zu erwarten und ein gutes Zeichen für Teamentwicklung.*

**3. Phase der Einigung auf Spielregeln, Etablierung von Normen**

Gegenseitige Unterstützung und Zusammenhalt bildet sich aus.
*Aufgabe für Steuerung: Klarheit des Auftrages, der Aufgaben und der Zielsetzung überprüfen; Kommunikationsregeln vorschlagen.*

**4. Phase Funktionale Teamstruktur zur Aufgabenerfüllung**

Probleme sind weitgehend gelöst und entschärft, konstruktive Aufgabenbewältigung möglich.
*Aufgaben für Steuerung: Moderation des Teamprozesses und der Themenbearbeitung als vorrangige Aufgabe betrachten.*

## 6.1: What Is the Purpose of the Project Completion Phase?

During the final phase of the project the project results are presented and accepted by the client. To carry out the completion of a project the completion must have been previously defined. Last, the project and the associated project group (project manager and project team) will be disbanded.

## 6.2: What Are the Tasks of the Project Manager Within the Completion Phase?

- Define acceptance conditions
- Create final report
- Perform final meeting with the client
- Obtain feedback from the project members
- Involve individuals in charge of implementation
- Recognize the performance of the project members
- Prepare the reintegration of the project participants
- Document the experiences
- Final party with project group

## 7: Describe the Stages of Team Building

### 1. Initial Stage of Team Building (Phase 1)

Team structure is characterized by high level of uncertainty.
*Task for group control: Ensure that everyone finds their seat.*

### 2. Phase of Turbulence, Conflict, Competition (Phase 2)

*Task for group control: Crises and conflicts are to be expected and are a good sign for team development.*

### 3. Phase of Agreement on Rules, Establishment of Standards (Phase 3)

Mutual support and cohesion is formed.
*Task for group control: Review the clarity of the order, the tasks, and objectives; Propose rules of communication.*

### 4. Functional Team Structure for Performance of Tasks (Phase 4)

Problems are resolved to the extent possible and defused, constructive task performance is possible
*Tasks for group control: Regard the moderation of the team process and the topic processing as a priority task.*

## 8.1: Was sind die Unterschiede zwischen klassischem und agilem Projektmanagement?

**Klassisches Projektmanagement**

Grundsätzlich stehen bei jedem Projekt drei Parameter im Mittelpunkt: Ziele, Kosten und Termine. In der klassischen Vorgehensweise werden als erstes die Ziele des Projekts festgelegt, die unter Einsatz verfügbarer Ressourcen zu bestimmten Terminen erreicht werden sollen. Dementsprechend werden nach dem Setzen eines Ziels Ressourcen- und Zeitpläne erstellt. Nun kann es bei der Umsetzung dieser Pläne dazu kommen, dass gegebene Ziele nicht mit dem vorhandenen Budget an Ressourcen und Zeit erreicht werden können. Tritt dieser Fall ein, werden als erstes diese zwei Komponenten verändert. Von der Änderung des Projektumfangs und somit der Ziele wird im klassischen Projektmanagement weitestmöglich abgesehen. Dies ist der Punkt, an den das agile Projektmanagement ansetzt.

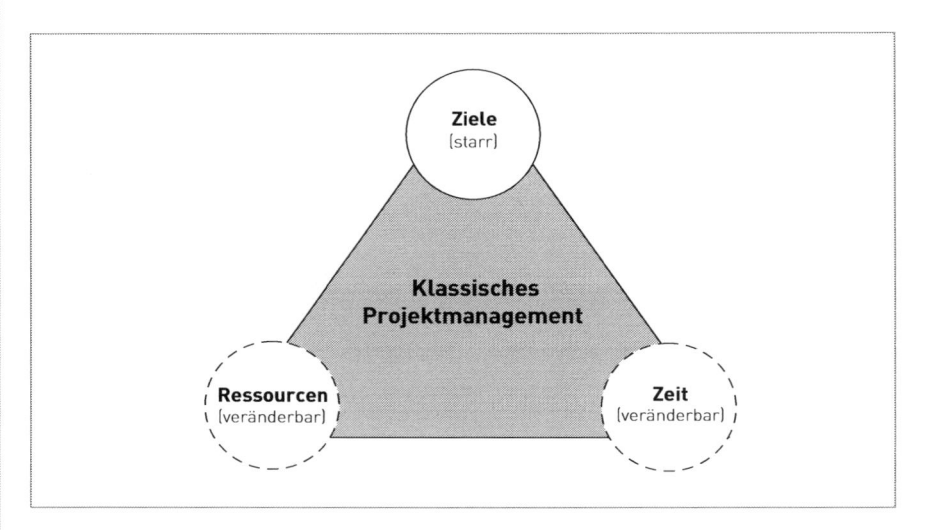

Abb. 67: Klassisches Projektmanagement (vgl. Wagener; Ziller (2012), S. 166).

**Agiles Projektmanagement**

Die Methoden des agilen Projektmanagements sehen von der traditionellen, starren Vorgehensweise ab und lassen eine dynamischere, flexiblere Herangehensweise zur Problemlösung zu. Im agilen Manifest[12] wird der Basisgedanke aller agilen Modelle sinngemäß wie folgt beschrieben:

---

12   Verfasst von Beck, Kent et al. (2001).

## 8.1 What Are the Differences Between Classical and Agile Project Management?

**Classic Project Management**

In principle, three parameters are at the heart of every project: objectives, costs, and milestones In the classic approach first the objectives of the project are established, which are to be achieved at specific dates with the use of available resources. Accordingly, after setting of the objective target resource plans and schedules are created. During the implementation of these plans it can happen that provided goals cannot be achieved within the existing budget resources and time. If this occurs, these two components are the first to be changed. In the classic project management the changing the scope of the project and therefore the objectives will be avoided as much as possible. This is the point at which the agile project management approach starts.

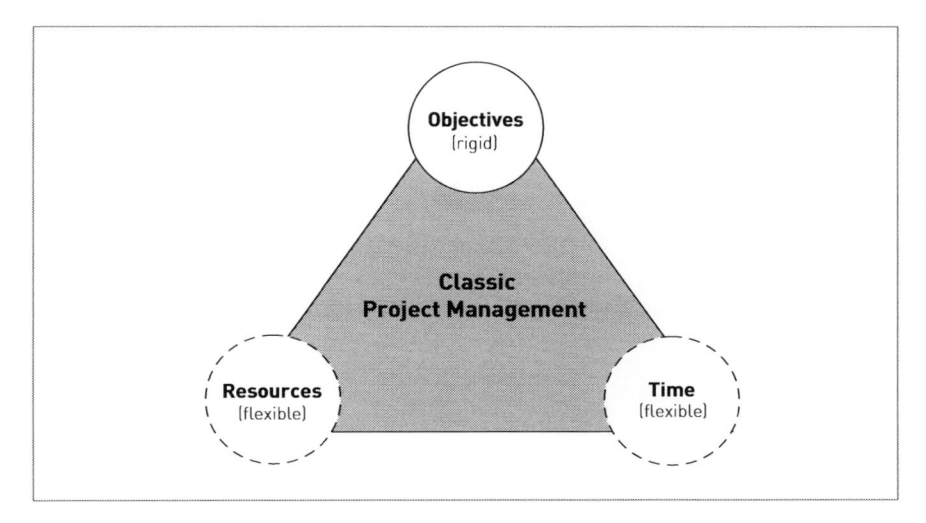

Fig. 67: Classic Project Management (cf. Wagener; Ziller (2012), S. 166).

**Agile Project Management**

See the methods of agile project management abstain from the traditional, rigid approach and allow a more dynamic, more flexible approach to problem solving. In the Agile Manifesto[12] the underlying thought for all agile models is described as follows:

---

12  Written by Beck, Kent et al (2001).

a) Der Mensch ist wichtiger als der Prozess.
b) Das entstehende Produkt ist wichtiger als eine umfassende Dokumentation.
c) Die Kooperation mit dem Kunden ist wichtiger als Vertragsverhandlungen.
d) Im laufenden Entstehungsprozess Änderungen am Produkt vorzunehmen, ist wichtiger als die strikte Verfolgung eines Plans.

Bei den agilen Projektmanagement-Methoden wird an erster Stelle der Projektumfang verändert. Die zur Verfügung gestellten Ressourcen (Kosten) und der gegebene Zeitrahmen bleiben möglichst unangetastet.

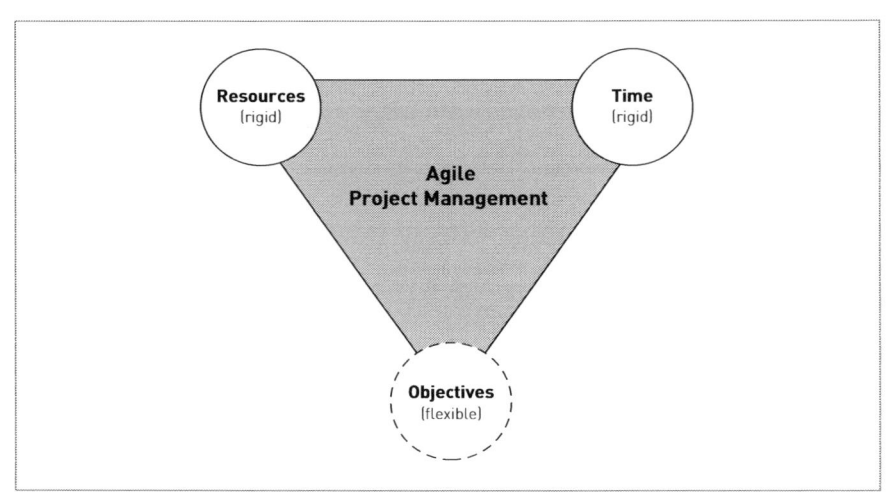

Abb. 68: Agiles Projektmanagement (vgl. Wagener; Ziller (2012), S. 169).

## 8.2: Aus welchen Komponenten setzt sich das Projektmanagementmodell Prince2 zusammen?

Zur Steuerung stellt Prince2 dem Projektmanager jeweils sieben Themen und Prozesse zur Verfügung. Neben den wiederum sieben Grundprinzipien und der Anpassungsmöglichkeit in das jeweilige Projektumfeld stellen dies die vier Bestandteile der Prince2 Methode dar.

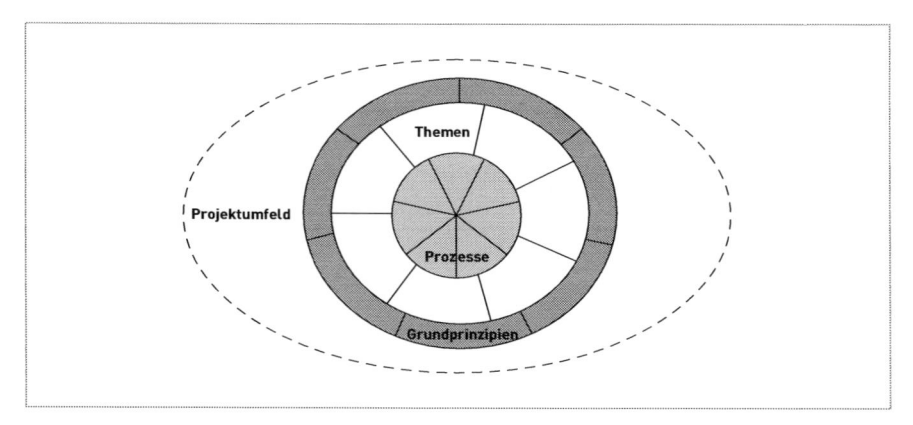

Abb. 69: Modell Prince2.

a) The human being is more important than the process.
b) The final product is more important than a comprehensive documentation.
c) The cooperation with the customer is more important than contract negotiations.
d) Is more important to make changes to the product in the current development process than to strictly follow a plan.

In the agile project management methods the project scope will be changed first. The available resources (cost) and the given time frame remain untouched as far as possible.

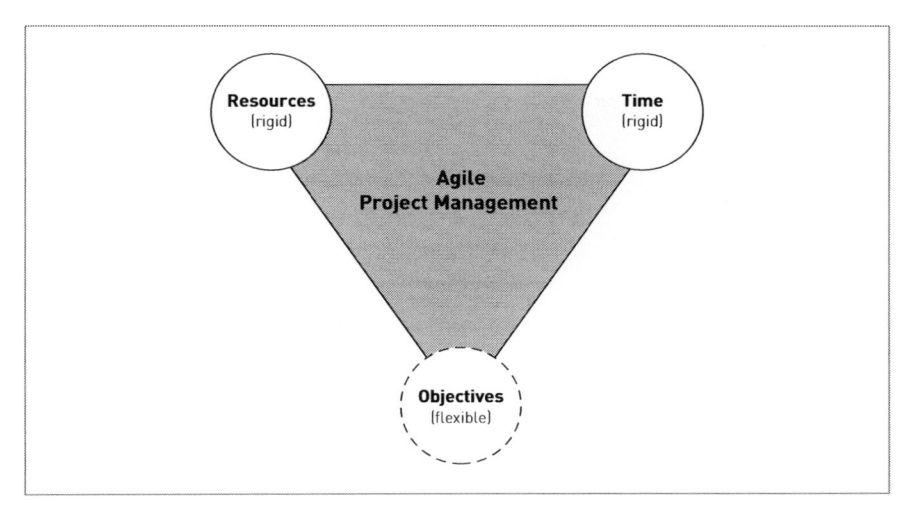

Fig. 68: Agile Project Management (cf. Wagener; Ziller (2012), p. 169).

## 8.2: Which Are the Components of the Project Management Model Prince2?

Prince2 makes seven topics and processes available to the project manager for the control of the project. In addition to the seven basic principles in turn and their adaptability in the respective project environment these four components represent the Prince2 method.

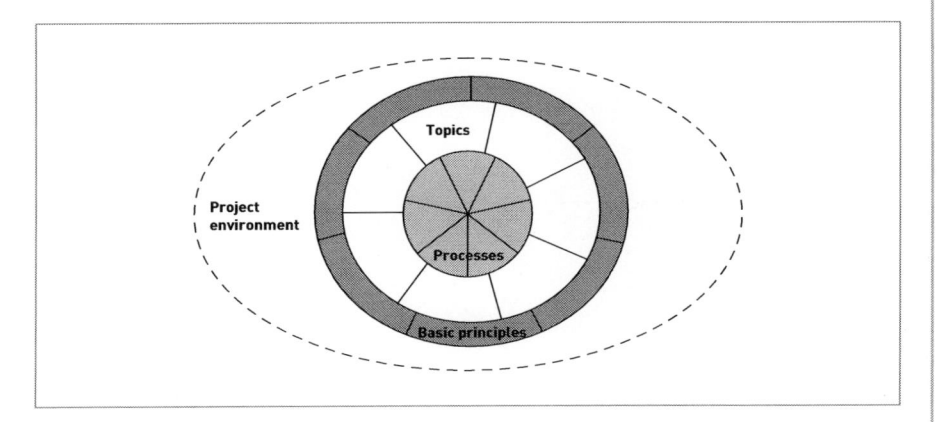

Fig. 69: Prince2 Model.

## 8.3: Welche Rollen sind bei Prince2 anzutreffen?

**Definierte Rollen und Verantwortlichkeiten**
Es sind drei unterschiedliche Rollen und Verantwortlichkeiten festgelegt:

| Rolle | Verantwortlichkeit |
|---|---|
| Vertreter geschäftlicher Interessen | Zielsetzung und Investition |
| Benutzer | Projektprodukte nutzen |
| Lieferanten | Ressourcen / Fachkenntnisse |

Tab. 39: Rolle und Verantwortlichkeiten Prince2.

## 8.4: Wie lässt sich Prince2 anpassen?

**Projektumgebung:** Die Projektmanagementmethode Prince2 zeichnet sich durch ihre Unabhängigkeit von Art und Größe des Unternehmens / des Projektes aus. Die Themen und Prozesse können individuell und universell angepasst werden, lediglich die Grundprinzipien müssen durchgehend berücksichtigt und eingehalten werden.

**Themen:** Bei den Themen ist eine Anpassung in Bezug auf Umfang und Ausprägung möglich.

**Produktbeschreibungen für Managementprodukte:** Es besteht die Möglichkeit verschiedene Managementprodukte zusammenzufassen.

**Rollenbeschreibungen:** Die verschiedenen Rollen lassen sich auf mindestens drei Personen reduzieren. Der Kunde kann gleichzeitig Benutzervertreter und Auftraggeber sein, der Projektmanager kann zusätzlich die Funktion des Teammanagers und der Projektunterstützung übernehmen. Zu diesen zwei Rollen wird noch ein Lieferantenvertreter benötigt.

**Prozesse:** Gegebenenfalls können mehrere Prozesse zu einem zusammengefasst werden. Zum Beispiel können die Vorbereitungsphase und das Initiieren eines Projektes in einem Prozess vorgenommen werden, wenn ein qualifiziertes und umfangreiches Projektmandat vorliegt.

## 8.3: What Roles Can Be Found in Prince2?

**Defined Roles and Responsibilities:**
Three different roles and responsibilities are defined:

| Role | Responsibility |
|---|---|
| Representative of commercial interests | Objectives and investment |
| User | Use project products |
| Suppliers | Resources / Expertise |

Tab. 39: Roles and Responsibilites Prince2.

## 8.4: How Can Prince2 Be Adapted?

**Project Environment:** The project management method Prince2 is characterized by its independence of the kind and size of the company / project. The topics and processes can be adjusted individually and universally, only the basic principles must be taken into account and complied with throughout.

**Topics:** The subject can be adjusted in relation to scope and expression.

**Product Descriptions for Management Products:** It is possible to summarize several management products.

**Role Descriptions:** The various roles can be reduced to a minimum of three persons. The customer can also be user representative and client, the project manager can in addition assume the function of the team manager and project support. Additionally to these two roles a supplier' representative will be required.

**Processes:** Several processes may be merged. For example, the preparatory phase and initiating of a project can be merged into one process if a qualified and extensive project mandate exists.

## 8.5: Aus welchen Komponenten setzt sich das Vorgehensmodell Scrum zusammen?

Die Komponenten des Vorgehensmodells „Scrum" lassen sich in drei Bereiche unterteilen. Diese umfassen Rollen, Zeremonien und Artefakte.

| Scrum | | | |
|---|---|---|---|
| Rollen | | Zeremonien | Artefakte |
| Scrum Team | Externe | | |
| Product Owner<br>Scrum Master<br>Entwicklerteam | Management<br>Customer<br>User | Sprint Planning<br>Sprint Review<br>Daily Scrum | Product Backlog<br>Sprint Backlog<br>Burndown Chart |

Tab. 40: Scrum-Komponenten.

## 8.6: Welche Rollen sind im Scrum anzutreffen?

**Rollen**
Die unterschiedlichen Rollen lassen sich in das Scrum Team und in außenstehenden Beteiligte einteilen. Im Scrum Team befinden sich der Product Owner, der Scrum Master und das Entwicklungsteam. Externe Beteiligte sind das Management, der Customer und der User.

## 8.5: Which Components Are Included in the Process Model Scrum?

The components of the process model "Scrum" can be grouped into three categories, these include: roles, ceremonies and artifacts.

| Scrum | | | |
|---|---|---|---|
| Roles | | Ceremonies | Artifacts |
| Scrum team | External | | |
| Product owner<br>Scrum master<br>Development team | Management<br>Customer<br>User | Sprint planning<br>Sprint review<br>Daily Scrum | Product backlog<br>Sprint backlog<br>Burndown chart |

Tab. 40: Scrum Components.

## 8.6: What Roles Can Be Found in Scrum?

**Roles**
The different roles can be divided into the Scrum team and external stakeholders. The Scrum team consists of the product owner, the Scrum master and the development team. External stakeholders are the management, the customer and the user.

## 8.7: Was ist unter den „Zeremonien" zu verstehen?

| 1. Sprint Planning Meeting | 2. Sprint Planning Meeting | Daily Scrum | Sprint Review | Retrospektive |
|---|---|---|---|---|
| Voraussetzung ist ein gepflegtes Product Backlog (PBL). D. h. es sollte:<br>– existieren<br>– nach Geschäftswert priorisiert sein<br>– Jeder Eintrag sollte ein Abnahmekriterium enthalten | Einträge des Sprint Backlogs werden in Aufgaben von maximal 1 Tag Aufwand aufgebrochen | täglich, stehend, < 15 min. | Präsentation und „Abnahme" der fertig gestellten Product-Backlog-Einträge | Was ist gut gelaufen?<br>Was kann verbessert werden?<br>Wer packt es an? |
| Das Team wählt so viele Einträge aus dem PBL aus, wie es denkt im Sprint umsetzen zu können | Ziel für den Sprint wird erstellt | Was habe ich seit gestern erledigt?<br>Was mache ich bis morgen?<br>Was hindert mich/hat mich gehindert? | Überprüfung des Sprint-Zieles | |
| Product Owner steht für etwaige Rückfragen bereit | Termine für Sprint Review und das tägliche Statusmeeting werden ausgemacht | Das Team aktualisiert:<br>– Sprint Backlog<br>– Burndown Chart (Wie viele Aufgaben sind noch zu erledigen?)<br>– Liste der Hindernisse (Impediment Backlog) | Feedback der Beteiligten, evtl. neue Einträge im PBL | |

Tab. 41: Übersicht Zeremonien Scrum.

## 8.7: What Means "Ceremonies"?

| 1. Sprint Planning Meeting | 2. Sprint Planning Meeting | Daily Scrum | Sprint Review | Retrospective |
|---|---|---|---|---|
| A prerequisite is a well-maintained product backlog. I. e. it should:<br>– exist<br>– be prioritized according to business value<br>– each entry should contain an acceptance criterion | Entries in the sprint backlog tasks are broken into a maximum of 1 day effort | Every day, standing, < 15 min. | Presentation and "acceptance" of the finished product backlog entries | What went well?<br>What can be improved?<br>Who does it? |
| The team chooses as many entries from the PBL, as it feels to be able to implement during the sprint. | The objective for the sprint is created. | What have I achieved since yesterday?<br>What do I do until tomorrow?<br>What hinders me/has hindered me? | Review of the sprint objective | |
| Product Owner is available for potential questions. | Dates for sprint review and the daily status meeting will be identified. | The team updates:<br>– Sprint backlog<br>– Burndown chart (how many tasks are still to be done?)<br>– List of obstacles (impediment backlog). | Feedback from the participants, possibly new entries in the PBL | |

Tab. 41: Overview Scrum Ceremonies.

## 8.8: Welche Artefakte werden verwendet?

| Product Backlog | Sprint Backlog | Burndown Chart | Impediment Backlog |
|---|---|---|---|
| beinhaltet alle erwünschten Eigenschaften und Ergebnisse | beinhaltet Aufgaben zur Erreichung des Sprintziels | zeigt die verbleibenden Aufgaben eines Sprints | Hier werden Hindernisse vermerkt |
| Priorisierung durch den Product Owner (nach wirtschaftlichem Nutzen und Risiko) | Einträge nach denen im Product Backlog gruppiert | wird täglich aktualisiert | kann zu neuen Aufgaben im Sprint Backlog führen |
| Änderungen jederzeit möglich | Organisationsbasis des Teams | steht im Idealfall am Ende des Sprints auf Null | wird vom Scrum Master gepflegt und verwaltet |
| kontinuierlich gepflegter Plan | Visualisierung auf Taskboard | | |

Tab. 42: Übersicht Artefakte Scrum.

## 8.8: What Artifacts Are Used?

| Product Backlog | Sprint Backlog | Burndown Chart | Impediment Backlog |
|---|---|---|---|
| Includes all the desired properties and results | Includes tasks for the achievement of the sprint objective | Displays the remaining tasks of a sprint | Obstacles are noted here |
| Prioritization by the product owner (for economic benefit and risk) | Entries grouped according to those the product backlog | Will be updated on a daily basis | Can lead to new tasks in the sprint backlog |
| Changes are possible at any time | The organizational basis of the team | At the end of the sprint is ideally set to zero | Is maintained and managed by the Scrum master |
| Continuously maintained plan | Visualization on task board | | |

Tab. 42: Overview Scrum Artifacts.

## Literaturverzeichnis | Bibliography

**Christe-Zeyse, Jochen (2004):** Controlling in der Polizei – Leitfaden für ein wirkungsorientiertes Management; Richard Boorberg Verlag; Stuttgart.

**Ebel, Nadin (2011):** Prince2: 2009™ – für Projektmanagement mit Methode. Addison-Wesley; München.

**Haug, Christoph V. (2003):** Erfolgreich im Team; Beck-Wirtschaftsberater im dtv; München.

**Holzner, Johann Peter; Schelle, Heinz (2005):** Projektmanagement für die Polizei – Systematische Darstellung für die Praxis; Richard Boorberg Verlag; Stuttgart.

**Kraus, Georg; Westermann, Reinhold (2006):** Projektmanagement mit System – Organisation, Methoden, Steuerung; Gabler; Wiesbaden.

**Litke, Hans-D. (2007):** Projektmanagement – Methoden, Techniken, Verhaltensweisen; Carl Hanser Verlag; München, Wien.

**Lock, Dennis (2007):** Projektmanagement; Wirtschaftsverlag Ueberreuther; Wien.

**OGC (2009):** Erfolgreiche Projekte managen mit Prince2; TSO Norwich; UK.

**Patzak, Gerold; Rattay, Günter (2004):** Projektmanagement – Leitfaden zum Management von Projekten, Projektportfolios und und projektorientierten Unternehmen; Linde; Wien.

**Peipe, Sabine (2011):** Crashkurs Projektmanagement; Haufe; Freiburg.

**Pichler, Roman (2007):** Scrum – Agiles Projektmanagement erfolgreich einsetzen; dpunkt.verlag; Heidelberg.

**Schelle, Heinz (2007):** Projekte zum Erfolg führen; Beck-Wirtschaftsberater im dtv; München.

**Schelle, Heinz (et al.) (1996):** Projekte erfolgreich managen, 3 Bände Loseblatt; TÜV-Verlag; Köln.

**Schwaber, Ken; Gloger, Boris (2011):** Scrum – Produkte zuverlässig und schnell entwickeln; Carl Hanser Verlag; München.

**Steinle, Claus (et al) (1995):** Frankfurter Allgemeine Buch; Frankfurt am Main.

**Wagener, Andreas (et al.) (2012):** IT-Projektmanagement: klassisch-agil. In: Kammerer, Sebastian (et al.) (Hrsg.) (2012); IT-Projektmanagement Methoden. Best Practices von Scrum bis Prince2; Symposium; Düsseldorf. S. 165–194.

**Witt, Frank-Jürgen (2002):** Lexikon des Controlling; Beck-Wirtschaftsberater im dtv; München.

## Quellen aus dem Internet | Sources from the Internet

**Angermeier, Georg:** Agiles Projektmanagement; unter: http://www.projektmagazin.de/glossarterm/agiles-projektmanagement (22.05.2012).

**Beck, Kent et al. (2001):** Manifesto for Agile Software Development; unter: http://agilemanifesto.org (22.05.2012).

**Berleb Media GmbH:** Cost Performance Index; unter: http://www.projektmagazin.de (28.05.2012).

**Berleb Media GmbH:** Projektmanagement Kompakt; unter: http://www.projektmagazin.de (22.06.2012).

**Berleb Media GmbH:** Schedule Performance Index; unter: http://www.projektmagazin.de (28.06.2012).

**Bundesministerium für Verteidigung:** V-Modell CD-ROM CBT-Programm, kostenloser Download und weitere Informationen unter: http://www.ansstand.de (19.03.2012).

**CCTA:** Prince2, Electronic online manual – the unique online guide to running Prince2 projects; unter: http://www.fee.unicamp.br (28.06.2012).

**GeProS (2003):** Frequnetly Asked Questions – Earned Value Analyse; unter: http://www.ges pros.com (18.06.2012).

**Gröger, Manfred; Schelle, Heinz:** Grundlagen Projektmanagement CBT-Programm; Bayerische Akademie für Verwaltungsmanagement GmbH / BstMI – kostenloser Download für Bayer. Behörden unter: http://www.verwaltungsmanagement.de/download/cbtpm/cbt/index.html (19.03.2012).

**Kana, Joseph Aurelien (2011):** Agile Testing – Scrum im Testing: eine interessante Herausforderng; in: blickpunkte Das Magazin rund um IT-Themen; Pentasys AG; unter: http://www.pentasys.de/uploads/blickpunkte/attachments/pentasys_blickpunkte_1106_agile_testing.pdf (25.05.2012).

**Kestler, Thomas:** Viel Scrum herum; unter: http://www.elevato.de/media/Scrum.pdf (25.05.2012).

**Maethner, Christoph:** Projektmanagment mit Prince2; unter: http://www.maethnerconsulting.de (28.06.2012).

**Peterjohann, Horst:** Projektmanagement: Earned Value Analyse. Eine Kurzübersicht; unter: http://www.peterjohann-consulting.de (18.06.2012).

**Die Beauftragte der Bundesregierung für Informationstechnik:** V-Modell des Bundes, unter: http://www.kbst.bund.de/statisch/HTML-Version_1.0/in dex.html?refer=http://www.kbst.bund.de/statisch/HTML-Version_1.0/250ffd4b6d1794.html (19.03.2012).

**Zyzik, Armin (2004):** Hilfmittel für den Projektalltag, Earned Value Teil 1–8; unter: http://www.1155pm.de (19.06.2012).

## Weiterführende Links zur ersten Orientierung
## Further Links for Basic Information

**Online-Lexikon Wikipedia:** http://de.wikipedia.org/wiki/ErnedValueAnalysis (19.07.2012).

**Online-Lexikon Wikipedia:** http://de.wikipedia.org/wiki/Prince2 (25.06.2012).

**Online-Lexikon Wikipedia:** http://de.wikipedia.org/wiki/Projektmanagement (11.05.2012).

**Online-Lexikon Wikipedia:** http://de.wikipedia.org/wiki/Scrum (14.05.2012).